Eighteenth-Century Europe

The 1680s to 1815

;

Eighteenth - Century Europe

The 1680s to 1815

STUART ANDREWS

CHIEF HISTORY MASTER AT REPTON SCHOOL

LONGMANS, GREEN AND CO. LTD
48, Grosvenor Street, London, W.1.
Associated companies, branches and representatives
throughout the world

© *Stuart Andrews 1965*
First Published 1965

Printed in Great Britain by
The Camelot Press Ltd., London and Southampton

TO B.W.T.

Preface

This book does not claim to be particularly original in content, but it may be thought a little unusual, even eccentric, in emphasis. I have tried to do at least three things:

1 To place most stress where earlier English works on the period have laid least, in the belief that the eighteenth-century revolution in political ideas, in artistic styles and in industrial techniques was ultimately more important than any revolution in diplomatic alignments or the arts of war.

2 To concentrate on those developments that throw light on the nineteenth century rather than those that reflect the afterglow of the seventeenth.

3 To quote extensively from contemporary documents, on the principle that what Frederick the Great wrote before a campaign is as much a part of history as what he did during it.

I know that some of the excursions into the history of ideas (especially Chapters 4, 6 and 17) will probably prove too sophisticated for normal A Level purposes, but I hope they may provide scholarship candidates with an introduction to political thought, besides affording at least a point of departure at under-graduate level. Textbook chapters on the fine arts all too often merely supply a shopping-list of names and dates. I have there-fore devoted the whole chapter on cultural developments (Chapter 15) to a single country in a single reign – the France of Louis XV – in the hope that this may reveal more about the taste of the age than any attempt to describe the cultural kaleido-scope of the entire century.

In spite of the modern historical habit of treating Europe as a single unit, I have followed national lines of division in dealing with internal developments, though I have tried to subdivide the chapters in such a way as to make comparison between states easier. The principal European states are discussed within the context of 'Enlightened Absolutism', partly because it pro-vides a convenient basis for comparison and partly because the term, however misleading as a label, does describe a reality. If we are going to discard the term, we shall need to invent a new one – and examiners at least have not discarded it yet. However, an attempt has been made to underline the military motives behind many of the reforms of 'Enlightened Absolutism' and to stress the social and economic limitations that obstructed the path of 'enlightenment'.

In quoting from contemporary sources I have not (except in the section on French literature) assumed a knowledge of foreign languages, though this has sometimes resulted in somewhat too literal translation. A selection of contemporary extracts too long for inclusion in the text will be found among the Appendices. I have perhaps been over-scrupulous in acknowledging sources, but I make no apology for using footnotes so extensively. Almost all the authorities cited ought to be found in a well-stocked school library, and if this book does not stimulate curiosity sufficiently to send its readers back to the shelves it will have failed in its primary purpose.

My debt to other historians is made clear in the text, but I must acknowledge debts of a more personal kind. To David Thomson, Master of Sidney Sussex College, Cambridge, who guided my early studies and without whose encouragement the book would never have been started, and to my wife whose patience enabled it to be finished; to Mr G. R. Searle of Peterhouse, Cambridge, Mr E. P. Dickins of the University of Keele, Mr J. Harris of St Dunstan's College, Mr W. B. Downing and Mr A. A. V. Rudolf of Repton School, all of whom read sections of the manuscript; to Miss Daphne Macnamara and Miss Frances Morrison who did the typing; and to my pupils at Repton and St Dunstan's, who have taught me more than they suppose and who saved me from my grosser absurdities. They are not to blame for such blemishes as remain.

S. M. A.

Repton, 1964

Contents

Preface   vii

PART I   THE OLD ABSOLUTISM   I

1   *The Last Years of Louis XIV*
    France   3
    The War of the Spanish Succession, 1702–12   11
    The Settlement of Europe at the Peace of Utrecht   16
    The Sequel to Utrecht, 1713–35   17

2   *Empires in Decline*
    Spain   20
    The Holy Roman Empire   24
    The Republic of Poland   28
    The Ottoman Empire   31
    Sweden   33

3   *Empires in the Making*
    Russia under Peter the Great, 1689–1725   38
    Prussia after the Great Elector, 1688–1740   43
    The Austrian Monarchy before Maria Theresa, 1705–40   45
    The First British Empire, 1689–1740   48

PART II   THE ENLIGHTENMENT   51

4   *The Scientific Background*
    Bacon and the Experimental Method   53
    Descartes and the Mathematical Method   56
    Copernicus Confirmed: Kepler and Galileo   59
    The Newtonian Synthesis   62
    Locke and Natural Law   65

5   *The Cult of Reason*
    The *Philosophes*   68
    Diderot and the *Encyclopaedia*   71
    Scepticism and Deism   73
    Utilitarianism and *Laissez-faire*   76
    Democracy versus Absolutism   78

CONTENTS

6   *The Seeds of Romanticism*
     Hume and the Attack on Reason   81
     Rousseau and the Return to Nature   85
     The Enlightenment in Germany   89

PART III   ENLIGHTENED ABSOLUTISM AT HOME   97

7   *The Economic Structure of Europe*
     The Survival of Feudalism   99
     The Zenith of Mercantilism   103
     The Birth of Industrialism   108

8   *Frederick the Great in Prussia, 1740-86*
     Frederick and the *Philosophes*   115
     Centralization in Government   117
     Law Reform   120
     Commercial and Economic Policy   122
     Religious Policy   124
     Education   125

9   *Catherine the Great in Russia, 1762-96*
     Catherine and the *Philosophes*   128
     Centralization in Government   130
     Law Reform   132
     Commercial and Economic Policy   135
     Religious Policy   137
     Education   138

10   *Maria Theresa and Joseph II, 1740-90*
     The Habsburgs and the *Philosophes*   140
     Centralization in Government   142
     Law Reform   144
     Commercial and Economic Policy   147
     Religious Policy   148
     Education   151

11   *Enlightened Absolutism in the Lesser European States*
     Naples and Tuscany   153
     Spain and Portugal   158
     Sweden and Denmark   165

CONTENTS

PART IV   ENLIGHTENED ABSOLUTISM ABROAD   171

12   *The War of the Austrian Succession, 1740-48*
    Silesia   173
    The War on the Continent   179
    The War in the Colonies   182

13   *The Seven Years War, 1756-63*
    The Diplomatic Revolution   185
    The War on the Continent   190
    The War in the Colonies   193

14   *The Expansion of Russia, 1763-96*
    The First Turkish War, 1768-74   199
    The Bavarian Succession War, 1778-79   202
    The Second Turkish War, 1787-92   206
    The Partitions of Poland   208

PART V   THE *ANCIEN RÉGIME* IN FRANCE   215

15   *The Age of Louis XV*
    The Court   217
    The *Salons*   221
    Literature   223
    Painting   226
    Sculpture and Architecture   229

16   *Absolutism in Decline*
    The Economic Situation   233
    The Administrative Machinery   237
    The *Parlements* and Religion   240
    The *Parlements* and Taxation   242

17   *Revolutionary Influences*
    The Example of England   246
    The Impact of America   251
    The Writings of the *Philosophes*   256

18   *Revolutionary Agents*
    The King   261
    The Nobles   264
    The Clergy   266
    The *Bourgeoisie*   268
    The Town Crowd   270
    The Peasants   271

CONTENTS

PART VI   THE FRENCH REVOLUTION   275

19   *The Experiment in Constitutional Monarchy*
     From Estates-General to Constituent Assembly   277
     The Reforms of the Constituent Assembly   282
     The Revolution and Europe   289

20   *The Republican Phase*
     The Legislative Assembly and the Fall of the Monarchy   293
     The National Convention and the Fall of the Girondins   297
     The Dictatorship of Robespierre   301

21   *The Return to Absolutism*
     The Fall of Robespierre   307
     Reaction   310
     The Rise of Bonaparte   315

22   *Napoleonic Europe*
     Napoleon in France   321
     The Grand Empire   327
     The Defeat of Napoleon   333

Epilogue   345

Appendices   349

     1   Royal family trees   349
     2   Other European monarchs   356
     3   Popes   358
     4   French currency   359
     5   Montesquieu and the Separation of Powers   359
     6   The American Declaration of Independence, 1776   361
     7   Arthur Young and the French crowd   362
     8   The Republican Calendar   363
     9   The Republic of Virtue   364
    10   Joseph II's instructions to his district commissioners, 1784   365
    11   Catherine the Great's Charter of the Nobility, 1785   366
    12   The Coalitions against France, 1793–1813   368
    13   Goethe and the Religion of Nature   369

Select Bibliography   371

Index   381

xii

MAPS

Europe in 1700   12

Europe in 1740   13

Rising and Declining Empires   25

The Growth of Prussia, 1688–1815   176–7

The Westward Expansion of Russia, 1682–1815   204

The Partitions of Poland, 1772–95   211

France before 1789   286

Revolutionary France   287

Europe in 1810   340

Europe in 1815   341

ACKNOWLEDGEMENTS

We are grateful to the following for permission to include copyright material:

The author's agents for material from *The Bourbons of Naples* by Harold Acton, published by Methuen & Co. Ltd; the Executive Council of the American Friends of Lafayette for material from *The Eighteenth Century Revolution*, edited by Peter Amman; Basil Blackwell & Mott Ltd for material from *Letters of Napoleon*, edited by J. M. Thompson, *Napoleon Bonaparte: His Rise and Fall* by J. M. Thompson, and *L'Ancien Régime* by Alexis de Tocqueville, translated by H. W. Patterson; G. Bell & Sons Ltd for material from *Travels in France* by Arthur Young; Cambridge University Press for material from *The New Cambridge Modern History*, Vols. v and vii; Jonathan Cape Ltd for material from *The Revolutionary Emperor* by S. K. Padover; Jonathan Cape Ltd and Holt, Rinehart and Winston, Inc. for material from *The French Revolution 1788–92* by Gaetano Salvemini, translated by I. M. Rawson; Professor William F. Church for material from *The Greatness of Louis XIV: Myth or Reality*; The Clarendon Press for material from *A Treatise of Human Nature* by David Hume and *The Eastern Question* by J. A. R. Marriott; Faber & Faber Ltd and Oxford University Press, Inc. for material from *Faust*, Part I, by J. W. von Goethe, translated by Louis MacNeice, copyright 1951 by Louis MacNeice; Hafner Publishing Co. Ltd for material from *The Social Contract and Discourses* by Jean-Jacques Rousseau; Longmans, Green & Co. Ltd for material from *Frederick the Great, Catherine the Great and Other Studies* and *Maria Theresa and Other Studies* by G. P. Gooch, and *Frederick the Great on Kingcraft* by Sir J. William Whittall; Longmans, Green & Co. Ltd and David McKay Company, Inc. for material from *An Introduction to Seventeenth Century France* by John Lough; Phaidon Press Ltd for material from *French XVIII Century Painters* by Edmund and Jules Goncourt, translated by Robin Ironside, and Princeton University Press for material from *The Philosophy of the Enlightenment* by E. Cassirer, *Eighteenth-Century Revolution in Spain* by R. Herr, and *Twelve Who Ruled: The Year of the Terror in the French Revolution* and *Age of Democratic Revolution*, vol. I, both by R. R. Palmer.

The maps on pages 25, 176–7 and 204 were based on some in *History of the Modern World* by R. R. Palmer, by permission of Alfred A. Knopf, Inc.

I

THE OLD ABSOLUTISM

The year 1700 did not mark the beginning of a new age. If the death of Charles II, last of the Spanish Habsburgs, may be seen as the end of an era, the War of the Spanish Succession that followed was also the last of Louis XIV's four wars, while Louis XIV himself did not die until 1715. And although 1700 saw the opening of the Great Northern War – it was the year in which the Swedes routed the Russians at Narva – the war was to end in the eclipse of Sweden and the emergence of Russia as a European power.

The 1680s perhaps have a better claim to mark a turning-point: the death of Colbert, the revocation of the Edict of Nantes, the accession of Peter the Great, the death of the Great Elector of Brandenburg-Prussia, the defeat of the Turks at the gates of Vienna, the English Revolution, the publication of Newton's *Principia*. The Scientific Revolution did not, of course, make its impact outside academic circles for another generation, and the period between the 1680s and the 1730s may perhaps be regarded as an interlude between the Age of Faith and the Age of Reason.

It can be seen as an interlude in other respects. Louis XIV, in spite of his ultimate political failure, remained the model for would-be absolute monarchs throughout Europe, while the rapid recovery of France showed that Louis' wars had not damaged her irreparably. Other great powers of the seventeenth century were now, however, in decline. Spain, in spite of apparent signs of rejuvenation, did not recapture her former dominance, while by 1740 the Turks, though not completely expelled from Europe, were no longer a threat to Vienna. The Austrian Habsburgs, having escaped from the Turkish menace, were now able to concentrate on building up their authority over their own territories, as compensation for the evident decline in their powers and prestige as Holy Roman Emperor. The decay of the Holy Roman Empire gave Prussia her opportunity in Germany, and, although there was little indication yet that she was prepared to take it, the events of 1740-42 would show how much useful preparation had been accomplished in the interim. Meanwhile Russia, having wrested command of the Baltic from Sweden, had asserted her right to be regarded as a European power and was poised to begin her advance westwards, at the expense of Turkey and Poland, that was to occupy the next two centuries.

Of the maritime nations, Spain and Holland, who had dominated seventeenth-century trade, were losing their commercial supremacy to England and France, a reversal of roles that would have taken place even without the Spanish Succession War. For the first half of the eighteenth century the wars continue to be mainly dynastic in motive and to carry dynastic labels, but even by the 1740s economic rather than dynastic issues are principally at stake. If in some ways the eighteenth century begins in the 1680s, in others it does not start until 1740.

I

The Last Years of Louis XIV

France

Napoleon I was to complain during his exile on St Helena: 'I asked for twenty years. Destiny gave me only thirteen.' In contrast, Louis XIV's reign of seventy-two years proved at least a generation too long for his reputation. The twenty-two years between the death of Mazarin in 1661, when Louis unexpectedly took up the reins of government, and the death of both Colbert and the Queen in 1683 mark the zenith of the *Roi Soleil*. But Louis XIV's marriage to Madame de Maintenon[1] in 1684, the revocation of the Edict of Nantes in 1685, and the opening of the War of the League of Augsburg in 1688 were all indications of the extent to which religious disputes and unsuccessful wars were to dominate the last thirty years of the reign. These were the years that inspired the harsh judgements of nineteenth-century French historians. Albert Sorel (1842–1906) laid at Louis XIV's door the blame for the French Revolution:

Louis XIV carried the principle of monarchy to its utmost extent, and abused it in all respects to the point of excess. He left the nation crushed by war, mutilated by banishments, and impatient of the yoke which it felt to be ruinous. Men were worn out, the treasury empty, all relationships strained by the violence of tension, and in the immense framework of the state there remained no institution except the accidental appearance of genius. Things had reached the point where, if a great king did not appear, there would be a great revolution.[2]

Fifty years earlier Guizot, historian and minister of Louis Philippe's 'Bourgeois Monarchy', had written:

[1] See below, p. 8.
[2] A. Sorel, *Europe and the French Revolution*, quoted in *The Greatness of Louis XIV*, ed. W. F. Church, D. C. Heath, Boston, 1959, p. 63.

3

It was not Louis XIV alone who was becoming aged and weak at the end of his reign: it was the whole absolute power. Pure monarchy was as much worn out in 1712 as was the monarch himself: and the evil was so much the more grave, as Louis XIV had abolished political morals as well as political institutions. . . .[3]

But historians have not been unanimous. Acton, Sorel's contemporary, described Louis XIV as 'by far the ablest man who was born in modern times on the steps of a throne',[4] while Voltaire claimed in his *Age of Louis XIV* (1751) that Louis XIV 'did more good for his country than twenty of his predecessors together'. Voltaire's tribute should warn us of the danger of drawing too firm a distinction between the absolutism of Louis XIV and that of Frederick the Great and his contemporaries: the example of Louis XIV probably did as much to shape the political practice of the eighteenth-century 'Enlightened Absolutists' as did the writings of the *philosophes*.[5]

Louis XIV, coming to the throne before his fifth birthday, was unable to remember a time when he had not been king, and this, together with his descent from Philip II of Spain, may help to explain his exalted view of kingship. Louis XIV's own memoirs contain such maxims as: 'Kings are absolute lords and have full authority over all people, secular and ecclesiastical; use it according to the needs of the state. Never hurry. Take long views. The King must know everything. Empires are only preserved by the same means by which they are created, namely vigour, vigilance and hard work.'[6] This advice to his son, though less pithy than the apocryphal *L'état c'est moi*, more explicitly conveys Louis XIV's view of monarchy.

The routine which Louis XIV drew up for himself on the day of Mazarin's death and which he almost invariably followed, provided for his devoting six to eight hours a day to state affairs, quite apart from the demands of court ceremonial. In 1661 he had required the secretaries of state 'to seal nothing without my order and to sign nothing without my consent', while Colbert

[3] F. Guizot, *History of Civilization in Europe*, trans. W. Hazlitt and quoted in Church, *op. cit.*, p. 59.

[4] Lord Acton, *Lectures on Modern History*, Macmillan 1950, p. 234.

[5] See Chapter 5 below.

[6] G. P. Gooch, *Louis XV*, Longmans 1956, p. 4.

thought it worthwhile to warn his son: 'Never as long as you live send out anything in the King's name without his express approval.'[7] This attention to detail recalls the picture of Louis' great-grandfather, Philip II, installed in the Escurial and patiently annotating the Spanish state papers with laborious marginalia. Not without reason has Louis XIV been called 'Louis the Administrator'.[8]

Such centralization of authority was to have fatal effects in the 1680s and more particularly after the death of Louvois in 1691 when Louis XIV assumed personal control over all the major departments of government. But as long as Colbert lived the system worked well. By Colbert's death in 1683 Louis had largely succeeded in substituting government by trained bureaucrats for the traditional government by the feudal nobility who had regarded office as their birthright.[9] Under Colbert, himself of *bourgeois* origin, the finances had been put on a sounder basis. This was achieved by curbing fraudulent tax-farmers and curtailing the tax-exemptions of clergy and nobility rather than by any large-scale reform of the system of taxation; but as early as 1667 Colbert had a surplus in the treasury.

Colbert's industrial and commercial policies were based on the principle of Mercantilism,[10] though his attempt to impose an industrial revolution by royal fiat on a country that was still predominantly agricultural was bound to fail. Luxury industries were introduced or revived in the 1660s: high-quality glass to compete with Venice; lace to rival Genoa; tapestries manufactured in the Gobelin works (which employed 800 workmen) to oust the tapestries of Flanders. Ambassadors were required to bribe foreign craftsmen to bring their skills to France. But increased production demanded new markets, and Colbert's attempt to expand France's external trade by the creation of chartered companies in the 1660s failed through lack of capital: not even Louis XIV's government could *compel* Frenchmen to invest.

---

[7] F. L. Nussbaum, *The Triumph of Science and Reason 1660–1685*, Harper 1953, p. 75.

[8] By the jurist and historian Pierre-Edouard Lemontey (1762–1826). See Church, *op. cit.*, p. 49, for an extract from his writings.

[9] For a discussion of the *Intendants* and their importance in the administrative system of the *ancien régime* see Chapter 16 below.

[10] See below, p. 103.

Colbert did, however, transform the French navy. It is estimated that by 1670 naval expenditure was more than forty times the 1661 figure. In 1661 there had been less than twenty vessels, some of them more than twenty years old; by 1667 France already had a navy that could present a credible challenge to those of England and Holland, and ten years later the number of French ships exceeded 200. Crews were less easily found, but by the 'sailor's roster' of 1673, all sailors were required to serve one year in three in the navy. Not until it met the combined English and Dutch fleets in 1692 did Colbert's navy suffer defeat.

While Colbert created a navy, Louvois reformed the army. The recruiting problem remained, but, by employing large numbers of foreign troops, an effective army of the unprecedented size of 400,000 was built up, equipped with uniform, elaborately disciplined, and drilled in the use of the bayonet. In 1688 the regular force was augmented by the creation of thirty militia regiments, although the companies of cadets maintained at most of the frontier towns, where they were taught mathematics and drawing as well as drill, had to be abandoned because they proved, in Voltaire's words, 'too difficult to discipline'. In the army as a whole, however, Martinet's methods gave Europe a new word for harshness. Du Metz developed artillery as an offensive siege weapon, while defensive engineering was reduced to a science by Vauban, who constructed or rebuilt 150 fortresses.

In spite of Colbert's vision of a unified legal system, the complexities and anomalies of French law remained largely untouched until the Revolution.[11] But certain sections of the law were at least codified. The Civil Ordinance of 1667 and the Criminal Ordinance of 1670 had systematized procedure. The Ordinance of Commerce of 1673 provided a codification of existing commercial practice, while the Marine Ordinance did the same for maritime law. The Colonial Code of 1685 gave legal definition to the status of slaves. Louis XIV's legal innovations may seem meagre when compared with those of the next century, but parts of his work were incorporated in the Napoleonic Codes.[12]

The policy of centralization when applied to religion had more far-reaching results. The Four Articles of 1682, drafted by Bossuet[13] and signed by thirty-four bishops, reasserted the traditional Gallican claim of royal supremacy in all but doctrinal matters: 'Kings and princes are not by the law of God subject to any ecclesiastical power nor to the keys of the Church with respect to their temporal government. ...'[14] But Gallicanism was anti-Protestant as well as anti-Papal. The Huguenots, numbering perhaps one and a half million out of a population of 19 million, still enjoyed the religious freedom granted to them in 1598 by Henry IV and confirmed by Richelieu at the Peace of Alais (1629). Yet as early as 1634 the Advocate General had openly affirmed that the Huguenots were 'suffered only by toleration and connivance, as men suffer a thing which they had rather be without'. In 1662 Bossuet had argued, in a sermon on the duties of kings, that the Church had striven so hard to strengthen royal authority that she deserved royal protection against heretics. Louis was probably less impressed by this argument than by Bossuet's further claim: 'The true religion being founded on certain principles makes the constitution of states more stable and more solid.' In 1665 Louis agreed to interpret in a hostile sense all existing edicts relating to the Huguenots, and in 1674 the king gave one-third of his profits from the *régale*[15] to create the *caisse de conversions*. This 'conversions bureau' offered financial compensation to Protestant ministers who turned Catholic, and the success of the scheme may have misled Louis into thinking that the Huguenots could easily be persuaded to change their religion.

Conversion by force was certainly cheaper than conversion by cash, and in 1681 the army was called in. Louvois wrote to a

---

[13] Bishop Bossuet, tutor to the Dauphin and the greatest preacher of the age, expounded, in terms that recall those of James I of England, the theory of Divine Right: 'Princes are gods and participate somehow in divine independence. ... There is only one God who may judge over their judgements and their persons.' Though he was careful to add: 'Without the divine judgement-seat absolute authority degenerates into arbitrary despotism.'

[14] The First Article.

[15] The right to enjoy the revenues of a vacant bishopric and to appoint to benefices within the bishop's gift. The Papacy opposed Louis' claim to the *régale*, but eventually (1693) recognized it in return for Louis' renunciation of the Gallican Articles of 1682.

dragoon commander whose troops were to be billeted on Huguenot families: 'It is His Majesty's wish that the utmost severity should be inflicted on those who refuse to adopt his religion.' In Poitou alone the dragonnades claimed 37,000 converts. Three thousand Huguenot families are thought to have left France in 1681, and in 1685, on the pretext that the Huguenot community no longer existed, the Edict of Nantes was formally revoked. Huguenot ministers were to leave France within ten days or go to the galleys; children were to be baptized by Catholic priests and brought up as Catholics. Thus, by what Bossuet hailed as 'the supreme achievement of your reign', Louis XIV not only drove out some 250,000 of his subjects (including many skilled artisans of the kind that Colbert had enticed into France) but also gave France's Protestant enemies an ideological motive for combining against her. Less obvious at the time, but more significant for the future, was the way in which Huguenot exiles in Holland provided a base from which to launch literary attacks on the *ancien régime*. The Huguenot Pierre Bayle,[16] who left France in 1681 to become professor of philosophy and history at Rotterdam, is now regarded as the herald of the French Enlightenment.

Historians have seen the revocation of the Edict of Nantes as the culmination of Louis XIV's absolutist policies. In Acton's view, 'the ardour of rising absolutism is the true cause of the Revocation'. Contemporary Frenchmen blamed a woman. Madame de Maintenon, who had secretly married Louis in 1684 but never bore the title of queen, was herself a convert from Protestantism, was known to hate the Jansenists,[17] and was on good terms with the more influential clergy. But in spite of Saint-Simon's vindictive charges, it seems unlikely that Madame de Maintenon's influence extended beyond the control she exercised over Louis' private life: she seems to have been content with improving the King's morals and increasing his piety. Louis once described her as a saint, and the patience with which she endured the monotony of life at court suggests some of the marks of martyrdom.

[16] See below, p. 73.
[17] For a discussion of the political importance of Jansenism see below, p. 240.

The odour of sanctity was not particularly prevalent in the atmosphere of Versailles where king, court and council resided from 1682. The concentration of the nobility in the King's presence, the employment of their time in the deliberately contrived intricacies of court ceremonial in which courtiers competed for the honour of wearing an embroidered coat, the semi-religious ritual of the *lever* and *coucher,* the promenades in the park, the hunting and hawking expeditions, the balls and ballets, concerts and masquerades – all these are well known. It is less often remembered how uncomfortable the rambling palace was. Saint-Simon was not the only one to complain of the all-pervasive stench, while Madame de Maintenon wrote: 'The King's apartment is so cold that if I live there long I shall become a paralytic; not a door or a window will shut and the wind recalls American hurricanes.'[18]

The pageant of Versailles, an impressive façade concealing internal squalor, is an apt symbol of the France of Louis XIV's last years. Contemporaries exaggerated the expense of the court, but as early as 1675 Colbert had warned Louis against undertaking schemes without considering how they were to be financed, and after Colbert's restraining hand was removed in 1683 expenditure increased. But war was the chief cause of the unbalanced budget. The War of the League of Augsburg,[19] which started in 1688, so exhausted France that by the Peace of Ryswick (1697) Louis had to agree to surrender almost all the German territories he had seized by the so-called policy of Reunions in the early 1680s. He was allowed to keep only Strasbourg, and was required to recognize William of Orange as King of England. With the peace, Vauban, whose fortresses had saved France from invasion, proposed the introduction of a tax of 10 per cent on all sources of income, to replace the unpopular *taille* which was borne chiefly by the peasants. A manuscript copy of Vauban's *Dîme Royale* was apparently well received by the King, but its publication in 1707 caused an outcry, and

[18] R. Ergang, *Europe from the Renaissance to Waterloo*, D. C. Heath, Boston, 1954, p. 471.
[19] A misleading title, since the League was soon absorbed in William III's Grand Alliance, the members of which included, besides the German states of the League, England, Holland, Spain, Austria, Savoy and Sweden.

Vauban died in disgrace. In 1715 expenditure was more than double the revenue, while the national debt stood at three thousand million livres. The Crown's financial problem remained unresolved until desperate remedies provoked the Revolution.[20]

In the last decade of the reign the volume of criticism grew. The effects of the long War of the Spanish Succession combined with natural hazards like the winter of 1709 to cause real economic distress. In May 1713 an *Intendant* describing conditions in Anjou wrote: 'This province is in a state of frightful misery through the dearth of corn. Half the people in the countryside are without bread; a great number have already died of hunger.'[21] But the most striking indictment of Louis XIV's last years is contained in Fénelon's famous letter, probably written in 1694, but surely never read by the King:

Your peoples are dying of hunger. Agriculture is almost at a standstill, all the industries languish, all commerce is destroyed. France is a vast hospital. The magistrates are degraded and worn out. It is you who have caused all these troubles. The whole kingdom having been ruined, everything is concentrated in you and everyone must feed out of your hand. . . . Your victories no longer arouse delight. There is only bitterness and despair. Sedition is boiling up. You do not love God; you only fear Him with a slavish fear. It is hell you are afraid of. Your religion consists of superstition and ceremonies. You relate everything to yourself as if you were God on earth.[22]

The description is no doubt exaggerated, but it is difficult to quarrel with Gooch's final verdict: 'The sufferings of the people were far more grievous in 1715 than on the eve of the Revolution in 1789. Such was the price his subjects had to pay for the greater glory of the *Roi Soleil*.'[23]

[20] See Chapter 18 below.
[21] French text in J. Lough, *An Introduction to Seventeenth Century France*, Longmans 1954, p. 273.
[22] Gooch, *op. cit.*, p. 15.
[23] *Ibid.*, p. 29.

The War of the Spanish Succession, 1702–12

Before 1789 all the major European states, with the exception of Venice, were monarchies, and in all these monarchies except that of Poland[24] the hereditary principle prevailed. Even in England, which had already executed one king, the fiction of James II's 'abdication' had to be invented to justify William III's accession, and even then the non-jurors remained to testify to the strength of the hereditary principle. Throughout the eighteenth century, therefore, the map of Europe was drawn and redrawn largely on dynastic lines: most of the wars of the century were, as their textbook titles suggest, dynastic wars, while Napoleon was to show his respect for the dynastic principle by marrying into the Habsburgs and installing his undistinguished relatives on the vacant thrones of Europe.[25]

The first war of the century was no exception. It had long been evident that the mentally defective Charles II of Spain would be the last male of the Spanish Habsburg line. As early as 1668, Louis XIV and the Emperor Leopold I, each of whom had married one of Philip IV's two daughters, had agreed to partition the Spanish Empire when Charles eventually died. On marrying Louis XIV, Maria Theresa had renounced her claim to the Spanish throne on condition that her dowry was paid: it never was, and her son the Dauphin could therefore boast a plausible claim. Margaret Theresa had made no such renunciation when marrying Leopold, and the marriage of her daughter Maria Antonia to the Elector of Bavaria produced another claimant, the Electoral Prince Joseph Ferdinand. The third candidate was the Archduke Charles, the younger son of Leopold by his second marriage. By the so-called First Partition Treaty of 1698, England, France and Holland agreed, without consulting the Emperor, that at Charles II's death the Spanish Empire should be divided between the three claimants, with the Electoral Prince taking the lion's share. But in 1699 Prince Joseph Ferdinand died of smallpox, and a second partition treaty provided for a

---

[24] See below, p. 28.
[25] See below, p. 346.

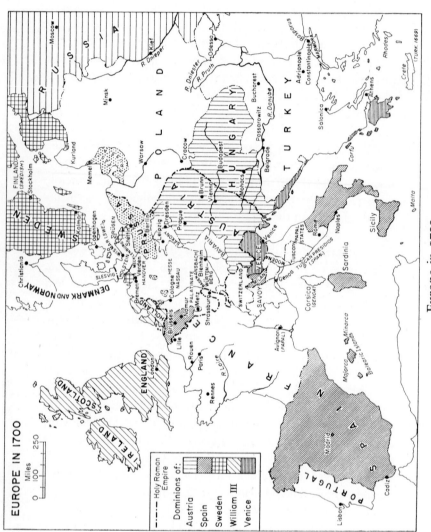

Europe in 1700

EUROPE IN 1740

Miles
0   100   250

Holy Roman
Empire

Dominions of:
Austria
Prussia
George II
Venice

Europe in 1740

RUSSIA

Moscow
Narva
Estonia
Livonia
Riga
Kurland
Lithuania
R. Dnieper
Kiev
Poltava
R. Dniester
Oczakov
R. Pruth
Jassy
Moldavia
Bucharest
R. Danube
Wallachia
Transylvania
Constantinople
Salonica
Chios
Athens
MOREA

TURKEY

FINLAND
(SWEDISH)
Stockholm
SWEDEN
Christiania
DENMARK AND NORWAY
NORWAY
Copenhagen
SWEDISH POMERANIA
Stralsund
Stettin
MECK-
LENBURG
Danzig
Thorn
Posen
Warsaw
Cracow
POLAND
EAST
PRUSSIA
Breslau
Oppeln
SILESIA
(PRUS. 1740)
Brünn
Moravia
Pressburg
Budapest
HUNGARY
Belgrade
(AUS. 1739)
Ionian Is.
Malta
(KNIGHTS OF ST. JOHN)

Bremen
HANOVER
Berlin
PRUSSIA
SAXONY
Dresden
Prague
BOHEMIA
AUSTRIA
Vienna
BAVARIA
TYROL
Venice
VENICE

HOLLAND
Netherlands
JULICH
Dettingen
NASSAU
HESSE
PALATINATE
WÜRT-
EMBERG
BADEN
ANSBACH
LORRAINE
SWITZERLAND
MILAN
SAVOY
PIEDMONT
PARMA
Genoa
(Rep.)
Tuscany
PAPAL
STATES
Rome
KINGDOM OF NAPLES
Naples
Sardinia
(SAVOY)

London
BRITAIN
IRELAND
Le Havre
Paris
R. Loire
Brest
Bordeaux
FRANCE
Lyon
Avignon
(Papal)
Marseille
Toulon
Corsica
(GENOA)
Minorca
(BRIT.)

Sicily

Saragossa
Barcelona
Madrid
SPAIN
Valencia
Oviedo
Santiago
Seville
Granada
Cadiz
Gibraltar (BRIT.)
Ceuta (SPAN.)
Tangier
Lisbon
PORTUGAL

EUROPE IN 1740

13

straightforward division between the Dauphin and the Arch-duke. [See family tree on page 352.]

In 1700 Charles II at last died, but not before his Council of State, anxious to keep the Spanish Empire in one piece, had persuaded him to make a will bequeathing the whole of the Spanish Empire to the Duke of Anjou, the Dauphin's second son, on condition that he never inherited the French throne. Only if Louis XIV declined to accept in the name of his seven-teen-year-old grandson would the entire Spanish inheritance pass to the Archduke Charles.

Louis accepted. Of course, he promised that the French and Spanish thrones would never be united, but the view of Europe was aptly if tactlessly expressed in the famous remark of the Spanish ambassador: 'The Pyrenees are no more.' An Austrian Habsburg on the Spanish throne would have revived the spectre of the Empire of Charles V; but the prospect of a Bourbon in Madrid was even more daunting: even if the French and Spanish thrones were never united, French influence would extend from the Netherlands to Naples and from Milan to Mexico. And it had all happened without a shot being fired. But when Louis XIV tried to exploit his advantage by obtaining the *asiento* (which gave France a monopoly in the slave trade to South America), by sending his troops to Milan and Belgium, and by seizing the Dutch frontier fortresses, William III was able to find the European support he had earlier lacked and revived the Grand Alliance of 1689.[26] Louis' retort was to hail James Edward as rightful King of England on his father's death in 1701. William himself died the next year, but thanks to Louis' provocative actions, the Tories under Anne directed the war that William had planned.

Louis XIV, supported only by Spain and Bavaria, was con-fronted by allied forces, which, though inferior in numbers, were led by two great generals, Marlborough and Prince Eugene of Savoy. The difficulties that beset cooperation between democracies were demonstrated in the dispute over the Anglo-

---

[26] The Grand Alliance of 1701 included England, Holland, the Empire, and Branden-burg; Portugal and Savoy joined later. Spain had been a member of the 1689 Alliance, but was now allied to France.

Dutch command which prevented Marlborough from moving his troops until half the campaigning season was gone. In what was left of it, he succeeded in forcing the French to retreat up the Rhine by threatening their lines of communications, but he was hindered by Dutch caution from chasing the French right out of the Netherlands, and 1703 brought only a few captured fortresses as the fruits of victory.

While Marlborough was halted on the Meuse, and the Methuen Treaties of 1703 with Portugal committed the allies to sending 12,000 'veterans' to the Peninsula in order to put the Archduke Charles on the Spanish throne, the French prepared to attack Vienna. They were thwarted by Marlborough's memorable march across Europe to the Danube where, with the help of Eugene of Savoy, the Franco-Bavarian army was defeated at the Battle of Blenheim (1704). But Marlborough was again prevented from following up his success. It was not until 1706 that the victory of Ramillies led to the French evacuating all the Netherlands except the fortresses of Mons, Tournai and Namur, while Eugene drove the French out of Italy. The following year saw an unsuccessful attempt to take Toulon and failure also in Spain, where an Anglo-Portuguese army persisted in its futile task of trying to impose 'Charles III' on the unwilling Spaniards.

Although 1708 brought the victory of Oudenarde, the fall of Lille and the capture of Minorca, even the Allies felt that the war had gone on long enough. Yet it was to drag on for five more years. In the negotiations that opened at The Hague, Louis was willing to concede all of the Allies' somewhat immoderate demands except the requirement that France should join the allies against Spain if Philip V did not abdicate in favour of Charles within two months. Louis preferred, as he put it, 'to make war on my enemies rather than on my grandson'.

The allied victory at Malplaquet in September 1709 was bought at the enormous cost of 20,000 men. A change of ministry in London and a change of monarch in Vienna paved the way to peace: in April 1711 the Archduke Charles succeeded his brother Joseph as Austrian Emperor, and the Tory ministers, who had no wish to see the union of Spain with Austria, opened peace negotiations. But the British attempt to make peace behind the backs of her allies provoked bitter recrimination when the plenipotentiaries met at Utrecht in January 1712. The Emperor fought on alone. Eugene was defeated by Villars at Denain; the Utrecht peace treaties were finally signed in April 1713; but it was not until 1714 that Austria and France made peace by the treaty of Rastatt.

The Settlement of Europe at the Peace of Utrecht

The Peace of Utrecht, signed in 1713, was not a single document but a series of treaties, not only between the allies and the defeated France and Spain, but also between members of the alliance themselves. The Spanish Empire was partitioned, but not merely among the original claimants. Louis XIV's grandson was confirmed as Philip V of Spain, on condition that the French and Spanish thrones were never united in the person of a single monarch. Austria, who had entered the war in the hope of keeping Spain within the Habsburg family and carrying Austrian influence over the Alps into Italy, received the Spanish Netherlands and most of the Spanish Mediterranean possessions: Milan, Naples and Sardinia. But Sicily went to the Duke of Savoy (henceforth to be 'King') for services rendered to the allied cause, while Britain kept Gibraltar (captured in 1704) and Minorca (captured in 1708).

Other British acquisitions were the concession of the *asiento*[27] from Spain, and Newfoundland, Acadia (Nova Scotia) and the Hudson's Bay territory from France. The chief of the Whig war aims was achieved in Louis XIV's recognition of the House of Hanover's right of succession to the English throne; in return France was allowed to keep Alsace, including Strasbourg. The Elector of Brandenburg's new title of 'King in Prussia' was acknowledged. The Dutch, who had fought to keep the French out of Belgium, were allowed to garrison eight 'barrier' fortresses on the Franco-Belgian border (instead of the nineteen

[27] The exclusive right to supply South America with slaves. It had been granted to France in 1702, and was now granted to the British South Sea Company, together with the right to send one ship a year to South America for general trade.

they had been promised in 1709) and were pledged to defend the Protestant succession in England.

France suffered temporarily from the economic exhaustion caused by the war, but she soon recovered.[28] Not so Holland, who may be regarded as the chief loser. The war dealt a fatal blow to her commercial supremacy, already challenged by England before the war began,[29] and her political importance in Europe declined proportionally. Spain, though she conceded the *asiento* and lost territory, emerged, paradoxically, somewhat stronger.[30] Austria, though angry at being cheated of her Spanish inheritance, had nevertheless ousted Spain from her dominant position in the Italian peninsula, and the Habsburg hold on Italy was further strengthened in 1720 when Sardinia was exchanged for Sicily.[31]

FAILURE FOR ENEMIES

The Sequel to Utrecht, 1713–35

In September 1715 Louis XIV died. He was succeeded by his five-year-old great-grandson. Louis' will left the control of France divided between his illegitimate son, the Duke of Maine, and the Duke of Orleans, his nephew. But Orleans quickly ousted Maine from his command of the household troops, and secured control of patronage, which Louis had intended to be left in the hands of the Council of Regency. Before he died, Louis had drafted instructions for his heir urging him to preserve good relations with his uncle, Philip V of Spain: 'Let the ties of blood and friendship ever unite you to the King of Spain and allow no reason or misunderstood political interest to separate you. That is the only way to preserve peace and the European equilibrium.'[32] Yet, as Voltaire wrote: 'the first war of Louis XV was against his uncle whom Louis XIV had established at such cost'.

Philip V, in defiance of the Utrecht Treaty, had in 1715 claimed the Regency in France. Philip's evident designs on the French throne led Orleans to look for allies among his erstwhile enemies. In 1716 secret negotiations were opened with England,

---

[28] See below, p. 233.   [29] See below, p. 107.   [30] See below, p. 22.
[31] See below, p. 18.   [32] Gooch, *op. cit.*, p. 27.

where the recent accession of George I seemed to promise a revision of diplomatic alignments; but memories of French encouragement of the Pretender proved too strong. By the autumn, however, with Peter the Great in Mecklenburg now threatening Hanover, the British government proved more amenable, and the so-called 'Triple Alliance' was signed at the Hague. England, France and (some months later) Holland agreed to 'guarantee all and every the articles of the Treaty of Utrecht so far forth as they concern the interests of each of the three Powers, and the succession to the thrones of France and Great Britain'. The British object was achieved: the Tsar withdrew from Mecklenburg, and the Anglo-French alliance lasted until the 1730s under the guidance first of Stanhope and later of Walpole and Townshend.

In August 1717 Philip V reopened the war by attacking Sardinia. Elizabeth Farnese, who, as Philip's second wife, saw little prospect of her sons ever inheriting the Spanish throne, was anxious to acquire Italian territories for her family. She was encouraged in this project by Cardinal Alberoni,[33] who, as the Duke of Parma's representative at the Spanish court, had engineered Elizabeth's marriage to Philip. The seizure of Sardinia was followed in 1718 by an attack on Sicily. In August, while Stanhope engaged in futile attempts at pacification in Madrid, Admiral Byng destroyed the entire Spanish fleet. Six months earlier the Emperor had joined England and France in what was called the 'Quadruple Alliance' – although Holland remained very much a sleeping partner. In 1719 a French army crossed the Pyrenees, while Alberoni's armada on its way to the west of Scotland was broken up by storms in the Bay of Biscay. Philip V made peace. He dismissed Alberoni and agreed to Stanhope's scheme which had been the basis of the Quadruple Alliance. Charles VI renounced his claims to the Spanish throne; Philip V renounced his claims to the former Spanish possessions in Italy, though not the rights of Elizabeth's eldest son to Parma, Piacenza and Tuscany; the Duke of Savoy exchanged Sicily for Sardinia in return for the Emperor's recognition of Savoy's right to succeed to the Spanish throne if the Bourbon line should fail.

[33] See below, p. 22.

Outstanding points of disagreement were to be settled at the Congress of Cambrai which met in 1721. The Congress was distracted by disputes over procedure, by Anglo-Dutch hostility to Charles VI's East and West Indian Trading Company established at Ostend in 1722, and by Spain's persistent demands for the return of Gibraltar, captured by the British in 1704. After four fruitless years the Congress broke up in confusion. Early in 1725 Spain, outraged by Louis XV's rejection of the Infanta and his betrothal to the Polish Marie Leszczynska, concluded an alliance with the Empire (the first Treaty of Vienna). England and France retorted with the Alliance of Hanover, which included Sweden and Denmark, and (for a time) Prussia. In 1727 Spain declared war and attacked Gibraltar, but the alliances did not operate, and the diplomacy of Fleury and Walpole restored peace. Spain had found that the Emperor was an unreliable ally, and in 1731 Imperial troops occupied Parma on the death of its duke. But diplomacy again prevailed. By the second Treaty of Vienna (March 1731) Charles VI agreed to withdraw from Parma and abandon the Ostend Company, in return for British approval of the Pragmatic Sanction.[34] In 1732 Elizabeth's son, Don Carlos,[35] formally took over the duchies of Parma, Piacenza and Tuscany, but three years later these were returned to the Emperor in exchange for the cession of Naples and Sicily to Don Carlos. This was the third Treaty of Vienna.[36] The essentials of the Utrecht Settlement seemed safe at last, though only four years later (1739) Spain went to war with England over the *asiento*.[37]

[34] See below, p. 47.
[35] See Chapter 11 below.
[36] See below, p. 47.
[37] The War of Jenkins' Ear. See below, p. 49.

2

Empires in Decline

Spain

The diplomacy of Elizabeth Farnese was prompted by a desire to acquire thrones and territories for her two sons rather than to enlarge the dominions of the Spanish crown, which she did not expect them to inherit.[1] Her diplomatic successes were won at the expense of retarding Spain's economic recovery, for Spain, more than most of her European rivals, desperately needed peace. The wars of the seventeenth century had cost Spain a succession of territorial losses. In the 1640s the Spanish Empire had been torn by revolts in Portugal, Catalonia and Sicily. Portugal successfully asserted her independence, and in 1648, after the Thirty Years War, Spain had finally to recognize the independence of the United Provinces. In 1659 the Peace of the Pyrenees secured French evacuation of Catalonia at the price of ceding Cerdagne and Roussillon to France. The Peace of Lisbon (1668) marked the failure of the attempt to regain Portugal: Spain kept Ceuta on the coast of Morocco, but all the remaining Portuguese possessions in Africa, the Far East and South America were finally relinquished. In the same year Spain allowed France to retain her conquests in the Netherlands, in return for the restitution of Franche-Comté – which the French captured again only six years later. The Peace of Nymegen (1678) confirmed the loss not only of Franche-Comté, but also of a strip of the Spanish Netherlands containing twelve fortresses, though these were returned to Spain by the Peace of Ryswick (1697). Thus even before the War of the Spanish Succession, the dismantling of the Spanish Empire in Europe was under way.

Even unsuccessful wars have to be paid for, and the second

[1] See above, p. 18.

half of the seventeenth century brought a period of inflation so disastrous that between 1680 and 1686 a drastic devaluation of the coinage was undertaken and all copper coins were withdrawn from circulation – without compensation. Wholesale prices on the home market fell by 45 per cent between 1680 and 1682,[2] while the wool trade of Segovia, described by the French envoy, the Marquis de Villars, as 'almost the only trade from which the Spaniards still derive money', slumped heavily because foreign merchants refused to buy wool at the old prices.[3]

But the financial measures of the 1680s cannot alone be blamed for a decline in trade that had started long before. Between 1575 and 1675 trade between Spain and the Indies had fallen by 75 per cent, while by 1660 the imports of bullion from Mexico and Peru had fallen to a small fraction of their sixteenth-century volume. The effect on home industry was noticeable before the 1680s: between 1663 and 1680, 7,000 silklooms closed down in Toledo, leaving only 500 by 1685. Population figures are less easy to establish: estimates vary between six and eight million. It seems probable that between 1600 and 1723 the population declined by as much as three million. Most of this decline took place in the first half of the seventeenth century, but if the population did grow somewhat in the second half, it can have done little more than make up the loss of the plague years 1648–54. And in February 1681 the Marquis de Villars wrote to Louis XIV from Madrid:

The galleons left on the 28th of last month. I am assured that in addition to the persons who sailed for business reasons, more than six thousand Spaniards have passed over to America for the simple reason that they cannot live in Spain.[4]

From 1685 to 1691 the Count of Oropesa was allowed to attempt some fiscal and economic reforms: he abolished many of the more superfluous military, judicial and administrative posts, and increased the hours of work in the civil service while

---

[2] E. J. Hamilton in *Economic History Review*, viii (1938), 2. (Reprinted in *Essays in Economic History*, ed. E. M. Carus-Wilson, Arnold 1954.) During the United States slump of 1929–33 commodity wholesale prices fell by 37 per cent.
[3] See R. T. Davies, *Spain in Decline 1621–1700*, Macmillan 1957, p. 151.
[4] *Ibid.*, p. 159.

reducing pay. He also curtailed court expenditure, but it was court opposition that contrived his dismissal. He was not replaced. In the last decade of Habsburg rule Spain was divided into three large governmental districts, each under a governor, presumably on the principle that a problem shared is a problem halved. The scheme was as irrelevant as it was unworkable, since the question of how Spain was to be governed was now being determined in Paris and Vienna, London and The Hague.

By a strange paradox the Bourbons, who had spent most of the seventeenth century trying to destroy Spain, began the eighteenth century by saving her. The War of the Spanish Succession[5] had robbed Spain of her territories in the Netherlands, the Mediterranean and Italy, but it had given her a new dynasty. And if the hypochondriac Philip V seemed poorly cast for the role of rejuvenating an aging empire, he nevertheless brought with him some energetic ministers. Jean Orry (1652–1719), though he could scarcely recast the whole fiscal system while Spain was still at war, succeeded in curbing the excessive court expenditure of the previous reign and greatly improved the efficiency of tax collection. The greatest testimony to Orry's methods was the success with which Philip defeated the allies of the Archduke Charles on Spanish soil and forced the rebellious provinces to recognize Bourbon rule. Aragon, Catalonia and Valencia lost their separate administrative councils as a penalty for supporting the wrong side, while the Council of Castile became the pivot of a centralized administration on the French pattern.[6]

The death of Philip's first wife in 1714 led to the exile of Orry; the arrival of Elizabeth Farnese marked the advent of Alberoni. In four years of feverish activity Alberoni took steps to stimulate agriculture and industry, such as the establishment of the cloth works at Guadalajara under the management of the Dutchman Ripperda; he started to reform the fiscal system replacing the various internal tariffs and taxes by customs duties at the ports and a single excise on salt; he remodelled the army

[5] See above, p. 11.
[6] The reign of Charles II had seen the disappearance of the *Cortes*. The *Cortes* of Castile last met in 1665 and that of Aragon in 1686. The *Cortes* of Catalonia and Valencia did not meet during Charles' reign.

and built up the navy, founding a naval college at Cadiz and setting up two shipyards. But Alberoni's reconstruction programme was cut short by the war of 1717–19, and his removal was one of the conditions of the peace.

Alberoni's successors, first Ripperda, and, after 1727, Patiño, continued his economic policy. Patiño built a new fleet to replace the one destroyed by Byng off Sicily in 1718, and in 1732 600 ships sailed from Alicante to capture Oran. Patiño also increased the yield from customs duties, and in 1737 the royal revenue stood at 211 million *reales* compared with 142 million under Charles II. But much of this increase was absorbed by the demands of Elizabeth Farnese's foreign policy and the cost of the new palace at San Ildefonso which Philip V hoped would rival Versailles. It was not until the accession of Charles III in 1759 that a policy of *ad hoc* reforms to meet the needs of war was replaced by a policy of comprehensive reform under the aegis of 'enlightened absolutism'.[7]

The condition of the Spanish Empire beyond the seas[8] is described by the Spanish authors of *Secret Notes on America* (1749):

The countries of the Indies, fertile, rich and flourishing . . . distant from their Prince and from his principal Ministers, governed by persons who often regard no interests but their own, . . . are now reduced to such a condition . . . that justice has no authority, and reason no power, to make any stand against disorder and vice.[9]

Charles V and Philip II had been conscientious in their selection of colonial administrators; Charles II used colonial posts as means of patronage or sources of revenue. Decisions were supposed to be referred to Madrid, but the channels of communication became so clogged that the viceroys sometimes waited years for answers to their letters. Philip V and his successors attempted to reorganize the government of the empire on French lines, and after the Seven Years War some success was achieved. But the sale of offices, though curtailed, was not abolished until 1812,

[7] See below, p. 158.

[8] In 1713 this embraced Mexico and all South America except Guiana (Dutch) and Brazil (Portuguese).

[9] *New Cambridge Modern History*, vii, p. 487.

and as late as the 1830s the Earl of Clarendon, British Ambassador in Madrid, could still remark: 'Spanish dynasties go and come; Spanish kings go and come; and Spanish ministers go and come; but there is one thing in Spain that is always the same – they never answer letters.'

The Holy Roman Empire

Most contemporaries found it easier, like Voltaire in his famous gibe, to define the Holy Roman Empire in terms of what it was *not*, rather than in terms of what it was. The seventeenth-century German jurist Pufendorf found the Empire impossible to classify: it was neither monarchy, nor aristocracy, nor democracy, nor even a mixture of all three; it was merely an indefinite association 'like that of the Greeks marching against Troy'. It was in fact an association of 360 independent states (or nearly 2,000, if all the Imperial Knights with their castles and few hundred acres are counted in) and the Emperor, though expected to guard the Empire from external attack, was internally little more than an umpire arbitrating between quarrelsome princes.

Geographically, the Empire embraced the area of the German language, with the exception of the Dutch, the Swiss, and those Germans who had long since settled on the Baltic shores. But Germany remained a mere geographical expression: there was no marked sense of nationality, and the Peace of Westphalia (1648) had given both France and Sweden, by virtue of their German conquests, a voice in the Imperial Diet. The same treaty had left Germany religiously divided, but the principle of *cuius regio eius religio* was not everywhere enforced: the Calvinist Electors of Brandenburg were content to rule over Lutheran subjects and even to find room for Jews; and when the Electors Palatine and the Electors of Saxony later turned Catholic, they did not attempt to convert their largely Protestant peoples. Thus the religious map of 1648 remained largely unchanged.

The Thirty Years War had caused grave economic damage within the Empire. After the war the population stood at perhaps twenty million, but many parts of Germany had suffered depopulation. In 1652 over 41,000 derelict houses and barns

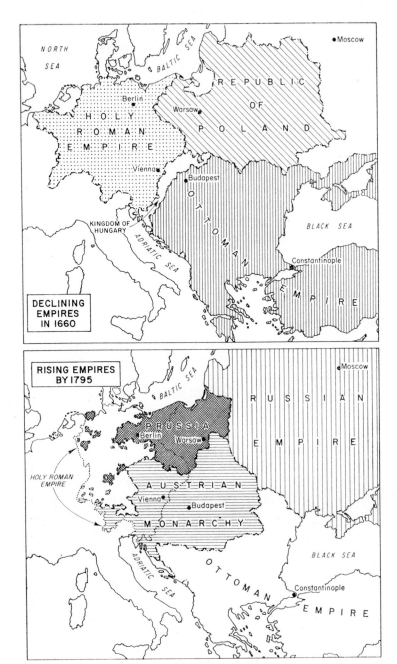

Rising and Declining Empires

were counted in Württemberg and about one-third of the arable land was deserted, while it has been estimated that 50 per cent of Brandenburg farms were uninhabited. Berlin lost only 25 per cent of its population, but Potsdam lost over 40 per cent and Munich 50 per cent.[10] The decay of the towns was hastened by fiscal expedients. The excise, first imposed in Saxony in 1640, had by the early eighteenth century been extended to most of the towns of Brandenburg-Prussia, and within twelve years of its imposition the population of the towns of Cleves had declined by more than 10 per cent. Hamburg and Leipzig continued to prosper, as did the Silesian linen industry, but they were exceptions to the general rule of economic decline. The Thirty Years War cannot be blamed for all the economic ills of the time, as contemporaries were inclined to claim; but it aggravated them to a greater extent than some historians have allowed.[11]

In the political sphere disorganization was only slightly less complete. Not all the 360 states were represented in the Imperial Diet which met at Ratisbon to discuss such matters as vagrancy, coinage, diplomacy and taxation. It comprised three houses or 'colleges': the Electors[12] (two Protestant and six Catholic), the Princes (thirty-seven ecclesiastical and sixty-three temporal), and the Free Imperial Cities. The third house had a subordinate role, since from 1653 it was allowed to vote only after the two upper houses had reached agreement. Such agreement was rare, particularly after 1663 when the college of princes was transformed from an occasional meeting of princes into a permanent meeting of their representatives, who had to refer every decision to their masters. When religious matters were discussed, Catholics and Protestants could claim the right of voting as separate chambers; and no action was possible unless both chambers agreed. A unanimous vote was also required for the levying of taxes. It is thus not surprising to find that discussion focused on such trivia as the date of Easter and the order of precedence for envoys. Sir George Etherege, writing from Ratisbon in 1688, remarked:

[10] N.C.M.H., vol. v., p. 435.
[11] *Ibid.*, p. 443, for a discussion of this.
[12] By 1700 the Electors were: Brandenburg and Hanover (Protestant); Bavaria, Cologne, Mainz, Trier, Saxony, the Palatinate (Catholic); the ninth elector (Bohemia) was the Emperor himself.

'Those who are unacquainted with the proceedings of this assembly would wonder that, where so many ministers are met and maintained at so great a charge to their masters, so little business is done and the little that is so slowly. . . .'[13]

When foreign danger threatened, however, the Diet showed greater dispatch. In 1681 it agreed on an Imperial army of 60,000, established an Imperial war-chest and empowered the Emperor to command the Imperial army or nominate a Field Marshal. The army was to be raised by the ten 'circles' into which the Empire was divided, but those states who already possessed a standing army were reluctant to lose control of it and in the event only those western 'circles' directly threatened by Louis XIV supplied contingents. But the number of troops raised proved sufficient to protect the Rhine frontier, and an Imperial army of 30,000 took part in the relief of Vienna in 1683.[14] The army was the one institution which gave the Empire a semblance of unity; Bismarck was not the first to demonstrate the unifying properties of 'blood and iron'.

The chief judicial institution of the Empire was the Aulic Council (*Reichshofrat*), of which the members were nominated by the Emperor and to which the subjects of the states could appeal, even against their prince. Only the four or five biggest states, like Bavaria and Saxony, were immune from its jurisdiction, and as late as 1770 it helped to force the Duke of Württemberg to make constitutional concessions to his Estates. The Imperial High Court (*Reichskammergericht*) was less effective. The Emperor could nominate only two of its fifty judges, though shortage of money in practice reduced the number of judges to a maximum of eighteen, so that in 1772 there were 61,233 cases still awaiting trial.

By the eighteenth century the Holy Roman Empire was little more than a polite anachronism in European diplomacy. But in its German context the Empire had more meaning. With all its faults it held together its half a dozen large states and 350 small ones in some kind of legal relationship. It lacked executive power and financial resources, but the *idea* of the Empire guaranteed the territorial integrity of its component states, so

[13] N.C.M.H., vol. v., p. 447.   [14] See below, p. 32.

that the Peace of Westphalia endured in all its essential features until the dissolution of the Holy Roman Empire in 1806. The Empire enabled Germans, for all their particularism, to think of themselves as Germans. And as early as 1748 David Hume had written: 'Germany is undoubtedly a very fine country, full of industrious people, and were it united, it would be the greatest power that ever was in the world'.[15]

The Republic of Poland

For almost 1,000 miles eastward from the frontiers of the Holy Roman Empire stretched the Republic of Poland. The third largest state in Europe (in 1700 only Russia and Sweden exceeded her in area), Poland was perhaps both too large and too racially heterogeneous for effective government. The Kingdom of Poland in the west and the Grand Duchy of Lithuania in the east formed the two main component parts, each with a separate administration, and the population included in addition German, White Russian, Ukrainian and Jewish elements. Three-quarters of the inhabitants were peasants and five-sixths of these were serfs whose conditions were probably worse than those elsewhere in Europe.[16]

Poland was called a republic because its king was elected, and the real political power lay with the nobles who elected him. The Polish aristocracy, ranging from the great magnates with private armies to a virtually landless gentry (the *szlachta*), amounted to perhaps a million, or a tenth of the population. However impecunious these nobles were, they jealously guarded their political rights. Their only duty was military service in time of war, and the seigneurial jurisdiction which they exercised on their estates was the only system of law that the country possessed. The central Diet, which met every two years, comprised representatives from fifty or sixty regional diets which were dominated by the aristocracy and from which the towns were excluded. This semblance of a central authority was

---

[15] W. H. Bruford, *Germany in the Eighteenth Century: the Social Background of the Literary Revival*, Cambridge 1935, p. 1.
[16] See below, pp. 101–103.

illusory: a single member of the Diet, by his exercise of the
liberum veto, could not only prevent the passing of a law of which
he disapproved, but could also dissolve the Diet and nullify all
the previous legislation of that particular session. Between 1652,
when the Diet was first 'exploded' in this way, and 1764, only
seven diets ran their full course, and almost a third were dissolved by the vote of one member. 'With a single word,' wrote
Vespazian Kochowski (1633–99), 'God created the world; with
the single word, *veto*, we destroy Poland.'[17]

So diffuse a legislative body could hardly hope to levy
adequate taxes. By 1750 the revenues of the King of Poland
were about one-thirteenth of those of the Tsar of Russia and
one-seventy-fifth of those of the King of France. It is not surprising that the Diet of 1719 should have refused to wage any
more wars. This lack both of unanimity and of money led the
Poles to look for a wealthy foreigner when the throne fell vacant.
John Sobieski, who ruled from 1674 to 1696, was the last Pole to
occupy the throne until 1763, and although he brought distinction to Polish arms by saving Vienna from the Turks in 1683,[18]
little subsequent success befell him. With the retreat of the
Turks, the Poles' temporary unity disintegrated, and Sobieski
failed to persuade the Diet to turn the Republic into a hereditary
constitutional monarchy.

For the next twenty years Poland became the scene of the
struggle in which Charles XII of Sweden tried to oust Augustus
the Strong of Saxony (who had become Augustus II, King of
Poland in 1697) and instal his own candidate, Stanislas Leszczynski.[19] Augustus, compelled to renounce the crown in 1706, was
able to return after the Russian defeat of the Swedes at Poltava
in 1709 and was finally guaranteed his Polish throne in 1717 by
the Treaty of Warsaw between Augustus and the *szlachta*,
signed under Russian auspices. This constitutional revision of
1717, 'the only legislative achievement of the whole Saxon
period',[20] weakened the king's position by subordinating him
even further to the Senators-Resident, members of the Upper
House of the Diet who acted as the King's Council when the

[17] F. L. Nussbaum, *The Triumph of Science and Reason 1660–1685*, Harper 1953, p. 144.
[18] See below, p. 32.   [19] See below, p. 35.   [20] N.C.M.H., vol. vii, p. 372.

Diet was not sitting. The army establishment was fixed at 24,000, which was too large for the financial resources of the Republic, yet too small to defend her long frontiers against foreign encroachment.

When Augustus II died in 1733 the European powers went to war in order to decide the Polish succession. Stanislas, former protégé of Charles XII, was now supported by France, since his daughter was Louis XV's wife. The French smuggled Stanislas into Poland and secured his election, but a fortnight later Russian and Saxon armies entered Poland to put the son of Augustus on the throne. Since Stanislas had no army, and France was hardly within helping distance, the advantage lay with Augustus. Stanislas fled to Danzig where he was besieged for nine months before admitting the hopelessness of his cause. The rest of the war was not fought on Polish soil and was really regarded as an excuse for the French and Spanish to attack Austrian territories in Italy. The Third Treaty of Vienna,[21] concluded in 1735, confirmed Augustus III as King of Poland and promised the Duchy of Lorraine to Stanislas as compensation. The remaining terms concerned the resettlement of the Italian peninsula.

During sixty years of Saxon rule Poland's territories were preserved virtually intact, but in 1734 Stanislas Leszczynski had inquired poignantly: 'How can a country subsist without justice in its law courts, without concord in its councils, without military discipline in the army, without money in the treasury ... ?'[22] Under Augustus III this system of constitutional anarchy persisted. He was succeeded in 1763 by Stanislas Poniatowski (Stanislas Augustus) who owed his election less to his Polish nationality than to the fact that he was a former lover of Catherine II of Russia. The new king seems to have tried to apply the principles of 'enlightened absolutism', but his mentors were to ensure his failure: in the very year of his accession, Catherine and Frederick the Great agreed that the elective kingship and *liberum veto* of the Polish constitution must be preserved. Poland was to be ended, not mended, and less than ten years

---

[21] See below, p. 47. The treaty was not finally ratified until 1738.
[22] N.C.M.H., vol. vii, p. 382.

elapsed before the first partition of 1772 marked the beginning of the end.[23]

The Ottoman Empire

The last of the Ottoman rulers to lead his troops in battle was the Sultan Murad IV, who had died of drink in 1640 at the age of thirty. His successors were more inclined to sleep than to fight, and preferred the pleasures of the harem to the rigours of the field. But in 1656 there had been a minority, and the Sultan's mother appointed as Grand Vizier an Albanian, Mohammed Kiuprili, whose family was to rule Turkey for forty years and who brought to the government a new energy and a new harshness: there are said to have been 50,000 executions in five years. Under his son Fazil Ahmed, who succeeded him as Grand Vizier, the Ottoman Empire reached its farthest limits: by 1675 it extended over three continents, embracing the Ukraine (lost in 1676) and the Balkans (including most of Hungary), and stretching as far afield as Algeria, the Upper Nile and the Persian Gulf.

The very extent and diversity of the Ottoman territories, with their twenty-five to thirty million people, forced the Turks to be relatively tolerant rulers. North of the Danube, the Christian princes of Transylvania, Moldavia and Wallachia continued to rule over their Christian subjects on payment of tribute to the Sultan. French traders within the empire were free to practise the Roman Catholic religion and to be tried by their own judges, who, though resident in Turkey, were appointed by the French king. The Greek Orthodox Church, to which most Christians in the empire belonged, remained autonomous and outside Moslem law; though this freedom was bought at the price of loss of rights and heavier taxes. Christians under the Turks in fact enjoyed greater toleration than Protestants in France after 1685. But this leniency on the part of the government was a measure of Ottoman weakness, and those outlying Turkish provinces adjoining Russia, Poland and the Habsburg lands were secured to the Sultan by the most tenuous

[23] See below, p. 208.

of ties. Even a succession of energetic Grand Viziers could hardly hope to keep those territories under Turkish control for long.

The Ottoman Empire was held together by its army, which was made up of feudal levies from the thirty-two provinces and a standing army of 50,000 Janissaries. This famous regular corps, founded in the fourteenth century, was based on a system of conscripting Christian children from the Balkans, converting them to Islam and subjecting them to rigorous military training. By the seventeenth century the Janissaries had somewhat deteriorated in their standards of discipline, and the decision during the reign of Mehmed II (1648–87) to confine recruitment to Moslems probably did more to hasten than retard this decline. But under the Grand Vizier Kara Mustapha, Fazil Ahmed Kiuprili's son and successor, the army of Mehmed II showed itself a real enough threat to Europe: in 1683 the Turks besieged Vienna. The two-months siege was raised just in time by John Sobieski, King of Poland, who appeared before the capital with a combined Polish-German army of 70,000 after a three-hundred-mile march from Cracow. The Turks withdrew, and in the cathedral the archbishop preached on the text: 'There was man sent from God, whose name was John.'

The relief of Vienna was the last great military effort of the disintegrating Republic of Poland. It also marked the beginning of the Turkish retreat from Europe. By 1699, when the Peace of Karlowitz was concluded, Habsburg forces led by Eugene of Savoy had driven the Turks out of Hungary: Budapest fell in 1687; in the same year the Venetians captured Athens (damaging the Parthenon, which the Turks had been using as an ammunition dump) and held it for six months; in 1696 the Russians seized the fortress of Azov at the mouth of the Don, though they had to surrender it again in 1711; in 1717 Eugene captured Belgrade and had advanced into Wallachia before the Treaty of Passarowitz (1718) halted his march on Constantinople.

The repulse of the Turks was a European victory and was seen as such by contemporaries. The Pope commemorated the event by creating twenty-seven cardinals, while a bibliography compiled by the municipal library of Budapest lists 1,600 separate items written in honour of the recapture of that city.[24] Not all the reconquered Balkan territories were retained. For twenty years the Habsburgs ruled what are now central Yugoslavia and western Rumania, but by the Peace of Belgrade (1739) these territories were restored to the Turks, who thus held Rumania and the whole of the Balkan peninsula except Catholic Croatia. The westward limit of the Ottoman Empire was thus fixed at a frontier that was to last until the upsurge of Slav nationalism in the nineteenth century, when Turkey came to be regarded as 'the sick man of Europe'.

Sweden

The Swedish Empire was a seventeenth-century creation. The territories which Gustavus Adolphus (1611–32) had won for Sweden in the Thirty Years War had been augmented by Charles X (1654–60), who followed up his indecisive Polish campaign of 1655–57 with a highly successful campaign against Denmark (1657–58), in which he surprised the Danes by marching the entire Swedish army across the frozen Great and Little Belts. But at his death the government devolved upon a council of regency, which soon became completely dominated by the magnates led by Magnus de la Gardie. The decline in the army under this regency was marked by the defeat of the Swedes by Brandenburg at Fehrbellin in 1675, and only the intervention of Louis XIV forced Denmark and Brandenburg to disgorge their Swedish conquests.

Charles XI (1660–97) had come of age in 1672, however, and, with the help of Johan Gyllenstierna, the King resumed the programme of 'reductions' (the recovery of alienated crown lands), reorganized the army, and deprived the *Riksdag* or Diet of its control over finance and administration. Swedish absolutism was formally recognized in 1693 by the Declaration of Sovereignty: the declaration of 1680 had required the king to govern 'according to the law'; after 1693 he was to govern 'according to his pleasure and as a Christian king'. As if to

---

[24] Nussbaum, *op. cit.*, p. 237.

underline the significance of the change, his son refused to take the traditional coronation oath.

When Charles XI died on Easter Monday 1697, a boy of fourteen inherited the titles of King of Sweden, Goths and Wends, Grand Duke of Finland, Duke of Scania, Estonia, Livonia, Karelia, Bremen, Verden, Stettin, Pomerania, Cassubia and Wenden, Prince of Rügen, Lord of Ingria and Wismar, Count Palatine of the Rhineland Palatinate in Bavaria, Duke of Jülich, Cleves and Berg ... Charles XII's scattered provinces scarcely deserve to be termed an Empire. They contained probably no more than three million people, compared with Poland's seven million. Much of the country was forest and there were perhaps twelve cities, modest, timber-built and widely dispersed. At least 80 per cent of the people were peasants, who enjoyed the then unusual distinction of owning the land they tilled.

Under Charles XI the country had been divided into military districts, and troops were installed in special soldier-crofts, or billeted on farms, where they cultivated their cabbage patch and were paid a nominal retaining fee by the government; they were also inspected from time to time. These territorial troops, who were to prove their worth in Charles XII's campaigns, were augmented by a number of regular regiments which garrisoned the outer provinces. The only road to a commission was through the ranks, and units like the crack Household Foot Guards of Stockholm contained many of the younger nobility.

These were the troops who accompanied Charles XII as he set forth in 1700, before his eighteenth birthday, to challenge the hostile coalition that had been formed the previous year by Denmark, Poland and Russia in expectation of an easy victory over the young king. The Danes had invaded Holstein, whose Duke was Charles' brother-in-law, but the arrival of the Swedes at the gates of Copenhagen was enough to persuade Frederick IV to sue for peace. Cheated of his prize, Charles had now to turn against Russia: Peter the Great had invaded Ingria and laid siege to Narva. It was at Narva, in November 1700, that Charles' force of 10,000 well-trained and well-equipped troops routed a Russian army at least four times their number and captured eighteen generals, 145 cannon and 151 colours, for the loss of about 700 officers and men. Conservative estimates put the number of Russian dead at 9,000.

Instead of following up his victory, Charles turned against Augustus of Saxony, whose recent election to the Polish throne[25] he was determined to dispute. However, in undertaking not merely the seizure of some suitable slices of Polish territory, but the actual dethronement of Augustus, Charles was setting himself a colossal task. His Swedish biographer[26] is uncompromising in his verdict: 'There is no doubt that his decision to depose Augustus is the great lunacy of Charles XII's life, corresponding to Napoleon's Spanish hallucinations.'

In the summer of 1701 Charles defeated the Saxons on the Dvina and raised the siege of Riga. From here he marched south to Warsaw, where he lingered from mid-May to mid-June 1702 before completing his southward march with the capture of Cracow. The following year saw the Swedish seizure of the Vistula fortress of Thorn and a period of recruiting in Polish Russia. In 1704 Charles returned to Warsaw in time for the election of his candidate Stanislas Leszczynski as King of Poland; he then continued his pursuit of Augustus as far south as Lemberg, only to discover that Augustus had given him the slip and was back in Warsaw. The chase continued, bringing Charles westward to the borders of Silesia, where he was as far from getting to grips with Augustus as ever.

The chief diversion of 1705 was the coronation of Stanislas in Warsaw; but the next year was expended in an eastward excursion to the Niemen where a Russo-Saxon army was annihilated. On completing the round trip, Charles did not stop at the Silesian frontier: by September he had reached Altranstädt, near Leipzig, where he signed a peace treaty by which Augustus agreed to renounce the Polish throne. Europe now waited to see whether Charles would attack the Emperor and so involve Sweden in the War of the Spanish Succession. But in August 1707 Charles moved eastward at the head of 43,000 men, on the road to Moscow. The Russians retreated. The spring of 1708 found Charles near Minsk where he issued his newly completed

[25] See above, p. 29.
[26] F. G. Bengtsson, *The Life of Charles XII*, trans. N. Walford, Macmillan 1960, p. 121.

infantry drill-book entitled *A Few Words of Command Relative to Wedges, the Formation of Squares, the Reforming of Ranks and the Changing of Wings*. The quartermasters had other things to think about: Peter employed the 'scorched earth' policy to be used with such effect against Napoleon and Hitler, while those crops that were not burned were ruined by the abnormal rain of 1708. The wet summer was followed by a freakish winter, and when Charles at last confronted the Russians at Poltava in June 1709 his force had shrunk to some 22,000. The Russians numbered 45,000 and, thanks to the nine years' grace which Peter had been allowed, were very different from the troops who had run away at Narva. Yet even these odds might have been overcome if a fever had not prevented Charles from directing the battle in person. In the event, as a contemporary put it: 'There was no right command in this battle, and every man did as he thought best.' More than 9,000 Swedes were killed or captured, and a further 13,000 surrendered. Charles struggled southwards with a few hundred survivors to seek asylum with the Sultan.

Charles stayed in Turkey for four years. He persuaded the Sultan to launch an attack on Russia in 1710, which merely gained Azov for the Turks. In 1712 the new Swedish army, on which Charles had built such hopes, had its stores and transports destroyed by the Danish fleet, and in 1713 a Turkish expedition to restore Stanislas got no farther than the Polish frontier. The Sweden to which Charles reluctantly returned in 1715 was in desperate need of peace. But in spite of bad harvests and war exhaustion, the energy and rigour of Baron Goertz raised a new army with which Charles was to fight one more campaign. In October 1718 he invaded Norway with 30,000 troops, and a month later was killed by a stray bullet at the siege of Fredrikshall.

Charles XII had made no provision for the succession. When urged to do so he is said to have replied: 'There is always some head which the crown will fit.' There were at least two. In the absence of a direct heir, the crown was claimed both by Charles' younger sister Ulrika Eleanora and by Duke Charles Frederick of Holstein-Gottorp, the son of his elder sister. Ulrika's husband,

Frederick of Hesse, was at the siege of Fredrikshall and acted so swiftly after the king's death as to arouse the suspicion that he had been privy to an assassination plot.[27] It is more likely that he had simply seen the need to be prepared for the probable eventuality of Charles' death in battle. In any case Frederick used his position as commander-in-chief to persuade the *Riksdag* to recognize his wife as queen. Goertz, who had been negotiating for the marriage of the Duke of Holstein to a daughter of Peter the Great, was brought to trial and executed. Goertz had been the chief instrument of Charles XII's absolutism, and his removal was symbolic. When in 1720 Ulrika abdicated in favour of her husband, Frederick I (1720–51) had to accept the new constitution imposed by the Estates. The *Riksdag* was to meet every three years and was to pass laws and levy taxes on its own authority. The Council, though appointed by the King, was nominated by and responsible to the *Riksdag*; and as President of the Council the King was merely allowed two votes – and a casting vote in case of deadlock. The absolute monarchy, which at Charles XII's accession had refused to be bound even by a coronation oath, had by 1720 been reduced to the chairmanship of a committee.

Meanwhile the series of treaties that followed Charles XII's death, culminating in the Treaty of Nystadt (1721), dismantled most of the Swedish Empire. Prussia and Hanover received territory, Denmark was allowed to occupy Holstein, Augustus was restored to the Polish throne. But the real beneficiary of the Great Northern War was Peter the Great: the collapse of Charles XII's absolutism meant the end of Swedish dreams of empire. Henceforth Russia, not Sweden, would dominate the Baltic.

[27] For a discussion of the mystery of Charles XII's death see M. Srigley's article in *History Today*, December 1963, and Professor Michael Roberts' letter in reply, February 1964.

3

Empires in the Making

Russia under Peter the Great, 1689–1725

'In a single reign, by the action of one man, Russia passed from lethargy and obscurity to a dominant position among the nations.' Lord Acton's verdict[1] on Peter I is too flattering, but even if much of Peter's celebrated policy of 'westernization' went little more than skin-deep, the Russia of Catherine the Great probably owed more to the example of Peter than to the exhortations of the *philosophes*.[2] Russia had been bypassed by both the Renaissance and the Reformation, but at Peter's accession she was not entirely isolated from Europe. Tsar Michael (1613–45), the first of the Romanovs, had reorganized his army under foreign officers; Artamon Matviev, the chief adviser of Peter's father, had a Scottish wife of liberal ideas and habits; Peter's nursery contained musical boxes and toy drummers made in Germany. But although the court showed signs of western influence and although the Russia Company's monopoly of trade between London and Archangel dated from 1555, the backwardness of Russia is more accurately reflected in the fact that serf law was first recognized as late as 1649.

Tsar Alexis (1645–76), Peter's father, was succeeded by his eldest son Theodore, who died only six years later. Peter, a younger son by a second marriage, was elected illegally, only to be overthrown by his half-sister Sophia, with the aid of the *Streltsi*.[3] Peter and his mother Natalia saw, but narrowly escaped, the butchery of their immediate relatives by the *Streltsi* in the

---

[1] Lord Acton, *Lectures on Modern History*, Macmillan 1906, p. 277.
[2] See below, p. 128.
[3] The *Streltsi* were formed in the reign of Ivan the Terrible (1547–84). They were a sort of praetorian guard, concentrated mainly in Moscow, where there were about twenty-two regiments of *Streltsi* in 1682, each about 1,000 strong.

rooms and passages of the Kremlin. Sophia, abetted by her lover Galitzin, posed as regent, with Peter and his half-brother Ivan as joint tsars. Peter, exiled to his country estates, learned in 1689 of a plot to murder him. With the *Streltsi* this time on his side, he ousted Galitzin and Sophia, and when Ivan died in 1696 Peter became sole ruler of Russia at the age of twenty-four. Whether or not the nightmarish events of his adolescence help to explain the more grotesque traits of Peter's character, the circumstances of his accession show clearly enough the need for a strong ruler.

Peter faced external as well as internal threats. Russia had passed the seventeenth century in a struggle for survival, first against Poland and then, after 1650, against Sweden and Turkey. There was in fact a real danger of Russian dismemberment and Peter's reforms were prompted in the first place by military necessity. So, perhaps, was his European tour of 1697–98. The first Russian ruler to travel abroad since the eleventh century, Peter took a great interest in things technical and military: besides showing an interest in medicine, dentistry and engraving, he visited sawmills and spinning mills and worked as a ship-wright at Amsterdam and Deptford. Here he lodged in the house of the diarist John Evelyn who recorded in his diary for 9 June 1698: 'I went to Deptford to view how miserably the Tzar of Muscovy had left my house after three months making it his court.' The general boorishness of Peter's behaviour – the ill-sustained attempt to travel incognito, the drunkenness of his retinue, and his own liking for practical jokes and fireworks – made it difficult for the European courts to take the Tsar seriously, and it is not surprising that his demand for a crusade against the Turks was ignored in Vienna. But in spite of the diplomatic failure of the mission, Peter recruited for service in Russia nearly a thousand experts (chiefly in mining and in military and naval engineering) and shipped 260 cases of naval stores and munitions back to Moscow.

Even before his visit to Europe Peter had attacked the Turks. In 1695, in order to gain an outlet into the Black Sea, he had tried to seize Azov, the Turkish fort at the mouth of the Don. He had failed dismally through lack of naval support, but, with the help of a hastily assembled flotilla of galleys, he succeeded at the second attempt in the summer of 1696. This first Turkish war dragged on until 1700; the second broke out in 1710, and Peter was forced to restore Azov to the Turks. It was left to Catherine the Great, by taking the Crimea and the northern seaboard, to establish Russia firmly on the Black Sea.[4]

Peter did succeed, however, in reaching the Baltic, and by his death in 1725 Russia held the eastern shore of the Baltic from Riga to Viborg. These territorial gains were made at the expense of Sweden.[5] After the crushing defeat which Charles XII inflicted on Peter at Narva in 1700, when 10,000 Swedes routed 40,000 Russians, the Swedish King diverted his attention to Poland. When at last, early in 1708, Charles invaded Russia with an army of 30,000, the combination of a severe Russian winter and a reorganized Russian army resulted in the virtual annihilation of the Swedes at Poltava in 1709. By Charles XII's death in 1718 Peter's armies had occupied Livonia and part of Eastern Finland, and the treaty of Nystadt (1721), which formally ended the Great Northern War (1700–21), confirmed the Russian conquests. Peter's control of the Baltic shore gave him 'a window to the west', a port that did not, like Archangel, become ice-bound in winter. As early as 1703 Peter began the building of St Petersburg, capital of Russia until 1919. The new city was symbolic not only in its name and its westward-looking position: the death of 200,000 labourers during its construction reflects the ruthlessness with which Peter pursued his westernizing policy.

The same ruthlessness is seen in Peter's suppression of the revolt of the *Streltsi* which cut short his European tour in 1698. Sophia and his wife Eudoxia, who were thought to be implicated, were shut up in a convent. The *Streltsi* were abolished in name and fact by torture, by wholesale execution, or, for the fortunate few, by exile to Siberia. This deprived Russia of her only corps of trained troops and the disaster at Narva in 1700 provoked Peter to strenuous efforts to reform the army. European-style clothing, equipment and discipline were introduced, while a

4 See Chapter 14 below.
5 For an account of Peter's relations with Sweden see p. 34 above.

system of conscription for life, which required each province to provide and maintain its quota, produced a regular army of 200,000 by 1725.[6] By the same date Peter had created a navy of forty-eight ships of the line, nearly 800 galleys and smaller vessels, and 28,000 sailors. He also planned, but barely began, a scheme to connect the Black Sea to the Baltic by a canal system linking the dozens of intervening rivers and lakes.

Military reorganization necessitated administrative and fiscal reform. In 1699 Peter had re-established the Prikaz of Accounts to control all state finance and record all expenditure made by the other *prikazy* (state departments). The Duma, originally a deliberative and legislative assembly of boyars,[7] had declined in importance and in 1711, on the eve of his departure for the Turkish wars, Peter transferred its functions to a new body: 'Having to absent ourselves frequently during the wars, we appoint the Senate as ruler.' The Senate, though it remained an informal body subject to the Tsar's pleasure, was intended to supervise the new provincial administration, set up in 1708, under which Russia was divided into ten *gubernia* administered by a governor with the help of a council elected by the nobles. These new provincial units were preserved by Catherine the Great, though she greatly increased their number. In 1718 the central state departments were reorganized. The old *prikazy* were replaced by nine (later twelve) administrative 'colleges' on the Swedish model, each with a board of twelve members[8] and each responsible for a different branch of government, with authority over the whole country.

The administrative reforms were intended to increase the revenues, which in fact rose from an annual average of 3.33 million roubles for the years 1705-7 to nearly nine million for 1724.[9] This increase came partly from the establishment of state monopolies in such commodities as salt, tobacco, cod liver oil

[6] The desertion rate was high. It has been estimated that in 1718 those who had avoided conscription numbered 45,000 and deserters 20,000.

[7] Originally confidential advisers of the Russian princes, the boyars had become, by Peter's reign, the first grade of a fully fledged aristocracy with the exclusive privilege of possessing lands and serfs.

[8] A president, vice-president, four councillors, four assessors and two secretaries, of whom one councillor or assessor and one secretary were to be foreign.

[9] V. Klyuchevsky, *Peter the Great*, trans. L. Archibald, Macmillan 1958, p. 176.

and oak coffins. Another source was the state encouragement of trade and industry. In 1696 the first ironworks had been established near Moscow; by 1725 there were eighty-six ironworks, fifteen cloth mills and six cotton mills. In 1710, 153 foreign ships had entered Archangel; by 1724, 240 were already using St Petersburg, and by Peter's death the value of Russia's exports was probably as much as double that of her imports. But the chief new source of revenue was the substitution of the poll tax for the old, unproductive 'household tax'. The new tax, announced in 1718 but not collected until 1724, was levied on all male 'souls' (contemporary estimates vary between five million and nearly six million) and imposed a much heavier burden on the already overtaxed peasant: after one year of operation the poll tax was 843,000 roubles in arrears. But Peter had balanced his budget.

Peter's attack on the Church originated from financial motives. After the defeat at Narva, Peter confiscated the bells of some 300 churches for making cannon, seized the monastic estates which then employed some 900,000 serfs, and limited the jurisdiction of Church courts. While the clergy as a whole were critical of Peter, the Church itself was divided over the liturgical innovations of the Patriarch Nikon, which had provoked the schismatic group known as 'Old Believers'. This made it easier for Peter, on Adrian's death in 1700, to leave the patriarchate vacant until 1721 when he finally abolished it, creating in its place a Holy Synod to manage Church affairs under the supervision of a lay official, the high procurator.

The clergy had objected to Peter's westernizing policy which seemed to involve, not merely greater military and administrative efficiency, but a complete reorientation of social customs. The calendar was reformed in 1700; the alphabet was simplified; nobles were encouraged to wear western clothes and were taxed if they continued to wear beards; 1714 saw the first company of Russian actors; in 1716, forty civil servants were sent to Berlin to learn German, while in 1717 appeared *The Honourable Youth's Mirror*, a manual on the manners of western society. In order to enforce his new policy, Peter compelled the nobles to enlist in either the army or the administrative service for life. In

1722 *The Table of the Grades in All Ranks of Military, Civil and Court Service* made a man's position in the hierarchy of fourteen degrees dependent on his position in the public service. The top eight grades carried the privileges of nobility.

It may be argued that Peter's reforms merely gave old institutions new names. Certainly the legal system remained largely unchanged: the new criminal code, which was applied to the whole population in 1716, was borrowed in its entirety from the new military code of 1715 and included various forms of the death penalty (from burning alive to impalement) for over 100 offences. The peasants, excluded from trade and exhausted by the poll tax, were treated either as cannon fodder or as cheap labour on government projects, while Peter extended serfdom by introducing it into industry. The money that might have been spent on education went on war. The administrative and ecclesiastical reforms survived, but they needed a strong ruler, and of Peter's six immediate successors three were women and one was a child.[10] But geographically at least Russia had moved west: Peter's Swedish conquests and the new port of St Petersburg had given Russia an entry into Europe.

Prussia after the Great Elector, 1688–1740

'Four Hohenzollern rulers in the space of a century and a half put Prussia on the map.'[11] When the first of Gooch's four Hohenzollerns, Frederick William the Great Elector (1640–88), died, Prussia was scarcely even a geographical expression. The Elector of Brandenburg ruled over a collection of scattered territories. In 1614 the Hohenzollerns, rulers in Brandenburg since 1417, had inherited the Rhineland duchy of Cleves and one or two other small west German territories; in 1618 had come, also by inheritance, the duchy of Prussia (East Prussia); at the Peace of Westphalia in 1648 had been added the bishoprics of Halberstadt and Minden, the archbishopric of Magdeburg, and eastern or Farther Pomerania, which was separated from ducal Prussia by the Polish territory of West Prussia. But even with all these

10 See below, p. 130.
11 G. P. Gooch, *Frederick the Great*, Longmans 1947, p. 1.

additions the Brandenburg lands, thinly populated and ravaged by war, famine and plague,[12] contained in 1688 less than one and a half million people – about half the population of seventeenth-century Holland.

Frederick III (1688–1713), the Great Elector's son, did not tax his own delicate constitution with anything more constructive than an attempt to emulate the court ceremonial of Versailles, but he created the kingdom of Prussia at least in name. In 1701 he gave military support to the Emperor Leopold I in return for the prize of kingship. His title was to be 'Frederick I, King in Prussia' and was to apply only to the duchy of East Prussia, not to his lands within the Empire. It was only after Frederick the Great had gained West Prussia by the first partition of Poland in 1772[13] that the style King *of* Prussia was confirmed.

If the Great Elector had not founded a state,[14] he had created an army: it was at the battle of Warsaw in 1657 that the men of Cleves, Brandenburg and ducal Prussia had acted together for the first time. The revenues from the Hohenzollern crown lands were still sufficient to meet the whole cost of the civil government, and the new taxes levied by the Great Elector, excises on consumer goods and a state salt monopoly, were collected by the army and spent on the army.

The Great Elector's grandson, Frederick William I (1713–40), continued to build up the army. He cut the expense of the royal household by three-quarters, spending 2,547 *thalers* on his coronation journey to Königsberg where his father had spent five million. He centralized the administration of the army, finance and the royal domains in the General Directory set up in 1723. He established a cadet corps to train the younger sons of the *Junkers* or landed nobility and in 1721 authorized those holding a captaincy to bring their own serfs into the army for a short period of service. Most of the rank and file were recruited from foreign mercenaries or by the new cantonal system of conscription introduced in 1733: the country was divided into

[12] The plague of 1709, combined with famine, is thought to have killed one-third of the population of East Prussia; in one year 18,000 died in Königsberg alone.

[13] See below, p. 208.

[14] In his will, the Great Elector tried to divide his lands between the sons of his first and second marriages, but this was successfully resisted by Frederick III.

cantons, each of which had to supply recruits for a particular regiment – a system which lasted until 1806. By these means Frederick William raised the size of his army from 38,000 at his accession to 83,000 at his death, while it has been estimated that troops comprised no less than one-fifth of Berlin's population of 100,000.

But Frederick William carefully avoided using his army. Frederick III had held aloof from the coalition of Russia, Denmark and Poland against Sweden in 1699, thus avoiding the humiliation which they suffered at the hands of Charles XII.[15] Frederick William supported Peter the Great in the later stages of the Great Northern War (1700–21) and by the Treaty of Stockholm (1720) received most of western Pomerania with its port of Stettin; but it was Peter's troops who had done most of the fighting. The comic aspects of Frederick William's character – his insistence on always appearing in uniform, his passion for collecting giant grenadiers from all over Europe and his delight in drilling them himself – must not be allowed to obscure the fact that 'the Sergeant-Major King' bequeathed to his son a war chest of seven million *thalers* and an army with which Frederick the Great was to astonish Europe.

The Austrian Monarchy before Maria Theresa, 1705–40

The virtual disintegration of the Holy Roman Empire during the Thirty Years War (1618–48) and the extinction of the Habsburg line in Spain in 1700 transformed the European position of the Habsburgs, but did not necessarily weaken it. Their retention of the Imperial title preserved their influence over the German princes, and if it also perpetuated their responsibility to defend Europe from the Turks, this was in any case a role which geography had forced on the Habsburgs. Leopold I (Holy Roman Emperor, 1658–1705) had entered the War of the Spanish Succession (1702–13) in an attempt to keep Spain in the Habsburg family.[16] But by the Treaty of Rastatt (1714) Leopold's son Charles VI had to content himself with the Spanish Nether-lands, Milan, Naples and Sardinia, although he was able in 1720 to exchange Sardinia for Sicily.[17] Apart from these Italian and Flemish possessions, the lands ruled over by the House of Habsburg comprised the old 'hereditary provinces' (Upper and Lower Austria, with adjoining Tyrol, Styria, Carniola and Carinthia), the kingdom of Bohemia (including Moravia and Silesia) and the kingdom of Hungary. During the seventeenth century, while failing to recatholicize Germany, the Habsburgs had nevertheless consolidated their hold over their non-German lands by retrieving Bohemia from Protestantism and Hungary from the Turks.[18]

The expulsion of the Turks did not automatically decide the destiny of Hungary. The peace of Szatmar in 1712 put an end to the civil war in which, since 1703, Francis Rakoczy had led the Magyars against the Emperor. At the Diet which met in 1712 at Pozsony an agreement was reached whereby Charles VI guaranteed the integrity of Hungary and the rights of the Estates, and promised to rule Hungary according to her own laws and not 'according to the pattern of other provinces'. The Diet also provided for the support of a standing army to supplement the traditional feudal levy, though the burden of taxes to maintain the army was to be borne by the peasants. Thus in order to protect their pockets, the Hungarian nobles were prepared to place in Habsburg hands a weapon which could be used against Magyars as well as Turks.

But if the Habsburgs had regained Hungary, the survival of their Empire nevertheless required that the crowns of all the constituent kingdoms should be inherited by one person, and it was the preservation of this dynastic unity that preoccupied Charles VI for the rest of his reign. The death of his brother Joseph I (Emperor, 1705–11) left Charles the sole male Habsburg heir: if he died childless, the succession ought to revert to the two daughters of Joseph I. But in 1713 Charles issued a declaration that, if the male line failed, all his territories (but not, of course, the imperial title) should pass to his own daughters. A son was born to Charles in 1716, but died the same year; two daughters followed, Maria Theresa in 1717 and Marianne a year later; hope of a male heir was abandoned. In 1720 Charles asked the

Diets of all his dominions for confirmation of his 1713 declaration. The Estates of the Habsburg lands in Germany, Bohemia, Italy and the Netherlands proved compliant and in 1722 even the Hungarian Diet, recently reminded that the Turkish threat was not yet dead, agreed. In December 1724 the declaration of 1713 was re-enacted, together with the approval of the various Diets; this was the famous 'Pragmatic Sanction'.

Charles then set about extracting promises of guarantee from the European powers. In 1725 he obtained Spanish recognition both of the Pragmatic Sanction and of his East and West Indian Trading Company newly established at Ostend. Prussia also agreed, provided that Maria Theresa married a German. The price of English and Dutch approval, however, was the abandonment of the Ostend Company (1731).

Charles' patient negotiations were interrupted in 1733 by another dynastic dispute: Austria, Russia and Prussia supported the claim of Augustus III of Saxony to the Polish throne, in opposition to France's candidate Stanislas Leszczynski.[19] The ensuing European war (1733-35) and the elaborate peace-making at Vienna (1735-38) resulted in the confirmation of Augustus III as Polish King, the marriage of Maria Theresa to Francis Stephen, duke of Lorraine, and the resettlement of the Italian peninsula: Naples and Sicily were ceded by the Empire to Spain, on condition that they remained a separate Bourbon kingdom; in return the Empire received Parma and Piacenza, while Francis Stephen exchanged Lorraine for Tuscany; Sardinia gained Novara and Vigevano. All the signatories recognized the validity of the Pragmatic Sanction.

Charles VI's dynastic preoccupations left him with little time for internal reorganization of his lands. To the chancelleries for Austria, Bohemia, Hungary and Transylvania, he added new chancelleries for the Netherlands and his Italian states. In a complicated administrative pattern, the chancelleries successfully asserted their authority over the Estates and municipalities. But it was left to Maria Theresa (1740-80)[20] to attempt a conscious centralizing policy in the considerable Empire which Charles had worked so hard to preserve.

[19] See above, p. 30.   [20] See below, p. 142.

The First British Empire, 1689–1740

In 1600 the British Empire did not exist; by 1689 the British were established in the West Indies, had three important footholds in India, and had founded all but one of the original thirteen colonies in North America. The thirteenth, Georgia, was colonized in 1732 and when General Oglethorpe returned to the colony in 1735 he brought with him not only John Wesley as chaplain, but an army to fight the Spaniards.

But it was France who was Britain's chief contestant in North America. By 1689 the French had founded Quebec and Montreal, and settled in the peninsula of Acadia (later Nova Scotia) and on the island of Cape Breton. La Salle, the explorer of the Great Lakes, had in 1682 sailed down the Mississippi and established the province of Louisiana, which, because of its climate and the incursions of hostile Indians, proved of strategic rather than of economic importance. The first clash between British and French in North America occurred in 1689 with the accession of William of Orange. During 'King William's War' the French and their Indian allies penetrated into New Hampshire and New York, while the British took Port Royal (1690) but not Quebec. By the peace of Ryswick in 1697 both sides restored their North American conquests. During the War of the Spanish Succession[21] the British again took Port Royal (1710) and conquered Acadia, renaming it Nova Scotia. By the treaty of Utrecht[22] France was forced to cede Nova Scotia and New-foundland to Britain, and recognized British sovereignty in the Hudson Bay area. The French retort to Utrecht was to build the fortress of Louisbourg to defend the St Lawrence estuary, while trying to keep the Acadians friendly to France through the influence of Jesuit missionaries. They were allowed some success by the slow pace of the British settlement of Nova Scotia, which did not receive its charter until 1749.

The Anglo-French struggle in India belongs to the second half of the eighteenth century,[23] but the East India Company had been granted a new charter by Cromwell in 1657 and,

[21] See above, p. 11.　　[22] See above, p. 16.　　[23] See below, p. 183.

although pushed out of the East Indies trade by the Dutch, was already well established in India by 1700. Bombay, so cholera-ridden that the average expectation of life for an Englishman was put at three years,[24] had been let by Charles II to the East India Company in 1668 for an annual rent of £10; by 1677 it had a population of 60,000. In the same year Madras, which the Company had almost abandoned but had fortified instead, was successfully defended against Sivaji the Maratha chief, while 1690 saw the first permanent British settlement of Calcutta. During the wars of 1688–1713 there was little Anglo-French conflict in India, largely because the native powers were too strong, but in 1707, with the death of the last Mogul Emperor to exercise real power outside Delhi, the way was left clear for the colonial powers to fight each other.

In the West Indies Spain had occupied the larger islands, such as Cuba, but the smaller ones, like Barbados, colonized in 1624, were left to the British, who had also succeeded in taking Jamaica from the Spaniards in 1655. These islands, with their sugar trade, proved more profitable than the thirteen mainland colonies put together, although by 1738 French St Domingo was exporting twice as much sugar as Jamaica. The plantations of the West Indies and Spanish South America depended on the cheap labour of negro slaves imported from Africa. By the treaty of Utrecht Britain secured for the South Sea Company the *asiento* or sole right of supplying slaves to South America, together with the privilege of sending one ship a year for general trade. Spain suspected that these concessions, far from stopping illicit trade on the part of the British, merely provided cover for it, and she accordingly insisted on the right to search all foreign ships at sea. But the freelance *guarda-costas*, which the Spanish authorized to enforce the right of search, ill-treated even legitimate traders, and in March 1738 their most famous victim, Captain Jenkins, took his complaint to Westminster. Legitimate or not, the British government supported his complaint to the point of war in 1739, although 'the War of Jenkins' Ear' soon became submerged in the European war which started in the next year. For Britain, the War of the Austrian Succession

---

[24] J. A. Williamson, *A Short History of British Expansion*, Macmillan 1927, p. 305.

(1740–48), like the Seven Years War (1756–63),[25] provided a convenient excuse for trying to enlarge her Empire in India and the Americas. The First British Empire was *not* acquired in a fit of absence of mind.

[25] See Chapters 12 and 13 below.

II

THE ENLIGHTENMENT

It is no paradox that the scientific discoveries of the seventeenth century were much more significant for the period of the Enlightenment than were the scientific discoveries of the eighteenth. In any age it takes at least a generation for the fruits of scientific research to be disseminated among intelligent laymen. The *philosophes* of the Enlightenment were laymen. They were not even philosophers, except in the sense that they popularized the new ideas in natural philosophy and political science that were the achievements of the seventeenth century. The *Encyclopaedia* collected and classified what was already known: it laid no claim to originality. What *was* new was the *philosophes'* assumption that there were uniform laws of nature – not only in physics, but throughout the whole range of human experience. This was, of course, little more than a guess. The true philosophers of the age – Hume, Rousseau, Kant – at least partially rejected the *philosophes'* rather naïve belief in the power of reason, but it was only when the French Revolution had demonstrated the limitations of rationalism in politics that the reaction towards religion and romanticism gathered force. In spite of the rise of Methodism in England and the strength of popular superstition in southern Europe, the prevailing temper of eighteenth-century thought was essentially rationalistic.

4

The Scientific Background

Bacon and the Experimental Method

The seventeenth century has been called the Century of
Genius; the century that followed deserves perhaps to be called
the Age of Encyclopaedias rather than the Age of Reason. But if
it is true that the chief contribution of the *philosophes* of the
eighteenth century was to popularize the scientific achievements
of the seventeenth, it is also true that the encyclopaedic impulse
had its birth in the seventeenth rather than in the eighteenth century. The debt of the French encyclopaedists to Francis Bacon,
James I's Lord Chancellor, was admitted by Diderot in the Pros-
pectus to the *Encyclopaedia*[1] of 1751: 'If we emerge from this
vast operation, our principal debt will be to the Chancellor
Bacon who sketched the plan of a universal dictionary of
sciences and arts. . . .'

Francis Bacon (1561–1626) would not have regarded himself
as a 'scientist', for the term was not coined until the nineteenth
century and the modern distinction between 'science' and 'philosophy' was not drawn: at the end of the seventeenth century
Newton was to entitle his great work *Philosophiae Naturalis Principia Mathematica* (*Mathematical Principles of Natural Philosophy*).[2]
But Bacon nevertheless has a strong claim to be regarded as one
of the pioneers of the scientific method, which may be briefly
defined as the method of inductive reasoning from observations
and verification by experiment.[2a] As early as 1592 Bacon, in a

---

[1] See below, p. 71.

[2] See below, p. 63.

[2a] Induction is the mode of reasoning from the particular facts to general conclusions;
deduction, in spite of its popular use in detective fiction, is the opposite method of
starting from self-evident axioms and proceeding by logical steps from the general to
the particular, in the manner of a geometrical proof.

composition written for a 'device'[3] in honour of the Queen's birthday, had complained: 'All the philosophy of nature which is now received is either the philosophy of the Grecians or that other of the Alchemists. ... The one never faileth to multiply words, and the other ever faileth to multiply gold.' Bacon's remedy was prescribed in a similar composition for the 'device' of 1594. The Queen's government should provide for the setting up of a library comprising books by authors both ancient and modern and in all languages, the creation of botanical and zoological gardens to facilitate the observation of plant and animal life, a museum in which inanimate objects were contained and classified, and a laboratory equipped for experimental research.

Bacon's thesis that true knowledge is useful knowledge was developed in *The Advancement of Learning*, published in 1605 and republished, revised and in Latin, in 1623. He put his ideas into more popular form in *The New Atlantis*, a scientific Utopia published a year after his death. The spirit of the work may be gauged from Bacon's description of Solomon's House with its 'great lakes both salt and fresh'; its 'parts and enclosures of all sorts of beasts and birds'; its 'furnaces of great diversities'; its 'sound-houses', 'perfume-houses', and 'engine-houses'; to say nothing of its 'houses of deceits of the senses, where we represent all manner of feats of juggling, false apparitions, impostures and illusions; and their fallacies'. The purpose of Solomon's House is summed up thus: 'The End of our Foundation is the knowledge of Causes, and secret motions of things; and the enlarging of the bounds of Human Empire, to the effecting of all things possible.'

If the words sound extravagant, they are not much more so than those in the charter of The Royal Society of London for Promoting Natural Knowledge, founded in 1660,[4] which set itself the task of 'promoting by the authority of experiments the science of natural things and of useful arts'. It is certainly not extravagant to regard the Royal Society as a monument to

---

[3] A contemporary description of an entertainment.

[4] The first charter of the Royal Society was sealed on 15 July 1662, but the first recorded meeting of the society was on 28 November 1660, when Robert Boyle, William Petty and Christopher Wren were among those present. The French *Académie des Sciences* was founded in 1666.

Bacon. In the words of Cowley's 'Ode to the Royal Society:'[5]

> Bacon, like Moses, led us forth at last.
> The barren wilderness he past,
> Did on the very border stand
> Of the blest promised land,
> And from the mountain top of his exalted wit,
> Saw it himself, and shew'd us it.

'Nullius in verba' ('take no theory on trust') was the motto proposed for the Royal Society by the diarist John Evelyn, and at first its members adhered to their original rule not to debate 'concerning any hypothesis or principle of philosophy' until they had 'a sufficient collection of experiments, histories and observations'. But the expense of experimentation accounted for the early financial difficulties of the Society, and by 1680 its members were discussing whether experiments 'should be made in order to prove a theory propounded'. This suggestion, opposed by William Petty,[6] ran counter to Bacon's insistence on the need for a complete record of observations before proceeding to formulate propositions. Bacon took it for granted that such completeness was attainable. As he wrote: 'The particular phenomena of the arts and sciences are in reality but as a handful; the invention[7] of all causes and sciences would be the labour of but a few years.'[8] He once suggested that a book about six times as big as Pliny's *Natural History* would be sufficient to contain all the facts necessary for the understanding of nature. In *The Great Instauration* of 1620 Bacon claimed to have provided an outline of just such a comprehensive encyclopaedia of natural philosophy. Apart from the grandiose plan, providing for six parts, little of the *Instauration* was written beyond the second part entitled *The*

---

[5] Quoted in B. Farrington, *Francis Bacon: Philosopher of Industrial Science*, Lawrence & Wishart 1951, p. 17.

[6] The father of statistics. In the preface to his *Political Arithmatick* (1690) he claimed as his object: 'To express myself in terms of Number, Weight or Measure; to use only Arguments of Sense, and to consider only such Causes as have visible Foundations in Nature.'

[7] In the sense of *discovery*.

[8] Cf. Newton's famous words: 'I do not know what I may appear to the world, but to myself I seem to have been only a boy playing on the seashore, and diverting myself in now and then finding a smoother pebble or a prettier shell than ordinary, whilst the great ocean of truth lay all undiscovered before me.'

New Organon or Directions concerning the Interpretation of Nature.
But the Baconian philosophy is epitomized in the words of the
preface: 'Nature cannot be conquered but by obeying her. ...
To be ignorant of causes is to be frustrated in action.'

Bacon has often been condemned as a pure empiricist, a mere
collector of data. It is true that he underestimated the importance
of mathematics, and disliked Galileo's[9] method of turning the
problem of motion into a problem of geometrical bodies moving
in geometrical space; but he himself denied the charge of mere
empiricism. He compared the empiricists to ants who collect
and heap together material of all kinds quite indiscriminately,
while he saw the pure philosophers as spiders, spinning webs out
of their own insides. The true philosophers, Bacon thought,
were a blend of both: like bees who collect pollen from flowers
and turn it into honey. Bacon's simile of the busy bee might
serve as an apt picture of the eighteenth-century *philosophe*.
Diderot was right to recognize his debt to Bacon.

Descartes and the Mathematical Method

If Bacon refused to admit the importance of mathematics,
Réné Descartes (1596–1650), the inventor of coordinate geometry,[10] made mathematics the very basis and structure of his
philosophy. Bacon had called for 'minds washed clean of
opinions', open minds which could devote themselves to the
impartial interpretation of facts; but to Descartes facts seemed
all too ambiguous, and his aim was therefore to discount the
observation of phenomena and take as his starting point those
facts which were so simple as to be self-evident, those 'innate
ideas' later to be attacked by Locke.[11] In Descartes' own words:
'My design was singly to find ground of assurance, and cast aside
the loose earth and sand that I might reach the rock or the clay.'

In his *Discourse on Method*,[11a] published in 1637, Descartes
expounded his famous principle of 'systematic doubt'. Suspi-

[9] See below, p. 61.
[10] Descartes showed that by the use of coordinates (*e.g.* graph paper) any algebraic
formula could be plotted as a curve in space, and that, on the other hand, any curve
in space, however complex, could be converted into algebraic terms.
[11] See below, p. 65.
[11a] *Discours sur la méthode de bien conduire la raison et chercher la vérité dans les sciences.*

cious of the evidence of the external world which reached him through his senses, Descartes was prepared to accept only the certainty of his own existence: 'Cogito ergo sum' ('I think, therefore I exist'). But this was only the starting point: from this premise he proceeded by logical steps, in the manner of a mathematical proof, to the acceptance of the world of external phenomena. As he put it, his aim was: 'to conduct my thoughts in such order that by commencing with objects the simplest and easiest to know, I might ascend by little and little, and, as it were, step by step, to the knowledge of the more complex.'

This was the mathematical or deductive method of Descartes. To represent his system as destructive scepticism is to misconstrue it: it was essentially constructive. Among the self-evident truths that Descartes admitted was the existence of God, which he described as a truth 'at least as certain as I ever judged any truth of mathematics'. The argument went as follows:

1 All things which we clearly and distinctly conceive are **true**.
2 Therefore God must exist, since we clearly and distinctly conceive Him.[12]
3 Therefore we can trust our senses, since God, being God, would not deliberately deceive us.

Thus Descartes, for all his much misunderstood 'systematic doubt', was prepared to deduce the whole universe from the axiom of God's existence, with all the logic of a demonstration in geometry.

There was nevertheless some excuse for misunderstanding, for Descartes drew a distinction between two kinds of reality: the world of 'thinking substance' (the realm of the conscious mind) and that of 'extended substance' (everything outside the mind). This was the celebrated 'Cartesian Dualism'. Descartes never gave any explanation of the connection between these two worlds except to imply that it was miraculous. But this divorce between the spiritual and the physical tended to lead to a purely materialistic interpretation of the physical world. Descartes may have

---

[12] 'I could not possibly be of such a nature as I am, and yet have in my mind the idea of God, if God did not in reality exist.' Descartes, *Meditations on the First Philosophy*, iii, p. 110.

started with God, but by banishing God from the physical universe he prepared the way for the Deists and the idea of natural religion.[13] At all events, in spite of Descartes' personal protestations of orthodoxy, Cartesianism was denounced by Calvinists, Lutherans and Catholics: Descartes died in exile in 1650 and in 1663 his books were put on the Index.

If Descartes was mathematical in his metaphysics, he was mathematical in his physics too. All matter ('extended substance') in the universe was to be accounted for in terms of motion and extension (crudely, 'speed' and 'size'). All physical phenomena were measurable and reducible to mathematical formulae. 'Give me motion and extension,' he wrote, 'and I will build you the world.' But the actual business of measurement and the conducting of physical experiments occupied a very subordinate place in Descartes' system. Experiments might be made to test which of a number of alternative explanations suggested by his reasoning was in fact the true explanation; their role was often to confirm a hunch or hypothesis, and experimentation would stop as soon as such confirmation had been obtained – on what Bacon would have regarded as very incomplete data. And it is characteristic of Descartes' approach to physical problems that he should have supposed that space was filled with fluid matter and that each planet exerted some influence on the matter immediately around it after the manner of a vortex or whirlpool; the sun's vortex accounted for the movement of the planets, each of which carried round with it a minor vortex of its own.

The mathematical method of Descartes nevertheless had a powerful influence on the men of the eighteenth century. Newton might contradict the vortex theory, but Locke, while rejecting Descartes' psychology, continued to cling to the ideal of mathematical certainty. As Professor Cobban puts it: 'Descartes, if the Enlightenment was to repudiate many of his doctrines, remains one of its founding fathers.'[14]

[13] See below, p. 74.
[14] A. Cobban, *In Search of Humanity*, Cape 1960, p. 46.

Copernicus Confirmed: Kepler and Galileo

Plato's Academy, in which Aristotle himself probably lectured, is supposed to have carried over its door the legend: 'Only Geometers Admitted.' It is less often remembered that Copernicus' attack on Aristotle's universe was based on geometry, not on observation. The Aristotelian universe, as modified by Ptolemy (c. A.D. 140), with its nine spheres revolving round the earth and its system of epicycles to account for the irregular movement of the planets, had become by Copernicus' day a complicated mechanism involving some eighty 'wheels'. Copernicus (1473–1543) was disturbed by this complexity, and to him the chief attraction of putting the sun, instead of the earth, at the centre of the universe was that the picture became very much neater: the number of 'wheels' was reduced from eighty to thirty-four, while the rotation of the *earth* on its own axis removed the need for all the spheres to make a complete revolution every twenty-four hours.

But the greater simplicity brought with it some difficulties. According to Aristotle and Ptolemy, while the earth was solid, the spheres were made of an ethereal, perhaps even a crystalline substance. The movement of the spheres was much more easily explained than the movement of so heavy a body as the earth, which Copernicus had now, so to speak, put into orbit. Again, Aristotle had explained the phenomenon of gravity by the tendency of all objects to be drawn towards the centre of the universe; how was it to be explained if the earth was not the centre? The answers which Copernicus gave to these questions show how much he remained a prisoner within the Aristotelian system of explanations. Copernicus explained the movement of the earth by the fact that all spherical bodies have a tendency to revolve, while gravity was explained by the tendency of all things to form themselves into spheres – the perfect shape, as the ancients believed. Copernicus' *De Revolutionibus Orbium Coelestium*, published at his death in 1543, contained only twenty-seven of his *own* observations; all the rest were those of other observers, mostly ancient. But Copernicus' calculations did at least give results closer to those ancient observations than Ptolemy's had done.

Copernicus may or may not have regarded his theory as a mere hypothesis.[15] Certainly he was more afraid of ridicule than of ecclesiastical censure. In dedicating *De Revolutionibus* to Pope Paul III, Copernicus wrote of 'the scorn which was to be feared on account of the novelty and the absurdity of the opinion'; it was not placed on the Index until 1616, while Luther had condemned Copernicus as a 'fool'.[16] The title of Galileo's book, *Dialogue Concerning the Two Principal World Systems* (published in 1632), suggests how slowly the Copernican theory gained acceptance, and it was only when improved observation began to confirm Copernicus rather than Ptolemy that the heliocentric view triumphed. Copernicus had kept the Ptolemaic 'spheres', but they no longer performed any obvious function and observation was soon to suggest that they did not exist. In 1572 a new star suddenly appeared. It was as bright as Venus, and when its position was calculated it was found to be among the fixed stars. Five years later a comet was observed: it was evidently in the upper skies, not in the sub-lunar sphere, and had thus apparently cut a path through what were supposed to be the impenetrable crystalline spheres. Thus a double blow was struck at the Aristotelian astronomy: the spheres were imaginary, and the perfect, immutable matter of the upper skies could suffer change. It is not easy for us today to recapture the sense of shock that this discovery produced.

The position of the new star of 1572 had been measured by the instruments of Tycho Brahe (1546–1601), who, even before the coming of the telescope, had greatly improved the accuracy of astronomical measurement and systematized the collection and recording of astronomical data. In 1576 Tycho established himself on a 2,000-acre island near Copenhagen. Here he pursued his astronomical studies for twenty years before moving (complete with library, printing press and instruments) to Prague, where he accepted the post of Imperial Professor of Mathematics.

[15] The preface to *De Revolutionibus* in which the new theory was pleaded as an hypothesis was inserted by Osiander without Copernicus' knowledge.

[16] Luther complained: 'This fool of a Copernicus wants to upset the whole of astronomy, but Scripture says that Joshua stopped the sun and not the earth.'

Tycho's successor at Prague was Johann Kepler (1571–1630), a far greater mathematician, who now inherited Tycho's astronomical observations and used them to dramatic effect. Copernicus had clung to the ancient view that the orbits of the planets were circular; Tycho's observations had shown that their behaviour could not be explained in terms of circular motion. Kepler, while accepting the heliocentric theory, suggested a number of different geometrical figures to describe the planetary orbits before, by a process of trial and error, arriving at his three famous laws:

1 The planets move in an elliptical orbit with the sun at one focus.
2 The line joining the planet to the sun sweeps an equal area in any equal length of time.
3 The square of the time of one complete orbit (T) bears a constant relationship to the cube of the mean distance (d) from the sun: $\dfrac{T^2}{d^3} = K$.

While Kepler was formulating laws on the celestial bodies, Galileo (1564–1642) was formulating laws on terrestrial bodies. It now seems unlikely that he ever conducted the famous experiment from the top of the leaning tower of Pisa,[17] but he was nevertheless the first great exponent of the experimental method. Galileo's contemporaries would describe the path of a projectile in accordance with *a priori* principles. Galileo sought to isolate the motion of the projectile from its other qualities by creating artificial conditions in which motion had its simplest form, 'inducing' principles of motion from his actual observations, and applying them to the description of the path of the projectile. In the apparently absurd picture of Galileo measuring the acceleration of a brass ball down inclined planes of varying length and inclination, we have a working model of the scientific method. And although it never seems to have occurred to Galileo to consider the planets as celestial brass balls, he came very close to Newtonian mechanics in claiming that motion and rest were

[17] Coresio (an Aristotelian) claimed to have tried the experiment in 1612 and found that the larger body fell faster than the smaller.

equally natural states of matter and that only *change* of motion needed a physical explanation: a moving body continued to move uniformly in a straight line unless deflected by a definite force.

But Galileo was an observer as well as an experimenter and, by means of his telescope constructed in 1609, he was able to remove some of the objections to the Copernican theory. Not only did he find that the heavenly bodies were more solid than had been supposed, thus making it easier to regard the earth as a planet, but the discovery of the moons of Jupiter showed that the earth was, at least, not the *only* centre. Even more important, Galileo found that the fixed stars looked *smaller* than with the naked eye, thus suggesting that they were more distant than even Copernicus had imagined. The idea of an infinite universe, first suggested by Bruno (1548–1600), had serious theological implications. If the Church had burned Bruno, it is not surprising that she disciplined Galileo. By his confirmation of Copernicus, Galileo did indeed seem to have 'abolished heaven'.[18]

The Newtonian Synthesis

The climax to the astronomical discoveries of the seventeenth century came when Sir Isaac Newton (1642–1727) showed that Kepler's celestial mechanics and Galileo's terrestrial mechanics were two aspects of one whole and could both be embraced in a single law: the law of universal gravitation. But the laws of Galileo and Kepler were only part of a more complicated pattern of discovery, and, in order to understand the scope of Newton's synthesis, it is necessary to recall the various ingredients which Newton worked into his solution.

Among the astronomical problems facing Newton's contemporaries were two particularly perplexing questions. If the earth was not the centre of the universe, why were falling bodies attracted to it? And if moving bodies moved uniformly in a straight line unless deflected by a force, as Galileo claimed, why did the planets revolve round the sun instead of flying off in a

---

[18] It was not until 1744 that Galileo's *Dialogue* was printed with papal licence at Padua, and then only with the sentence on Galileo and his recantation included in the same volume.

straight line? William Gilbert's theory of gravity as magnetic attraction (1600) had been extended by Kepler to the planets. He considered that attraction between the heavenly bodies was mutual, but he did not apply his theory to the universe as a whole; he did not, for instance, regard the stars as 'bodies' like the planets, and he saw the sun as the source of the power which pushed the planets round their orbits. In 1665 Alphonse Borelli argued that the planets would gravitate to the sun, but for their centrifugal tendency. In 1673 Huygens published a mathematical formula for centrifugal force, but did not apply it to the planets. In 1674 Robert Hooke (member of the Royal Society since 1663) formulated the law that all heavenly bodies exerted an attraction on one another and that the attraction between two bodies became greater the closer they were together.

It remained for Newton to fuse all these elements into a single law. He had virtually succeeded by 1666, but he put the work aside for twenty years and it was not until 1687 that his *Mathematical Principles of Natural Philosophy* was published. Here he enunciated his law of universal gravitation: all matter moves as if every particle attracts every other particle with a force proportional to the product of the two masses and inversely proportional to the square of the distance between them. And the completeness of the synthesis is illustrated by the fact that if Newton's *general* law was true, all three of Kepler's *particular* laws[19] could be shown to be true also.

Newton had thus solved 'the problem of the skies' with a mathematical answer, so confirming Galileo's view that 'philosophy . . . is written in mathematical language, and the letters are triangles, circles and other geometrical figures, without which means it is humanly impossible to understand a single word'.[20] But Newton had not *explained* gravity, nor had he tried to suggest *why* one particle attracted another. As he retorted once: 'Pray do not ascribe that notion to me, for the cause of gravity is what I do not pretend to know.' Nor must it be thought that Newton had things all his own way at first. Huygens and Leibnitz both criticized the Newtonian system, and

[19] See above, p. 61.
[20] *The Age of Reason*, ed. S. Hampshire, Mentor Books 1956, p. 33.

although Descartes' vision of space filled with whirlpools to account for the movement of the planets seems absurd today, it commanded support in France until well into the eighteenth century. Both Newton and Descartes were great geometers, but the clue to Newton's ultimate victory lies in the fact that his mathematical answer was grounded firmly on observational verification. No one had *seen* a Cartesian vortex.

The experimental method bore fruit not only in the celestial mechanics of Newton, but in the non-mechanical sciences as well. It was Newton himself who constructed a reflecting telescope and who, by a series of careful experiments, showed that white light, far from being simple, was composed of the primary colours of the spectrum. As he claimed at the beginning of his *Opticks*, not published until 1704: 'My Design ... is not to explain the Properties of Light by Hypotheses, but to propose and prove them by Reason and Experiments.' Meanwhile Robert Boyle (1627-91), author of the *Sceptical Chymist* (1690) and the famous law on the pressure of gases, saw that Aristotle's four elements were too few to account for observed phenomena; and although his investigation of the air stopped just short of the discovery of oxygen, his work formed a basis on which Lavoisier was to build in the next century.[23a] William Harvey's *De Motu Cordis*, describing his discoveries on the circulation of the blood, had been published in 1628, with a dedication in which Harvey professed 'to learn and teach anatomy not from books but from dissections, not from the tenets of Philosophers but from the fabric of Nature'.[21] Or, as he put it in the first chapter, his method was 'through ever wider and more meticulous inquiry, involving frequent examinations of the insides of many different living animals and the collation of many observations'.[22] The fact that Harvey also based his work on observations and experiments made in sixteenth-century Padua is a reminder that the experimental method was not invented by Bacon. But it is no exaggeration to say with Professor Cobban that Harvey 'did for the human body what the new astronomy was doing for the heavenly bodies'.[23]

[21] W. Harvey, *De Motu Cordis*, trans. Franklin, Blackwell 1957, p. 7.
[22] *Ibid.*, p. 24.   [23] A. Cobban, *op. cit.*, p. 37.   [23a] See below, p. 112.

Locke and Natural Law

In the eyes of the eighteenth century, Newton's greatest achievement lay in his restoration of order to the universe. Copernicus' heliocentric universe had preserved the medieval order, and the displacement of the earth from the centre was probably not as much of a psychological shock as is often claimed.[24] But with the subsequent disappearance of the celestial spheres, the movements of the heavenly bodies seemed to be thrown into a state of disorder which could be described but not explained. Here Newton came to the rescue by showing that there *was* a universal order, even if it had to be described in abstract terms capable of mathematical expression.

Newton's success in astronomy encouraged the hope that all branches of knowledge could be similarly reduced to a few simple laws which any educated man could understand. This cult of simplicity is reflected in Newton's own law of parsimony: 'We are to admit no more causes of natural things than such as are both true and sufficient to explain their appearances ... for Nature is pleased with simplicity and affects not the pomp of superfluous causes.' The notion of natural order is also to be found in Alexander Pope's *Essay on Man*, begun in 1732, though not published until 1784. As he wrote in the preface: 'The Science of Human Nature is, like all other sciences, reduced to a few clear points: there are not many certain truths in this world.'

This optimistic belief was also held by John Locke (1632–1704). He described his *Essay concerning Human Understanding* (1690) as an inquiry into 'the original, certainty and extent of human knowledge'. The origin of human knowledge Locke placed firmly in the world of empirical fact: all ideas came through the senses, and the so-called 'innate ideas' of Descartes were not innate at all, but rather the lessons of early experience. With an empiricist's zest for the collection of data, Locke listed the peculiar customs that prevailed in different parts of the world and then asked: 'Where, then, are those innate principles of justice, piety, gratitude, equity, chastity?' But although he

[24] The psalmist had asked, 'What is man that Thou art mindful of him. . .?'

dismissed 'innate ideas', Locke nevertheless believed that mathematical certainty could be achieved in ethics and politics: 'Where there is no property there is no injustice is a proposition as certain as any demonstration in Euclid.' Politics and ethics, no less than mechanics, were governed by natural laws.

To the men of the middle ages, 'natural law' or 'the law of nature', had meant God's law for governing the world, and the interpreter of natural law had therefore been the Church. Thus, when the Church suffered disparagement during the period of Renaissance and Reformation, the notion of natural law suffered too.[24a] But in the eighteenth century, thanks to Newton's laws, natural law recovered credit: it was to be interpreted now, not by the Church, but by Reason. In the words of Pope's famous couplet:

> Nature and Nature's laws lay hid in night:
> God said, 'Let Newton be!' and all was light.[25]

To Locke, natural law was God-given, but nevertheless simple and discoverable: it 'teaches all men who will but consult it, that being all equal and independent no one ought to harm another in his life, health, liberty or possessions'.[26] The execution of God's law was in the hands of men, who could execute it effectively only in society. Hence the idea of the 'social contract': each individual surrenders his own right to execute the law of nature, transferring it into the hands of a legislature. The law of nature must be taken as the constant guide in framing the laws of society, 'an eternal rule to all men, legislators as well as others', and the legislature must take care not to infringe the individual's right of private property, since the security of property was, in Locke's eyes, the object of government. If such 'natural' rights were infringed, the trust between rulers and ruled had been broken and the ruled were entitled to rebel. Locke refused, however, to believe that revolutions would be frequent, and if the right to rebel were

---

[24a] This is something of an oversimplification since even in medieval times some philosophers had distinguished between natural law and divine law.
[25] A. Pope, 'Epitaph Intended for Sir Isaac Newton'.
[26] J. Locke, *Second Treatise of Civil Government*, Blackwell 1948, p. 5.

denied, he complained, 'they may as well say upon the same ground that honest men may not oppose robbers or pirates because this may occasion disorder and bloodshed'.[27]

Locke's *Civil Government*, though not published until 1690, had been written before the 1688 Revolution in England. His arguments nevertheless formed a useful justification of the English Revolution.[28] Locke's natural rights did not in fact differ greatly from the rights which the average Englishman enjoyed in 1690; but they were far beyond those of the average Frenchman. When Locke's ideas reached first Europe, then America, they looked much more revolutionary than they had done at home.

Locke died in 1704, but he was to exert a double influence on the eighteenth century: his psychology of sensation affected both the encyclopaedists and educationists of the age, while his political ideas and even his language were re-echoed in the manifestoes of both the American and the French revolutions.[29]

[27] J. Locke, *op. cit.*, p. 111.

[28] It used to be thought that Locke was trying to justify the deposition of Charles I. But it now seems more likely that Locke, as the close friend and sometime secretary of Shaftesbury, was defending the idea of resistance to the government of James II.

[29] See below, pp. 253 and 282.

5

The Cult of Reason

The 'Philosophes'

The Enlightenment, like all such portmanteau labels bestowed by historians, eludes precise definition. The belief in the rationality of man and in his ability to improve his environment by increasing his knowledge was at least as old as the Renaissance. The fifteenth-century boast of Alberti[1] that 'man can make what he will of himself' might have served as the slogan of the Italian Renaissance. But in the sixteenth and seventeenth centuries the Counter-Reformation reclaimed much of Europe from Protestantism; and, as France, Germany, the Netherlands, even England, were torn by religious conflict, the optimism of the Renaisance humanists began to seem misplaced.

The seventeenth-century Scientific Revolution, however, put new weapons into the hands of the rationalists. Newton, in expounding his gravitational theories on the movement of the heavenly bodies and the action of the tides, had written: 'I wish we could derive the rest of the phenomena of Nature by the same kind of reasoning from mechanical principles . . . but I hope the principles here laid down will afford some light either to this or some truer method of philosophy'.[2] Newton was thinking of the world of inanimate objects, but the so-called *philosophes* of the eighteenth century set themselves the task of similarly illuminating the laws of *human* nature, of discovering in ethics, economics and politics general laws comparable to the law of universal gravitation. They accepted Descartes' belief in the mathematical neatness of nature and in the existence of a few simple under-

[1] Leone Battista Alberti (1404–72). Venetian painter, poet, philosopher, musician and architect. His chief work, *De Re Aedificatoria*, was translated into Italian, French, Spanish and English

[2] *From Absolutism to Revolution: 1648–1848*, a collection of documents edited by H. H. Rowen, Macmillan 1963, p. 4.

lying principles,[3] but they sought to discover those principles by the inductive method of Bacon and Newton: the collection and classification of facts, and the testing of conclusions by observation and experiment. The *philosophes'* insistence on the appeal to experience was fortified by Locke's psychology of sensation, which dismissed the Cartesian notion of innate ideas and held that all ideas came through the senses.[4] Voltaire, the doyen of the *philosophes,* admirably summed up their attitude in his *Treatise on Metaphysics* (1734):

We must never make hypotheses; we must never say: Let us begin by inventing principles according to which we attempt to explain everything. We should say rather: Let us make an exact analysis of things. . . . When we cannot utilize the compass of mathematics or the torch of experience and physics, it is certain that we cannot take a single step forward.

'Reason', then, was not so much a body of knowledge as a method: the faculty of discovering the right answer by induction from the collected facts. And underlying this attitude was the assumption that there *was* a right answer to every question, that all problems from bridge-building to law-making could be answered with the same certainty as could a mathematical problem. These two threads of empiricism and mathematical neatness run throughout the thought of the Enlightenment and account for much of its complexity and apparent contradiction.

If the formative influences on the *philosophes* were largely English, the *philosophes* themselves were French.[5] Although the Enlightenment is often known as the 'Aufklärung', we shall later suggest that the German manifestation of the movement was untypical.[6] The extent to which the Enlightenment was a French phenomenon is best measured by a bare list of its principal French works:

1733 Voltaire's *Philosophical Letters* (*Letters on the English*)
1738 Voltaire's *Elements of the Philosophy of Newton*

---

[3] See above, p. 56.
[4] See above, p. 65.
[5] For the influence of English ideas on the *philosophes* and for the influence of the writings of the *philosophes* on the French Revolution see Chapter 18.
[6] See below, p. 89.

1746 Diderot's *Philosophical Thoughts*
1748 Montesquieu's *Spirit of Laws*
1748 La Mettrie's *Man as Machine*
1749 First volume of Buffon's *Natural History*
1749 Rousseau's *Discourse on the Arts and Sciences*
1749 Condillac's *Treatise on Systems*
1751 First volume of Diderot's *Encyclopaedia*
1753 Voltaire's *Essay on Manners*
1755 Rousseau's *Discourse on the Origins of Inequality*
1756 Holbach's *Christianity Unmasked*
1758 Helvétius' *On the Mind*
1758 Quesnay's *Economic Tableau*
1759 Voltaire's *Candide*
1762 Rousseau's *Social Contract*
1762 Rousseau's *Émile*
1772 Last volume of the *Encyclopaedia*

D'Alembert, mathematician and co-editor of the *Encyclopaedia*, commented in his essay *Elements of Philosophy* (1759) on the flowering of philosophical works around the midpoint of the century. He went on to give his own character sketch of the Age of Reason:

If one considers without bias the present state of our knowledge, one cannot deny that philosophy among us has shown progress. Natural science from day to day accumulates new riches. Geometry, by extending its limits, has borne its torch into the regions of physical science which lay nearest at hand. The true system of the world has been recognized, developed and perfected. . . . Thus from the principles of the secular sciences to the foundations of religious revelation, from metaphysics to matters of taste, from music to morals, from the scholastic disputes of the theologians to matters of trade, from the laws of princes to those of peoples, from natural law to the arbitrary law of nations . . . everything has been discussed and analyzed, or at least mentioned.[7]

---

[7] E. Cassirer, *The Philosophy of the Enlightenment*, Eng. trans., Beacon Press 1955, pp. 3–4.

Diderot and the 'Encyclopaedia'

The notion that everything could be 'discussed and analyzed, or at least mentioned' led to the attempt to classify knowledge alphabetically. We have already noticed Bacon's scheme for a universal dictionary of knowledge,[8] and in 1728 the English Quaker, Ephraim Chambers, had published in two volumes *A Cyclopedia or Universal Dictionary of the Arts and Sciences*. But, like Bayle's *Historical and Critical Dictionary* (1697),[9] it was the work of one man, whereas an encyclopaedia was a project demanding a team. Diderot, born at Langres in 1713 and educated, like Voltaire fifteen years earlier, at a Jesuit college in Paris, was already working on a translation of Robert James' six-volume *Medicinal Dictionary* when in 1746 he was commissioned by the publisher Le Breton to edit a ten-volume encyclopaedia.

The task that Diderot and his co-editor d'Alembert set themselves is best described in Diderot's own words:

The aim of an *Encyclopaedia* is to assemble the knowledge scattered over the face of the earth; to explain its general plan to the men with whom we live, and to transmit it to those who will come after us, so that the labours of past centuries may not be useless to future times; so that our descendants, by becoming better informed, may in consequence be happier and more virtuous; and so that we may not die without having deserved well of the human race.[10]

The team assembled to carry out this ambitious task included Voltaire, Montesquieu, Rousseau, Buffon, Holbach, Turgot (later Louis XVI's finance minister)[11] and Condorcet, who drafted the ill-fated French constitution of 1793.[12] These distinguished contributors often wrote on unexpected subjects: Voltaire was the author of an article on hem-stitching, while Rousseau (less surprisingly, since he had written an opera) contributed the sections on music.

---

[8] See above, p. 53.   [9] See below, p. 73.
[10] G. R. Havens, *The Age of Ideas*, Peter Owen 1957, p. 295.
[11] See below, p. 262.   [12] See below, p. 300.

In February 1752, by which time the first two volumes had appeared, further printing, reprinting and sale of the *Encyclopaedia* were forbidden by the King's Council on the grounds that it tended 'to destroy royal authority, establish the spirit of independence and revolt, and under obscure and equivocal terms, lay a foundation for error, corruption, irreligion and incredulity'. In spite of this prohibition, publication continued at the rate of one volume a year until 1757, and by this date there were nearly 4,000 subscribers compared with 2,000 in 1751. In March 1759 the Council officially revoked the privilege granted to Le Breton in 1746 and publication stopped. Even now composition and printing continued, but the team was beginning to break up. In 1759 Rousseau withdrew from the project in protest against d'Alembert's article on Geneva in Volume VII, in which he had recommended setting up a theatre in the city. Soon after Rousseau's defection, d'Alembert himself withdrew complaining that he was 'worn out with the affronts and vexations of every kind which this work draws down upon us'. Even Voltaire advised that the work of publication should be moved to Switzerland.

For the next seven years Diderot worked on alone. He determined that the remaining ten volumes should be held up until all were completed and then published simultaneously. In 1764 Diderot was enraged to discover that Le Breton had, on his own initiative and after Diderot had corrected the proofs, removed from the text all portions which might invite government censure. These last, expurgated volumes were sent to subscribers in 1765–66, bearing the name of a Swiss publisher and thus keeping, however implausibly, within the letter of the law. The eleven volumes of plates, making a total of twenty-eight in all, were completed in 1772, one year after the *Encyclopaedia Britannica* had made its shy debut with a mere three volumes.

Much of the *Encyclopaedia* escaped the dual censorship of Le Breton and the government, by stating revolutionary views obliquely, often by suggesting unflattering comparisons with England. In his article on 'Torture', for instance, Diderot remarks that 'in England all torture has been abolished'. Similarly the article on 'Refugees' is used to convey an attack on religious persecution:

Refugees. The name given to French Protestants whom the revocation of the edict of Nantes has forced to leave France to seek refuge in foreign lands. . . . Since that time France has seen herself deprived of a great number of citizens who have taken to her enemies arts, skills and resources which they have often used against her. . . . The persecuting spirit ought to be suppressed by every enlightened government. . . .

The *Encyclopaedia* was the manifesto of the Enlightenment. Its moving impulse was the belief in the beneficial effects of the diffusion of knowledge; its comprehensiveness was a demonstration of the empirical method. Subtly, but surely, it spread its influence among those who could not only read, but read between the lines.

Scepticism and Deism

The *Encyclopaedia* condemned religious intolerance, but the case for toleration had already been impressively stated before the close of the seventeenth century. Locke's celebrated *Letter Concerning Toleration* appeared in its Latin version in 1689 and was translated into Dutch and French before appearing in English. In 1686, one year after Louis XIV's revocation of the Edict of Nantes, Pierre Bayle (1647–1706) had published *A Philosophical Commentary on Christ's Words 'Compel Them to Come In'*, which, in the words of the *Encyclopaedia* itself, 'exhausts the subject' of toleration.

Bayle, the son of a Huguenot pastor, was professor of philosophy at the Protestant Academy of Sedan at the age of 28. In 1681 he exchanged this chair for that of philosophy and history at the École Illustre in Rotterdam, but twelve years later was deprived of his post at the instigation of the Protestant theologian Jurieu, who had described toleration as 'a dangerous principle leading unquestionably to indifference in religion'.[13] As if by way of demonstration, Bayle's *Historical and Critical Dictionary* published in 1697 attacked not merely intolerance, but the

---

[13] Jurieu's attack on Bayle's *Philosophical Commentary* was published anonymously at Rotterdam in 1687 and entitled *Religion, Conscience and the Prince*. (*To destroy the dogma of Religious Indifference and Universal Toleration.*)

Christian Church as a whole. The key word was *critical*: Bayle would take nothing on trust and he saw no reason why the Bible should not be subjected to the same close textual criticism as other books. Within less than fifty years Bayle's *Dictionary* had run to nine French editions, two English and one German. It was the ancestor of the *Encyclopaedia* and its influence on the *philosophes* was profound: in their scepticism, as in their science, the *philosophes* were popularizers of the seventeenth century, rather than pioneers in their own right.

It was Voltaire (1694–1778) who most vigorously took up Bayle's attack on the Church. In 1726 Voltaire had been released from a spell of imprisonment in the Bastille on condition that he went to England. In 1729 he returned to France determined to popularize both the philosophy of Locke and the physics of Newton. Voltaire's *Philosophical Letters* first appeared in London in 1733. The first four essays, on the Quakers, draw an ironic contrast between French ceremoniousness and English simplicity: Voltaire's Quaker repudiates baptism on the grounds that 'we do not think that Christianity consists in throwing on the head cold water mingled with a little salt'. English tolerance in religious matters is summed up in Voltaire's memorable phrase: 'An Englishman, like a free man, goes to Heaven by the road that pleases him.'[14] Other letters in the volume concern Bacon, Descartes, Locke and Newton; and in 1738 Voltaire published *Elements of the Philosophy of Newton*.

Descartes had taken the existence of God as the very basis of his philosophy, reserving his 'systematic doubt' for the physical world – what he called the world of 'extended substance'. But, unless one accepted Descartes' dualistic view of the universe, there was every reason for viewing even the existence of God with scepticism. Pascal (1623–62), though himself a believer, had gone so far as to admit that unaided reason could not establish the certainty of God's existence, but could merely demonstrate its probability: the existence of God was a good bet. Newton's physics seemed greatly to have improved the odds in favour of God's existence by revealing a universe whose order implied a

---

[14] For the practical consequences of Voltaire's attack on the Church in France see Chapter 17.

master-planner – the famous argument from design.[15] But God was nevertheless confined to the role of architect of the universe, 'the eternal Geometer', or, according to William Paley (1743–1805) the heavenly watchmaker who had created the intricate and interlocking mechanism, had set it in motion and then left it to run by itself. Subsequent providential intervention was ruled out: God did not tamper with the works. Knowledge of God was thus limited to the certainty of his existence: he was knowable, not through supernatural revelation, but through the observation of natural phenomena. This approach to God through physics rather than metaphysics was the so-called 'natural religion' or Deism of the eighteenth century. It was left to Bishop Butler and David Hume to demonstrate the limitations of the experimental method and so to demolish the foundations on which Deism rested.[16]

The demise of Deism was hastened by a physical event, the Lisbon earthquake of All Saints Day 1755 when between 10,000 and 15,000 people, most of them at worship in the churches, were killed in a matter of minutes.[17] So disastrous a natural phenomenon could not easily be regarded as the act of the Christian God of love; it was scarcely less difficult to fit it into the design of the Deists' eternal geometer. Voltaire became less confident in his Deism, and his *Candide* (1759) was an indictment of optimism, defined by Candide as 'the mania for pretending all is well when all is ill'. Candide's long line of misfortunes included his arrival in Lisbon at the time of the earthquake. Diderot, who had earlier said that he was a Christian 'because it is reasonable to be so', is supposed to have asserted on his deathbed in 1784: 'I do not believe in God the Father, God the Son, or God the Holy Ghost.'

If the scepticism of the Enlightenment was compounded of many contrasting elements, its practical effect was to attack established Christianity as the chief buttress of unenlightened

[15] An argument memorably expressed in Addison's hymn, 'The spacious firmament on high . . .', even if Addison's universe is described in pre-Newtonian terms and Addison himself was no Deist.

[16] See below, p. 84.

[17] For a readable account of the earthquake and its effect on eighteenth-century thought see T. D. Kendrick, *The Lisbon Earthquake*, Methuen 1956.

governments. Voltaire, with his war-cry of *Écrasez l'infame*, reserved his bitterest attacks for the Catholic Church in France, while Holbach's main charge in *Christianity Unmasked* (1756) was that religion, by inspiring fear of an invisible tyrant, had made men subservient to kings.

Utilitarianism and 'Laissez-Faire'

By attacking Christian metaphysics the *philosophes* undermined Christian ethics also: if there was no God to enforce the Ten Commandments, what was to be the basis of morality? Was it to be, as Hobbes (1588–1679) had asserted in *Leviathan*, merely the command of the king? The *philosophes'* answer was that it must be the command of an *enlightened* king who would legislate in accordance with the natural laws of morality and with the well-being of his subjects in view. Helvétius (1715–71), the chief of the French 'utilitarians', claimed in his preface to *On the Mind* (1758) that he had tried to treat ethics like any other science and to make it as empirical as physics. But he was quick to make generalizations. 'Men are not bad' he asserted 'they are merely subject to their own interests. . . . The thing to complain of is not the badness of men, but the ignorance of legislators.' According to Helvétius, it was absurd to expect men to be virtuous in a vicious environment: 'Good laws are the only means of making men virtuous.'

The same assumption led the Italian Beccaria (1738–94) to assert: 'It is better to prevent crimes than to punish them. This is the fundamental principle of good legislation which is the art of conducting men to the *maximum* of happiness and to the *minimum* of misery, if we may apply this mathematical expression to the good and evil of life.' It was precisely this mathematical approach to ethics that Jeremy Bentham (1748–1832) developed. Much influenced by Beccaria's *Crimes and Punishments* (1764) from which he borrowed the phrase 'the greatest happiness of the greatest number', Bentham sought to apply the empirical methods of a botanist to the codification of laws. His aim was to devise a comprehensive system of classification in which there should be no room for a bad law.

Starting from the assumption that 'mankind is under the domination of two sovereign masters, pleasure and pain', Bentham concluded that 'the business of government is to promote the happiness of society by punishing and rewarding'. The criminal law was to be based purely on deterrence, though the penalty was not to exceed what was sufficient to deter, while positive legislation was to be determined on the 'greatest happiness' principle, or what Helvétius had called 'the principle of the utility of the public'. As Bentham put it in *Principles of Morals and Legislation* (1789): 'The interest of the community then is what? – the sum of the interests of the several members who compose it.'[18] The confidence that the 'pleasure–pain calculus' would provide a precise answer was, of course, characteristic of the *philosophes*' belief in reason. In his *Fragment on Government* (1776) Bentham had asserted: 'Men, let them but once clearly understand one another, will not be long ere they agree.'[19] It therefore followed that if men were allowed to pursue their *enlightened* self-interest, the interest of the community as a whole would be served. The function of government was thus merely to provide conditions in which enlightened self-interest had free play. Bentham's social arithmetic may seem logically absurd, but the test of utility was a useful yardstick with which to measure anachronistic institutions, and the *practical* effect of the Utilitarians' teaching proved considerable in the next century.[20]

Bentham assumed that, given a sound system of positive laws, the amount of government intervention necessary to secure the greatest happiness of the greatest number would be small indeed. There were those who wanted to curtail governmental action still further. In 1776, the year of Bentham's *Fragment* and the American Declaration of Independence, the Scotsman Adam Smith published his *Inquiry into the Nature and Causes of the Wealth of Nations*, in which he called for the removal of all governmental regulation and restriction of trade. Although he won the support of the Younger Pitt, Smith's ideas did not seriously influence government policy in England until the 1820s.

---

[18] J. Bentham, *A Fragment on Government and an Introduction to the Principles of Morals and Legislation*, Blackwell 1948, p. 126.
[19] Bentham, *op. cit.*, p. 103.   [20] Particularly in England in the 1830s.

In France, however, similar ideas gained currency much earlier. The 'Physiocrats' or *philosophes economistes*, led by Quesnay (1694–1744) and including politicians like Mirabeau and Turgot in their number, looked for laws of nature in the realm of economics. They held that the production, circulation and distribution of wealth were governed by natural laws comparable to those controlling the physical world, and that governments should not attempt to interfere with them. Quesnay defined economics as a system of laws 'susceptible of a demonstration as severe and incontestable as those of geometry and algebra'. The basis of their teaching was the absolute inviolability of private property: free trade merely meant the natural right of the farmer to grow what he pleased and sell it where he pleased.

But although the principle of *laissez-faire* was to become a dogma in the nineteenth century, the physiocrats were untypical of the Enlightenment as a whole. Most of the *philosophes* clung to the prevailing economic policy of Mercantilism.[21] *Laissez-faire* was the antithesis of Enlightened Absolutism: the *philosophes* were mercantilists precisely because they were not democrats.

Democracy versus Absolutism

The Encyclopaedists, while accepting natural law, natural rights, natural religion and a natural economy, nevertheless insisted that ideas and social institutions depended also on geographical, historical and economic conditions. This characteristically eighteenth-century tension between natural order and the confusion of empirically observed fact is nowhere more marked than in Montesquieu (1689–1755). In his late twenties Montesquieu, already President of the Bordeaux Parlement, had read to the Academy of Bordeaux a number of scientific papers on such topics as *Causes of the Echo* and *Functions of the Kidneys*. Through failing eyesight, he abandoned his physical experiments, but not before he had observed under the microscope the effect of heat and cold on animal tissues. This seems to have led him to his belief in the importance of climate in the formation of national

[21] See below, p. 103.

characteristics. In his *Persian Letters* (1721), which purported to be *bona fide* descriptions of France by two Persian visitors to Paris (but were, of course, a biting satire on France under the Regency), Montesquieu asserted the relativity of political institutions: the best government, he argued, was that which 'leads men in the way best suited to their dispositions'. On the other hand, 'Justice is eternal and does not depend on human conventions'. Montesquieu had not abandoned natural law.

This mixture of natural rights and 'natural sites' persisted in Montesquieu's greatest work, *Spirit of Laws*, published in 1748. Taking his types of government from Aristotle rather than deriving them from his own observation, Montesquieu in the early books of *Spirit of Laws* defended the republic as the best form of government. But Book XI shows the influence of his travels in Europe and England between 1728 and 1731. Here he enunciates the famous doctrine of the separation of powers,[22] which was to have such a profound effect on the shaping of the American and French constitutions. Book XIV is entitled 'Laws in their Relation to the Nature of the Climate'. Montesquieu comes to the conclusion that a republican form of government is suitable only for small states, whereas a country as large as France requires a monarchy. And he implies that it should be a monarchy modelled on that of England, rather than on that of Louis XIV.

What Montesquieu seems most to have admired about England was the habit of free discussion. As he wrote in *Spirit of Laws*:

In a free nation it is very often indifferent that individuals should reason well or ill; it suffices that they reason: thence springs the liberty which is a security against the effects of reasoning – whereas in a despotic government, it is equally pernicious whether they reason well or ill; their reasoning is alone sufficient to shock the principle of that government.

Voltaire had also applauded the English constitution in his *Philosophical Letters* (1733):

The English nation is the only one on earth which has succeeded in regulating the power of its kings by resisting them; and which

---

[22] See Appendix 5. Cf. below, p. 253.

after repeated efforts has established that wise government under which the prince all powerful for good is restrained from doing ill; in which the nobility are great without insolence and without vassals, and in which the people share in the government without confusion.

But it is important to remember that the England that Montesquieu and Voltaire admired was the England of George II, where less than half a million Englishmen had the vote, not the England of Lloyd George. Voltaire, 'conservative in all things save religion', was later to write a flattering history of *The Age of Louis XIV* (1751), while one of the most fervent admirers of Montesquieu, and perhaps his greatest disciple, was the Whig politician Edmund Burke (1729–97), now regarded as the prophet of British Conservatism.

The *philosophes* were well aware of the dangers of absolutism, even when enlightened. Diderot admitted that 'one can abuse one's power in order to do good as well as to do evil'. But the philosopher-king remained their political *beau idéal*. The physiocrats, while urging *lassez-faire* principles in economics, were the most ardent champions of absolutism in politics. In the words of Le Trosne: 'In France reforms that can change the face of society can be effected in a moment, whereas in England even important measures may be obstructed by party spirit.' Rousseau was to defend democracy, but his political ideas were not taken seriously until the failure of 'Enlightened Absolutism' stood revealed.[23] Meanwhile most of the *philosophes* found their hero in Frederick the Great.

[23] *The Social Contract* (see below, p. 86) seems to have been the *least* read of all Rousseau's writings up to 1789.

6

The Seeds of Romanticism

Hume and the Attack on Reason

The Encyclopaedists, for all their emphasis on observation and experiment as the only means of increasing knowledge, based their empiricism on an unproven hypothesis: the neatness or *uniformity* of nature. Newton's law of universal gravitation[1] implied the uniformity of nature in the physical world; Locke deduced from Natural Law a system of 'natural rights' that belonged to all men everywhere.[2] The aim of the Encyclopaedists was, by describing and analyzing the world, to reveal the underlying uniformity of nature not only in physics, but also in politics, ethics, economics and aesthetics. Yet they found that the more facts they collected and classified, the more complex and uncoordinated the picture seemed to become. Locke had listed the divergent customs in different countries and had cited their bewildering variety to disprove the existence of 'innate ideas'; though he did not allow this to undermine his belief in Natural Law. Montesquieu,[3] in his search for universal political principles, admitted that national dispositions and customs were shaped by climate. Yet he could not bring himself to excuse the 'vices' of tropical lands (he could not condone cannibalism[4] or the Sultan's harem) and his belief in Natural Law thus led him to regard some climates as 'unnatural' and even to insist that governments must mitigate the evil effects of a vicious climate.

The limitations of the experimental method were, of course, freely admitted by contemporary scientists. Newton had stressed that he was seeking to describe *how* the force of gravity operated,

---

[1] See above, p. 63.   [2] See above, p. 65.   [3] See above, p. 79.
[4] M. E. de Montaigne (1533–92), in his essay on cannibals, had pretended to argue that cannibalism was merely a local custom no less legitimate than Parisian customs.

not to explain *what* gravity *was*.[5] In his *Treatise on Light* (1690) Huygens had been at pains to emphasize that it was impossible in physics to achieve the certainty of mathematics: in physics only such hypotheses were tenable as could be tested by immediate experience. And in 1717 s'Gravesande, in his inaugural address as professor of mathematics and astronomy in the University of Leyden, admitted that scientific prediction on the evidence of past experiments was based on the axiom of the uniformity of nature, an axiom which could not in itself be proved.

The so-called scepticism of Hume lay in his demonstrating those limitations already admitted by physicists and in elucidating their philosophical implications. David Hume (1711–76), another of those Scotsmen of genius who illuminated the century of Dr Johnson, was from 1752 librarian of the Faculty of Advocates in the University of Edinburgh, where he wrote his *Natural History of Religion* (1755) and his five-volume *History of England* (completed 1761). In his early twenties he had spent three years in France, when he had written *A Treatise of Human Nature* (1738), later republished in a revised form. The aim of the work was what Hume called 'the science of MAN':

We must, therefore, glean up our experiments in this science from a cautious observation of human life, and take them as they appear in the common course of the world, by men's behaviour in company, in affairs, and in their pleasures. Where experiments of this kind are judiciously collected and compared, we may hope to establish on them a science which will not be inferior in certainty, and will be much superior in utility, to any other of human comprehension.[6]

However much these words may suggest the sentiments of the Encyclopaedists, Hume soon set out to show how little *certainty* could be achieved by the experimental method. The idea of cause and effect, he pointed out, was based on the experience of finding two objects in constant conjunction, and arguing from this experience to the assumption that the two objects would occur in conjunction in the future. Yet it was impossible in the

[5] Cf. above, p. 63.
[6] D. Hume, *A Treatise of Human Nature*, Dent 1911 (Everyman's Library), vol. i, pp. 7–8.

first place to *prove* by empirical means that constant conjunction implied cause and effect: we could not prove that event *A* was caused by event *B*; we could only say that event *A* followed event *B*. The connexion of cause and effect, then, was not implicit in the facts; it could only be arrived at by intuition. Secondly, there was no logical justification for arguing from past experience to future prediction, unless we *assumed* the uniformity of nature:

We suppose, but are never able to prove, that there must be resemblance betwixt those objects of which we have had experience, and those which lie beyond the reach of our discovery. . . . We have no other notion of cause and effect, but that of certain objects, which have been *always conjoined* together, and which in all past instances have been found inseparable. We cannot penetrate into the reason of the conjunction.[7]

Hume was not denying the existence of cause and effect; he was merely arguing that reason alone cannot explain it, and that our belief in causation must therefore stem from some other source. His thesis was, as he put it, 'that all our reasonings concerning causes and effects are derived from nothing but custom; and that belief is more properly an act of the sensitive than of the cogitative part of our natures'. Understanding through feeling rather than through thinking: this is the point at which Hume challenges rationalism and seems to join hands with the Romantics.

When Hume turned in the *Treatise* to discuss morality, he was again ready to assert the supremacy of feeling over thought: 'We speak not strictly and philosophically when we talk of the combat of passion and reason. Reason is and ought to be the slave of the passions, and can never pretend to any office than to serve and obey them.'[8] We distinguish virtue from vice, not by intuition, nor by logic, but by sensation, by the feeling of pleasure or pain that we derive from the contemplation of a character or action. 'Morality, therefore, is more properly felt than judged of.'

Hume's political theory was a development from his psychology. He dismissed the 'social contract'[9] on both logical and historical grounds. Political obligation did not rest on an original

[7] *Ibid.*, i, pp. 94-5   [8] *Ibid.*, ii, p. 127.   [9] See below, p. 86.

contract but on the mixed basis of human selfishness and human sympathy. Man is a social animal, but his aptness for society is due, according to Hume, not to man's ability to overcome his selfish interests by reason, but to his sympathetic ability to make his neighbour's interests his own. Social instinct rather than social contract is the basis of the state.[10]

By exposing the dubious foundations on which the belief in universal natural laws rested, Hume dealt a fatal blow at Deism.[11] If, as Hume argued, causation could not be proved empirically but could only be grasped intuitively, what became of the Deists' claim that the existence of God, the First Cause, could be inferred from observation of the orderliness of nature? And how orderly was nature, anyway? As Hume remarked in *The Natural History of Religion*:

What a noble privilege it is of human reason to attain the knowledge of the Supreme Being; and, from the visible works of nature, be enabled to infer so sublime a principle as its Supreme Creator! But turn the reverse of the medal. Survey most nations and most ages. Examine the religious principles which have, in fact, prevailed in the world. You will scarcely be persuaded that they are anything but sick men's dreams. . . . The whole is a riddle, an enigma, an inexplicable mystery. Doubt, uncertainty, suspense of judgement, appear the only result of our most accurate scrutiny concerning this subject.[12]

According to Hume, men's ideas and behaviour were determined by irrational feelings as much as by rational thinking, and religion itself was essentially irrational: superstition and the fear of the inexplicable were the roots of our belief in God. A rational religion was a contradiction in terms. Hume's arguments undermined the foundations of natural religion, but they also struck at the premises of the Enlightenment itself: the uniformity of nature and the rationality of man. Hume's *Natural History of Religion* may have remained, in Ernst Cassirer's phrase,

---

[10] Hume's account of sympathy was probably his most important contribution to moral theory. The best short statement of his argument is perhaps that in Hume, *op. cit.*, ii, pp. 287 ff.

[11] See above, p. 74.

[12] E. Cassirer, *The Philosophy of the Enlightenment*, Eng. trans., Beacon Press, Boston, 1955, p. 181.

'an isolated phenomenon in the intellectual history of the Enlightenment'; but it signposted the route, through Kant,[13] to Romanticism.

Rousseau and the Return to Nature

Jean-Jacques Rousseau (1712–78), the contemporary and sometime friend of Hume, occupies a similarly ambivalent position in the history of eighteenth-century thought. *The Social Contract or Principles of Political Right* (1762) has been called 'the book of all books that is most talked of and least read'. The customary abbreviation of the title is in itself a source of misunderstanding, for it suggests that the 'social contract' was Rousseau's invention, whereas it had long been a commonplace of political thought. Similarly Rousseau's conception of the state of nature is remembered in the popular caricature of the 'noble savage' or in the familiar words of *The Social Contract*: 'Man is born free; and everywhere he is in chains.'

Until 1759 Rousseau contributed to the *Encyclopaedia*,[14] and it is ironical that his first attack on 'Reason' should have been launched at the instigation of Diderot. In 1749 Rousseau wrote his *Discourse on the Arts and the Sciences* in answer to the prize essay question set by the Academy of Dijon: 'Has the restoration of the arts and sciences had a purifying effect upon morals?' Diderot advised him against defending the affirmative view: 'All the mediocrities will take that road and only find commonplace ideas on it; whereas the opposite view opens up a rich field for philosophy and eloquence.'[15] This may explain the rhetorical and one-sided arguments of the *Discourse* with its conclusion that 'luxury, profligacy and slavery have been in all ages the scourge of the efforts of our pride to emerge from that happy state of ignorance in which the wisdom of providence has placed us'.[16] Polemical though the *Discourse* may have been, d'Alembert devoted the preface of the *Encyclopaedia* to refuting its assertions, and Rousseau himself seems to have been carried away by his

---

[13] See below, p. 89.   [14] See above, p. 71.

[15] W. Boyd's edited version of *Émile*, entitled *Émile for Today*, Heinemann 1956, p. 179.

[16] J-J. Rousseau, *The Social Contract and Discourses*, Everyman 1947, p. 129.

own eloquence. He returned to the attack in *Discourse on the Origin and Foundation of Inequality among Men* (what Voltaire called 'your second book against the human race') published in 1755. Rousseau devoted half the book to a description of the state of nature in which man lived by 'satisfying his hunger at the first oak, and slaking his thirst at the first brook; finding his bed at the foot of the tree which afforded him a repast; and, with that, all his wants supplied'.[17]

Rousseau was not so naïve as to suppose that man could return to the state of nature or indeed that such a state had ever existed. Society was inevitable, but Rousseau wanted to justify it on different grounds from those advanced by his contemporaries. The notion that society is based on an original contract, either between all the individuals comprising society or between the people and the government, can be traced back to the Greeks and was common in the political writings of the sixteenth and seventeenth centuries. To Hobbes (1588–1679) the contract was one between the individual members of society whereby they agreed to surrender to a sovereign their power to execute the 'laws of nature': once the contract was made the subjects were bound to submit without question to the sovereign's will. Unlike Hobbes, Locke believed in a God-given Natural Law, and his notion of the contract incorporated the idea of a trust between the government and the governed: if the government infringed the 'natural rights' of the citizen, the citizen was entitled to rebel.[18]

Although Rousseau clung to the current doctrine of Natural Law and discussed political obligation in the customary terms of the social contract, he gave the contract a new interpretation. He refused to draw a distinction, much less recognize a contract, between society and the sovereign: the individual surrendered his freedom, but he surrendered it to the community as a whole. Rousseau would not allow representative government.[19] Each citizen must be able to say, *L'etat c'est moi*. Government was defined by Rousseau as 'an intermediate body set up between

[17] *Ibid.*, p. 163.   [18] Cf. above, p. 66.
[19] Rousseau Everyman edition, p. 78: 'The people of England regards itself as free; but it is grossly mistaken; it is free only during the election of members of Parliament.'

the subjects and the Sovereign . . . charged with the execution of the laws and the maintenance of liberty'.[20] Government was thus reduced to the role of what Rousseau called 'supreme administration', and while the executive power was thus delegated, the legislative power remained in the whole body of citizens.

Legislation was determined by Rousseau's elusive conception of 'the General Will'. He seems to say that the body of citizens will always legislate in the interests of the community at large, and yet to deny that this means merely the rule of the majority. But where does the general will reside when a motion is carried by a bare majority? In his refusal to face this question Rousseau revealed how much he shared the Encyclopaedists' faith in the rationality of man: given the full facts, the right answer would be obvious.[21] Thus Rousseau explains in a footnote: 'To be general, a will need not always be unanimous.'[22] The implication is that it usually will be. It follows that the individual citizen who finds himself at variance with the general will is mistaken in his judgement. As Rousseau remarked with regard to morality: 'Right men's opinions, and their morality will purge itself. Men always love what is good or what they find good; it is in judging what is good that they go wrong.'[23] That is why, in his famous phrase, the individual must be 'forced to be free'.

Thus Rousseau, though making the individual his starting-point, ended by glorifying the state. The same shift from individualism to collectivism is found in his writings on education. In his Considerations on the Government of Poland, written in 1773 at the request of a Polish patriot, he expounded his idea of a national education: 'Young Frenchmen, Englishmen, Spaniards, Italians, Russians, are all much the same when they leave college. A Pole at twenty should be different; he should be nothing but a Pole.'[24]

Yet Rousseau had earlier defended a 'natural' system of education. In Émile (1762) he had written: 'We must choose between making a man or making a citizen. We cannot make both.'[25] Émile is an account of how to make a man. The boy's education must proceed at a pace dictated by his own needs rather than his

[20] Ibid., p. 47.   [21] Cf. above, p. 71.   [22] Everyman edition, p. 21.
[23] Ibid., p. 105.   [24] Emile for Today, p. 191.   [25] Ibid., p. 13.

tutor's knowledge. He must not be taught the three Rs until he has himself seen their value; his vocabulary must be curtailed since it is a disadvantage for children 'to have more words than ideas and be able to say more than they think';[26] until the age of twelve, the tutor's aim should be 'not to save time but to waste it' so that the mind can 'remain inactive until it has all its faculties'. Early education should in fact be negative: 'It consists not in teaching virtue and truth, but in preserving the heart from vice and the mind from error.'[27] Elementary science and geography might be introduced between the ages of twelve and fifteen, but they must be learned from nature, not taught from books; Émile's first book was to be *Robinson Crusoe*; the study of history must be deferred until the age of eighteen, since there can be no 'real knowledge of events without a knowledge of their causes and effects', and even then Rousseau would have preferred biography to history.[28] It is easy to smile at the absurdities of Rousseau's child-centred educational system, but it would be difficult to overestimate the influence of *Émile*, by way of Pestalozzi and Froebel, on the educational practice of the nineteenth and twentieth centuries.

Rousseau was not so absurd as the inconsistencies in his writings and the ineptness of his private life[29] often make him seem. 'All my ideas are consistent,' he protested in *The Social Contract*, 'but I cannot expound them all at once.' Even his political ideas made sense in the city state of Geneva in which he had grown up. He admitted that 'the larger the state, the less the liberty', and even asserted, in agreement with Montesquieu, that 'liberty, not being the fruit of all climates, is not within the reach of all peoples'.[30] Rousseau's disciples seldom paid attention to his more cautious qualifications.

Diderot described the gulf between Rousseau and the rest of the *philosophes* as 'the vast chasm between heaven and hell'. Certainly, by his attack on the contemporary praise of progress, Rousseau unwittingly fathered the 'back to nature' school of Romantics; his political theories could lead to Robespierre's

---

[26] *Ibid.*, p. 28.   [27] *Ibid.*, p. 41.   [28] *Ibid.*, p. 107 ff.
[29] Rousseau's unattractive private life is urbanely described in H. Nicolson, *The Age of Reason*, Constable 1960, though he somewhat exaggerates Rousseau's 'Romanticism'.
[30] Rousseau, Everyman edition, p. 64.

republicanism or to Hegel's idealism; his educational theories laid stress on the development of the *individual* intelligence. Yet for all his links with Romanticism, Rousseau shared at least one important assumption with the *philosophes*: he believed in the rationality of man – although he may be said to have substituted the idea of 'original innocence' for that of 'original ignorance'. As Cassirer remarks, 'Rousseau did not overthrow the world of the Enlightenment; he only transferred its centre of gravity to another position'. The shift was a subtle one, but its implications were to prove spectacular and would have surprised Rousseau himself.

The Enlightenment in Germany

What Englishmen call 'The Enlightenment' is more commonly known as the *Aufklärung*. Yet Professor Cobban can ask provocatively: 'Did the *Aufklärung* ever really become translated into German?'[31] This paradox is best illustrated in the person of Immanuel Kant (1724–1804), who has been variously regarded both as the last defender of the Enlightenment and as the first prophet of Romanticism. How did Kant himself define the *Aufklärung*?

Enlightenment is man's exodus from his self-incurred tutelage. Tutelage is the inability to use one's understanding without the guidance of another person. This tutelage is self-incurred if its cause lies not in any weakness of the understanding, but in indecision and lack of courage to use the mind without the guidance of another. 'Dare to know' (*sapere aude*)! Have the courage to use your own understanding; this is the motto of the Enlightenment.[32]

The appeal is still to reason, but it is to the *individual* intellect rather than to the more universal and impersonal 'Reason' of the *philosophes*.

The emphasis that Kant laid on the individual was perhaps partly due to the extreme Protestant atmosphere of German pietism in which he grew up. But he was also much influenced by Newtonian astronomy. His first major work was *Theory of*

---

[31] N.C.M.H., vol. vii, p. 111.
[32] Cassirer, *op. cit.*, p. 163.

the Heavens: An Essay on the Constitution and Origin of the Universe Treated According to Newtonian Principles (1755), which propounded the theory of the nebular origin of the solar system. It was Kant who, in the *Critique of Pure Reason* (1781), resolved the contradiction running through the Enlightenment as a whole: the difficulty in reconciling the belief in the order of the universe with the confusion of data collected by empirical observation. Kant's conclusion was that order was in the mind of the beholder: 'Our intellect does not draw its laws from nature, but imposes its laws on nature.' The law of universal gravitation was Newton's law, not Nature's: the neatness of nature did not lie in the facts themselves, but in the pattern which the human mind imposed on those facts. The facts of the external world were real enough, but it was the individual intellect which systematized them. Kant called this his 'Copernican Revolution', reminding us that Copernicus himself had not discovered new facts, but had devised a new framework into which to fit the old facts.

Kant's insistence on the primacy of individual reason was carried into the sphere of ethics. The individual must himself decide whether to obey the command of authority, however exalted:

Much as my words may startle you, you must not condemn me for saying: every man creates his God. . . . For in whatever way . . . the Deity should be made known to you – even . . . if he should reveal Himself to you – it is you . . . who must judge whether you are permitted (by your conscience) to believe in Him, and to worship Him.

It is easy to see why Kant has been hailed as a Romantic. He himself violently rejected the advances of Fichte (1762–1814), but, in spite of Kant's protests, the German Romantics continued to regard themselves as his disciples. Kant's appeal to conscience was qualified by his notion of the 'categorical imperative': act in such a way that the principle on which you act is capable of becoming a universal law. And he did, after all, sketch a plan for a League of Nations. But Kant's 'categorical imperative' was as open to misunderstanding as Rousseau's 'general will'.

In 1740 a Frenchman, Mauvillon, in his *French and German*

Letters, had challenged the Germans to name a single German writer who had a European reputation or whose works did not consist largely of translations. German parochialism was perhaps partly due to unintelligibility – to the Germanic tendency to regard obscurity as a mark of profundity, in contrast to the French identification of truth with clarity. But it was also due to the political divisions of eighteenth-century Germany, which deprived her of a cultural centre such as a metropolis like Paris could provide. In spite of the stimulus which Luther's Bible had given to the development of the German language, French and Latin remained the language of European letters, while Frederick the Great banished German from his court.[33]

The first half of the eighteenth century had seen the proliferation of journals on the model of the English *Spectator*: 182 of these so-called Moral Weeklies appeared in Germany between 1713 and 1761, though more than one-third were published in Hamburg or Leipzig. From the 'eighties onwards, reading clubs and circulating libraries became increasingly popular among the middle classes, and in 1806 a provincial journalist could write: 'Formerly, reading was the affair of the scholar and the truly cultivated man. Now it is a general habit, even of the lower classes, not only in the towns but in the country too.'[34]

But this was literature of an ephemeral kind. Goethe and Schiller did not find a reading public waiting for them, and the so-called *Sturm und Drang* (Storm and Stress) movement of the period 1770–78 was a writers' revolt against an uncongenial literary environment. It was a young man's revolt: in 1770 Herder, the father of the movement, was twenty-six, Goethe twenty-one, Lenz and Klinger[35] not yet twenty. Led by Herder, anthropologist, philosopher of history, collector of folk-songs, and protagonist of Gothic art, they turned their backs on French culture, taking Thomson, Gray, Shakespeare, and the newly discovered Ossian as their heroes. They championed the German language since, in Lenz's phrase, 'it gave more ample feeling to the mind'. They repudiated all teachers and critics, and were

[33] See below, p. 115.
[34] W. H. Bruford, *Germany in the Eighteenth Century*, Cambridge 1935, p. 283.
[35] Lenz and Klinger were both writers of plays and novels. Klinger wrote the play *Sturm und Drang*.

opposed to all restraint upon the life of the emotions and its artistic expression, since they regarded the true artist as one who communed directly with Nature. The origin of all knowledge was sensual. 'Feeling may err,' wrote Herder, 'but it can only be corrected by feeling.'

Goethe (1749–1832) and Schiller (1759–1805) were greatly influenced by the *Sturmer*. Goethe's *Werther* (1774), which describes the attitude of mind so typical of the movement, became a European bestseller, and seems to have produced a spate of suicides in Germany at least. At the age of twenty-six Goethe moved to Weimar where he obtained a post at the ducal court. Here he reacted against the sentimental oversimplifications of the *Sturmer* and applied himself to science.

Goethe was a keen observer of nature. His objections to Newton's theory of the composition of light never carried much conviction, but his patient collection and comparison of skulls led to his discovery of the intermaxillary bone in the human jaw, while Charlotte von Stein at Weimar had to deal with urgent requests for 'mosses of all sorts, if possible with the roots, and *wet*'. Goethe's scientific studies confirmed his belief in the 'harmony of nature'. Leibnitz (1646–1716) had held that there was a universal harmony underlying the apparent diversity of nature, a view immortalized in Pope's *Essay on Man*[36] and ridiculed in the figure of Dr. Pangloss in Voltaire's *Candide*. Goethe's view of nature was coloured by his reading of Spinoza (1632–77), whose pantheistic notion of God was of a force pervading all nature: God and Nature were not in opposition; they were identical.

Goethe sought the universal principle underlying nature in what he called the *Gestaltung* (or formative process) and the *Metamorphose* (or transforming process). Indeed, he once said that he wanted to discover a single law of change running through all realms of nature – chemistry and geology, botany and zoology, ethics and aesthetics. According to Goethe, human

[36] All Nature is but art unknown to thee;
   All chance, direction which thou canst not see;
   All discord, harmony not understood;
   All partial evil, universal good.
   And, spite of pride, in erring reason's spite,
   One truth is clear, Whatever is, is right.

nature was to be studied, not in isolation, but as an aspect of Nature: man must not wrestle with Nature, but must learn to accept her, 'to regard the external world with love,' as he put it. Well might Goethe claim that he moved 'in a region where metaphysics and natural science overlap'.

The philosophy of Goethe, then, was one not of analysis, but of synthesis – a synthesis that could embrace feeling and thought, Nature and God, pleasure and pain. Nowhere is this more clearly revealed than in the pages of *Faust*, the writing of which was spread over nearly sixty years. When the first part of *Faust* was published in 1808 the legend was over 200 years old, but Goethe transformed the satirical tragedy of the man who sells his soul to the devil into what can perhaps best be described as a portrait of European man in his intellectual development from Renaissance to Enlightenment. Faust's opening monologue asserts 'the impossibility of knowledge', but, while following the promptings of Mephistopheles in the quest for pleasure, Faust is torn between the material and the infinite, between his love for the rustic Gretchen and the celestial Helen. It is perhaps not too fanciful to see in this a statement of the tension between romanticism and rationalism in eighteenth-century thought as a whole. The play is not a bundle of contradictions but a union of opposites. Faust finds his ultimate salvation not through grace but through works, in his self-imposed task of reclaiming land from the sea. Thus Faust conquers Nature by cooperating with her:

> I find this wisdom's final form:
> He only earns his freedom and his life
> Who takes it every day by storm.[37]

Faust's divided love reminds us of the duality in Goethe himself: German by inheritance, Greek by adoption. Goethe and Schiller recalled the Germans to a study of classical Greece, after the reaction of the *Sturm und Drang* against contemporary French classicism had led to an exaggerated respect for the German language, Gothic architecture and Nordic literature. Lessing (1729–81), one of the chief leaders of the attack on

[37] J. W. von Goethe, *Faust*, trans. L. MacNeice, Faber 1951, p. 287. For further extracts see Appendix 13.

French classicism, had appealed to the example of classical Greece in support of his call for drama that embodied a moral purpose and was more than mere entertainment. This kind of classicism was, like that of Goethe, classicism of a somewhat romantic hue. Goethe's admiration for ancient Greece, fostered by his visit to Italy of 1786–88 and reflected in *Iphigenie* (1787), *Tasso* (1790), and even in *Faust*, was almost a form of escapism, a nostalgia for the time when beauty was truth and truth beauty. But this interest was not purely antiquarian, for the Greek ideal was to shape the future: Schiller's writings on aesthetics asserted that the world could be saved through art.

Schiller sought to apply Kant's philosophy to the world of art: beauty in art was the expression of the ethical freedom of the individual artist who had achieved a balance between sensuality and reason, between the senses and the intellect. As Schiller himself expressed it:

Let not each man be like the next, but let each one be like the Highest! How shall this be achieved? Let each be complete in himself.

Through his friendship with Goethe, Schiller helped to mould *Faust*, and his own plays, covering a quarter of a century from *The Robbers* (1781) to *William Tell* (1804), gave him a German, if not a European reputation second only to Goethe's. At Schiller's death, Goethe paid his own poetic tribute:

> Vanished that comet, yet our way he's lighting,
> Eternal light with his own light uniting.

The German writers of the *Aufklärung* were in many ways untypical of the European movement as a whole. They repudiated the extreme sentimentality of the *Sturm und Drang*, yet their emphasis on the individual intelligence, their mystical conception of nature, their acceptance of emotion as the chief guide to understanding, their belief in the moral function of art, are all ideas more closely akin to nineteenth-century Romanticism than to eighteenth-century Classicism. They were not nationalists. Schiller despised patriotism in his youth, and his first patriotic play was written under the stress of the Napoleonic Wars, while as late as 1808 Goethe had a famous interview with Napoleon.

Yet the German nationalist historian Treitschke (1834–96) commended Goethe and his contemporaries for preserving what he called 'the abiding value of the German spirit'. And Professor Bruford remarks: 'It would hardly be too much to say that the liberals of 1848 were still fighting for a Germany worthy of Goethe, Schiller and Kant.'[38]

[38] Bruford, *op. cit.*, p. 296.

III

ENLIGHTENED ABSOLUTISM
AT HOME

'Enlightened Absolutism', or 'Enlightened Despotism' as it is more often called with a typically British conviction that absolutism and despotism are synonymous, has become an increasingly imprecise term since it was first used by the *philosophes* in the second half of the eighteenth century. The title of 'Enlightened Despot' (which was not used by eighteenth-century rulers themselves) has been bestowed on monarchs as separated in time as Frederick William I of Prussia and Napoleon III of France. This seems to be stretching the term beyond the point of usefulness. In this book the term is taken to mean those eighteenth-century monarchs who were familiar with the ideas of the Enlightenment and who carried out a programme advocated by the *philosophes*: the abolition of irrationalities and inconsistencies in administration and judicial procedure through a policy of centralization and codification, the introduction of more humane punishments, the granting of freedom of worship and the curbing of the powers of the Church, the stimulation of trade and industry by the encouragement of the latest technical innovations, the patronage of the arts and sciences and the extension of education, the alleviation of the lot of the peasantry.

It may be objected that policies such as these were pursued long before the *philosophes* commanded a public, and that eighteenth-century monarchs needed no prompting from armchair philosophers to enable them to see the political advantages to be derived from such reforms. All this is true: Frederick the Great was not the kind of ruler to allow humanitarian principles to impede military efficiency. Yet the fact that he and his fellow monarchs chose to patronize men of letters and to frame their edicts in the language of the Enlightenment is in itself significant. No doubt these monarchs had good political reasons for doing what the *philosophes* urged, but their measure of success owed something to the growing belief that such reforms were in themselves desirable. (It would surely be unduly cynical to argue, by comparable reasoning, that the advent of the twentieth-century welfare state was due solely to the demands of two world wars.)

Of course, the success of enlightened absolutism was only relative. Even the most enlightened of eighteenth-century monarchs were powerless to implement the whole of the *philosophes'* programme in the face of a semi-feudal society in which commercial policy was still regarded as the continuation of war by other means and where industry was as yet only localized and on a small scale. It was as unrealistic in Prussia as in France to expect the landed classes voluntarily to relinquish their power and privileges.

7

The Economic Structure of Europe

The Survival of Feudalism

The simultaneous impact of the French Revolution and the Industrial Revolution seriously weakened the position of the landed aristocracy throughout Europe, but not until the nineteenth century. Before 1789 the European nobility were very much on the offensive. In almost every major country in Europe they improved on their seventeenth-century position, while in France itself it was a revolt of the nobility that precipitated the Revolution.[1] The French Estates-General had its rough counterparts in the Estates of the Holy Roman Empire, the Austrian Netherlands and Hungary, in the Diets of Poland and Sweden; and all these representative bodies, like the British Parliament itself, were dominated by the nobility. Nobility meant different things in different countries, of course. The Polish and Hungarian aristocrats had more in common with the English gentry than with the French nobility; the Spanish grandees[1a] had lost their political power, whereas in Russia and Prussia the status of nobility was closely connected with service to the state.

In Sweden war gave the aristocracy a chance to regain political power lost in the previous century. The death of Charles XII in battle in 1718 and a disputed succession enabled the Diet (*Riksdag*) to impose the Constitution of 1720.[2] This vested power in the four Estates, but, since the nobility enjoyed double representation on the committees of the Diet, it was the nobles who effectively controlled the government until

---

[1] For a discussion of the economic condition of the French nobility and of the extent to which feudalism had survived in France see Chapter 18.

[1a] See below, p. 161.

[2] See above, p. 37.

Gustavus III's *coup* in 1772.[3] Out of a population of about one and a half million in Sweden proper there were in 1718 perhaps 10,000 nobles, whose privileges included partial exemption from taxation and (after 1723) a monopoly of the highest state appointments.[4] This monopoly was gradually eroded during the century, but it was not until 1809 that public office was thrown open to members of all the Estates.

The Polish nobility (*szlachta*) enjoyed even greater political power, though in the condition of eighteenth-century Poland it was power of a somewhat negative kind. The number of *szlachta* has been put at anything from 725,000 to one and a half million, of whom perhaps only twenty or thirty families were great magnates, like the self-styled princes of the Czartoryski family, who owned between them eleven castles and fifteen towns. The *szlachta* controlled church appointments, the law, the Diets and such local government as existed. They were exempt from taxation and military service, and by the exercise of the *liberum veto* could frustrate the decisions of the Diet.[5]

The Hungarian Diet was composed almost exclusively of nobles, and nine-tenths of its legislation was concerned with the interests of the nobility, so that Charles VI's promise in 1712 to respect the laws and liberties of Hungary[6] meant in fact the guaranteeing of the political dominance of the nobles. They comprised 5 per cent of the total population, they monopolized the chief offices in church and state, they were alone allowed to own land, and after 1741 they were exempt from taxes. Central government was largely controlled by the magnates (two or three hundred families), while local government was in the hands of the landed gentry. At the bottom of the aristocratic hierarchy and without political power were the 'sandalled' or 'seven-plum-tree' nobles, who owned little or no land and who amounted to nearly half the total number.[7] The leading magnates spent much time in Vienna and intermarried with the Austrian aristocracy. While the eldest sons of the Imperial

---

[3] See below, p. 166.

[4] For a detailed analysis see ed. A. Goodwin, *The European Nobility in the Eighteenth Century*, Adam & Charles Black, 1953, p. 141.

[5] See above, p. 29.   [6] See above, p. 46.

[7] Goodwin, *op. cit.*, p. 125.

nobility inherited the family estates, the younger sons sought commissions in the Imperial army, sinecures in the Church, or posts at the Imperial Court. Charles VI's court at his accession is said to have numbered 40,000 persons, while at the death of Maria Theresa there were nearly 1,500 chamberlains.[8]

In Prussia the political role of the nobility[9] was effective rather than decorative. There was no central Prussian Diet and the provincial diets had lost their political powers in the previous century. But the social and fiscal privileges of the nobility had been confirmed in 1653, and in the eighteenth century the nobles became more important in administration. Frederick William I showed a preference for burgher bureaucrats, but under Frederick the Great all but one of the ministerial appointments went to nobles.[10] Administratively as well as militarily Frederick II's state rested on the support of the *Junker* class, as the *Landrecht* of 1791 explicitly recognized: 'The nobility, as the first estate in the state, most especially bears the obligation, by its distinctive destination, to maintain the defence of the state, both of its honour without and of its constitution within'.[11]

Peter the Great's Table of Ranks of 1722 saw a similar attempt to identify aristocracy with bureaucracy.[12] The result was a multiplication of titles of nobility until by the 1760s the British ambassador put the number of nobles at half a million in a population of twenty-eight million. The fate of the Legislative Commission of 1767–68 illustrates Catherine II's dependence on the nobility early in her reign, while her Charter of Nobility (1785) confirmed the legal, fiscal and feudal privileges of the nobles.[13]

Governments so dependent on the support of the nobility could not be expected to abolish serfdom, and it was in Russia and Poland that the lot of the peasants was hardest. Serfdom in Russia was not a medieval institution: it had originated in the sixteenth century and was greatly extended under Peter the Great and Catherine the Great, so that by 1797 there were nearly

[8] *Ibid.*, p. 104.
[9] The *Junkers* were gentry, proud of their birth but managing their own estates and economically comparable with the English squirearchy.
[10] Michaelis as Postmaster-General was the exception.
[11] See below, p. 121.   [12] See above, p. 42.   [13] See Appendix 11.

twenty million serfs in a population of thirty-six million (nearly 56 per cent). The census of 1718 had drawn no distinction between serfs and peasants, and the new burdens imposed by Peter, conscription in 1705 and the poll tax of 1718, fell on peasant and serf alike. Thus the legal distinction between privately-owned serfs and state-owned peasants did not in practice imply much economic advantage for the peasant. The serfs performed labour services (*barschina*) for their lords on two or three days a week, though in less productive agricultural regions they paid instead an annual money due (*obrok*), which rose from two roubles in the 1770s to as much as five in the 1790s. In Poland, too, feudal dues increased during the eighteenth century and labour services were required three days a week. Of the seven or eight million serfs, those on crown and church lands were slightly better off than those who were privately owned, but Polish literature of the day abounds in pleas for a lightening of the peasants' load,[14] and not until 1768 was the Polish lord deprived of the power of life and death over his serfs.

In general the serf suffered most east of the Elbe. In East Prussia the recognized three days' labour services a week sometimes rose to five or even six; the serf had little security against eviction, while the *Gesindedienst* (menial service in the lord's kitchens or stables) lasted until Stein's reforms of 1807-9.[14a] In West Prussia, where serfdom was medieval in origin, conditions were more closely akin to those in France. In Bohemia the labour services (*robot*) had been fixed at a maximum of three days a week in 1775 but, in spite of the attempts of Maria Theresa and Joseph II to improve the serfs' lot, serfdom survived in the Habsburg Empire until 1848.

The condition of the serfs was scarcely improved by the gradual conglomeration of landed estates. The *latifundium* of a Hungarian magnate might extend to anything from 20,000 to 50,000 acres, while the acreage of the Esterházy family at one time ran into millions.[15] These, together with the Schwarzenbergs of Bohemia and Prince Radziwill of Poland (whose estates equalled half the area of Ireland) were, of course, the most

[14] See *The Cambridge History of Poland 1697–1935*, C.U.P. 1941, p. 79.
[14a] See below, p. 338.　　[15] Goodwin, *op. cit.*, p. 129.

spectacular examples. But the prevalence of primogeniture ensured that there was a general tendency towards larger estates. The Russian Entail Law of 1714 required estates to be left in their entirety to a single son or relative; this was a reversal of an existing tradition, as was Leopold I's authorization in Hungary in 1697 of the *fidei-commissa* (a land-trust system designed to keep estates intact even when the male line failed) which had been current in the Austrian lands for a century. Frederick the Great failed to persuade the *junkers* to resort to the *fidei-commissa*, but he repeatedly forbade the sale of noble land to non-noble purchasers without explicit royal consent.

Catherine II's Charter of Nobility (1785) had confirmed the Russian nobles in 'the right to purchase villages'. It also recognized their right 'to possess, not only the surface of the lands belonging to them but also whatever minerals or plants may be present in the depths beneath the soil or waters, and likewise all metals extracted therefrom. . . .' And many of the leading eighteenth-century Swedish ironmasters were men of noble birth. But elsewhere in Europe (apart from England) land was more highly regarded for the crops, rents and dues it yielded than for the minerals it concealed. There is something sadly symbolic about the Bialystok palace of the Polish Branicki family, which had more horses in its stables than books in its library.[16]

The Zenith of Mercantilism

Adam Smith, in his *Wealth of Nations*,[17] credited the economic theories of the eighteenth century with a coherence that they did not possess. The system of strict government regulation of trade and industry, which he attacked and for which he coined the name 'mercantilism', had evolved more as a haphazard response to the harsh facts of commercial competition than as the product of a preconceived body of principles. Indeed one of the most succinct statements of mercantilist theory appears in James I's Book of Rates of 1608: 'If it be agreeable to the rule of nature to prefer our own people before strangers, then it is much

[16] *Cambridge History of Poland 1697–1935*, p. 75.   [17] See above, p. 77.

more reasonable that the manufactures of other nations should be charged with impositions than that the people of our own kingdom should not be set on work.' And in 1666 Colbert had written of the Dutch: 'It is certain that their whole power has hitherto consisted in trade; if we could manage their trade, they might find it more difficult in the future to carry out their preparations for war than they have hitherto done.'

Underlying Colbert's argument was the contemporary assumption, shared by no less an authority than William Petty,[18] that there was only a finite amount of trade in the world and that one nation's profit therefore implied another's loss; though few writers went so far as the German T. L. Lau, who in 1719 argued that plague, war and famine in a neighbouring state were to be welcomed since they increased the relative prosperity of one's own.[19] The aim of economic policy was to secure a favourable balance of trade or, as Thomas Mun (1571-1641), the English prophet of mercantilism, had written, 'to sell more to strangers yearly than we consume of theirs in value'. The balance was to be achieved by encouraging the import of raw materials and discouraging their export, by encouraging the export of manufactured goods and discouraging their import. Since 1696 England had had a special office under the Inspector General of Imports and Exports for keeping watch on the balance of trade; France followed suit in 1726.

Yet the eighteenth century saw widespread criticism of the mercantilist system. Petty himself, in his *Political Arithmetic* published posthumously in 1690, while accepting the importance of the balance of trade, had insisted that wealth did not lie solely in money and that it was foolish to forbid the export of bullion. Another Englishman, Nicholas Barbon (d. 1698), had pointed out in his *Discourse on Trade* (1690) that 'the prohibiting of any foreign commodity doth hinder the making and exportation of so much of the native [commodity] as used to be made and exchanged for it'. Some of the merchants agreed with him. To protect the woollen industry against competition from calico, the British government in 1721 prohibited all 'printed, painted,

[18] See above, p. 55.
[19] M. S. Anderson, *Europe in the Eighteenth Century*, Longmans 1961, p. 75.

stained or dyed' calicoes. But fifteen years later the woollen manufacturers themselves supported the partial repeal of the Act since, they argued, to stop such imports from Africa and the West Indies would 'prejudice and prevent the exportation of woollen goods to those places'. In France, Boisguilbert (d. 1714) used the phrase *laissez-faire la nature* (leave nature alone) when calling for a free trade in grain, while the Dutchman Bernard de Mandeville (d. 1733) put the case for free trade in his famous *Fable of the Bees: or Private Vices, Publick Benefits*. In the 1750s, with Vincent de Gournay (1712–59) as intendant of commerce, the French government took some tentative steps in the direction of free trade, and the same decade saw the opening of the physiocrats' campaign in defence of *laissez-faire*.[20]

But in spite of attempts to discredit mercantilist theories, mercantilist policies continued to be practised by the major European states. Frederick the Great's economic policies were modelled on Colbert's, while his fellow monarchs, though they might flirt with free trade ideas, remained mercantilists at heart.[21] The Peace of Utrecht (1713) had provided for a commercial treaty between England and France, but the British Parliament had rejected the proposal, so that Adam Smith was able to complain two generations later that 'those mutual restraints have put an end to almost all fair commerce between the two nations'.[22] It was probably the loss of the American colonies rather than the writings of Adam Smith that persuaded the British government to reappraise its economic policy. Pitt's free trade treaty with France was signed in 1786, but during the Napoleonic wars both countries reverted to militant mercantilism;[23] and it was not until 1849 that the Navigation Acts were finally repealed.

Exploitation of colonial trade through navigation acts was the principal pillar of eighteenth-century mercantilism. The British colonies enjoyed a greater degree of self-government than the French. (In 1753 Dupleix was recalled from India because he had ventured on territorial conquest instead of concentrating on commercial development.) But both governments saw colonial

---

[20] See above, p. 77.   [21] See Chapters. 8–11 below.
[22] There was, of course, a good deal of smuggling.   [23] See below, p. 332.

policies in terms of exploiting natural resources rather than of civilizing backward peoples. 'The white man's burden' was a figment of the nineteenth-century conscience. By 1789 France's colonial trade amounted to about 400 million *livres* – well over a third of her total imports and exports. Between 1698 and 1774 England's colonial trade had increased fivefold to 33 per cent of her total overseas trade, while the total tonnage of the British merchant fleet increased from 260,000 in 1702 to 695,000 in 1776. This growth may have been because of the Navigation Acts or in spite of them. The combined effect of the Acts of 1651, 1660, 1663 and 1673 was to require all goods imported from or exported to the British colonies to be carried in British or colonial ships; 'enumerated' articles (the original list was lengthened at least three times during the eighteenth century) were to be exported only to England or another British colony, and all imports to the colonies were to be put on board ship in England.[24] In 1736 a further Act required every British ship to have one set of sails made in England.

Colbert's creation of a French navy[25] had been matched by his encouragement of the mercantile marine through paying bounties of five and six *livres* a ton for ships built in France and by protecting French fisheries with higher tariffs against foreign fish. Colbert's tariff barriers against foreign manufacturers were maintained by his successors, and the letters patent of 1717 and 1727 attempted to regulate French colonial trade in the manner of the Navigation Acts. Colbert's trading companies failed, but John Law's Company of the Indies,[26] reconstituted and reorganized in the 1720s, played an important role in French commercial prosperity in the eighteenth century.

The West Indies were the pivot of both French and British colonial systems. Sugar, tobacco, cotton, indigo and dyewoods were the first 'enumerated' commodities under the Navigation Acts, and between 1713 and 1792 England imported £162

[24] Thus French brandy could not go direct from Bordeaux to Boston even in English ships. For further details on the Navigation Acts see S. B. Clough and C. W. Cole, *Economic History of Europe*, D. C. Heath, Boston, 1952, pp. 343-51.

[25] See above, p. 6.

[26] See below, p. 236.

million worth of goods from her own West Indian islands, compared with £104 million from India and China combined.[27] France's West Indian possessions were even more profitable: St Domingo alone produced more sugar than all the British West Indies together, and in 1763 the British government seriously considered exchanging Canada for Guadeloupe.[28] The wealth of the West Indies depended on the slave trade. The French government paid a premium for every negro transported to the new world, while in England the slave trade was still defended as the most important branch of English commerce. It is easy to see why: not only the West Indian sugar plantations but the rice, indigo and tobacco production of the American colonies depended on slave labour. In New England, West Indian sugar was made into rum, which was then traded in Africa for slaves, who in turn produced more sugar to be made into rum. The system was as neat as it was lucrative.

The Dutch also had a foothold in the West Indies and, in spite of the theoretical restrictions of the *asiento* treaty,[29] were the biggest slave-traders on the West African coast. In the East Indies the Dutch continued to control the spice trade, though by 1750 coffee production in the islands had become almost as important; but their trade with the Indian mainland declined in the face of British and French competition. Between 1709 and 1750 the British East India Company doubled the value of its imports and exports, and increased its ships from eleven to twenty, while in the 1740s the French Company of the Indies had thirty ships on its route from France, via West Africa, India and the East Indies, to the Far East. Sweden, Denmark, Hamburg, Prussia and Austria all attempted to exploit the East Indies trade by founding rival companies, but only the Danish survived for any length of time.

Such commercial ventures were a recognition of the way in which the focus of European trade had changed since the seventeenth century. No longer was Europe itself the chief sphere of seaborne commerce, as it had been when timber and corn, wine and wool, salt and herrings were the staple

[27] R. R. Palmer, *A History of the Modern World*, Knopf 1956, p. 229.
[28] See below, p. 197.   [29] See above, p. 16.

commodities of European trade. In the 1660s Colbert had estimated, probably rather unreliably, that three-quarters of the ships
engaged in European trade were Dutch. Certainly the Navigation Acts had been directed primarily against Holland, and in
1728 Defoe could still describe the Dutch as 'the Carriers of the
World, the middle Persons in Trade, the Factors and Brokers of
Europe'. But from the 1730s onwards, as other European countries developed their merchant fleets and port facilities, and as
colonial trade grew so rapidly in volume, Holland ceased to be
the entrepôt of Europe, though Amsterdam remained Europe's
financial capital at least until the American war and perhaps until
the French Revolution. The chief factor in the economic decline
of Holland was her lack of industrial resources, and perhaps
even a reluctance to admit their importance. As late as 1824 a
Dutch writer thought that Dutch trade was better balanced than
the British, since as much as 70 per cent of British exports were
manufactures.[30]

The Birth of Industrialism

England's industrial pre-eminence in the eighteenth century is
beyond dispute, however much historians may haggle over the
term 'revolution'. Although France and England were well-
matched rivals in overseas trade, England enjoyed several
important advantages helpful to industrial development. Both
countries had improved internal communications – the French
corvée produced roads as good as the British turnpikes – but by
1800 England had twice the canal mileage of France and, until
the Revolution, French internal trade was still hampered by
tolls and tariffs. French farming, based on a system of peasant
proprietorship, was less amenable to improvements requiring
capital investment, while French industrialists could command
fewer sources of capital[31] than their British counterparts. England
was also luckier in the distribution of raw materials: she had
more coal, and it was situated near her iron deposits (as in the
Midlands) or within easy reach of the South Wales ports.

[30] Ed. E. M. Carus-Wilson, *Essays in Economic History*, Vol. I, Arnold 1954, p. 269.
[31] See below, p. 236.

British coal production rose during the century from two and a half million tons to some ten million tons, or about 90 per cent of the world output. French production in 1800 was still under a million tons, although a century earlier it had been a bare 75,000 tons. Belgium, whose annual output in 1700 had been about a third of that of the Durham and Northumberland coalfields alone, had the most important coal industry on the Continent in 1800. By the middle of the nineteenth century Germany had overtaken Belgium, but only after the mines of Upper Silesia had started large-scale production in the 1840s.

In the production of iron British superiority was less impressive. As a result of Peter the Great's exploitation of the iron ore of the Urals, Russia produced more pig-iron in 1718 than England did in 1740; and as late as the 1790s Russian iron was exported to England. British production in 1790 was only about 40 per cent more than the French, while her output of 250,000 tons in 1800 amounted to less than half the combined continental production. Much of Europe's iron was produced on a small scale. It is estimated that as late as 1846 three-fifths of the pig-iron produced in France was smelted in small charcoal furnaces, while it was not until 1847 that the first coke blast-furnace was built in the Ruhr.[32]

Even in the textile industry, the first to benefit from technical inventions on a large scale, the domestic system rather than factory organization remained the rule. The introduction of steampower necessitated the concentration of machines into factories, but the first Manchester steamloom factory was not set up until 1806, and as late as 1830 it was calculated that there were still 240,000 handlooms in England and Scotland as against 60,000 powerlooms. There was, of course, an inevitable timelag between the invention of a new technique and its widespread adoption and, in spite of Watt's engine, water remained the chief motive power in the eighteenth century. It was the Age of Invention rather than the Age of Industrialization.

If the more obvious manifestations of industrialism did not appear until the following century, the eighteenth century saw the beginnings of the population explosion that was perhaps the

[32] S. B. Clough and C. W. Cole, *op. cit.*, p. 411.

most important ingredient in the Industrial Revolution. It has been estimated that Europe's population rose from about 118 millions in 1700 to nearly 188 millions in 1800. France's population seems to have risen from about nineteen millions in 1715 to twenty-six millions in 1789, while the population of England and Wales rose from about six millions in 1720 to nearly nine millions in 1801. In Germany the population of Prussia rose from an estimated 2,380,000 in 1740 to 5,750,000 in 1783, while that of Saxony rose from 1,600,000 to two million between 1722 and 1802.[33] Territorial changes conceal the rate of population growth in Russia and the Habsburg Empire, but the increase seems to have been comparable. Certainly the population of Moscow rose from 150,000 early in the century to 250,000 in 1812, while Vienna with 226,000 in 1800 was the largest city after London, Paris, Naples and Moscow. The urban population of Europe remained small by modern standards. Only about 10 per cent of Frenchmen lived in towns at the time of the Revolution, while in Russia the proportion was as low as 4 per cent.

Whatever the reasons for the population increase, and they are much debated, the need for improved food production is obvious. Although the open-field system of agriculture still survived in half the English counties by 1760, subsistence farming had long since begun to give way to farming for market, while in the Netherlands from the seventeenth century onwards the cultivation of flax, hops and tobacco developed together with market-gardening and fruit-growing. Holland was in fact the home of many of the new techniques for which the British tend to take the credit, but parts of Italy could also boast a prosperous agriculture. Grosley, whose *Observations about Italy and the Italians* appeared in 1764, described the dairy-farming district of Lodigiano as 'possibly the most fertile canton in Europe', while Arthur Young, on the eve of the French Revolution, thought that the irrigation system of East Piedmont and Milan was 'possibly the most important in the world'.[34] Farther south it was a different story. Sicily, once the granary of Southern

[33] W. O. Henderson, *The Industrial Revolution on the Continent*, Cass 1961, p. 7. Prussia had, of course, gained in territory during this period.
[34] M. Vaussard, *Daily Life in Eighteenth-century Italy*, Allen & Unwin 1962, p. 32.

Europe, lost 30,000 of its inhabitants in the famine of 1763–64, and in 1787 Goethe found a traditional three-year cycle of beans, corn and fallow, since, as the peasants told him, 'manure works greater miracles than the saints'.[35]

Not all European peasants were as poor as the Sicilians, but over much of the Continent the organization of agriculture remained manorial. This did not necessarily rule out improvements. The Hungarian magnates sank a good deal of capital in land reclamation and new agricultural techniques, and organized the large-scale export of their produce. Frederick the Great, though resisting enclosures, encouraged the adoption of British farming methods.[36] In France, Duhamel du Monceau published six volumes on the new techniques between 1751 and 1760, while the physiocrats campaigned for more efficient agriculture. Although turnip cultivation did not become common in Europe until the next century, it was advocated in France before the Revolution. Louis XVI, no less than 'Farmer George', encouraged stockbreeding experiments on his farm at Rambouillet, and actually tried to break down the prejudice against potatoes by wearing a potato-flower in his buttonhole.

Mechanization in farming and the use of artificial fertilizers were nineteenth-century developments. Meikle's threshing machine, invented in 1786, was still a rarity even in English counties by 1830, while Sir Humphry Davy's *Elements of Agricultural Chemistry* did not appear until 1813. But Davy's work is a reminder of the importance of scientific as well as technological advances in the eighteenth century. It is true that the developments in pure science in the century after Newton bore little relevance to the technology of the age of steam; but they pointed the way to the later industrial revolutions of the twentieth century.

Newtonianism had triumphed by the 1730s. Fontenelle, as Permanent Secretary of the *Académie des Sciences* from 1699, fought a spirited rearguard action in defence of Descartes,[37] and

---

[35] J. W. von Goethe, *Italian Journey 1786–1788*, trans. W. H. Auden and E. Mayer, Collins 1962, p. 253.
[36] See below, p. 122. [37] See above, p. 56.

as late as 1752 (at the age of 95) published a work in support of the vortex theory. But Voltaire's popularization of Newton's works defeated the Cartesians, and as early as 1732 the Italian Count Francesco Algarotti had published *Il Neutonianesimo per le donne* (Newtonianism for the Ladies).[38] Newton's reputation proved something of an obstacle to further discovery, and it was left for Laplace in the last decade of the century to extend Newton's astronomy by developing the nebular hypothesis for the origin of the solar system. The nebular theory was presented, as Laplace himself put it, 'with the bravado that must inspire everything that is not the result of observation and calculation'. Laplace's universe was no longer the observable and comprehensible universe of the *philosophes*:

If we now reflect on this profusion of stars and nebulae scattered throughout space and on the vast distances that separate them, the imagination, astounded by the grandeur of the Universe, will have difficulty in conceiving that it has limits.[39]

The microscope achieved for the biological sciences what the telescope had done for astronomy. Invented at about the time that Galileo first used a telescope, the microscope had been used in the seventeenth century to study the life of a silkworm, to examine the structure of skin tissues, to classify insects and to reveal the sex difference in plants. The Dutchman Antony van Leeuwenhoek (d. 1723) seems to have been the only man before the nineteenth century to observe bacteria under the microscope. The Swedish botanist Linnaeus (1707–78) relied on the instrument for his elaborate system of classifying plants, which led him on to the further classification of animals and minerals, thus preparing the way for Lamarck (1744–1829), whose views on evolution were first published in 1801.

Lavoisier, born only a year before Lamarck but executed in 1794, brought about a 'Copernican' revolution in chemistry. His formulation of the oxygen theory of combustion – that combustion was the result of the combination of the burning substance with oxygen – disposed of the tenacious belief in phlo-

[38] Ed. H. H. Rowen, *From Absolutism to Revolution. 1648–1848*, Macmillan 1963, p. 97.
[39] Quoted in French in R. Mousnier and E. Labrousse, *Le XVIIIᵉ Siècle: Révolution Intellectuelle, Technique et Politique*, Presses Universitaires de France 1955, p. 30.

giston. As he said in a memoir presented to the *Académie* in 1783:

Chemists have made phlogiston a vague principle, which is not strictly defined and which consequently fits all the explanations demanded of it. Sometimes it has weight, sometimes it has not; sometimes it is free fire, sometimes it is fire combined with earth; sometimes it passes through the pores of a vessel, sometimes these are impenetrable to it. It explains at once causticity and non-causticity, transparency and opacity, colour and the absence of colour. It is a veritable Proteus that changes its form every instant![40]

And in words reminiscent of Diderot's definition of the aims of the *Encyclopaedia*[41] he added:

It is time to lead chemistry back to a stricter way of thinking, to strip the facts, with which it is daily enriched, of the additions of rationality and prejudice, to distinguish what is fact and observation from what is system and hypothesis, and, in short, to mark out, as it were, the limit that chemical knowledge has reached, so that those who come after us may set out from that point and confidently go forward to the advancement of the science.[42]

Lavoisier's *Elementary Treatise on Chemistry* (1789) listed thirty-three elements, though he realized that this was only a beginning:

Chemistry in subjecting to experiments the various bodies in Nature aims at decomposing them so as to be able to examine separately the different substances that enter into their composition. .... Chemistry advances towards its goal and its perfection by dividing, subdividing and resubdividing; and we do not know what the limit of its achievements may be.[43]

Two years later he was able to write: 'All young chemists adopt the theory and from that I conclude that the revolution in chemistry has come to pass.'

The invention of the fire-balloon owed little to Lavoisier's theory of combustion, but Lavoisier took great interest in the work of the two Frenchmen (the brothers Montgolfier) who in June 1783 demonstrated the buoyant properties of heated air – though they attributed the buoyancy to the levity of the smoke.

[40] D. McKie, *Antoine Lavoisier: Scientist, Economist, Social Reformer*, Constable 1952, p. 116.
[41] See above, p. 71.   [42] McKie, *op. cit.*, pp. 116–17.   [43] *Ibid.*, p. 217.

In September they repeated the experiment at Versailles before the King and Queen, when a sheep, a cock and a duck became the first balloon passengers. Benjamin Franklin realized that he was witnessing the infancy of air travel.[44] Hot air was soon replaced by hydrogen (then known as 'inflammable air'), to which Lavoisier himself had devoted so much study, and at the end of 1783 Lavoisier was one of the commissioners who reported to the *Académie* on the problems and possibilities of the new invention.

Lavoisier's interest in ballooning is a reminder that the eighteenth century did not recognize the modern distinction between pure and applied science. But the point at which pure and applied science became most closely identified was in the early experiments with electricity. About 1745 the invention of the Leyden jar had proved that electricity could be stored, and it was a spark from a Leyden jar that led Franklin to conclude that lightning and electricity were identical. In 1772 John Wesley was using what *The Westminster Journal* called 'an Electrical Machine' to cure ailments ranging from gout to toothache, while in the 1790s Galvani's treatise on animal electricity (published in 1791, the year of Faraday's birth) and Volta's discovery of the voltaic pile or battery heralded a second industrial revolution. And it was Davy, inventor of the miner's safety lamp and writer on soil chemistry, who in 1810 used a battery of 2,000 cells to produce a four-inch arc of electric light before an astonished audience at the Royal Institution.

[44] Cf. his celebrated reply when questioned about the usefulness of a balloon: 'What use is a newborn baby?'

8

Frederick the Great in Prussia
1740–86

Frederick and the 'Philosophes'

Frederick II (1740–86) inherited from his father a country of
two and a half million inhabitants, an annual revenue of
7,000,000 *thalers*,[1] and an army of 83,000 men. His first act was to
stake this legacy in a European war.[2] Yet Frederick William I
(1713–40)[3] had earlier suspected that his son was more of a
scholar than a soldier. At the age of 18 Frederick had tried to
run away from court, but the project was discovered, and he
was not only imprisoned but also forced to watch the execution
of the friend who had helped to plan the flight. It was not until
after his marriage (at his father's direction) in 1733 that Crown
Prince Frederick was allowed to set up house on his own at
Rheinsberg. Here he read widely in Latin and French literature,
dabbled in philosophy and science, and surrounded himself
with men of letters.

His correspondence with Voltaire began in 1736 and continued, on and off, for forty years. On his accession in 1740
Frederick moved to Potsdam where Knobelsdorff, architect of
the Berlin Opera House, built the royal palace of Sans Souci.
It was at Potsdam that Voltaire visited him four times between
1740 and 1743 and found the atmosphere so French that he could
report that he was still in France. In 1737 Voltaire had written
to Frederick: 'You think like Trajan, you write like Pliny, you
talk French like our best writers. Louis XIV was a great king

---

[1] The *thaler*: a silver coin current in northern Germany before 1871, when it was
superseded by the mark; *thalers* continued to circulate for the rest of the nineteenth
century at the rate of three *thalers* to the mark.

[2] The War of the Austrian Succession, 1740–48. See below, p. 173.

[3] See above, p. 44.

and I respect his memory; but his voice was not so human. I have seen his letters; he could not spell. Under your auspices Berlin will be the Athens of Germany, perhaps of Europe.'[4] Two years later Voltaire commended Frederick's *Antimachiavel* as 'a book worthy of a prince, and I do not doubt that an edition of Machiavelli, with this refutation at the close of each chapter, would be one of the most precious monuments of literature'.[5] But however effusive the terms of their early letters, the friendship showed signs of strain by the time of Voltaire's fifth visit in 1750. At the beginning of 1752 Voltaire sent to Potsdam an advance copy of *The Age of Louis XIV*, but by the end of the year he had mortally offended Frederick by his attack on Maupertuis, President of the Prussian Academy. Their correspondence continued, but things were never the same again. 'Voltaire is the most malevolent madman I ever met,' complained Frederick; 'he is only good to read.'

For twenty years Frederick also corresponded with d'Alembert,[6] who had been a member of the Prussian Academy since 1746 and who hailed Frederick as 'a prince greater even than his fame, a hero at once *philosophe* and modest, a king worthy of friendship, in fact a true sage on the throne'. The Prince de Ligne, who frequented most of the European courts, was equally fulsome in his praise of Frederick:

The King's encyclopaedic range enchanted me. The arts, war, medicine, literature, religion, ethics, history and legislation were discussed: the great epochs of Augustus and Louis XIV, good society among the Romans, the Greeks and the French; the chivalry of Francis I; the frankness and valour of Henri IV; the renaissance of letters since Leo X; anecdotes of clever men; the slips of Voltaire, the touchiness of Maupertuis. ... He talked of everything imaginable in a rather low voice.[7]

Frederick gave little encouragement to German scholars, however. He withheld his patronage from Lessing and Winckelmann[8] and, although he revived the Prussian Academy[9] as the

---

[4] G. P. Gooch, *Frederick the Great*, Longmans 1947, p. 151.

[5] Gooch, *op. cit.*, p. 158.   [6] See above, p. 70.

[7] Gooch, *op. cit.*, p. 142.   [8] See below, p. 230.

[9] Founded in 1700 by Frederick I, at the instigation of Leibnitz, but neglected by Frederick William I.

Academy of Science and Literature, in 1786 only five out of the eighteen Academicians were German.

How genuine was Frederick's interest in literary pursuits? *Les Matineés du Roi de Prusse, écrites par lui-même, A.D. 1764*, purports to be advice written by Frederick to his nephew and heir. Its authenticity remains somewhat suspect, but the remarks about the *philosophes* seem to have the full Frederician flavour:

I have done all I could to gain for myself a reputation in literary matters, and I have been more fortunate than Cardinal Richelieu, for, thank God, I pass for an author; but, between ourselves, the race of *beaux esprits* is an accursed one. They are a people insupportable for their vanity. Such a poet would refuse my kingdom if he were obliged to sacrifice one of his fine verses. As it is a profession which draws us away from the occupations of the Throne, I only compose when I have nothing better to do; and, to give myself more ease, I have at my court some *beaux esprits* who take the trouble to write down my ideas.

You saw with what distinction I treated d'Alembert on his last trip. I always made him take his meals with me, and I did nothing but praise him. You were surprised at the great attentions which I paid this author. You do not, then, know that this philosopher is listened to in Paris as an oracle, that he does nothing but speak of my talents, of my virtues, and everywhere he relates that I have all the characteristics of a true hero and a great king. Moreover I like to be praised, and d'Alembert never opens his mouth but to tell me obliging things. Voltaire is not of such a character, therefore I drove him away. . . . I forgot to tell you that, in the midst of my greatest misfortunes, I always took care to pay the *beaux esprits* their pensions. These philosophers describe war as the most frightful folly when it touches their pockets.[10]

Centralization in Government

Frederick's literary and philosophical interests were the occupation of his leisure hours, and after 1740 he did not allow himself much leisure. The centralization of Prussian government had been largely completed by Frederick William I, and had been

---

[10] This translation from the *Matinées*, together with the original French text, appears in Sir J. W. Whittall, *Frederick the Great on Kingcraft*, Longmans 1901, pp. 31–32.

prompted by military necessity. It was chiefly to ensure the efficient collection of the Excise, which maintained the army, that the traditional town councils had been replaced by small bodies of paid officials, appointed for life and responsible to the central government. The councils were placed under the supervision of the Local Commissary (*Steuerrat*), who was responsible for a number of towns. In country districts similar supervision was exercised by a Rural Commissioner (*Landrat*), who was, however, always a *junker*[11] and who fulfilled the functions of policeman, Justice of the Peace, tax-collector and recruiting officer all in one. It was the efficiency of these local officials that enabled Frederick to exploit the slender financial resources of Prussia sufficiently to fight three wars in two decades.[12]

At the centre of government Frederick William I had in 1723 established the General (Finance and Domains) Directory. This worked through fifteen provincial War and Domains Chambers, which were in turn served by the Local Commissaries in the towns, Rural Commissioners in the country, and Crown Bailiffs on the royal estates. This machinery was not Frederick the Great's creation, but he established over it a personal control that was as novel as it was complete. The General Directory comprised four ministers, each of whom was entrusted with *all* the affairs of a particular group of provinces and with *certain* matters concerning the country as a whole: one minister combined the post of Master of the Mint with his regional responsibilities. There was no Prime Minister and the principle of collective responsibility prevailed: decisions had to be signed by all four ministers. The King stayed at Potsdam and communicated with his ministers in Berlin only by letter: they sent him reports, he replied with directives. When he found the General Directory too slow for his purposes, he created a new functional ministry responsible directly to himself. Thus in 1742 he set up a ministry for newly conquered Silesia, in 1746 one for military administration, and, at intervals throughout the reign, a number of ministries for economic affairs.[13] There had been a Foreign Office even

[11] See above, p. 101.
[12] The first Silesian War, 1740–42, the second Silesian War, 1744–48 (see below, p. 179), and the Seven Years War, 1756–63 (see below, p. 189).
[13] See below, p. 123.

in his father's time, but Frederick preferred to act as his own foreign minister, writing direct to every Prussian ambassador abroad. In wartime, he combined in his own person the functions of both ministry of war and general staff.

Frederick set himself to be master of every department of government, believing, as he once said, that a coherent system of government must spring, like Newton's law of gravity, from a single agile mind.[14] Rising at four in summer and five in winter, Frederick devoted ten hours a day to state affairs, four to study and writing, and two to recreation. A calendar on his desk reminded him of the business of the week and indicated when reports and replies were due. His civil servants were recruited by public examination, and he tried to make them work as hard as he did himself by inserting at strategic points in the bureaucratic hierarchy an agent called a *Fiscal*, who kept a watch for irregularities and reported them to the King. Between May and August Frederick toured his territories in person, and in the autumn he inspected the army.

In contrasting his system of government with that of France where, he claimed, 'everything is decided by Court intrigues', Frederick summarized his political philosophy in words that have become famous:

A well-conducted government must have a system as coherent as a system of philosophy, so that finance, police and the army are co-ordinated to the same end, namely the consolidation of the state and the increase of its power. Such a system can only emanate from a single brain, that of the sovereign. Idleness, pleasure-seeking and imbecility are the causes which keep princes from the noble task of securing the happiness of their people. The sovereign is the first servant of the state.[15]

Yet Frederick was also the sternest critic of his own system. However hard the King worked, things would go wrong:

With the best will in the world he can make mistakes in the choice of his agents; he can be misinformed; his orders may not be punctually executed; injustices may never reach his ear; his officials may

---

[14] W. L. Dorn, *Competition for Empire 1740–1763*, Harper 1940, p. 54.
[15] Gooch, *op. cit.*, p. 282.

be too severe; in a word, the ruler of a large kingdom cannot be everywhere. Such is and such will be the destiny of things on earth that man will never attain to the state of perfection required for the happiness of the peoples, and therefore in governing, as in everything else, we must be content with what is least defective.[16]

The weakness of Frederick's highly centralized system was that it was centralized in his own head. As Mirabeau remarked: 'If ever a foolish prince ascends this throne, we shall see the formidable giant suddenly collapse and Prussia will fall like Sweden.'[17]

Law Reform

The defects in the administration of justice derived from the fact that it was still, at Frederick's accession, largely in the hands of the manorial and civic courts. Frederick William I had set himself the modest aim of ensuring that all civil suits should be settled within the year, but even this eluded him, and the Chief Justice Samuel von Cocceji (1679–1755) urged his proposals for reform in vain.

Cocceji's schemes to institute a single centralized judicial system with a standardized procedure, to replace the hereditary jurisdiction of the nobility with a body of wholetime, trained officials, and to introduce a single codification of Prussian law, all received a more sympathetic hearing from Frederick II. The first two of Cocceji's aims had been all but achieved by 1750: each province was left with only one central court, judges were better paid but were forbidden to take fees and fines, and the nobles were forced to reform the conduct of their manorial courts. The effect of the simplification of procedure was most clearly shown in Pomerania where 3,000 outstanding cases were settled in a single year.

The complete reform of civil procedure was not, however, achieved until 1781 when Cocceji's successor, Johann von Carmer (1721–1801), assisted by the jurist Suarez, issued the *Prozessordnung*. The new civil code, the Prussian *Landrecht*, though based on Cocceji's draft, was not completed until 1794, eight

---

[16] *Ibid.*, p. 294.   [17] *Ibid.*, p. 296.

years after Frederick's death. But Carmer and Suarez had done their work well: the *Landrecht* remained in force until 1900. The preamble to the 1791 version of the new code spoke with the voice of the Enlightenment:

The welfare of the state in general, and of its inhabitants in particular, is the aim of civil society and the general objective of the laws. The laws and ordinances of the state should restrict the natural liberty and rights of citizens no further than the general welfare demands.[18]

In the 1794 *Landrecht* these clauses were deleted – presumably because the French Revolution had made them sound too dangerous.

In fact, of course, the civil code of 1794 ratified the predominance of the landed aristocracy. Nobles, burghers and peasants remained clearly defined classes, each with their separate taxes, their separate property rights, and their separate function in the state. These divisions were preserved in the interests of military necessity: the peasants provided the rank and file of the army, the *junkers* its officer class. Serfdom remained firmly fixed on all but the most westerly parts of Prussia. Frederick tried to lighten the burden of the serfs on the crown estates, but he could not afford to antagonize the *junker* class on whom his army and his administrative system relied. Nor was Frederick prepared to deprive the provincial chambers of their jurisdiction in matters affecting 'the public interest', which meant in practice the security of the state revenues. Yet, while admitting these qualifications, the rationalization of the judicial system during Frederick's reign undeniably made the ordinary citizen much more secure in the enjoyment of his civil rights. As Gooch remarks, 'Frederick's system was better than any regime in Europe except where constitutional government prevailed, and it formed a bridge between feudalism and the modern democratic state'.[19]

[18] R. R. Palmer, *The Age of the Democratic Revolution: The Challenge*, Oxford 1959, p. 510.
[19] Gooch, *op. cit.*, p. 295.

Commercial and Economic Policy

Frederick the Great was a Mercantilist.[20] As he told his officials: 'Two things are conducive to the welfare of the country: (1) To bring money in from foreign countries. This is the function of commerce. (2) To prevent money from leaving the country unnecessarily. This is the function of manufactures.'[21]

Frederick continued the policy of attracting settlers from neighbouring states. The swamps along the lower Oder were drained, and the land settled by 50,000 immigrants: native Prussians were excluded, and foreigners were promised exemption from military service for three generations as an additional incentive. If a fire occurred in a Saxon town, Frederick would tell one of his officials to look out for suitable people who might be prepared to make a new home in Prussia. After the Seven Years War, 40 million *thalers* were spent on a recovery programme, which provided peasants in devastated areas with free grain, fodder, cattle and building timber; 35,000 spare army horses were also distributed.

In an age before blotting paper, Brandenburg was known as 'the sandbox of the Holy Roman Empire', and Frederick indirectly admitted the aptness of the gibe, in a letter to Voltaire:

I confess that with the exception of Libya few states can boast that they equal us in the matter of sand. Yet we are bringing 76,000 acres under cultivation this year as pasture. This pasture feeds 7,000 cows, whose dung will manure and improve the land, and the crops will be of more value.[22]

Frederick showed great interest in the growing of turnips, and the potato and even sugar beet were introduced from England, though the peasants were suspicious until the poor grain harvests of 1770–72 taught them prudence. But the most important of all the eighteenth-century agricultural innovations, the consolidation of holdings by enclosure, was not greatly encouraged, for fear of disrupting the cantonal recruiting system.

[20] See above, p. 103.
[21] N.C.M.H., vol. vii, p. 313.
[22] W. F. Reddaway, *Frederick the Great and the Rise of Prussia*, Putnam 1908, p. 310.

In his efforts to encourage industry Frederick attracted immigrant spinners, set up rural schools to train spinners and weavers, and established cotton mills. Bounties were paid to silk growers, government warehouses were built for the storage of silk, and an attempt was even made to persuade schoolmasters and other citizens who had time for gardening to grow mulberry trees. By the end of Frederick's reign the silk exports of Brandenburg were valued at over a million *thalers*, more than half of which were sent outside Prussian territories, while Brandenburg woollen exports reached almost the same figure. During the Seven Years War the secret of porcelain manufacture was stolen from Dresden, and the production of Prussian porcelain was stimulated by royal example: porcelain replaced gold and silver on Frederick's dinner table and became his standard gift to fellow monarchs. Attempts to foster the Prussian tobacco industry were less successful because the quality of the leaf was laughably inferior to the Virginian product; but Frederick was quick to conclude a commercial treaty (1785) with the new American republic, and Virginian tobacco was now to be admitted in exchange for Prussian textiles and porcelain.

In general Frederick clung to the Colbertist principle of protecting home industries by high external tariffs, while stimulating internal trade by abolishing internal tolls and by cutting canals to improve communications. After the Seven Years War, state subsidies were devoted to fostering industrial schemes such as iron production in Westphalia, mining in Upper Silesia, trading companies like the Levant Company and the Russian Company, and the establishment of state monopolies in salt, sugar, porcelain, tobacco and coffee. Government encouragement of industrial and commercial development was further reflected in the creation of new ministries: Commerce and Industry in 1741, Excise and Tolls in 1766, Mines in 1768 and Forestry in 1770.

Frederick seems to have been interested in industry chiefly as a means of increasing state revenues, and in 1766 a revised system of indirect taxation (the *Regie*) was introduced under the supervision of de Launay and some 200 French officials. The general principle was that of reducing taxes on necessities and increasing those on luxuries, but Frederick could not resist raising the excise on beer, salt, tobacco and coffee. The British ambassador, Sir Andrew Mitchell, wrote home: 'The new projects of excise have really alienated the affections of the people from their sovereign to a degree hardly to be described.'

Nevertheless, more efficient taxation, together with the beginnings of industrial development, British subsidies during the Seven Years War (four million *thalers* a year from 1758), and a systematic depreciation of the currency, enabled Frederick to pay for his wars, more than double the size of his army, and leave behind at his death a war-chest of over fifty-two million *thalers*. And if we are tempted to mock Frederick's narrow mercantilism, it is worth remembering that Prussia proved sufficiently attractive for some 300,000 immigrants to settle there during his reign.

Religious Policy

In religious matters Frederick II was the most tolerant ruler in Europe. In the first of his Political Testaments, written in 1752, he expounded his views on religious toleration. He himself was a Deist: 'All religions, when one looks into them, rest on a system of fable more or less absurd.' But religious beliefs must be respected because they were important to those who held them. Persecution was bad politics: it led only to disunity in the state and the emigration of useful citizens.

Frederick described his position as 'neutral between Rome and Geneva', but, although he tried to keep on good terms with the Pope, the Testament revealed scant respect for papal claims:

The Pope is an old neglected idol in his niche. He is at present the chief almoner of Kings. His thunderbolts are no more. His policy is known. Instead of laying peoples under an interdict and deposing sovereigns as of old, he is content if no one deposes him and lets him say mass quietly in St Peter's.[23]

In 1773 Clement XIV was persuaded to dissolve the Society of Jesus, the members of which had already been expelled from Portugal, France and Spain. Frederick promptly offered them

[23] Gooch, *op. cit.*, p. 284.

asylum: 'Since my brothers, the very faithful and apostolic Catholic Kings have driven them out, I, very heretical, gather up as many of them as I can.' But he did not extend the same toleration to Jews. An edict of 1750 debarred foreign Jews from settling in Prussia, except on payment of an exorbitant sum, and excluded Prussian Jews from all civil office, from the professions, and from the practice of most trades, including agriculture. Wealthy Jews were encouraged to *invest* in industry, however, and were, of course, heavily taxed. 'As for the Jews,' Frederick wrote, 'they are poor devils who in substance are not as bad as people think; they pay well, and, after all, it is only fools that are their dupes.'

Education

Frederick's refusal to suppress the Jesuits may have been prompted by his need for teachers. 'The more one advances in age,' he wrote to d'Alembert, 'the more one is convinced of the harm done to society by the neglected education of youth.' Frederick did little to help higher education. The universities of Halle and Königsberg were kept desperately short of funds throughout his reign, while his Academy of Science and Literature was an association of expatriate *philosophes* rather than an educational establishment.[24] Nor did Frederick abolish censorship. In 1769 Lessing wrote to a friend:

Do not tell me anything about your freedom to think and write in Berlin. This freedom may be summarized as solely that of saying as many *sottises* against religion as one likes. . . . Let one man stand up in Berlin for the rights of the subject and against exploitation and despotism, as now happens even in France and Denmark, and you will soon find out which country is to this day the most slavish in Europe.

Meanwhile Frederick's schoolmasters were recruited from among his discharged soldiers. A scheme for a national system of education, the *Landschulereglement*, was proposed in 1763, but was not carried out through lack of funds, and the Prussian primary school system remained far inferior to the Austrian.

[24] See above, p. 116.

Frederick was probably not wholly convinced of the political advisability of universal education:

It is enough for the people [he wrote] to learn only a little reading and writing. . . . Instruction in the country must be planned so that they only receive that which is most essential for them, but which is designed to keep them in the villages and not influence them to leave.

But apart from such considerations, Frederick was not prepared to foot the bill. In 1786 twelve million *thalers* out of a total revenue of twenty-two million were spent on the army. Not for the last time was national education sacrificed to the needs of national defence.

Frederick described himself as '*philosophe par inclination politique par devoir*', and his order of priorities remained that of the politician. Nowhere, perhaps, is this more clearly reflected than in the words he wrote to the Electress of Saxony in 1765: 'While the coffers of the Great Powers remain empty, we can cultivate the sciences at our ease. The recent blood-letting was so copious that I expect to finish my course in peace.' He was to be disappointed. In 1778 the ambitions of Joseph II involved him in the War of the Bavarian Succession. Frederick condemned 'this enthusiasm of the young Caesar for war' as vigorously as an earlier generation had condemned his own seizure of Silesia. And when in 1779 peace was concluded Frederick accepted it with resignation:

Imperfection is our destiny. Man has to content himself with approximations. . . . Will peace be more secure? We can only guess. Anything is possible. Our eyes cannot pierce the future. We can merely trust to Providence or rather to Fate, which will shape the future as they have shaped the whole history of mankind.[25]

The 'enlightenment' of the youthful scholar-prince seems to have given place to the cynicism of the retired general. The truth probably is that, once he became King, Frederick relegated philosophy to his leisure hours. Where the reforms advocated by the *philosophes* seemed to make for the smoother running of a military and mercantilist state, Frederick was ready to adopt

[25] For Frederick's foreign policy see Chapters 12–14 below.

them; where they seemed more likely to impair his absolutism, he ignored them. 'I labour with both hands,' Frederick had written to Voltaire in 1742, 'one for the army, the other for the people and the arts.' The implied division of effort is instructive.

9

Catherine the Great in Russia
1762–96

Catherine and the 'Philosophes'

In the middle years of her reign Catherine wrote her own epitaph: 'In 1744 she went to Russia to marry Peter III. Eighteen years of tedium and solitude caused her to read many books. When she came to the throne she wished to do good and strove to introduce happiness, freedom and prosperity.'[1] It is not a bad summary as far as it goes. When the fourteen-year-old daughter of Christian August of Anhalt-Zerbst left her native Stettin to marry the Grand Duke Peter and take the name of Catherine, she knew nothing of Russia and could speak no Russian. Peter was probably not as repulsive as Catherine depicted him in her *Memoirs*, but he was mentally backward and thoroughly childish in his interests,[2] so that we may believe Catherine's claim that 'when he left the room the dullest book was a delight'. French was her second language, and among the books she turned to were the writings of Voltaire and Montesquieu.

Catherine was later to tell Voltaire that 'since 1746 I have been deeply in your debt', but their correspondence did not begin until 1763 when he was sixty-nine and she thirty-four. In the previous June, Catherine had seized power in the traditional Russian manner of a palace revolution: she rode into St Petersburg and was proclaimed Empress by the Archbishop; Peter III signed his abdication and duly died a few days later, apparently poisoned by Alexis Orlov, brother of Catherine's current lover.

[1] G. P. Gooch, *Catherine the Great and Other Studies*, Longmans 1954, p. 107.
[2] Gooch goes so far as to cite the mental instability of Paul, Catherine's son, as proof that Peter III was indeed his father – a fact disputed at the time.

Voltaire commented laconically: 'Like the Jesuits, Providence makes use of every means, and a drunkard's death from colic teaches us to be sober.'[3]

Catherine and Voltaire never met, but their fulsome exchanges continued until the latter's death in 1778. As the author of a history of the reign of Peter the Great, Voltaire was particularly interested in Catherine's achievements:

If Peter the Great had chosen Kiev or some more southernly spot I should now be at your feet, despite my age. I have never wished to go to Rome. . . . But I die of regret not to see deserts changed into proud cities, and 2,000 leagues of territory civilized by heroines. It is the finest of revolutions. My heart is like the lover; it turns always towards the North. D'Alembert is very wrong not to have made the journey, for he is still young.[4]

When, at the age of seventy-five, Voltaire at length offered to come to St Petersburg, Catherine forbade the visit: 'I know you are in delicate health. I admire your courage, but I should be inconsolable if it were to suffer from the effort. Neither myself nor Europe would forgive me.'[5]

How sincere were these compliments? In his correspondence with d'Alembert, Voltaire referred to Catherine in more measured terms, but when Voltaire died Catherine wrote to Grimm demanding 'a hundred complete copies of the works of my master so that I can distribute them. They will form citizens, geniuses, heroes and authors, and will foster a thousand talents.'[6] And it was not until the French Revolution that Houdon's famous bust of Voltaire was removed from Catherine's gallery of the great.

Catherine's letters to Grimm were in lighter vein, and in 1787 she told him to burn them. Grimm (1723–1807), the son of a Lutheran pastor, had won his way into the Paris *salons* before he was thirty and edited a confidential journal of Parisian literary and social gossip, the *Correspondance Littéraire*. Diderot contributed items, and subscribers included the King of Poland and Karl August of Weimar, who passed on his copy to Goethe. Frederick

---

[3] Gooch, *op. cit.*, p. 58. [4] Gooch, *op. cit.*, p. 61.
[5] Gooch, *op. cit.*, p. 64. [6] Gooch, *op. cit.*, p. 70.

the Great held aloof, but Catherine herself subscribed 1,500 roubles a year. She and Grimm first met in 1773. He declined her first offer of a post, but returned for a second visit and stayed for almost a year. He then agreed to act as her confidential agent in Paris, responsible for purchasing works of art.

The Empress was a keen patron of the arts. She bought the Walpole collection and gave Sir Joshua Reynolds a gold snuff-box for his painting of the infant Hercules strangling serpents, a symbolic representation of the new Russian state. She greatly embellished St Petersburg, notably by her extensions to the Winter Palace: in 1765 the Frenchman, Vallin de la Mothe, designed the Hermitage Pavilion, to which she later added an art gallery and a theatre. Catherine also bought Diderot's library, leaving him in possession as librarian until his death. She greatly admired the *Encyclopaedia*,[7] and wrote to Diderot in 1774: 'I cannot dispense with it for a single day; despite all its faults it is an essential and excellent work.' She had earlier tried unsuccessfully to persuade Diderot to transfer its publication to Russia. Diderot himself refused to move to St Petersburg permanently, but he paid one visit in 1773 when he overwhelmed Catherine with his exuberance. Wearied by his insistent demand for reforms, she admitted to him the limitations of her 'enlightened absolutism': 'You only work on paper, while I, poor empress, work on human skin, which is much more ticklish.'[8]

Centralization in Government

In the thirty-eight years between the death of Peter the Great and the accession of Catherine, Russia had seen no fewer than six rulers. Peter had personally disposed of his son, thus leaving two daughters by his second marriage and an infant grandson; he had meant to nominate his successor, but had died before doing so. His widow ruled as Catherine I until her death in 1727. Peter's young grandson succeeded as Peter II, but died of small-pox in 1730, the last surviving male of the Romanov line. He

---

[7] See above, p. 71.

[8] For a fuller version of this famous remark see J. M. Thompson, *Lectures on Foreign History*, Blackwell 1945, p. 357.

was succeeded by Anna (1730-40), daughter of Peter I's deceased stepbrother Ivan.[9] Anna nominated her sister's grandson Ivan as her successor, but Ivan VI was ousted within the year by Elizabeth, Peter I's second daughter. And it was Elizabeth (1741-62) who arranged Catherine's marriage to her nephew, later Peter III (1762-63). [See family tree on p. 354.]

During this period of dynastic turmoil the Russian nobility[10] had reasserted their privileges. By his Table of Ranks (1722)[11] Peter I had tried to replace the old aristocracy of the blood by a new aristocracy based on state service, but Peter III's edict of 1762 releasing the nobles from the obligation to do state service did little more than formally recognize the independence that they had regained for themselves during the intervening forty years. Catherine inherited Peter I's machinery of government, but the machine no longer worked. At her accession she found that the pay of the troops that had fought in the Seven Years War was many months in arrears, that the navy was, in her own words, fit only to catch herrings, and that nearly half the state revenues failed to reach the exchequer.

Catherine tried to regain personal control. She rose at five a.m., lit her own fire and often worked fifteen hours a day. Her room had separate tables assigned to different subjects, and she employed four secretaries. She attended debates in the Senate, questioned officials and private citizens, and, in her early years at least, made long tours of inspection. Catherine is notorious for the number of her favourites. It is possible to trace an unbroken succession of at least a dozen from Saltikov and Stanislas Poniatowski, later King of Poland,[12] through the long ascendancy of Gregory Orlov, to Potemkin and the string of young men in their early twenties through whom he influenced the Empress in her later years. Catherine owed her throne to the Orlovs, and their influence was reflected in their positions: Gregory was grand master of artillery, Alexis admiral of the fleet, and Theodore procurator-general. But it was Catherine who ruled.

[9] See above, p. 39.
[10] A rather vague term covering almost the whole of the landowning class in Russia. Pares, in *A History of Russia*, Cape 1937, prefers the term 'gentry'.
[11] See above, p. 43.   [12] See below, p. 208.

Peter I's successors had experimented with various forms of central council, and Catherine seems to have considered creating a permanent Council of State; but in the event she fell back on occasional councils of varying composition. The permanent organ of government was the Senate, instituted by Peter I. Its members were appointed by the crown and directly responsible to it. Catherine retained the Senate, but allowed it a less significant role than it had played under Elizabeth. Peter's system of 'colleges'[13] had largely broken down; Catherine reduced their number, and allowed those departments dealing with military, naval and foreign affairs to complete their development into independent ministries.

Catherine's chief constitutional reforms were in local government. She was convinced of the need for decentralization by the Pugachev rebellion,[14] and in 1775, the very year of its suppression, she turned to the reform of provincial administration. She replaced Peter I's unwieldy *gubernia* with fifty smaller *gubernia*, each of 300,000 to 400,000 inhabitants and each subdivided into 'districts' of 20,000 to 30,000. Each *gubernium* was presided over by a governor assisted by collegiate boards of officials nominated by the central government, together with an Office of Public Welfare to supervise health, education and poor relief. *Gubernia* were grouped into larger units under a Governor-General. The districts were administered by various courts elected by the nobles, who also elected an official called an *ispravnik* or corrector, responsible for police and poor relief. Each district had an Assembly of Deputies which met every three years.

Peter I's attempt to discipline the nobles from the centre was thus finally abandoned: Catherine was content to recognize her reliance on them and to entrust the control of the provincial administration to the only ruling class that Russia possessed. Russia was too large for complete centralization.

Law Reform

Catherine's dependence on the nobility was the limiting factor in the legal innovations of her reign. Peter I's instructions for the drafting of a new legal code had never been implemented. Catherine now devoted three hours a day to preparing a draft of her own, which emerged as the *Nakaz* or *Instructions to the Commissioners for Composing a New Code of Laws*. Of the 655 paragraphs, 250 came straight from Montesquieu[15] and 100 from Beccaria, whose *Crimes and Punishments* had appeared in 1764.

The *Instructions* opened with an uncompromising assertion of absolutism: 'The sovereign is absolute. The extent of the empire necessitates absolute power in the ruler. Any other form of government would have ruined it. The aim of monarchy is the glory of the citizen, the state and the sovereign.'[16] Later articles asserted that all men were equal before the law, that the object of administration should be the prevention rather than the punishment of crime, that capital punishment should be used sparingly, that 'all maiming ought to be abolished', and that serfdom ought to be rare and could only be justified by the needs of the state, though it was added that it would be dangerous to free all serfs at once.

The *Instructions* attracted some notice in Europe. Voltaire described it, with typical effusiveness, as 'the finest monument of the century', and Frederick II made Catherine a member of the Berlin Academy on the strength of it. Within four years of its completion the *Instructions* had appeared in twenty-four foreign versions, while the French government forbade its entry into France.

The *Instructions* were intended to guide the deliberations of an assembly summoned to discuss law reform. The Legislative Commission which met in Moscow in 1767 comprised 564 members: 208 representatives from the towns, 161 from the nobility, seventy-four from the peasants (though not the serfs), and twenty-eight from government officials; the remaining eighty-eight came from marginal territories, especially from the Cossack communities.[17] The representatives brought *cahiers*

---

[15] See above, p. 78.   [16] Gooch, *op. cit.*, p. 93.

[17] G. S. Thomson, *Catherine the Great and the Expansion of Russia*, E.U.P. 1947, p. 104. Pares, *op. cit.*, gives slightly different figures.

setting forth their grievances: the majority wanted more local self-government, many wanted to pay taxes in cash instead of in kind, the merchants wanted their monopolies respected. The peasant deputy from Archangel brought a list of 195 grievances, and several deputies made eloquent speeches on behalf of the peasants.[18] But how little real relief the peasants could expect was shown by the articles deleted from the draft: the paragraphs suggesting that each peasant should be guaranteed food and clothes, that the nobility should be allowed to punish only as masters and not as judges, and that there should be peasant judges and a peasant jury system, were all struck out. Well might Catherine complain of the fate of her _Instructions_: 'Every part provoked disagreement. I allowed them to cancel what they pleased, and they omitted over half my draft.'[19]

Modern historians have agreed with contemporaries in viewing the whole episode as a propaganda stunt. Certainly the outbreak of the Turkish war in 1768 was used as an excuse for suspending the Legislative Commission after 200 sittings extending from August to April, during which not a single law had been formulated. But many of the nineteen sub-committees of the Commission continued in session, some of them until 1775, and a measure of judicial reform did emerge: civil cases were separated from criminal, and the nobility, the town-dwellers and the crown peasants each came under the jurisdiction of their own system of courts. It seems likely that Catherine genuinely wanted reforms, but that the Legislative Commission convinced her of their impracticability.

Catherine certainly made no serious attempt to abolish serfdom, even before the Pugachev rebellion. Her Imperial Free Economic Society offered a prize for an essay on the condition of the peasant, but forbade the publication of the winning essay because it recommended peasant proprietorship of land. In 1765 permission had been given to landowners to send recalcitrant serfs to Siberia on their own initiative, and the right of appeal which the peasant had at least formally possessed was removed. Serfdom was actually extended by Catherine: she introduced it into the new lands of White Russia and the Ukraine, and she

[18] Pares, _op. cit._, p. 286.   [19] Gooch, _op. cit._, p. 92.

added 800,000 to the number of private serfs by granting crown lands to her favourites. In 1797 there were some 19,500,000 privately owned serfs and about 14,500,000 state- and church-owned peasants, out of an estimated population of thirty-six million.

The statistics illustrate the size of the problem facing Catherine, and it is perhaps not surprising that she shrank from tackling it, nor that she preferred instead to strengthen the position of the landowning classes. In 1785, four years before feudalism was finally abolished in France, the Charter of the Nobility (or Letter of Grace to the Nobility)[20] formally recognized the nobles as a separate estate and confirmed their traditional privileges. Peter III's edict of 1762 exempting them from state service was reaffirmed, as was their exemption from personal taxation, corporal punishment, and the billeting of troops. They could not lose their rank, life or estates, except by judgement of their peers. They were granted the exclusive right to set up factories and sink mines. In return they were required to ensure that the serfs paid the poll tax and discharged their compulsory military service. The armies that faced Napoleon would be armies of serfs, and serfdom was not finally abolished in Russia until 1861.

Commercial and Economic Policy

The central fact in Catherine's economic policies, as in those of her other 'enlightened' contemporaries, was the need to find men and money for the army. If the vested interests of the nobles were one obstacle in the way of a liberal policy, her own interest in territorial aggrandizement was another. The annual expenditure during her reign rose from seventeen million to seventy or eighty million roubles. Much of this money was expended in conquests that added (according to one estimate) nearly 220,000 square miles of territory to her empire. Yet Russia's population remained both too sparse and too poor.

In 1771 Pugachev, a Don Cossack, appeared among the Cossacks of the Urals, where the hardships of the workers in the

[20] See Appendix 11.

salt-mines combined with peasant grievances to provide raw material for revolt. Posing as Peter III, Pugachev in 1773 took several forts and besieged Orenburg (Chkalov). Catherine, with presumably unconscious irony, sent Marshal Bibikov, who had presided over the Legislative Commission, to check Pugachev's progress. On arrival Bibikov reported that this was not just another Cossack revolt, but the result of genuine and general discontent. He blamed 'the blindness and ignorance, the incompetent and dishonest officials, the weak and stupid officers'. Pugachev, after taking several of the Volga towns, threatening to march on Moscow, and hanging 500 priests and officers in three months, was eventually defeated by generals Panin and Michelson, assisted by famine. Pugachev was brought in an iron cage to Moscow and executed in 1775. Catherine refused to have him tortured; he was, however, drawn and quartered.

It was against this background of social discontent, of which Pugachev was only the most spectacular expression, that Catherine tried to pursue her policy of economic liberalism. Within a fortnight of her accession she had abolished most of the state monopolies which Elizabeth had farmed out to individuals. She continued the earlier efforts of Shuvalov, Elizabeth's chief minister, to establish internal free trade. The export of corn was permitted, and other export duties were abolished. Exports of flax, hemp, furs and skins, iron and naval stores increased, notably to England. Catherine showed great interest in road and canal building, while in 1774 the treaty of Kutchuk Kainardji[21] gave Russia access to the Black Sea, the Bosporus and the Dardanelles. Commercial treaties were concluded: with Poland in 1775, Denmark 1782, Turkey 1783, Austria 1785, and Naples, Portugal and France in 1787. The protective tariff of 1767 was replaced by a more liberal tariff in 1782. By 1793, however, Catherine had jettisoned her liberal views, and her last years saw a return to mercantilist policies, for which the disorder of the national finances provided sufficient excuse.

During Catherine's reign the value of Russian foreign trade increased from twenty-one million roubles in 1762 to an average of ninety-six million between 1794 and 1798. Even allowing for

21 See below, p. 202.

the depreciation of the currency by 25 per cent, this was a notable increase. But few of Russia's exports were manufactures. Potemkin's cloth factory which employed 9,000 was exceptional. The urban population had risen from 328,000 in 1724 to 1,300,000 in 1796, but this was still only a tiny fraction of the total population. The merchants remained a somewhat under-privileged class. Much of Russia's trade was in the hands of foreigners, and Russian merchants were still forbidden to own serfs or lands. In 1785 a charter for the towns provided for an elected mayor and town council who were to manage the town's financial affairs, but as no provision was made for levying rates, urban self-government existed only on paper. In a letter to Grimm in 1781 Catherine claimed to have founded 144 towns.[22] Perhaps she was joking. Certainly when the Governor of Archangel went to the formal opening of the town of Kem, he found that no such town existed. Potemkin is remembered for the dummy villages that are alleged to have lined the route when Catherine toured the Crimea with Joseph II in 1787.[23] He is less often given credit for the agricultural reconstruction of the Ukraine and the Crimea, which were pacified and settled not only with serfs but with German colonists, while the port of Sebastopol was built under the direction of Jeremy Bentham's brother. Yet Catherine returned from her triumphal tour of 1787 to find Moscow in the grip of famine. The celebrations that were to have been held in the Kremlin had to be cancelled.

Religious Policy

Catherine continued Peter I's policy of subordinating the Church to the State.[24] One of Peter III's last acts had been to appropriate the remaining Church lands, and this was confirmed by Catherine in 1764, though she had been expected to revoke it. She was at once condemned by the Archbishop of Rostov, who protested to the Synod, complaining that the Church had been plundered more heavily in Russia than in Turkey. The Archbishop was, of course, unfrocked and sent, first to a monas-tery, and later into solitary confinement. Catherine's secularization

[22] J. M. Thompson, *op. cit.*, p. 359.   [23] See below, p. 207.   [24] See above, p. 42.

of Church lands deprived the Orthodox Church of political independence: henceforth the clergy were paid by the State.

The partitions of Poland [25] brought Catherine large numbers of Catholic subjects. She allowed them religious freedom and remained on polite terms with the Papacy, although when the Society of Jesus was dissolved in 1773 she did not expel the Jesuits from Russia. She extended toleration to the Jews and admitted wealthy Jews to municipal office. In 1785 she lightened the disabilities of the Old Believers.[26] Catherine seems genuinely to have shared the *philosophes'* belief in toleration, though no doubt she thought it good politics too.

Education

'It is clear,' Catherine once wrote, 'that education is at the root of all good and evil; a new race or new fathers and mothers must therefore, so to speak, be produced by means of education in the first instance.'[27] Yet she tried to build her educational system from the top down. In 1764 she separated the Academy of Fine Arts, previously a department of Peter I's Academy of Science, from its parent body and gave it a new foundation. It was to supervise all branches of art throughout Russia and to provide classes in painting, etching and engraving, architecture, fine metalwork, and the making of mechanical instruments. In addition to such courses, the Academy provided a general education, followed by specialization in one or more of the arts, for some 200 boys from six to fourteen. In the same year she founded the Smolny Institute for the daughters of noblemen. In 1763 she had established the College of Medicine, while her decision to be inoculated against smallpox has been called her greatest contribution to the Enlightenment.

Her scheme of education was nothing if not sophisticated. Even in the naval academies the course included fine arts, with dancing and acting, while some of the provincial schools for the nobility held dances twice a week.[28] Not all the children of the nobility went to school. Many families engaged private tutors

---

[25] See Chapter 14 below.   [26] See above, p. 42.
[27] *Cambridge Modern History*, 1909, vi, p. 692.   [28] Pares, *op. cit.*, p. 295.

from abroad: Marat's brother taught the Saltikov children, while the future Alexander I was taught by the Swiss La Harpe. In 1767 Princess Daschkov took her son to England where he attended Westminster School before going on to Edinburgh.

In 1764 Catherine had sent a commission to report on British universities and schools. She accepted the recommendation that a national system of primary education should be set up to provide instruction in religion, reading, and perhaps a little writing and arithmetic. There may have been 300 free public primary schools in Russia by Catherine's death, but they were all in the towns, and, in general, elementary education was left to village schools run by the clergy and private schools provided by benevolent landlords. In Russia, as elsewhere in Europe, universal education was viewed with suspicion: a peasant might learn to forge a passport.

'Catherine was in theory a disciple of the *Aufklärung*, and in practice an absolute monarch.'[29] It would be difficult to improve upon this epitaph, except by stressing the practical limitations on her absolutism. Catherine was evidently influenced by the ideas of the *philosophes*, but the size of Russia, the political power of the nobles, and her own programme of conquest[30] all prevented their being put into practice. Peter I was probably her greatest hero: no name appears more frequently in her letters. And Catherine was the only exponent of 'enlightened absolutism' who lived long enough to see the graver excesses of the French Revolution. Under its impact her regime became as repressive as any in Europe: Novikov, Russia's leading publicist, was imprisoned; Raditchev, author of *Journey from St Petersburg to Moscow*, was dispatched to Siberia; even the circulation of Catherine's own *Instructions* was forbidden.

[29] C.M.H., vi, p. 699.
[30] For Catherine's foreign policy see Chapters 13–15.

10

Maria Theresa and Joseph II
1740–90

The Habsburgs and the 'Philosophes'

Maria Theresa (1740–80) and her son Joseph II (1765–90) provide an instructive commentary on the strengths and weaknesses of 'enlightened absolutism', not only in the contrast they present to their fellow monarchs on other European thrones, but also in the contrast they present to each other. As a result of Charles VI's patient diplomacy,[1] Maria Theresa succeeded to the Habsburg dominions in 1740, though the Imperial title, which could not descend to a woman, was bestowed at length in 1742 on Charles of Bavaria. At his death three years later the title reverted to the Habsburg family with the election of Francis of Lorraine, Maria Theresa's husband. When Francis died in 1765 Joseph succeeded him as Emperor and ruled the Habsburg territories jointly with his mother until her death in 1780.[2]

The Pragmatic Sanction[3] had been an attempt to preserve the Habsburg Empire from internal disintegration as much as from external attack. When Maria Theresa came to the throne at the age of twenty-three, she faced rebellion in Hungary as well as Prussian aggression in Silesia. The reforms which she introduced between the end of the Silesian wars and the start of the Seven Years War were dictated by the harsh necessity of securing Austrian survival rather than by the promptings of the *philosophes*. Maria Theresa was too devout a Catholic to approve of Voltaire, and if her political reforms seemed to owe something to Montesquieu it was not because she had herself read him.[4]

[1] See above, p. 47.
[2] She had nearly died of smallpox in 1767.
[3] See above, p. 47.
[4] Cf. Catherine the Great, p. 133 above.

Indeed she was later to forbid the teaching of English at the universities 'because of the dangerous character of this language in respect of its corrupting religious and ethical principles'.

Joseph, though nominally co-regent after 1765, was allowed a say only in the affairs of the royal household, public finance and the army. A memorandum which he drew up in 1765, at the age of twenty-four, reflects the impatient idealism that he had to bridle as long as his mother lived. 'The service of God is inseparable from the service of the state', he asserted. And by service to the state he meant military service: every young noble on completion of his education should serve unpaid for at least three years in the army. 'The pay of soldiers should be raised or that of civilians should be reduced so that they are treated alike.' To ensure the success of his reforms a good police, organized on military lines, would be needed. The memorandum ends on a characteristic note: 'If my ideas are not approved, let us hear no more of them and not pick and choose, since their merit lies in their comprehensiveness.'[5]

Joseph refused to visit Voltaire, but he was well-read in the works of the *philosophes*, and in 1769 he met Frederick the Great at Neisse, in Silesia. Joseph wrote enthusiastically to his mother: 'We talked of legislation, of Voltaire, of a hundred things that it is impossible to recount.' Frederick was less fulsome. He thought Joseph was 'anxious to learn but lacked patience to instruct himself'. He saw him as 'a man devoured by ambition who is brooding over some great plan, who is temporarily held in leash by his mother, but is fretting to throw off the yoke'.[6] When in 1780 Joseph at last became sole ruler, he tried to convert the theorizing of twenty years into the practice of a decade. This was to set a killing pace: he could scarcely have worked harder had he *known* that he had less than ten more years to live. Joseph's claim to 'have made philosophy the law-maker of my empire'[7] was no idle boast; but in doing so he became the only eighteenth-century monarch to pursue the principles of the *philosophes* beyond the bounds of practical politics. He was

[5] G. P. Gooch, *Maria Theresa and Other Studies*, Longmans 1951, p. 27.

[6] Gooch, *Frederick the Great*, p. 73.

[7] In a letter to Cardinal Herzan. See S. K. Padover, *The Revolutionary Emperor*, Cape 1934, p. 220.

the Enlightenment's aptest pupil and its most spectacular failure.

Centralization in Government

The subjects of Maria Theresa spoke ten languages, and the only political unity they possessed was that of allegiance to the Habsburg family. Charles VI had tried to ensure the preservation of these tenuous dynastic ties by means of the Pragmatic Sanction, signed by the Estates of the Empire as well as by the monarchs of Europe; but he had done nothing towards giving his territories centralized political institutions. Preoccupied with his quest for signatures, Charles had bequeathed to Maria Theresa an army and a civil service that had not been paid for two years, and an administrative system that was a century behind those of France and Prussia.

The inadequacy of the financial and military administration based on the traditional provincial assemblies or Estates was amply demonstrated in the early stages of the War of the Austrian Succession. Maria Theresa found that in the whole of Silesia she could not raise sufficient resources to support two cavalry regiments, while Frederick II's quartermasters kept a whole army supplied despite longer lines of communications. While the war lasted Maria Theresa could not afford to tamper with the administrative machine, however antiquated, particularly when she was surrounded by councillors whom she herself described as 'too prejudiced to give useful advice and too respectable and meritorious to be dismissed'.[8] But in Kaunitz, who was made Chancellor in 1753, she found a foreign minister who was a match for Frederick II,[9] while in Haugwitz she discovered an administrator of genius.

Haugwitz demanded a standing army of over 100,000 and called for a corresponding increase in the annual military budget from nine million to fourteen million florins. This was to be met by extending taxation to cover all property, including that of the nobles, and as early as 1748 he persuaded the estates of all the Austrian and Bohemian lands (except Carinthia) to sign contracts for increased taxation for ten years in advance.

This veiled attack on the independence and traditional privileges of the Estates was quickly followed by the replacement of the separate Bohemian and Austrian court chanceries by a single high court of justice (*Hofrat*) and a single ministry for all internal affairs (*Directorium in publicis et cameralibus*) in all the Habsburg lands except Hungary, Milan and the Netherlands. Haugwitz himself presided over this *Directorium*, which was in 1762 itself divided into the Exchequer (*Hofkammer*) and the Chancery (*Hofkanzlei*). Alongside these were a reorganized council of war (*Hofkriegsrat*), and a new directory of commerce on the Prussian model. Above them, and controlling all of them, stood the Council of State, established in 1760.

The reforms in Vienna were matched by a reorganization of the provincial administration. Austria and Bohemia were divided into ten *gubernia*, each with a high court and an administrative council, which were directly dependent on the central government in Vienna. To these new *gubernia* the provincial estates surrendered all their traditional administrative functions. Dorn comments: 'Thus with a single stroke of the pen Maria had effected a political, constitutional and administrative revolution. This marks the end of Bohemia as an independent state.'[10] The local agent of the *gubernium* was the *Kreishauptmann* or district officer, a salaried official who combined the functions of the Prussian local commissary and *Landrat*,[11] and whose role resembled that of the French *intendant*. In Prussia the growth of bureaucracy had been curtailed by Frederick's need to retain the support of the *junker* class; Maria Theresa was less dependent on the Bohemian nobility, and Habsburg bureaucratization was accordingly more complete.

Maria Theresa did not, however, try to extend her centralizing policy to Italy or the Netherlands, where the existing chanceries were allowed to pursue their routine unchallenged. Indeed she had come close to losing Hungary at the outset of her reign, and even if we reject the traditional story of her winning over the Hungarian magnates by appearing before the Diet at Pressburg in 1741 with her infant son in her arms, feminine charm and eloquence were certainly the chief weapons with which she

---

[10] Dorn, *op. cit.*, p. 48.   [11] See above, p. 118.

secured Magyar loyalty. While Hungarian independence remained nominally intact, more and more business was gradually transferred from Budapest to Vienna. The central directories extended their jurisdiction over Hungary, while traditional Budapest officials like the Palatine, who directed all internal Hungarian affairs, lent their support to the interests of the dynasty. By bribes and blandishments – diplomatic posts, court dignities, generalships, titles, schools for their children – Maria Theresa succeeded in enticing the Magyar nobles, the ruling class of Hungary, into the service of the state. Whereas they had been traditionally hostile to the Habsburgs, they now intermarried with the Bohemian and Austrian aristocracy, and some of them even learned to speak German.

In contrast to such seductive methods, Joseph II tried to Germanize Hungary at one stroke. The crown of St Stephen was transferred to Vienna; German was made the official language; the Hungarian Diet was deprived of all authority; a separate *gubernium* was established for Hungary and another for Transylvania, each under a Viennese governor; the traditional feudal military levies (the *noble levée* which had raised 25,000 troops in 1742) were forbidden and conscription introduced instead.[12] This drastic policy, coupled with Joseph's attempt to abolish serfdom,[13] provoked a rebellion in Hungary in December 1789. The new year opened with a revolt in Brussels in protest against Joseph's policy of subordinating the Austrian Netherlands to Vienna: he had abolished the local provincial estates, and divided the country into nine circles, each under an *intendant*. A few weeks before his death Joseph rescinded most of his Hungarian edicts, but it was left to his successor, Leopold II, to recall the 'United States of Belgium' to their allegiance.

Law Reform

Haugwitz's administrative reorganization applied the principle of the separation of powers demanded by Montesquieu in his *Spirit of Laws* published in 1748. In 1749 the Bohemian and

---

[12] Conscription had been introduced in Austria and Bohemia in 1771.
[13] See opposite page.

Austrian chanceries gave place to separate judicial and administrative bodies.[14] But Haugwitz's reforms were not inspired by
Montesquieu, and Maria Theresa's reign saw only an empirical
and piecemeal approach to the problem of law reform. Reform
was certainly needed: within a single province the same offence
might involve penalties from a light fine to mutilation or death.
In 1753 a commission of lawyers was appointed to gather evidence for a new civil code, but, having collected eight volumes
of decrees by 1767, it then reported that to promulgate a
new comprehensive code at one stroke would cause chaos; it
therefore recommended no change. A new criminal code introduced in 1770 retained the use of judicial torture, though this
was abolished in 1776 at the instigation of Joseph and Kaunitz.

Maria Theresa had no intention of depriving the gentry of
their rights over their peasants, though she tried to stop the
worst feudal abuses. In 1771 a commission was appointed to
settle disputes between landlord and serf, and after the famine of
that year an attempt was made to fix the maximum number of
days that a peasant could be required to work on his lord's land.
The provincial Estates, dominated as they were by the nobility,
showed little willingness to reduce these labour services (the
robot) and in 1775 the *Urbarium*, which limited the *robot* to a
maximum of three days a week, was imposed on Bohemia by
imperial decree. When the lords still proved recalcitrant, the
impatient peasants rose in revolt: 15,000 of them besieged
Prague itself. The government called out the army and the
rebellion was harshly suppressed. Maria Theresa was confirmed
in her determination to go no farther in concessions to the
peasants.

Joseph, however, was convinced that his mother had not gone
far enough, and he wasted little time in tackling the problem
once he was in sole command. Yet even Joseph did not try to
abolish serfdom at the stroke of a pen. In 1781, 'in the name of
reason and humanity', he abolished the serfs' personal dependence on their lords – though the *robot* was retained. The peasants
were now to be allowed to own land, marry whom they
pleased, take up new trades, and move from place to place at

14 See above, p. 143.

will; they were also granted the right of appeal to crown officials in criminal cases. Maria Theresa had already introduced these reforms on the crown estates; Joseph now applied them to all lands in Austria and Bohemia, and extended them to Transylvania in 1783 and to Hungary in 1785. The next stage was even more ambitious. In 1782 Joseph had ordered a land survey of all the Habsburg territories, and in the following year it was decreed that all lands, irrespective of the status of their occupier, were equally liable to taxation. Joseph had expected the survey to take six months; it took four years, and it was not until 1789 that a single land tax was at last introduced. All land in all the provinces except Belgium and Lombardy was subject to the new tax, which was fixed at 30 per cent of gross income. Of this figure about $13\frac{1}{2}$ per cent was to go to the state, while the remainder was divided between landlord and parish. Thus both the *robot* and the tithe had been commuted to cash payments: 'Money is to be the sole and unalterable scale for payments of feudal obligations, and neither the manorial lords nor the clergy may demand anything else but cash.'[15] Joseph died before this decree became effective. The opposition it provoked from those peasants who found their new taxes heavier than their old dues forced him to suspend its execution. Leopold revoked the land tax and restored the *robot*, though this action also resulted in a peasant rebellion.

Although Joseph abolished feudal courts in Hungary, he retained them elsewhere for civil cases, and contented himself with establishing new higher courts. The Penal Code (1787) and the Code of Criminal Procedure (1788) made men equal before the law, gave wider opportunities for appeal to higher courts, and abolished the death penalty in most cases. 'A death sentence', Joseph wrote, 'has never the same effect as a lasting heavy punishment carries with it; for the first is quickly over and forgotten, but the other is long before the public eye.'[16] Only the first part of the proposed Civil Code was published during Joseph's reign: the law of persons and property appeared in 1786. The Code was finally completed in 1811 under Francis I, Joseph's nephew, and lasted until 1918.

---

[15] Padover, *op. cit.*, p. 285.   [16] Ergang, *op. cit.*, p. 508.

Commercial and Economic Policy

The Habsburg system of government by bureaucracy was extended to commerce and industry. The loss of Silesia,[17] with its mineral resources and its access to the Oder and Elbe rivers, had been a serious setback to the economic development of the Habsburg territories, but from about 1770 Bohemia became an important industrial area. Its flax-spinning industry employed over 200,000 domestic workers, mostly women, and by the 1770s a textile factory at Nova Kydne in Bohemia employed 1,400 spinners and 100 weavers, though only about 300 of these worked inside the factory walls. Government officials were expected to try to stimulate production, to restrict guild monopolies, and to suppress brigandage on the roads. Joseph II even tried to develop the port of Trieste, where he established an East India Company: it proved as complete a failure as Charles VI's Ostend Company.[18]

But mercantilist influence began to wane more quickly under the Habsburgs than under Frederick the Great, who remained a mercantilist to the end, and Catherine the Great, who returned to mercantilism in her last years.[19] In his memorandum of 1765[20] Joseph had written: 'To foster our commerce I should exclude all foreign merchandise except groceries. . . . Every business man who proves that he has brought 100,000 florins into the country should receive certain honours and privileges.' And the tariff union of Bohemia, Moravia, and the Austrian duchies in 1775, which created the largest free trade area in Europe,[21] was still compatible with high external tariffs and could be justified on mercantilist principles. But Joseph II, impressed by the arguments of Turgot, the physiocrat and sometime French finance minister,[22] came round to the view that 'nothing is more necessary than liberty for commerce and industry'. Government regulations on industry were therefore relaxed and government

[17] See Chapters 12 and 13 below.   [18] See above, p. 19.
[19] See above, p. 136.   [20] See above, p. 141.
[21] France was still divided by internal tariff barriers. See below, p. 234.
[22] See below, p. 262.

subsidies greatly reduced, although in the case of textiles and metallurgy they were restored before Joseph's death; and the agriculture of the German-speaking provinces remained protected by tariffs on Hungarian grain and wine.

Commercial policy was, of course, affected by fiscal considerations. Between 1748 and 1760 a series of reforms for the first time imposed a systematic property and income tax on the nobility and clergy, and converted the peasants' tax from one on persons to one on income. Financial burdens remained uneven: the peasants still paid twice as much as the nobles, and Bohemia contributed twice as much as Hungary. But in 1775 the budget balanced for the first time. Joseph nevertheless found the financial situation sufficiently daunting. He complained to Leopold at his accession: 'In financial matters I cannot find a single soul who understands me or has a single idea of the elements of the thing. In all honour I don't know how I am going to manage.'[23] In 1786 revenue stood at eighty-eight million against an expenditure of eighty-five million. But the following year saw war against the Turks, and at Joseph's death the budget was twenty-two million florins in the red, to say nothing of an accumulated debt of nearly 400 million. The proposed land tax of 1789[24] had been an attempt to remedy this desperate situation.

Religious Policy

Joseph disagreed with his mother over religious policy. Under Maria Theresa the privileged position of Roman Catholicism as the official religion of the Empire was jealously guarded. It is true that she followed the French lead in expelling the Jesuits, but she did so only in order to preserve the Habsburg–Bourbon alliance and only when it became clear that Pope Clement XIV would be forced by diplomatic pressure to dissolve the Society of Jesus, as he did in 1773. The Jews remained almost without civil rights: they were forbidden to own real estate, to hold office, or to practise crafts; they were required to wear distinguishing patches of yellow; they were excluded from the

[23] G. Bruun, *The Enlightened Despots*, Holt, New York 1947.
[24] See above, p. 146.

schools. In the 1770s a campaign of persecution was launched against the Moravians, a Protestant sect tracing its ancestry back to John Huss (1373–1415) but greatly revived in the 1720s under the influence of Count Zinzendorf.[25] In 1777 Joseph wrote to his mother protesting against the expulsion of the Moravians:

Half and half methods are not in my line. Either full liberty of worship or the expulsion of *all* who do not share your beliefs. . . . That souls may not be damned after death it is proposed to expel them and to forfeit all the advantages we could derive from excellent cultivators and good subjects during their life. . . . It is for the Holy Spirit to enlighten the heart; your laws can only challenge its operations.[26]

Maria Theresa's reply was characteristically paradoxical: 'No persecution, but still less indifference or toleration! That is my programme.' Eventually it was Kaunitz who secured a change of policy, and the Moravians were allowed to worship in their own homes.

In 1781 Joseph decreed full toleration to all except atheists and Deists: this included the right to hold property, to build schools, to enter the professions, and to be eligible for political and military office. Meanwhile the Catholic Church was nationalized. The bishops were forbidden to receive papal bulls and decrees without royal consent, and were required to take an oath of submission and fidelity to the Emperor. Marriage was made a civil contract and education was secularized. New state seminaries were established and made compulsory for would-be clerics. More than 700 of the 2,163 monasteries in the Austrian territories were closed, including all those of the contemplative orders. The sixty million florins obtained from the confiscation of monastic property were applied to education, poor relief and the raising of clerical stipends. Joseph did not tamper with doctrine, but he did forbid religious processions and pilgrimages, restrict the use of incense and music, substitute the vernacular for Latin in services, and cut fifteen saints' days out of the calendar on the ground that they interfered with work. In an

[25] John Wesley owed his conversion to the Moravians.
[26] Gooch, *op. cit.*, p. 50.

attempt to reverse this policy of 'Josephism', Pope Pius VI even journeyed to Vienna in 1782; but a month of negotiations came to nothing.

Joseph's policy of toleration seems to have been based on principle rather than, as in the case of Frederick the Great, on political expediency. As he wrote to van Swieten, the court physician:

Tolerance is an effect of that beneficent increase of knowledge which now enlightens Europe, and which is owing to philosophy and the efforts of great men; it is a convincing proof of the improvement of the human mind, which has boldly reopened a road through the dominions of superstition, which was trodden centuries ago by Zoroaster and Confucius, and which, fortunately for mankind, has now become the highway of monarchs.[27]

Joseph's toleration extended to the abolition of the system of censorship, which under Maria Theresa had not allowed even the Roman Index of forbidden books to be published in the Habsburg territories. Even now freedom of the press was not absolute. A poem on toleration by Alxinger, the leading Austrian poet of the day, had to be published in Leipzig to escape Joseph's censorship, while the *Nine Day Prayer to the Mother of God* was banned because it contained 'fabulous miracles, apparitions, revelations, and such things, which would lead the common man to superstition, arouse disgust in the scholar, and finally give non-Catholics an opportunity to ascribe such weaknesses to the Catholic religion itself'.[28] Meanwhile the persecution of the Deists continued and the discussion of clerical celibacy was forbidden. No doubt Joseph continued to regard himself as a Catholic, yet, whatever his intention, Joseph's reforms helped to make scepticism and irreligion fashionable. Both the Hungarian public prosecutor and the Supreme Chancellor, Count Kollowrat, commented on the contempt that students showed for religion, although it is characteristic that Kollowrat blamed the Commission for Education and Censorship for ignoring the religious attitudes of the professors they appointed.

[27] Padover, *op. cit.*, p. 206.   [28] *Ibid.*, p. 215.

Education

Maria Theresa tried to improve the Austrian school system. She established the *Theresianum*, where children of the nobility were educated alongside her own children, and in 1774 a national and centralized system of education was set up. Attendance was made compulsory during the summer months for children of six to eight years, and during the winter months for those from nine to thirteen, though these provisions were impossible to enforce. Latin schools (*gymnasia*) were established in every district for children from twelve years upwards, and the main ingredients of the curriculum were grammar, syntax, rhetoric and poetry.

Maria Theresa went so far as to say that 'the school system is and always will be a political institution'. Joseph adopted the same attitude in his dealings with the universities, which he regarded chiefly as training grounds for civil servants. 'Nothing must be taught the youth which they will use very rarely or perhaps not at all for the benefit of the state', he wrote. In the University of Vienna, German was made compulsory for all lectures, and the study of all modern languages except Serbo-Croat was dropped; only official textbooks were allowed, and standard methods of teaching were laid down. 'Good God', exclaimed Mirabeau, 'even their souls are to be put into uniform!'

Joseph's reply to an appeal for ending educational censorship might serve as an epitaph on his whole political philosophy: 'The father of a family who holds the welfare of his children at heart must not allow himself to be turned from a salutary course because of ill-judged complaints.' Joseph was obstinate, but he was not a dreamer. In Austria, as in Prussia, centralization in government had been motivated by the needs of war; and in Austria, as in France, a sound financial system depended on the curtailment of aristocratic privilege and the encouragement of a prosperous middle class. Joseph alone of the monarchs of the Enlightenment was ready to risk a frontal assault on the privileged orders, but his well-intentioned attempt to raise the status of his peasants to that enjoyed by their French counterparts *before* the Revolution was frustrated by the excesses of the peasants themselves.

Joseph found his aims equally thwarted by what he regarded as the excessive demands of the middle classes whose political aspirations his own reforms had done so much to arouse. He tried to apply the brake by tightening up press censorship in 1789, and bequeathed to his successor a secret police that was required to 'discover any discontent arising among the people, all dangerous thoughts and especially any incipient rebellion, and to nip these in the bud where possible'.[29] But even Joseph seems to have realized that this was not enough. 'I lack servants of every sort,' he complained, 'either for planning or for executing my designs.'[30] Joseph, in spite of his secret police, illustrates the crucial weakness of 'enlightened absolutism': the monarch was never sufficiently absolute to succeed in being enlightened.

Maria Theresa's work has been described as 'the addition of modern wings to a feudal castle'. Yet she laid the foundations of the state that was to last, with many modifications, until 1918. She converted Austria from a dynastic expression into a political unit. Indeed, it was through her policy of cautious centralization, and perhaps also because more ambitious reforms were at least attempted under her son, that the Habsburg Empire survived both the French Revolution and the Napoleonic Wars to emerge as the Austria of Metternich.

---

[29] E. Wangermann, *From Joseph II to the Jacobin Trials*, Oxford 1959, p. 38. Pages 37–44 give an illuminating account of the methods of the secret police.
[30] See Appendix 10.

I I

Enlightened Absolutism in the Lesser European States

Naples and Tuscany

In 1734, after more than two centuries of Spanish rule and twenty years under the Austrian Habsburgs, Naples became an independent kingdom under Don Carlos, eldest son of Elizabeth Farnese and Philip V.[1] His mother's diplomacy had gained for him the duchies of Parma, Piacenza and Tuscany,[2] and in the spring of 1732 Carlos had entered Florence amid music and fireworks. But the War of the Polish Succession[3] enabled Elizabeth to play for higher stakes: by the Treaty of the Escurial (1733) France guaranteed Carlos in his possession of the three duchies and implied approval of any attempt he might make to seize Naples and Sicily. By mid-March 1734 Carlos was in Rome where he issued a proclamation to the people of the Two Sicilies 'in the name of Don Carlos, by the grace of God Infante of Spain, Duke of Parma, Piacenza and Castro, etc., Hereditary Grand Prince of Tuscany and Generalissimo of the armies of His Catholic Majesty in Italy'. In May he was given a tumultuous welcome in Naples; in November the last Austrian fortress on the mainland fell, and by the following summer the Austrians had been chased out of Sicily. The Third Treaty of Vienna (1735)[4] confirmed Carlos as Charles III of the Two Sicilies, provided that he surrendered his northern duchies and on condition that the thrones of Spain and Naples were never joined.

Charles, who became King at the age of eighteen, remained at first very much under his mother's influence. Santo Stefano, his chief councillor of state, merely interpreted Elizabeth

---

[1] See above, p. 18. [2] See above, p. 19.
[3] See above, p. 30. [4] See above, p. 47.

Farnese's wishes, and Montealegre, who replaced him in 1738, proved even more dependent on direction from Madrid. In the War of the Austrian Succession, Charles had to follow Spain: he sent an army to help Montemar in central Italy and recalled it only when the British fleet threatened to bombard Naples.[5] But Charles' period of tutelage ended with the death of his father in 1746. Philip V was succeeded by Ferdinand, son of his first marriage, and the rule of Elizabeth Farnese ended abruptly.

Charles quickly demonstrated his independence. In 1750 he told the Sardinian ambassador:

I rise at five in the morning, read and attend to memorials till eight, when I dress and proceed to the State Council. I hope to make this kingdom flourish again and relieve it from taxes, especially since this year I have finished paying all the debts contracted during the last war and still have 300,000 ducats in savings to put into my treasury. To prove this I have refused the usual voted tax from the Sicilian Parliament, a larger sum than any voted previously, telling them I had no present need of it, and that they were to save it until it was required. Apart from which I have revoked a tax, and devote all my attention to improving the welfare of my subjects, since I wish to save my soul and go to Heaven.[6]

Four years later the British ambassador could write of Charles:

He is in many things his own Minister, passing several hours every day alone in his cabinet; has too good an opinion of his own judgement; and is so positive and obstinate that he is seldom induced to alter his resolutions. He has very high notions of his prerogative and his independency, and thinks himself the most absolute monarch in Europe.[7]

Charles' chief minister since the departure of Montealegre in 1746 had been the ineffective Fogliani, and on his dismissal in 1755 the post of Prime Minister was abolished. Bernardo Tanucci, who had been Minister of Justice since the 1730s, now took over foreign policy and became Charles' chief adviser. Tanucci had done his best to reduce bribery, make the criminal law less barbarous and rescue the judicial system from

[5] See below, p. 180.
[6] H. Acton, *The Bourbons of Naples*, Methuen 1957, p. 66.
[7] *Ibid.*, p. 73

the disrepute into which it had fallen. The codification of Neapolitan law, entrusted to Domenico Cirillo, was, however, hopelessly bungled.

Tanucci's reforms were nevertheless sufficient to antagonize the nobility, who in 1700 had numbered 119 princes, 156 dukes, 175 marquesses, 42 counts and 445 barons on the mainland alone, to say nothing of the 20,000 people (in a population of about five million) who sought to acquire the prestige of nobility through gaining privileged judicial and governmental posts. The nobles had jurisdiction over four-fifths of the people, controlled the municipal government of Naples and could obstruct the voting of taxes in the Sicilian Parliament. The clergy were more vulnerable. In 1741 a Concordat concluded with Pope Benedict XIV had empowered Charles to tax ecclesiastical property, to curtail clerical jurisdiction and privileges, and to limit the number of clergy.[8] But Tanucci, who fully exploited the judicial provisions of the Concordat and was bitterly hostile to the Jesuits, was no *philosophe* in his attitude to the Church: Voltaire's works were banned. In 1754 the Cardinal Archbishop of Naples was forced to resign for trying to introduce the Inquisition by stealth, but Charles' attempt to encourage the Jews to settle in Naples was frustrated by the popular outcry it provoked.

Charles was left to give evidence of enlightenment in less material ways. Although singularly unmusical himself, he gave great encouragement to the opera, and the San Carlo opera house was begun in March 1737. It was opened in November of the same year with a performance of Metastasio's *Achille in Sciro*. The prologue spoke of 'the new sublime and spacious theatre, vaster than which Europa hath not seen' and the chorus shouted 'Long Live Charles!' Metastasio was the Imperial Court Poet at Vienna, but he had started his career in Naples and most of the works performed in the early years of San Carlo were his. In 1738 his *Demetrius* was staged to commemorate Charles' marriage to Maria Amalia,[9] while in 1752 came *La Clemenzia di Titus* with music by Gluck. In that year the Royal Academy of

[8] Nearly 4 per cent of the population of the city of Naples in 1700 were clergy.
[9] Daughter of Augustus II of Saxony (Augustus III of Poland).

Design was opened to supplement the Neapolitan Academy of Art, already founded by Charles, and his court attracted a number of gifted artists, though Naples proved less of a magnet than Madrid.[10] The King seems at this stage to have been more interested in hunting: he spent the year moving from one game preserve to the next and imposed particularly harsh penalties on poachers.[11] Meanwhile the art treasures that had been moved from Parma to Naples in 1737 were left to moulder for years on a dark staircase before being properly housed at Capodimonte.

Charles III's palaces were intended to rival those of his great-grandfather Louis XIV. Portici, Capodimonte and Caserta all began, like Versailles, as hunting lodges. The grandest was Caserta, sixteen miles north of Naples and designed in 1751 by Vanvitelli, architect to Pope Clement XII. Five storeys high and thirty-seven bays long, the façade seemed even more massive than Vanvitelli had envisaged, since the roof pavilions and cupola were never built. Henry Swinburne, who saw it in the 1770s, said it reminded him of a monastery, though he admitted it was 'a dwelling spacious and grand enough to have lodged the ancient masters of the Roman world'. Relics of the Roman world embellished the royal villa at Portici, for in 1711 its previous owner, Prince d'Elbeuf, had discovered the theatre at Herculaneum and stolen its decorative marble – to the delight of his guests and the despair of later archaeologists. Charles III's intention was more scholarly, but archaeology was in its infancy and the excavations at Herculaneum were entrusted to a colonel of engineers in the Neapolitan army. In spite of methods more suited to military engineering, much of real worth was rescued, and the assistance of a Swiss engineer Karl Weber soon led to a more scientific approach. In 1748 attention shifted to the site that was soon to reveal Pompeii, though not until 1763 was the identity of the lost city put beyond doubt.[12] The classification of the finds had been committed to Fogliani's cousin, Baiardi, who instead of compiling a catalogue produced five introductory volumes describing the labours of Hercules and the mythical origin of Herculaneum. A catalogue at last appeared in 1755,

[10] See below, p. 164.   [11] See Acton, *op. cit.*, p. 50–51.
[12] See M. Brion, *Pompeii and Herculaneum*, Elek Books 1960.

the year of the foundation of the Royal Herculanean Academy. Two years later the first folio of *The Antiquities of Herculaneum* was published, under royal supervision. But when Winckelmann[13] visited the museum at Portici in 1758 he was scathing about the amateurism of the excavators.

The Herculanean Academy was not Charles' sole contribution to education. The curriculum of the University of Naples was pruned of much jurisprudence and theology, and experimental physics, astronomy, botany and chemistry were introduced instead. In 1755 the Abbé Antonio Genovesi became the first at a European university to lecture on political economy. His theories resembled those of the *philosophes* and he gave a course of lectures on Montesquieu and d'Alembert. 'My lessons have given birth to a great movement', he wrote, 'and all classes are asking for books on economy, the arts and agriculture, and this is a good beginning.'[14] Charles III's commercial policy, though praised by Genovesi, was chiefly confined to concluding commercial treaties with Turkey, Holland and England, and to encouraging the porcelain industry with the help of Saxon experts sent by his father-in-law.

The construction of the Royal Hostel for the Poor, started in 1751, seems to have been inspired not by the *philosophes* but by the Dominican preacher Father Rocco, who also solved the problem of street-lighting in Naples by inviting the devout to maintain illuminated shrines on the darkest corners, the only regular system adopted before 1806. All the magnificent mansions with which Naples was adorned during Charles' reign could not hide the poverty of the streets. It was said that in a population of 300,000 it was the profession of 15,000 people to run ahead of a carriage and of 15,000 others to run behind. Naples was better policed than most Italian cities,[15] but the famine of 1764 was to expose the inability of the government to deal with the problems posed by so large an urban population: 8,000 desperate women petitioned the Archbishop to exhibit the relics of Saint Janarius, the city's patron saint, in an effort to invoke the intervention of Providence.

[13] See below, p. 230.   [14] Acton, *op. cit.*, p. 98.
[15] See M. Vaussard, *Daily Life in Eighteenth Century Italy*, Allen & Unwin 1962, p. 121.

The Tuscany that Charles had left in 1734 also experienced the touch of enlightened absolutism. Leopold, younger brother of Joseph II of Austria, sponsored reforms similar to those attempted in Naples: feudal courts were subordinated to the central courts, the Inquisition was suppressed (though only temporarily), clerical revenues were taxed, and a more equitable system of taxation introduced. In law reform Leopold went further than Charles III. A keen admirer of Beccaria,[16] Leopold authorized the abolition of torture and of the death penalty, while a uniform criminal procedure was imposed. But by the time he left Tuscany in 1790 Leopold had provoked serious resentment by tampering with the liturgy of the Church to a greater degree than even his brother had dared to do.[17] In Tuscany, as in Naples, popular superstition defeated the apostles of enlightenment. Leopold's attempt to enlist clerical support by calling a General Assembly of Bishops in 1787 was a failure, while the mere rumour that the Bishop of Pistoia proposed to remove from Prato the famous but probably spurious girdle of the Virgin led to the sacking of the bishop's palace.

Spain and Portugal

In September 1759 Charles III of Naples became Charles III of Spain. During the twenty-eight years that had elapsed since Charles had last seen his native country, his half-brother Ferdinand VI (1746–59) had continued the work of centralization begun by Philip V.[18] In 1749 Ferdinand had divided most of Spain into administrative provinces and had appointed as 'intendant' the royal governor of the chief city of each province. But in Charles III's Spain, unlike the France of Louis XIV's last years, royal absolutism was still obstructed by the Church.

Charles inherited the Concordat concluded by Ferdinand in 1753 by which the Pope had surrendered his right of appointment to bishoprics and his claim to the revenues of vacant sees, while recognizing the royal right to tax church property. The victory of royal absolutism was not complete, however, for the interests of the Papacy were jealously guarded both by the

[16] See above, p. 76.   [17] See above, p. 149.   [18] See above, p. 22.

Society of Jesus and by the Inquisition. In Spain, as in France, opposition to the claims of Rome tended to become identified with Jansenism.[19] The Spanish 'Jansenists' seem to have had no doctrinal connexion either with the French Jansenists or with Cornelius Jansen of Ypres; the title was a term of abuse bestowed by the Jesuits on those writers who opposed the theological and moral teaching of the Society of Jesus and who impugned the infallibility of the Pope. In 1761 the papal nuncio in Spain received a brief from Rome condemning as Jansenist a catechism devised by a French abbé. Somewhat unusually, Charles III forbade publication of the brief. When the Inquisitor-General defied the King, Charles not only exiled him from Madrid to a monastery, but decreed that future papal briefs or bulls must receive explicit royal permission before they were published in Spain.

Charles soon faced a more serious challenge. The Marchese di Squillace, whom he had brought from Naples and who was already unpopular because of Spain's poor showing in the later stages of the Seven Years War,[20] provoked further resentment in March 1766 by reviving an ancient law forbidding the wearing of the customary broadbrimmed hat and long cape – on the grounds that they made the recognition of criminals more difficult. The Madrid crowd, already angry at the high price of bread, which they attributed to Squillace's grain policies, attacked the minister's house and that of foreign secretary Grimaldi. Charles was forced to dismiss Squillace and revoke the edict on dress; the King left his capital, vowing never to return. Disturbances spread to the provinces, but the Count of Aranda now emerged as the restorer of order. Charles returned to Madrid and within a year Aranda had repudiated the King's concessions. Although primarily bread riots, the troubles of 1766 were blamed on the Jesuits, and in 1767 Charles took the opportunity of decreeing the expulsion of the Order, thus following the example of Portugal and France. Aranda effortlessly enforced the edict, and even discussion of the episode was forbidden.

The expulsion of the Jesuits did not imply the end of the

Inquisition. In 1768 Charles laid down the procedure it was to adopt in the censorship of books and in 1784 he asserted his right of intervention in all cases involving grandees, ministers and royal officials. Having emasculated it to this extent, he was content to let the Inquisition live on. Charles did, however, take steps to reduce the numbers of the clergy: over a dozen edicts regulated the discipline of religious houses and diminished the number of monks, abolishing one order entirely. Even so, in 1788 there were still nearly 200,000 clergy and religious officers in a population of ten million; only Portugal could boast a higher proportion.

Yet in spite of the continuing dominance of the Church the Enlightenment did cross the Pyrenees. Indeed it was a Benedictine monk, Benito Feyjóo, university professor of Oviedo, who led the way in the popularization of foreign ideas. His *Teatro critico universal* began to appear in 1726 and nine volumes had been published by 1739. He defended the experimental method of Bacon, expounded the ideas of Newton and Descartes, and referred in his essays to over 250 foreign works, most of them French. In 1750 Ferdinand VI had prohibited the publication of works attacking Feyjóo, while fifty years later an admirer wrote somewhat extravagantly: 'Thanks to the immortal Feyjóo spirits no longer trouble our houses, witches have fled our towns, the evil eye does not plague the tender child, and an eclipse does not dismay us.'[21]

The economic theories current in Charles III's Spain were the mercantilist doctrines of Colbert rather than the free trade teaching of the physiocrats, although one writer in 1788 referred admiringly to '*el profundo Político Smith*'. Montesquieu was described by another Spanish writer in 1769 as 'one of the greatest statesmen of our century', although none of his works seems to have appeared in Spanish before 1820. A translation of Beccaria's *Crimes and Punishments* was published in 1774, though with a cautionary preface that it must not be construed as an invitation to break the laws of church and state. Rousseau's works were put on the Index in 1764, thereby ensuring their

[21] Herr, *The Eighteenth Century Revolution in Spain*, Princeton University Press 1958, p. 40.

greater popularity, and the ideas of *Émile* were current even if a copy of the book was publicly burned in Madrid in 1765. Indeed the four-volume novel *Eusebio*, published in the 1780s, borrowed freely from *Émile*, while the fact that a French translation of *Robinson Crusoe* was put on the Index was perhaps an indirect tribute to Rousseau's influence.[22]

In 1763 a Spanish journalist had written: 'Through the effect of many pernicious books that have become the fashion, such as those of Voltaire, Rousseau and Helvétius, much coolness of faith has been felt in this country.' In fact, however, it was not the scepticism of the *philosophes* that appealed to the Spaniards: the *History of Charles XII* seems to have been the only work of Voltaire to appear in Spanish before 1788, and there is little evidence to suggest that any of his writings enjoyed the clandestine popularity of *Émile*. Charles III's government seems to have looked kindly on the propagation of the *philosophes'* scientific, social and political ideas, and Aranda himself had met Voltaire, Diderot and d'Alembert when he was in Paris in the 1750s. But government blessing did not extend to the *philosophes'* attack on the Church. As late as 1787, in his instructions to his newly created Junta de Estado (Council of State), Charles proclaimed: 'The first of my obligations and of all my successors is to protect the Catholic religion in all the dominions of this vast monarchy.'

Of the ten million Spanish subjects of Charles III in 1787, nearly half a million claimed to be noble – more than in France with over twice the population. The Spanish nobility were divided into three broad social strata. At the top were the Grandees of Spain, 119 families by 1787; below them were some 500 *títulos*, who, like the grandees, managed not only their own family estates but also lands over which the King had given them seigneurial jurisdiction and from which they exacted feudal dues. The poorest nobles, the *hidalgos*, were often landless, and although they enjoyed certain privileges, such as freedom from arrest for debt, they were not exempt from taxation. In 1770 Charles revoked the edict of 1682 which had forbidden the

---

[22] *Robinson Crusoe* was the first book that Émile was allowed to read. See above, p. 88.

hidalgos to undertake manual labour, in order, he said, 'to avoid the disadvantage of their living idle or badly occupied and becoming a charge on society'.

The condition of the peasantry varied greatly from one part of Spain to another. In the north the land was held in return for a quitrent (*censo*) fixed for a term of lives, which left the peasant almost in the position of landowner. Rents could be raised only when leases fell in, and in 1763 the Council of Castile ruled that tenants could not be evicted unless they proved negligent. Even in the corn-growing areas of central Spain peasant ownership was not uncommon, but in the south between two-thirds and four-fifths of the peasants were landless labourers, while those who were tenants held their land on short leases. In the province of Seville two-thirds of the land belonged to towns and cities. One of Charles III's first acts had been to provide for supervision of municipal finances, and in 1766 special officials, elected by all local taxpayers, were empowered to intervene in municipal government, particularly in matters relating to finance and food supplies. Charles could not afford to buy back the seigneurial rights of the nobility, but he required the judges they appointed to be approved by the Council of Castile. More direct attempts to improve agriculture included the compulsory distribution of uncultivated land among landless peasants, though the land often went to the rich rather than the poor, and the provision of credit schemes to enable farmers to buy seed. The grazing rights of the migrant sheep industry (the *Mesta*) were also curtailed, a measure made easier by the fact that raw wool was becoming a less attractive export than corn: the heyday of the Spanish merino sheep was over.

Spanish textile industries showed signs of expansion, however. Toledo failed to revive her silk industry,[23] but the number of looms in Valencia grew from just over 3,000 in 1769 to about 4,000 in 1787. (The silk looms of Lyon decreased from 11,000 to 7,500 during the same period.) The government encouraged the industry by restricting the export of raw silk and setting up a royal silk factory. Meanwhile the woollen industry profited by the abandonment of the guild system and, together with the

---

[23] See above, p. 21.

developing cotton industry, revealed a degree of technical sophistication that surprised foreign visitors. The iron industry of the Basque provinces was helped by a law of 1775 forbidding the importation of foreign hardware, while the cutlery and ordnance industries of Catalonia grew steadily. Joseph Townsend wrote of the manufacture of cannon at the royal foundry at Barcelona in 1786: 'It is impossible anywhere to see either finer metal, or work executed in a neater or more perfect manner.' About the same date Arthur Young found in Barcelona 'every appearance as you walk the streets of great and active industry'. He was also impressed by the flourishing maritime commerce of the city.

External trade benefited from the ending of the monopoly of Seville and Cadiz in the American markets. Trading companies on the model of Colbert's had been set up by Philip V and Ferdinand VI, and in 1765 Charles threw open the West Indies trade to Barcelona and half a dozen other ports; in 1778 Spanish ports were permitted to trade with all parts of America except Mexico and Venezuela. By 1790 the Philippines were the only exception to the principle of free trade for all Spaniards within the Empire. Internal commerce was fostered by gradually standardizing the different tax structures of the various provinces and by successively reducing the *alcabala* – a tax payable whenever goods or property were sold. Less easy to remove were the physical obstacles imposed by bad roads and lack of inland waterways. Philip V had embarked on a scheme of highway construction in which all roads would lead to Madrid; Charles carried out further improvements, particularly along the Mediterranean coast. But road transport remained costly, and so a start was made on canal building. By the 1780s a canal had been cut from Tudela to Saragossa and plans made for continuing it to the sea, while work on another to run from Segovia to the Bay of Biscay had already begun.

The arts and sciences no less than commerce profited from foreign example. The expulsion of the Jesuits had been followed by a government attempt to reform the administration and curriculum of the twenty or so Spanish universities. From the early 1770s the Imperial College of Madrid offered courses in experimental physics, logic and 'the law of nature and of nations', and in 1787 its professor of physics was giving a series of public lectures on 'experimental philosophy'. In 1770 the Council of Cadiz ordered all universities to draw up new curricula. The University of Salamanca protested, defending the superiority of Aristotle and complaining that 'the Englishman Juan Lochio . . . besides being very obscure should be read with caution'.[24] But between 1772 and 1776 the universities of Santiago, Oviedo, Saragossa and Granada all reformed their curriculum, and Valencia followed suit ten years later. The Royal Academy of Fine Arts had been founded in 1752. By the 1760s Mengs (1728–79) and G. B. Tiepolo (1696–1770) were both working in Madrid; in the 1770s Mengs was commissioned to reorganize the Royal Tapestry Factory and Goya (1746–1828) was chosen to do some of the cartoons. Goya became Deputy Director of Painting at the Academy in 1785 and was appointed court painter in the following year.

Perhaps Charles III did no more than Voltaire had praised Louis XIV for doing, but he nevertheless came closer to the ideal of the philosopher king than most of his contemporaries. He had come to the Spanish throne after twenty-five years as King of Naples. He did not have to reckon with a politically powerful nobility. He was also very lucky in his ministers. Floridablanca, who succeeded Grimaldi as foreign secretary in 1776, had become by Charles' death in 1788 more of a colleague than a minister, so that a French observer could write at the end of the reign: 'The stability of ministers is one of the most remarkable features of the Court of Spain.'[25]

Portugal's enlightened despot was a minister. From the accession of Joseph I in 1750 until the King's death in 1777, the Marquis of Pombal was the effective ruler of one of the wealthiest yet most economically backward countries in Europe. Nowhere else in Europe was the Church so dominant nor, thanks to the riches of Brazil, so affluent; yet in a bare decade Pombal broke its power. The Inquisition was forbidden to put

[24] Herr, *op. cit.*, p. 165.　　[25] *Ibid.*, p. 233.

heretics to death without government approval; the Jesuits were expelled first from Court and then from the country; their seminaries were turned into secular colleges, and the University of Coimbra began to teach the natural sciences. Scarcely had the Church been disciplined before an attempt to assassinate the King in 1758 gave Pombal an excuse to crush the most powerful of the nobility. Having removed the two chief obstacles to royal absolutism, Pombal devoted his remaining seventeen years in power to carrying out the conventional programme of an 'enlightened' monarch. His success showed what enlightened absolutism could achieve when it was truly absolute.

Sweden and Denmark

The half-century between the death of Charles XII and the accession of Gustavus III is known to Swedish historians as the 'Age of Liberty'. It might more aptly be called the age of licence. The Constitution of 1720[26] had been intended to restore the Council to the central position it had occupied in the mid-seventeenth century, and as long as Count Horn remained dominant in both Council and *Riksdag* this aim was achieved. But with Horn's defeat and retirement in 1738, power passed to the *Riksdag*, which became the scene of bitter struggles between the rival parties, the 'Hats' and the 'Caps'. This purely domestic party strife had diplomatic implications since France supported the Hats and Russia the Caps. The failure of the Hats' policy in the Austrian Succession War was marked by their acceptance of the Russian candidate, Adolphus Frederick of Holstein, as heir to the Swedish throne. The accession of Adolphus Frederick in 1751 did not end the party struggles, and Sweden's intervention in the Seven Years War on the side of France did further damage to her economy while failing to improve her diplomatic position. By 1765 power had passed to the Caps, but their reliance on Russian support and their failure to solve the economic problems made them as unpopular as the Hats had been. The scene was set for Gustavus.

Gustavus III (1771–92) came to the Swedish throne at the age

[26] See above, p. 37.

of twenty-five. When the news of his accession reached him, he was in Paris enlisting the support of the French court in a bid to strengthen the political position of the Swedish monarchy. On his return to Stockholm he made an attempt to reconcile the two parties in the *Riksdag*, but the commoners construed it as a device to safeguard the privileges of the nobility, and the move failed. The King lost patience. On the morning of 19 August 1772, while his lieutenants were already fomenting insurrection in the provinces, Gustavus won over the palace guard, persuaded it to arrest the Council, and sent it to secure all strategic points in the capital. The people of Stockholm welcomed this bloodless *coup*, and when, two days later, the *Riksdag* was presented with a new constitution it was in no mood to resist. Not for nothing was Gustavus the nephew of Frederick the Great.

The royal *coup* ended the anarchy of the 'Age of Liberty'. But if the period had been one of political confusion and diplomatic disgrace, it had also been a time of intellectual and artistic ferment. The Academy of Science had been founded in 1739 and the Royal Academy of Painting and Sculpture in 1768. In the 1740s Carl Linnaeus (1707-78)[27] was professor of botany at Uppsala University, where Anders Celsius, inventor of the centigrade thermometer, was professor of astronomy until his death in 1744. Linnaeus was elected a member of the Royal Society, and in 1788 a Linnaean Society was founded in London. It was in London, too, that Emanuel Swedenborg (1688-1772) wrote his chief mystical works, culminating in *The True Christian Religion* published just after his death. Swedenborg is now more highly regarded for his pioneering work in a variety of scientific fields, from paleontology to physiology, though he himself claimed that it was through a study of nature that he had been led to God. Swedenborg was not honoured as a prophet in his own country: Gustavus III's tastes were theatrical rather than theological, and the Swedish court busied itself with imitating Versailles. The King himself adapted French plays to Swedish historical themes and even acted in the rococo theatre built at the royal palace of Drottningholm in the 1760s. The Swedish Opera was inaugurated in the 1770s and an Opera House

[27] See above, p. 112.

opened in 1782. The Academy of Belles-Lettres, founded in 1753, was revived in 1786 as the Academy of Belles-Lettres, History and Antiquities, and in the same year Gustavus founded the Swedish Academy, on the French model, to promote the 'purity, strength and beauty of the Swedish language'.[28]

Royal munificence required more revenue. The attempt o set up a royal monopoly in the distilling trade, previously in the hands of the peasants, proved a financial failure, but the disastrous economic legacy of the 'Age of Liberty' was repaired in other ways. Gustavus appointed Liljencratz, a physiocrat, as Minister of Finance. The redemption of paper currency and the reform of the coinage, which had been bungled by the Caps, were carried through smoothly in the late 1770s and early 1780s, though the King's extravagance made a later return to paper money inevitable. The establishment of a free trade in corn and the encouragement of enclosure were in accordance with physiocratic principles, but in industry mercantilist policies prevailed: iron production was deliberately limited in order to inflate prices, though as late as 1780 Sweden still exceeded the British output.

The Constitution of 1772 was theoretically a balanced constitution on Montesquieu's model. The Council was responsible only to the King, who was bound to consult it on judicial and diplomatic questions; the King could not declare an aggressive war without the consent of the *Riksdag*, which was supposed to share with the King control over legislation and taxation, though its rights were vaguely defined and it could be summoned and dismissed at royal pleasure. One of Gustavus' first acts had been to forbid the 'hateful and abominable' party names, and the press law of 1774 considerably curtailed the freedom of political discussion established under the Caps in 1766. But the acclaim with which the press law was received suggests that Stockholm had expected complete press censorship; certainly the abolition of extraordinary courts, the reduction in the number of capital offences, the prohibition of torture and the granting of religious toleration could not be regarded as reactionary measures. But the chief sphere of reform was military. Under Karl Sparre's

---

[28] The Academy now awards the Nobel Prize for Literature.

direction the army was brought up to strength, equipped with modern weapons and a new drill book, and supplied with reserves of grain and ammunition. The construction of fortresses continued and a partially successful attempt was made to modernize the navy.

Gustavus had not built up his armed forces for purely cere-monial duties. By agreeing in 1764 to preserve the existing constitutions of both Poland and Sweden, Catherine II and Frederick II had shown that they intended Sweden to share Poland's fate. Gustavus' *coup* of 1772 had upset their plans, and it was clearly only a matter of time before Sweden would go on to the offensive. In 1780 Sweden's Baltic enemies, Russia and Denmark, had joined with Gustavus in the League of Armed Neutrality against England,[29] but three years later it was only the threat of Russian reprisal that deterred Gustavus from going to war with Denmark in an effort to seize Norway. In 1786 the *Riksdag* rejected the King's proposal to maintain the army by taxation instead of by the system of local self-help introduced by Charles XI;[30] Gustavus suspected that the obstruction of the nobles had been fortified by Russian subsidies. Accordingly he used the outbreak of the Russo-Turkish war in 1787 as an oppor-tunity to attack Russia. The new Swedish navy proved a match for the Russian, but did not achieve the decisive victory needed to secure the advantages of surprise, and when the army was ordered to advance without naval support some of the officers resigned. The intervention of Denmark provoked a more patriotic spirit in the Swedish ranks, but it also halted the advance on St Petersburg. Gustavus had to turn to defend Göteborg from the Danes, while mutinous Swedish officers were treating with the Russians in an effort to proclaim an independent Finland. Fortunately for Sweden, the mediation of England and Prussia, who were jealous of Russia's Baltic ambitions, persuaded the Danes to make peace, which left Gustavus free to crush the Finnish conspiracy.

In 1789 Gustavus felt strong enough to summon a new *Riksdag*. He opened the session by proposing a secret committee to discuss with him the best means of 'preserving the safety,

[29] See below, p. 252.   [30] See above, p. 34.

security and independence of the realm'. When the nobles objected, the King ordered them out of the chamber and invited the commoners to join with him in a 'union to assure the future well-being of Ourselves and the Kingdom'. Having arrested the leading members of the opposition, Gustavus proceeded to impose a new constitution – the Act of Union and Security. The King was now to enjoy full legislative freedom: the *Riksdag* would be consulted only when he thought fit, and he was free to declare even an aggressive war. The Council became an indeterminate group of Councillors chosen by the King, and all but the highest court and official appointments were declared open to 'all subjects of whatever birth or condition'. Only in financial matters was the King to be dependent on the *Riksdag*, though grants were to continue 'until the next *Riksdag*', not for a fixed period, as the nobles wished. The defeat of the nobles was epitomized in Article II of the Act of Union: 'All subjects enjoy the same rights, under the protection of the laws; hence the royal high court to which cases are evoked must be composed of noble and non-noble members. Great and small persons must be judged by the legal tribunals.'[31]

Gustavus III's revolution of April 1789 provides an instructive contrast to events in France later the same year. For the last three years of his life, the most completely absolute enlightened monarch in Europe devoted his energies to trying to restore the *ancien régime* in France. A lucky naval victory at Svenskund enabled Gustavus to extricate himself from the Russian war in 1790, but he would have needed more than luck to accomplish the fantastic schemes that he was now cherishing. He put his court into Polish costume, in preparation for his projected seizure of the Polish crown, and offered to lead a crusade to rescue the French royal family. In June 1791 he actually came to Aachen where he hoped to meet Louis XVI after his flight to the frontier. Such extravagant gestures belonged to the world of opera rather than to the theatre of politics. And it was at the Opera House in Stockholm in March 1792 that Gustavus was assassinated while taking part in a masked ball. His death did not

---

[31] For the full text see R. R. Palmer, *The Age of the Democratic Revolution*, Vol. I, Oxford 1959, p. 512.

destroy enlightened absolutism in Sweden, but the manner of his dying seems curiously characteristic of the manner of his rule.

Denmark's kings in the later eighteenth century were less dynamic characters than Gustavus, and the adoption of enlightened policies depended on the royal ministers. The population, even with Norway included, was a mere two million, and the efforts of Moltke and the elder Bernstorff during the reign of Frederick V (1746–66) to stimulate agriculture and industry met with limited success. Christian VII (1766–1808) was not yet seventeen when he came to the throne and was already on the verge of insanity. By 1770 political power had passed into the hands of the German Struensee, the King's physician and the Queen's lover. Struensee carried through a programme of enlightened reforms – confiscation of church revenues, freedom of worship, abolition of censorship and judicial torture, provision of hospitals – but he provoked opposition by what was regarded as a high-handed attempt to Germanize Danish society, and in 1772 he was removed by a *coup d'état* and executed. Struensee's fall postponed enlightened reforms for more than a decade. It was not until 1784 that Crown Prince Frederick and the younger Bernstorff revived Struensee's programme. They went farther. Serfdom had been abolished in 1702, only to be restored thirty years later by a decree binding all peasants to their estates so long as they were liable to military service (that is, from their fourteenth to their thirty-sixth year). Now, in 1788, the serf was freed from this bondage to the land, while a series of measures to improve the legal and economic status of the peasants soon followed. Bernstorff died in 1797, but he had kept Denmark out of the Revolutionary Wars, and the consequent prosperity of Danish agriculture, in a wartime period of high corn prices, hastened the complete emancipation of the peasants: by 1807 more than half of them owned the land they tilled. In Denmark, at least, the Napoleonic Wars completed what enlightened absolutism had begun.

IV

ENLIGHTENED ABSOLUTISM
ABROAD

There was nothing self-evidently 'enlightened' about the policies pursued when the interests of 'Enlightened Despots' came into conflict. The cynicism of Frederick the Great's diplomacy does not pale appreciably in comparison with Hitler's, while Catherine owed her title of 'Great' to her conquests. In the wars and diplomacy of the period from 1740 onwards the central issues of the next century can already be discerned: the Prussian challenge to Austria in Germany, the Russian challenge to Austria in the Balkans, the competition for Polish and Turkish territory.

Why did the *philosophes* acquiesce in policies of aggression? Partly no doubt for fear of losing their pensions and their public, but also because it seemed the easiest way of extending the blessings of enlightened absolutism to the Slavs of Catholic Poland and Moslem Turkey. And although historians have condemned the Partitions of Poland as a crime, it must at least be admitted that, from another point of view, this seemingly discreditable episode could be seen as a proof that even rival states could reconcile their conflicting territorial ambitions by the aid of reason.

But the rivalry between the central European powers must not be allowed to efface the colonial and commercial duel between England and France. Their continuing competition remained a constant theme throughout the War of the Austrian Succession, the Seven Years War, the struggle for American independence, and ultimately the Revolutionary and Napoleonic Wars. Not for nothing have the middle decades of the eighteenth century been dubbed the 'Competition for Empire'.

12

The War of the Austrian Succession, 1740–48

Silesia

The death of the Emperor Charles VI in October 1740 meant that the Pragmatic Sanction[1] would be put to the test at last. It is easy to make fun of this famous document. It is true that Charles VI would have done better to take his ministers' advice and devote his energies to administrative reform within his diverse and disunited territories. But the agreement was signed by every important European state except Bavaria, and we must not assume that all eighteenth-century statesmen necessarily shared the modern contempt for treaty obligations. The fact that the Pragmatic Sanction had been ratified by all the Habsburg territories as early as 1724 ensured that Charles VI's subjects had long been prepared for the accession of his daughter, and in 1740 there seemed little immediate likelihood that England or Spain (already at war with each other),[2] France or Russia would challenge Maria Theresa; Charles Albert of Bavaria, though anxious to do so, could not wage war alone.

But Charles VI was not the only European monarch to die in 1740. In October the Empress Anna of Russia (1730–40) was succeeded by the infant Ivan VI, and, during the period of palace intrigues that intervened before Elizabeth became Empress a year later, Russia temporarily ceased to count in European diplomacy. This deprived Maria Theresa of a possible ally.

The most significant death, however, had occurred in May 1740 when the twenty-eight year old Frederick II of Prussia succeeded his father Frederick William I, who had so assiduously avoided using either his army or his war-chest.[3] It was

[1] See above, p. 47.   [2] See below, p. 49.   [3] See above, p. 44.

Frederick the Great who was to give the signal for the general repudiation of the Pragmatic Sanction. His reasons for doing so are best expressed in the frank words of his own memorandum:

Silesia is the portion of the Imperial heritage to which we have the strongest claim and which is most suitable for the House of Brandenburg. It is consonant with justice to maintain one's rights and to seize the opportunity of the Emperor's death to take possession. The superiority of our troops, the promptitude with which we can set them in motion, in a word the clear advantage we have over our neighbours, gives us in this unexpected emergency an infinite superiority over all other powers of Europe. If we wait till Saxony and Bavaria start hostilities, we could not prevent the aggrandizement of the former which is wholly contrary to our interests. If we act at once we keep her in subjection and by cutting off the supply of horses prevent her from moving. England and France are foes. If France meddles in the affairs of the Empire England could not allow it, so I can always make a good alliance with one or the other. England could not be jealous of my getting Silesia, which would do her no harm, and she needs allies. Holland will not care, all the more since the loans of the Amsterdam business world secured on Silesia will be guaranteed. If we cannot arrange with England and Holland we can certainly make a deal with France, who cannot frustrate our designs and will welcome the abasement of the Imperial house. Russia alone might cause us trouble. . . . All this leads to the conclusion that we must occupy Silesia before the winter and then negotiate. When we are in possession we can negotiate with success. We should never get anything by mere negotiations except very onerous conditions in return for a few trifles.[4]

By the time his terms were presented in Vienna, Frederick's troops were already crossing into Silesia. Meanwhile he explained to his uncle George II of England that he was invading Silesia in order to preserve the Habsburg Empire: 'I have no other purpose than the preservation and real benefit of the House of Austria.'[5] It all sounds very modern. For propaganda purposes, Prussia appealed to Charles VI's promise in 1728 that he would defend Hohenzollern claims to the Rhenish provinces

---

[4] G. P. Gooch, *Frederick the Great*, Longmans 1947, pp. 6–7.
[5] Gooch, *op. cit.*, p. 8.

of Jülich and Berg: Charles' later repudiation of these claims was alleged by Frederick to be sufficient excuse for his own flouting of the Pragmatic Sanction. But the real motive for annexation was geographical rather than dynastic. Prussia was a collection of scattered provinces strung out from the Rhine to the Niemen; the acquisition of Silesia would form at least a solid central block, besides increasing Prussia's population by half and greatly augmenting her economic resources.

Louis condemned Frederick's invasion of Silesia as folly. He was nearly proved right. At Mollwitz in April 1741 the Prussian cavalry was routed and Frederick fled with it; but the well drilled and disciplined infantry stood their ground and saved the day. With a mere 22,000 men and three dozen field guns Prussia had, at the first encounter, defeated the Habsburg army, however narrowly. The diplomatic repercussions of this inconclusive engagement led Reddaway to describe Mollwitz as 'one of the decisive battles of the world'.[6] Its immediate effect was to encourage the other European powers laying claim to parts of the Habsburg inheritance to join with Prussia in the process of dismemberment. Charles Albert of Bavaria, who had married one of Joseph I's daughters, demanded both the Imperial title and the Bohemian crown; Augustus II of Saxony, husband of the other daughter, claimed Moravia; Philip V of Spain, successor to the Spanish Habsburgs, asserted his right to succeed to all the Habsburg lands; and even Sardinia put in a bid for Milan.

But the most decisive intervention was that of France. Fleury had only just succeeded in defeating the French war party. The fall of Chauvelin, the aggressive French foreign secretary, in 1737 had made easier the final ratification of the Third Treaty of Vienna, by which France had agreed with Austria to abandon the claims of Stanislas Leszczynski to the Polish throne in exchange for the much more useful prize of the Duchy of Lorraine.[7] That was in November 1738. In the previous month Fleury had concluded an alliance with Sweden, where the pro-French faction had ousted the pro-Russian, while

---

[6] W. F. Reddaway, *A History of Europe from 1715 to 1814*, Methuen 1951, p. 164.
[7] See above, p. 47.

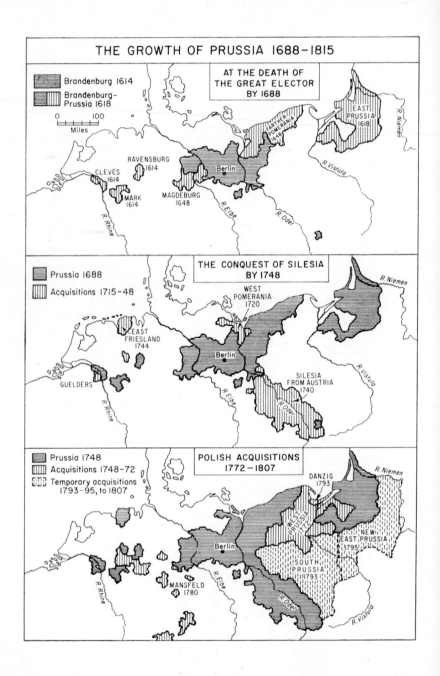

THE GROWTH OF PRUSSIA 1688-1815

AT THE DEATH OF THE GREAT ELECTOR BY 1688

Brandenburg 1614
Brandenburg-Prussia 1618

0 — 100
Miles

RAVENSBURG 1614
CLEVES 1614
MARK 1614
MAGDEBURG 1648
FARTHER POMERANIA 1648
Berlin
EAST PRUSSIA 1618
R. Niemen
R. Vistula
R. Elbe
R. Oder
R. Rhine

THE CONQUEST OF SILESIA BY 1748

Prussia 1688
Acquisitions 1715-48

EAST FRIESLAND 1744
GUELDERS
WEST POMERANIA 1720
Berlin
SILESIA FROM AUSTRIA 1740
R. Niemen
R. Vistula
R. Elbe
R. Oder
R. Rhine

POLISH ACQUISITIONS 1772—1807

Prussia 1748
Acquisitions 1748-72
Temporary acquisitions 1793-95, to 1807

DANZIG 1793
Berlin
MANSFELD 1780
WEST PRUSSIA 1772
NEW EAST PRUSSIA 1795
SOUTH PRUSSIA 1793
R. Niemen
R. Vistula
R. Elbe
R. Oder
R. Rhine

176

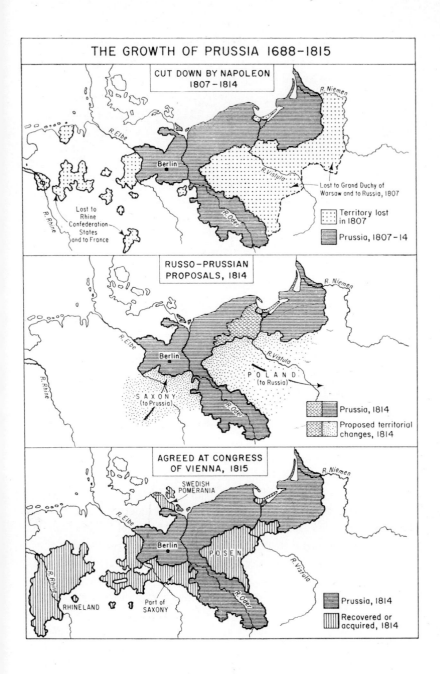

THE GROWTH OF PRUSSIA 1688-1815

CUT DOWN BY NAPOLEON
1807 - 1814

R. Niemen

R. Elbe

Berlin

R. Vistula

Lost to Grand Duchy of
Warsaw and to Russia, 1807

R. Oder

R. Rhine

Lost to
Rhine
Confederation
States
and to France

:::: Territory lost
in 1807

▓ Prussia, 1807-14

RUSSO-PRUSSIAN
PROPOSALS, 1814

R. Niemen

R. Elbe

Berlin

R. Vistula

P O L A N D
(to Russia)

R. Rhine

S A X O N Y
(to Prussia)

R. Oder

Prussia, 1814

Proposed territorial
changes, 1814

AGREED AT CONGRESS
OF VIENNA, 1815

R. Niemen

SWEDISH
POMERANIA

R. Elbe

Berlin

P O S E N

R. Vistula

R. Rhine

RHINELAND

Part of
SAXONY

R. Oder

Prussia, 1814

Recovered or
acquired, 1814

Villeneuve, French ambassador at Constantinople, bolstered up Turkish resistance sufficiently to secure the defeat of the Austrians in the field and so halt the advance of their Russian allies. The Peace of Belgrade (1739) was a triumph for French diplomacy.[8] By 1740 Fleury was content to rest on his laurels and had no wish to engage in a fresh war against Austria. But he was now eighty-six and the initiative passed to the anti-Austrian party led by the Comte de Belle-Isle. The reversal of Fleury's pacific policy meant that what had started as the revolt of one German prince within the Empire was now converted into a world war. France was resuming the role which she had played in the time of Charles V and during the Thirty Years War – that of trying to weaken the Habsburgs by splitting the Empire. Perhaps there was also the fear that if Maria Theresa's husband, Francis of Lorraine, secured the Imperial title he might try to recover his former duchy, which had since gone to Stanislas Leszczynski, father-in-law of Louis XV. In June 1741 Prussia and France agreed to fight together, and to support Charles Albert's candidature in the forthcoming Imperial election.

In a matter of months Franco-Bavarian forces had secured for Charles Albert the archduchy of Austria and the Bohemian crown; at the end of January 1742 he was duly elected Emperor as Charles VII, the first non-Habsburg for 300 years. Frederick viewed these successes with some misgivings. France had become dangerously dominant, and it looked as if Bavaria and even Saxony were making gains at the expense of Prussia. In October 1741, when the French and Bavarians had invaded Bohemia instead of marching on Vienna, Frederick decided to double-cross his allies. By the secret convention of Kleinschnellendorf in that month Frederick agreed to halt his offensive so that the Austrian armies could march against the French, while Maria Theresa undertook to surrender the besieged fortress of Neisse after a token resistance. The truce was short-lived, but in the following May, after a second victory at Chotusitz, Frederick reopened negotiations through the British ambassador at Vienna. Frederick was prepared for some hard bargaining, but the ambassador, instead of first offering Maria Theresa's *minimum*

[8] See below, p. 199.

concessions, at once proposed the cession of the whole of Silesia to Prussia. Reddaway comments: 'The region comprising the rich coalfields of after years was yielded to a Prussian negotiator whose instructions would have permitted him to let it go.'[9] The bargain was sealed in the Treaty of Berlin in July 1742.

The Silesian phase of the war was briefly reopened in August 1744 when Frederick, seeing that Austrian successes against Bavaria were placing his own gains in jeopardy, took the field in order, as he put it, 'to restore liberty to the Empire, dignity to the Emperor, and tranquillity to Europe'. Frederick's army had all but reached Vienna when it was forced, by French inaction and 17,000 Prussian desertions, to fall back on Silesia. The Emperor's death in 1745 thus came at an inopportune moment for Frederick. Bavaria bought herself out of the war by supporting the candidature of Francis of Lorraine in the Imperial election. France was now fully embroiled in war with England.[10] Yet Frederick managed to consolidate his position in four victories: at Hohenfriedberg in Silesia in June, at Soor in Bohemia in September, at Hennersdorf in November, and at Kesseldorf near Dresden in December. By the Treaty of Dresden, Christmas Day 1745, Maria Theresa reluctantly conceded Silesia, while Frederick recognized Francis I, who had been elected Emperor three months before.

Prussia's seizure of Silesia meant that there were now two major powers in Germany. The loss of a million German subjects ensured that the Habsburg Empire would henceforth contain proportionately fewer Germans and more Slavs and Magyars. Both these facts were to have momentous consequences in the next century, while making a Habsburg war of revenge a more immediate probability.

The War on the Continent

While Prussia appropriated Silesia, the other combatants pursued aims of their own. The plan which Belle-Isle had forced on the reluctant Fleury was no less than the partitioning of the whole Habsburg Empire by means of a Franco–Bavarian

---

[9] Reddaway, *op. cit.*, p. 171.   [10] See below, p. 183.

alliance, supported, it was hoped, by Prussia and Saxony.[11] In August 1741 France persuaded Sweden to intervene against Russia, Austria's nominal ally, while the Nymphenburg agreement between Bavaria and Spain (May 1741) led in December to the landing of Spanish troops in Italy and an advance northwards by combined Spanish and Neapolitan forces. This threat, though not immediately formidable, was sufficient to persuade Charles Emmanuel of Savoy and Maria Theresa to strike a bargain: Charles Emmanuel promised to defend Maria Theresa's lands, but reserved his own rights to a share in the Milanese and left himself free to repudiate the agreement at one month's notice. The checkmate on the Italian front became complete in 1742 when the British fleet, by threatening to bombard Naples, forced Charles III to recall his Neapolitan contingents from the north, and, by blockading the coast, prevented the Spanish army from being reinforced by sea.

The British role in the continental war was somewhat ambiguous. George II alone of the signatories of the Pragmatic Sanction stood by it, but fears for the safety of Hanover persuaded him to remain neutral at first. Walpole's fall early in 1742 left the way clear for the pursuance of a more active war policy, but it was not until the end of that year that a British army of 16,000 reached the Netherlands to join the Hanoverian, Hessian and Dutch contingents that were to comprise the 'Pragmatic Army'. The Dutch troops arrived late, and when the army eventually began its advance, with George II at its head, it was lucky to escape being cut off by the French. The victory at Dettingen in June 1743 owed more to French incompetence than to allied initiative, but it encouraged Carteret to continue his continental campaign, though from now on the British contribution was to be in money rather than men. The Treaty of Worms (August 1743), by which Sardinia, in return for the cession of part of the Milanese, agreed to combine with Austria to expel the Bourbons from the whole of Italy, was underwritten by a British promise of an annual subsidy of £200,000.

[11] Prussia pursued an independent policy (see p. 178) while Saxony changed sides, signing a defensive alliance with Austria in December 1742, and was finally knocked out of the war in 1745.

The Treaty of Worms may have prevented Charles Emmanuel from changing sides again, but it did so at a high price. Within a month France retorted by promising to fight Austria and England until Gibraltar and Minorca had been recovered for Spain and an Italian duchy procured for Don Philip.[12] Moreover the fact that the treaty guaranteed the Pragmatic Sanction without mentioning Silesia was perhaps an additional reason for Frederick's decision to repudiate the Treaty of Berlin and re-enter the war in August 1744.

The Treaty of Dresden (1745)[13] settled the disputes over Silesia and the Imperial crown for which the war had nominally been fought. But the war went on. In Italy the ambitious schemes of D'Argenson, the new French foreign minister, to expel both Austrians and Spaniards and set up a federation of states were cut short by his dismissal in 1746, while Elizabeth Farnese's direction of Spanish policy was ended by her husband's death in the same year. Ferdinand VI, Philip V's second son by his first marriage, made the mistake of replacing Gages, his father's most successful general. The Bourbon victories in Italy in 1745, culminating in Gages' defeat of the Sardinians at Bassignano in September, were followed by the campaigns of 1746 in which the Austro-Sardinian forces drove the French and Spaniards out of Northern Italy. After the capture of Genoa, Austria favoured an attack on Naples, but Sardinia refused to assist further Habsburg aggrandizement, and Provence was invaded instead. The invasion failed: Belle-Isle proved more than a match for the ill-coordinated Austro-Sardinian armies, and the revolt of the Genoese clinched the matter.

Meanwhile the French invasion of the Netherlands, launched by Maurice de Saxe in 1744, was well under way. By the end of 1746 Ypres, Tournai, Brussels, Antwerp, Charleroi and Namur had all fallen. In 1747 Saxe entered Holland, and his defeat of Cumberland's allied army at Laufeldt, near Maastricht, placed the Dutch in such peril that troops were hired from Russia. Now that she had made peace with Sweden the Empress could at last afford to intervene. But before the Russian corps could arrive in Europe, Louis XV, by now weary of the war,

---

[12] Elizabeth Farnese's second son.   [13] See above, p. 179.

had called off Saxe's campaign, and peace negotiations had opened at Aix-la-Chapelle.

The War in the Colonies

On the head of Frederick is all the blood which was shed in . . . every quarter of the globe. . . . The evils produced by his wickedness were felt in lands where the name of Prussia was unknown, and in order that he might rob a neighbour whom he had promised to defend, black men fought on the coast of Coromandel and red men scalped each other by the Great Lakes of North America.[14]

Macaulay's rhetoric was not altogether just, for the commercial phase of the war had begun before Frederick invaded Silesia. In 1739 England and Spain had gone to war, nominally over Captain Jenkins' ear, but in fact to settle the disputed *asiento* which had been granted to England at the Peace of Utrecht.[15] The Spaniards thought, quite rightly, that the British monopoly of the slave trade to the Spanish West Indies was being used as a cover for illicit trading beyond the annual ship for general trade that the Treaty of Utrecht allowed. Spanish belligerence was further reinforced by her unwillingness to reconcile herself to the loss of Gibraltar and Minorca.[16]

France welcomed the Anglo-Spanish war, for her merchants, who much resented the British hold on Spanish trade, now saw a chance for their own goods to infiltrate into the Spanish West Indies. British merchants, already well aware of the growth of French trade, particularly in West Indian sugar, were demanding war with France as early as 1740. As Sir Matthew Dekker wrote in that year: 'Because the Incumbrances on our Trade at present have given the French so much the Start of us in time of Peace, that War seems absolutely necessary to obstruct their growing power.'[17]

But for the time being England fought only Spain. Admiral Vernon, after successfully destroying the fortifications at Porto-

---

[14] Lord Macaulay, *Essays and Lays of Ancient Rome*, Longmans 1886, p. 667.
[15] See above, p. 16. [16] See above, p. 16.
[17] V. H. H. Green, *The Hanoverians, 1714–1815*, Arnold 1948, p. 145.

bello, failed to take either Cartagena or Santiago de Cuba. He therefore contented himself with disrupting Spanish trade with the Americas. Only one treasure fleet got through to Spain, while Vernon was explicitly ordered to give what protection he could to British ships trading with the Spanish colonies.

England and France eventually went to war in 1744. The French Canadians began a series of frontier raids on Nova Scotia and Massachusetts, while using Louisbourg (the port which they had built at the mouth of the St Lawrence) as a base for privateering in the New England fishing-grounds and for general harrying of colonial shipping. In 1745 an expedition organized by the Governor of Massachusetts and supported by a detachment from the West Indies squadron blockaded Louisburg and captured it. But the fact that the bulk of the British fleet was engaged in blockading the coast of Italy[18] prevented the British colonists from following up their success. Nor was France able to assist her settlers: a strong squadron which attempted to recapture Louisbourg in 1746 was beaten off and left to limp back to France, narrowly escaping interception and destruction by Anson. Neither France nor England could afford to devote any further forces to the war in Canada, which had thus proved little more than a curtain-raiser to the sterner conflict of ten years later.[19]

It was not until September 1744 that the news of Anglo-French hostilities reached India. Here the contestants were the two rival East India Companies, the British with its bases at Calcutta and Madras, the French at Chandernagore and Pondicherry. This was purely a commercial war, for the deeper political implications of the struggle were not fully understood at the time. The possibility of some sort of compromise between the two companies was dissolved by the arrival of Barnett's squadron in the Indian Ocean, where he cut the French trade routes and seized a number of East Indiamen. Dupleix, the able governor of the French East India Company, determined to defeat the British on land. He attacked Madras in 1746, by which time La Bourdonnais had arrived with his squadron from Mauritius, and Barnett's death had deprived the British of the

[18] See above, p. 180.   [19] See below, p. 194.

initiative needed to challenge him. Madras fell, and Dupleix, re-inforced by 1,200 men left behind by La Bourdonnais, succeeded in holding the town against an assault by the Nawab of Arcot, who enjoyed immense numerical superiority. The arrival of Boscawen in 1748 restored British control of the sea, but his force of fourteen men-of-war and 4,000 European troops failed to capture Pondicherry before the war ended.

The Peace of Aix-la-Chapelle (1748) restored the colonial *status quo*; the French gave back Madras while the British surrendered Louisbourg. In Europe the fruits of eight years of war seemed equally frugal. France restored the Netherlands to Austria. Prussian retention of Silesia was guaranteed, though Prussia did not sign the treaty and the guarantee was so worded that it was probably valid only if Prussia in turn guaranteed the remaining terms of the treaty. These were concerned chiefly with Italy: Charles Emmanuel kept the lands that Maria Theresa had promised him in the Treaty of Worms,[20] with the exception of Piacenza which was given to Don Philip together with the duchy of Parma. Spain promised to allow England to retain the *asiento* until 1752.

The Italian terms of the treaty were a sign that Maria Theresa had abandoned hopes of a Habsburg hegemony in Italy. A truce was at last called to the Habsburg–Bourbon struggle in the peninsula, and Charles Emmanuel of Savoy could now breathe freely. But Maria Theresa did not surrender Silesia with such good grace: she would willingly have relinquished the Netherlands if she could have kept Silesia. Yet, paradoxically, the war had made Austria stronger by providing the stimulus to military and administrative reform[21] that peacetime conditions could not have provided. Habsburg resources would soon be sufficient to sustain a war of revenge, and there was already more than a hint that when that war came Maria Theresa would look for support to Versailles rather than to London.

[20] See above, p. 180.
[21] See above, p. 142.

13

The Seven Years War, 1756–63

The Diplomatic Revolution

To a generation of historians who saw history largely in military
and diplomatic terms, the reversal of alliances that preceded the
Seven Years War seemed so spectacular as to deserve to be
called 'the Diplomatic Revolution'. Historians have argued as to
whether this 'revolution' caused the war and have hotly debated
whether Frederick the Great's invasion of Saxony in 1756 was
an act of aggression or of self-defence.[1] But on one point at least
there is general agreement: all the European powers who had
signed the Peace of Aix-la-Chapelle in 1748[2] were dissatisfied
with its terms. England and France had merely exchanged their
colonial conquests, thus deferring the conflict in India and
North America. Prussia, though she had gained Silesia, saw that
she would have to fight to keep it. Austria had retained the
Netherlands which she would gladly have surrendered, made
concessions in Italy which she could afford but nevertheless
begrudged, and lost Silesia which she was determined to regain.

The constant factor in European history since the fifteenth
century had been the antagonism between the French monarchy
and the Habsburgs. The emergence of Prussia as a result of the
Austrian Succession war transformed the situation: there were
now two major German powers within the Empire, and the
nineteenth-century struggle between Austria and Prussia was
thus foreshadowed. Anton von Kaunitz (1711–94) was one of
the first to see the implications of this new situation. In 1749
when Maria Theresa required her ministers to make written
suggestions on future foreign policy, Kaunitz alone offered a

---

[1] For a summary of the historiography of the origins of the war see H. Butterfield,
Man on His Past, Cambridge 1955, Chapter V.
[2] See opposite page.

185

complete reappraisal. Austria must recover Silesia. In order to do this the Franco-Prussian alliance must be disrupted and Austria herself must find allies. Holland was a broken reed; England was too preoccupied with colonial ventures and would never risk losing Hanover in a war to destroy Prussia; but Russia might be bought either by subsidies or even by the cession of East Prussia, which lay outside the Empire. But best of all, France, in spite of centuries of hostility, might be persuaded to acquiesce in the destruction of Prussia, and the Austrian Netherlands might be a suitable bait since Austria could scarcely hope to defend them. Such was Kaunitz's plan. Maria Theresa accepted it, though it was not formally sanctioned by the Austrian ministers until August 1755.

If Austrian diplomacy was quick to adapt itself to changed conditions, British diplomacy continued to move in traditional grooves. The Duke of Newcastle, though not as incompetent as he is often depicted, is the classic example of the dangers of long diplomatic experience. Having controlled British policy since the 1720s, he was reluctant to admit that the traditional Austrian alliance was moribund, and preferred to believe, in true Walpolean fashion, that every nation had its price and that British guineas could buy the simultaneous support of Prussia, Austria and Russia. Austria, who felt that England had let her down in the Austrian Succession war, declined to strengthen her Netherlands garrison merely to please the British, and would agree to defend Hanover only in return for a promise of British support in an attack on Prussia – a frank violation of the Aix-la-Chapelle treaty.

Anglo-Austrian relations were scarcely improved by George II's part in the attempt to secure the election of Archduke Joseph as King of the Romans.[3] The Electors demanded subsidies in return for their support, while the Elector Palatine went so far as to claim territorial compensation. George II, having promised to secure Joseph's election, nevertheless supported the demands of the Elector Palatine, and the role of the British diplomats in the inconclusive negotiations of 1750–52 served to antagonize rather than mollify Maria Theresa.

[3] Heir-presumptive to the Imperial title.

Austria's evident coolness was all the more alarming to England in view of Dutch determination to remain neutral in return for a French guarantee of non-interference. Newcastle turned to Russia. In September 1755 the British ambassador, Hanbury Williams, negotiated a subsidy treaty with Bestuzhev, Elizabeth's minister: Russia agreed to keep 55,000 men on the borders of Livonia to intimidate Prussia, in return for a subsidy of £100,000 in peace and £500,000 in war. It was a high price, but Newcastle believed that the treaty had guaranteed peace. Yet it started a chain reaction that was to end in war.

The immediate effect of the subsidy treaty was to persuade Prussia to come to terms with England, whose value as an ally Frederick had earlier been inclined to doubt. By the Convention of Westminster, signed in January 1756, England and Prussia agreed to guarantee the neutrality of Germany and to combine to prevent the passage of other foreign troops through Germany. British wishes were not altogether met for the Austrian Netherlands were excluded from the guarantee, but George II could feel that the security of Hanover had been strengthened.

The news of the Convention of Westminster provoked a furore in Paris. Louis XV was angered less by the content of the treaty than by the fact that Prussia had concluded it without consulting France, who was technically Prussia's ally. Louis had insisted on treating Prussia as the junior partner in the Franco-Prussian alliance; Frederick's action seemed to have reversed the roles. Frederick was surprised by the violence of the French reaction. In February 1756 he had assessed the situation thus:

It is an axiom that it will never be a French interest to foster the aggrandizement of the new House of Austria. We know the great efforts of Richelieu to diminish the power of the old House of Austria and what it cost France to succeed. Can one ever believe that a French Minister would wish to commit such a glaring error against the most essential interests of his country?[4]

But Frederick, like Newcastle, had learned his history too well. As early as 1750 Kaunitz had been sent to Paris to canvass the idea of a Franco-Austrian alliance, but by the time he

[4] G. P. Gooch, *Frederick the Great*, Longmans 1947, p. 33.

returned to Vienna to become Chancellor in 1753 he had done little more than convince Louis XV of Austrian friendship. Two years later Starhemberg, the Austrian envoy in Paris, was instructed to reopen negotiations on the quiet. He conveyed, through Madame de Pompadour, Kaunitz's proposals: Austrian neutrality in the Anglo-French war that had by now broken out,[5] French occupation of Ostend and Nieuport for the duration of the war, and transference to Don Philip of some territory in the Netherlands in exchange for his Italian duchies. In return for these concessions Kaunitz demanded financial rather than active assistance from France in an Austro-Prussian war, though France would be expected to acquiesce in the partition of Prussia, and, of course, to repudiate the Franco-Prussian alliance.

France refused to break with Prussia until provided with proof of Prussia's hostility. Instead she proposed to Austria a mutual guarantee of the other's territories and of the territories of the other's allies (except England) in return for Austrian neutrality in the Anglo-French war, the exclusion of the British troops from the Netherlands, and Austrian help in preventing Russian auxiliaries from passing through Germany. Such a bargain would be of little benefit to Austria in her proposed attack on Prussia, yet Kaunitz was so anxious for some sort of agreement that in January 1756 he was ready to accede to most of the French demands. But before the month was out, news of the Convention of Westminster provided the French with the evidence of Prussian fickleness that Kaunitz had been unable to supply. The French now agreed to abandon the Prussian alliance, but made it clear that they would not cooperate in an Austrian attack on Prussia and insisted that, although Austria was entitled to recover Silesia, the rest of Prussia must not be partitioned. Thus the first Treaty of Versailles between France and Austria in May 1756 was no more than a mutual defensive alliance and a mutual promise of neutrality.

In itself this treaty did not make an Austrian attack on Prussia possible. The conspiracy to despoil the King of Prussia had its centre not in Paris, nor in Vienna, but in St Petersburg. Russia had good reason to suspect Prussia: Frederick seemed to

[5] See below, p. 194.

be encouraging Swedish belligerence in the Baltic, and his Political Testament of 1752[6] actually discusses the possibility of gaining Swedish Pomerania in return for supporting Sweden's ambition to recover Livonia. Russia had regarded the British subsidy treaty[7] as a means of meeting this threat, and she accordingly resented the fact that England had used this treaty to persuade Prussia to sign the Convention of Westminster. In March 1756 a new council was set up in St Petersburg, ostensibly to discuss the subsidy treaty but in fact to produce a plan for the destruction of Prussia. In April this council agreed to offer Austria an army of 80,000 if a joint Austro-Russian attack on Prussia were launched during 1756, and to continue the war until Silesia was recovered. Almost simultaneously the Austrian ambassador told Bestuzhev of the Austro-French negotiations and proposed a triple attack on Prussia when France had been brought into alliance. The Russians were reluctant to wait for France, however, and it took all Kaunitz's skill to persuade Elizabeth and Maria Theresa to agree to postpone the attack until 1757.

Although in August 1756 Starhemberg reported to Vienna that the French had at last yielded on all crucial points, it remains doubtful whether even by this stage France had agreed to an offensive alliance. Thus when on 29 August Frederick II started the Seven Years War by invading Saxony, Kaunitz's offensive coalition was not yet complete. It may be that Kaunitz had calculated that Frederick would walk into the trap. 'We shall succeed sooner or later in our great scheme,' Starhemberg had written, 'and perhaps the King of Prussia himself will be our most effective helper.'[8] Certainly Frederick had known since 1753 that Augustus of Saxony was trying to do a deal with Austria at Prussia's expense. But France was a more formidable foe than Saxony, and it was only Frederick's invasion of Saxony that persuaded France finally to throw in her lot with Austria. By the second Treaty of Versailles (May 1757) she pledged herself to the 'total destruction of Prussia', and promised a subsidy of twelve million *livres* and an army of 100,000, besides paying for an additional 10,000 German mercenaries; only when

[6] Gooch, *op. cit.*, p. 286.   [7] See above, p. 187.   [8] N.C.M.H., vol. vii, p. 455.

Austria had recovered Silesia would the terms offered to France in 1755 apply.[9] By the convention of St Petersburg (January 1757) Russia finally adhered to the first Versailles treaty and, by a further treaty in February, put her entire army at Austria's disposal in return for subsidies, which were paid in French *livres*. Kaunitz had triumphed: he had secured his anti-Prussian coalition at a price far below what he had expected to pay, and Frederick appeared the aggressor.

The War on the Continent

The fact that Frederick struck the first blow meant that Russia no longer had to reckon with Austrian attempts to postpone the war,[10] while Austria was able to bring in France at once by invoking the first Treaty of Versailles, which had been a purely defensive alliance.[11] The Convention of Westminster[12] had also been a defensive treaty, and England was not therefore bound to come to Prussia's aid. Yet she could hardly hold aloof: she was already at war with France[13] and could not ignore the fact that France's ally held the Netherlands, while the defence of Hanover hinged on Prussian assistance. The collapse of New-castle's peace policy led to his replacement by Pitt, who had earlier deplored a continental commitment for the sake of Hanover, but who now energetically embarked on his policy of winning Canada on the plains of Germany.

By the time Pitt formed his ministry in 1757 the Prussian offensive had somewhat misfired. Frederick had overrun Saxony quickly, but not quickly enough: a spirited defence by the Saxon army entrenched in the highlands above Dresden delayed the Prussians for a month, just long enough to prevent Frederick from invading Bohemia before winter. Frederick was thus reduced to paper warfare. The archives in Dresden were ransacked for evidence of a Saxon conspiracy against Prussia and the *Mémoire Raisonné* was circulated to the courts of Europe in an attempt to justify Prussian action. This manifesto was a remarkable understatement of the Prussian case, for most of the

---

[9] See above, p. 188.   [10] See above, p. 189.   [11] See above, p. 188.
[12] See above, p. 187.   [13] See below, p. 194.

evidence Frederick had found pointed to Russia rather than Saxony as the arch-conspirator, and Frederick, believing that the British could restrain Russia, was anxious to avoid giving offence at St Petersburg.[14]

When Frederick at length invaded Bohemia in the spring of 1757, he failed to take Prague and lost half his infantry at the battle of Kolin in June. During the summer Sweden invaded Pomerania and Russia overran East Prussia. And to complete Frederick's discomfiture, the British 'Army of Observation' under Cumberland agreed to disband under the Convention of Klosterseven (September 1757).

Before the year was out Pitt repudiated the Convention and reformed the British force, entrusting it to the command of Frederick's cousin, Ferdinand of Brunswick. Meanwhile Prussia had set about saving herself. While the Russians and Swedes contented themselves with their initial gains in the Baltic, and the Austrians moved slowly on Silesia, Frederick brought the combined French and Imperial army to battle at Rossbach in November and routed it. He now turned to drive the Austrians from Silesia. A month after Rossbach, Frederick with 30,000 troops out-manoeuvred an Austrian army of 80,000 at Leuthen and allowed the Austrian general Daun to extricate little more than one-third of his force. These unexpected victories persuaded the British to invest more heavily in the Prussian cause: by the subsidy treaty of April 1758 Britain promised £670,000 on the understanding that neither country should make a separate peace. By the beginning of April Brunswick's army had driven the French back across the Rhine, and in the following year it was Brunswick's troops who met a powerful French thrust against Hanover and repulsed it at the battle of Minden (1 August 1759).

From this point England and France virtually dropped out of the continental war, which resolved itself into a struggle between Prussia and the Austro-Russian coalition. The effectiveness of this coalition was impaired by Kaunitz's reluctance to meet the Russian demand for the annexation of East Prussia and part of Poland. Kaunitz seems to have expected his allies to fight for

[14] See Butterfield, *op. cit.*, p. 144.

Austrian interests without compensation. He might have kept France as an active partner if he had been ready to allow immediate French occupation of the Austrian Netherlands. Disappointed in the west, France looked east to Poland where her encouragement of the anti-Russian faction actually hindered the offensive against Prussia by delaying the movement of Russian troops through Poland. In August 1758 Frederick, having failed to take Olmütz after a two-month siege, marched to defend Brandenburg against Russian invasion and won a bloody victory at the battle of Zorndorff. In October Daun defeated Frederick at Hochkirk, but failed to exploit his victory, leaving the Russians to continue the fighting. In the summer of 1759 Loudon's Austrians and Saltikov's Russians combined to produce an army of 80,000 which at Kunersdorf inflicted on Frederick the most crushing defeat of his career. But his enemies could not agree on how to use their victory: Saltikov refused to assist in the seizure of Silesia and withdrew to Poland, while Daun fell back on Bohemia rather than risk another battle. On the way he captured Finck and 12,000 Prussians at Maxen, but Frederick was left with Silesia and most of Saxony still in his possession.

If lack of coordination among her enemies was one reason for Prussia's survival, Frederick's own astonishing resilience was the other. In spite of the heavy losses of 1757–59 (and his victories were often as costly as his defeats) Frederick was still able in 1760 to put 100,000 troops into the field against 223,000 of his opponents. Though he was still gravely outnumbered, the caution of his enemies enabled him to achieve the effect of being in two places at once. In August he defeated Loudon's army at Liegnitz in Silesia before it could link up with the forces of Daun and Lacy. Ignoring a joint Austro-Russian threat to Berlin, Frederick attacked Daun's army at Torgau and defeated it. The Austrians again fell back upon Dresden, leaving most of Saxony in Prussian hands. In July 1760 Frederick bombarded Dresden in a siege described by Carlyle as 'one of the rapidest and most furious . . . anywhere on record'. Frederick was driven off by superior Austrian forces before he could breach the defences, and Boswell was not the only contemporary to think that the destruction of Dresden was an act of sheer wantonness:

'It gave me great pain to see the ruins made by the Prussian bombardments. I hated the barbarous hero. He was under no necessity to bombard Dresden. It was from mere spite that he did it.'[15]

The remainder of the continental war was, in Carlyle's phrase, 'like a race between spent horses'. No great battles were fought in 1761, though the Austrians took Schweidniz, the chief fortress of Silesia; but by the end of the year the Prussian army had dwindled to a mere 30,000. At this moment, with Prussia reduced to such desperate straits, Bute, who had replaced Pitt in October, declined to renew the subsidy treaty[16] unless the prohibition on peace negotiations was deleted. For the third time in half a century England had left an ally in the lurch.[17] In January 1762 Frederick told his foreign minister that Prussia's only chance of continuing the war lay in an alliance with the Turks. In the event, salvation came from an even more unlikely quarter. In that same month Elizabeth of Russia, who had resisted French and Austrian pressure to make peace,[18] at length died, and Peter III not only made peace with Prussia but concluded a military alliance with her. This surprising news confirmed Bute in his determination to withdraw the subsidy: it was one thing to devote money to saving Prussia from extinction, but it was quite another to finance an alliance designed to prolong the war in order to enable Russia to attack Denmark. At the end of 1762 England and France came to terms[19] and both withdrew their troops from Germany. Meanwhile Sweden had been glad to make peace on the basis of the 1756 position. Maria Theresa had no course but to renounce Silesia.

The War in the Colonies

The colonial phase of the Seven Years War was a continuation of that of the War of the Austrian Succession. The Peace of Aix-la-Chapelle had marked no more than an uneasy truce in

---

[15] *Boswell on the Grand Tour: Germany and Switzerland 1764*, Heinemann 1953, p. 129.

[16] See above, p. 187.   [17] In 1711–13, in 1733–34 and in 1761–63.

[18] N.C.M.H., vol. vii, p. 483.   [19] See below, p. 197.

the Anglo-French struggle for overseas empire, and the two nations were again at war before hostilities reopened in Europe. Although Louisbourg was restored to France in 1748, its strategic importance at the gateway to the St Lawrence had been demonstrated, and in the 1750s the British built Halifax as a counterpoise. Both countries were engaged in westward expansion at the expense of Indian tribes, and Duquesne, the new Governor of Canada, sent expeditions southward down the Ohio with the object of linking French Canada with those French settlements on the Mississipi above New Orleans. These ambitions threatened the westward expansion of Virginia, and when in 1753 the French built Fort Duquesne on the Ohio, the British replied by building Fort Necessity. The surrender of this new British fort to Duquesne in the summer of 1754 led to the opening of negotiations which were nevertheless intended to give both sides time to plan for a war which they regarded as inevitable, but for which they were unprepared.

The Anglo-French war actually started in the Mediterranean when the French landed troops on Minorca and Admiral Byng, failed to relieve the island.[20] But nowhere was Pitt's strategic insight more clearly shown than in his realization that Canada was the key to maritime and commercial supremacy. The British conquered Canada because Pitt had built up a North American army of 20,000 regulars and 22,000 colonial volunteers. He was accused of investing too much British money in the European struggle, but his subsidization of Prussian arms helped to divert French attention from North America and ensured that British superiority there was maintained.

While Amherst and Boscawen attacked Louisbourg, and Forbes crossed the Alleghenies to deal with the Ohio forts, Abercrombie and Howe invaded Canada from the south. Abercrombie's army suffered a severe setback at Ticonderoga in July 1758, but Pitt's three-pronged attack succeeded nevertheless. The British blockade kept the French short of food, while the scarcely veiled hostility between the French regular troops and the French Canadian settlers was personified in the disputes

---

[20] The execution of Byng prompted Voltaire's famous remark that in England they shoot an admiral from time to time *pour encourager les autres*.

over strategy between Governor-General Vaudreuil and General Montcalm. In the autumn of 1758 Montcalm appealed to Paris for reinforcements without which, he claimed, Quebec could not be defended. He received 300 recruits, some gunnery experts and two provision ships.[21]

Choiseul, who became French foreign minister in December 1758, hoped to save Canada by the invasion of England, but, before he had managed to collect a fleet of transports for this enterprise, Wolfe took Quebec in September 1759. The British had only 9,000 troops to Montcalm's 15,000, but Wolfe's daring won him the advantage of surprise, while Montcalm was hampered by Vaudreuil's interference. After an uncertain winter in which the British were cut off by ice from their naval support, the conquest of Canada was completed in the summer of 1760 with the capture of Montreal.

Seventeen-fifty-nine – Pitt's 'year of glorious victories' – was decisive in all theatres of the colonial war. The French West Indies had suffered an indirect blow in 1758 when Keppel's capture of Gorée off the Senegalese coast stopped the supply of slaves. In the spring of 1759 the sugar island of Guadeloupe was captured, though the other West Indian islands did not fall until after the surrender of Martinique in 1762. In the late summer and autumn of 1759 Choiseul's scheme for the invasion of England was finally frustrated by the British naval victories at Lagos (Boscawen) and Quiberon Bay (Hawke).

The same year saw a turning-point in India. The lesson of the 1740s had been that success in India depended on support from the sea.[22] On land the French had double the British numbers, but lacked comparable leadership. Dupleix had been recalled in disgrace in 1754, but his successors proved no more of a match for Clive than he had been. The battle of Plassey in June 1757, when Clive's 3,000 put to flight the Nawab of Bengal's army of 50,000, not only avenged the treatment of British civilians at Calcutta[23] in the previous year, but also convinced other Indian princes that the future of India lay with the British.

Lally-Tollendal, the French commander, though a good

[21] Dorn, *Competition for Empire 1740–1763*, Harper 1940, p. 361.
[22] See above, p. 183.   [23] In the 'Black Hole'.

general, was a tactless politician, and the fact that he had been assigned the dual task of reforming the French East India Company and simultaneously defeating the British meant that he could hardly hope to succeed in either. In 1758 he laid siege to Madras, but Pocock succeeded in frightening off D'Aché's squadron so effectively that it stayed in hiding at Mauritius for a year. Deprived of naval support, Lally called off the siege, but when the monsoon drove Pocock back to Bombay, Lally tried again with a strengthened force. He was on the point of success when in February 1759 Kempenfelt arrived with supplies and 1,000 men. The raising of the siege marked the failure of the French in India: they retained numerical superiority but ran desperately short of money. Pocock again chased D'Aché's squadron away, and the arrival of Sir Eyre Coote's contingent gave the British the advantage of numbers. In January 1760 the French were routed at Wandewash, and a year later Pondicherry was finally starved into surrender.

The closing stages of the colonial war were fought against Spain. Bernis' attempts during 1757 and 1758 to persuade Spain to enter the war in support of France had come to nothing: Ferdinand VI's queen, daughter of John V of Portugal, was pro-British in sympathy. But Ferdinand had died in 1759, to be succeeded by his half-brother Charles of Naples, whose antipathy to England no doubt owed something to the action of the British fleet in 1742.[24]

Choiseul was quick to exploit this new opportunity. While opening peace negotiations with Pitt, he set about bringing Spain into the war. The Family Compact,[25] signed in August 1761, guaranteed the territories of all branches of the Bourbon family in France, Spain and Italy, pledged the kings of France and Spain to a permanent alliance, and bound Spain to declare war on England before 1 May 1762. Pitt, knowing of these negotiations, tried to persuade the cabinet to strike a decisive blow at Spain before she declared war, but Bute prevailed and Pitt resigned. When war broke out in January 1762, however,

[24] See above, p. 180.
[25] This was the third 'Family Compact'. The first had been the Treaty of the Escurial (see p. 153 above) in 1733; the second had been the Franco-Spanish alliance of 1743 (the Treaty of Fontainebleau).

it was Pitt's plan that secured the capture of Havana and Manila, while Portugal, far from excluding British ships from her ports as the Bourbon powers hoped, used British troops under Burgoyne to throw back the Spanish from her frontiers. As soon as Choiseul saw the feebleness of his new-found ally, he accepted the need for an immediate peace, though it was Bute who re-opened the negotiations.

The colonial war was ended by the Treaty of Paris (February 1763) which was signed by Britain, France, Spain and Portugal. It confirmed British conquests in India and North America, though it allowed France to retain her Newfoundland fishing rights and her trading stations (though not her garrisons) in India. The West Indies were divided: England kept St Vincent, Tobago, Dominica and Grenada, but restored the remainder, including Guadeloupe, Martinique and St Lucia. In Africa the British restored the island of Gorée but retained Senegal. Bute was condemned at home for being too lenient to France, but it is doubtful whether England could have kept the West Indies and Gorée without prolonging the war, though the British merchant interests would willingly have exchanged Canada for Guadeloupe. Spain recovered Havana and Manila, but was compelled to cede Florida to England, to accept the loss of Minorca, and to abandon her hopes of regaining Gibraltar; as compensation she was given New Orleans and Louisiana west of the Mississippi. Spain paid heavily for her brief intervention.

The European phase of the war was formally concluded five days later in the Treaty of Hubertusburg, signed by Austria, Prussia and Saxony. The pre-war position was restored: Maria Theresa conceded the loss of Silesia and joined with Frederick II in a pledge of mutual friendship, while Frederick for his part promised the electoral vote of Brandenburg in support of Archduke Joseph in the Imperial election. Paradoxically, however, the outcome of the war in Europe proved more decisive than that of the colonial war. At the cost of one-ninth of her population (500,000 of 4,500,000) Frederick had vindicated his state's position as a European power. But he had lost his allies in the process: France and England had both turned their backs on him, thus forcing him slowly, but surely, into the arms of

Russia.[26] Austria had made her bid for supremacy and had failed: henceforth she would be on the defensive. France had contrived to fight on four continents at the cost of her military prestige in Europe; not until the revolutionary armies attacked Austria in 1792 would the reputation of French arms be restored. But outside Europe British magnanimity (or stupidity) had allowed France to remain a major maritime power. The Anglo-French struggle for command of the sea had not yet been decided.

[26] See below, p. 200.

14

The Expansion of Russia
1763–96

The First Turkish War, 1768–74

Peter the Great's northern conquests[1] had given Russia a port on
the Baltic, but although he took Azov in 1696 he lost it again in
1711, so that at Peter's death in 1725 Russia's access to the Black
Sea was still barred by the Turks. Russia and Turkey had first
come into conflict during the reign of Ivan the Terrible
(1533–85), and a century later had fought in the Ukraine, then
a dependency of Poland. In the eighteenth century Polish problems repeatedly bedevilled Russo-Turkish relations: in 1710
Charles XII of Sweden had enlisted the help of the Sultan in his
fruitless attempt to restore Stanislas Leszczynski to the Polish
throne,[2] while, in the War of the Polish Succession,[3] the Turkish
alliance with France in support of Stanislas' claims was the
pretext for Russia's attack on Turkey in 1735. The Russians
seized Azov and Oczakov, and overran the Crimea and much of
Moldavia, but their Austrian allies were defeated and concluded
a separate peace with the Turks at Belgrade (1739). Thus Russia
was also forced to come to terms: she was allowed to keep
Azov (provided its fortifications were demolished) and could
trade on the Sea of Azov and the Black Sea – in Turkish ships.
That the Ottoman Empire had gained a reprieve was in part due
to French diplomatic pressure at Constantinople, where
Villeneuve's encouragement seems to have stiffened the Turkish
will to resist.

In 1734 Montesquieu had written:

The Turkish Empire is now in approximately the same state of
weakness as that in which the Greek Empire once was; but it will

---

[1] See above, p. 40.　　[2] See above, p. 35.　　[3] See above, p. 30.

last longer. For if any prince should endanger this empire in pursuit of his conquests the three commercial powers of Europe know their business too well to refrain from coming immediately to its defence.[4]

Partition was not yet under discussion, but at Catherine the Great's accession Marshal Münnich, whose triumphant Balkan campaign had been cut short in 1739, put forward a strong plea that the Empress should take up the cause of the Greeks and Slavs under Ottoman rule. Catherine could hardly follow Münnich's advice without the help of a powerful ally. Austria would not approve Russian ambitions in the Balkans, any more than France and Britain would welcome Russian ships in the Mediterranean. That left Prussia.

Frederick the Great, who owed his survival in the Seven Years War to the accession of Catherine's husband in 1762,[5] was anxious to renew the short-lived alliance with Russia that had lapsed at Peter III's death. On the very day that the peace of Hubertusburg (1763)[6] was signed Frederick wrote to Catherine:

The King of Poland is ill and I hear from Warsaw that he is not expected to live long. If he dies unexpectedly there is a danger that the intrigues of the different courts may rekindle the fires of war so recently extinguished. I am ready, Madame, to consider any steps you may propose, and to save time I will explain my own attitude. Of all the pretenders to the Polish throne it is only princes of the House of Austria whom sound policy compels me to veto, and I imagine that the interests of Russia point in the same direction. I may add that a Piast [Polish nobleman] would suit both of us best. Profound secrecy will be necessary to prevent intrigues among those to whom such a solution would be unwelcome.[7]

Augustus III of Poland died in October 1763. In April 1764 Frederick and Catherine agreed to guarantee one another's territories and to support the candidature of Stanilas Poniatowski, a Pole and a former lover of Catherine. Five months later Stanilas was unanimously elected, thanks to a show of Russian military force and £300,000 in Russian bribes. 'Nothing seems to me more admirable,' wrote Frederick to Catherine,

4 J. A. R. Marriott, *The Eastern Question*, Oxford 1918, p. 141.
5 See above, p. 193.   6 See above, p. 197.
7 G. P. Gooch, *Frederick the Great*, Longmans 1947, p. 64.

'than your accomplishment of so many great deeds as it were without effort or resort to coercion or force. God said, Let there be light, and there was light.'[8] Frederick and Catherine were determined that Poland should not be given a new lease of life. By their treaty in April they had agreed to preserve both the Swedish and Polish constitutions, and in 1768 the Polish Diet declared the *liberum veto*[9] and other obstructive archaisms to be integral, essential and irrevocable parts of the Polish constitution.

Not all the Poles proved so pliant. The 'Confederation of the Bar' was formed to drive out the Russians and safeguard the supremacy of the Roman Catholic Church. The patriots found foreign allies. The French government was not pleased to see a Russo-Prussian rapprochement, and Choiseul wrote to Vergennes urging him to enlist the help of the Turks: 'True, the Turks are hopelessly degenerate, and the attempt will probably be fatal to them, but that does not concern us so long as we attain our objects.'[10] Catherine was not yet ready to fight the Sultan, but the activities of Russian agents in the Balkans since 1765 had already provoked the Turks; now Russian troops, by pursuing fugitive Poles into Turkish territory, provided the final pretext. In September 1768 Turkey declared war on Russia, in defence of the liberties of Catholic Poland. Vergennes had triumphed by persuasion alone: the funds that the French government had allowed him for bribes were returned intact to Paris.

It was just as well for France, for the money would have proved a poor investment. In 1769 a Turkish army was routed on the Dniester, and the Russians occupied Jassy and Bucharest. The next year a Russian fleet left the Baltic and, with English encouragement, English stores and an English admiral,[11] made its way down the Channel and across the Bay of Biscay to the Mediterranean, where Alexis Orlov was waiting to assume command. The Greeks rose in revolt, but Orlov failed in his

---

[8] W. L. Reddaway, *A History of Europe from 1715 to 1814*, Methuen 1951, p. 263.
[9] See above, p. 29.
[10] Marriott, *op. cit.*, p. 146.
[11] Admiral John Elphinstone. See G. S. Thomson, *Catherine the Great and the Expansion of Russia*, E.U.P. 1947, p. 136.

attempt to send troops to their aid and, leaving the Greek rebels to the vengeance of the Turkish army, continued the campaign by sea. He met and defeated the Turkish fleet off Chios, and then destroyed it by fireship as it lay at anchor. Meanwhile Russian armies had conquered the Crimea, taken the Turkish forts on the Danube and Dniester, and occupied Moldavia and Wallachia. Austria was alarmed. In the summer of 1771 she threatened intervention by signing a secret treaty with Turkey, but Frederick the Great was anxious to prevent Austrian participation, and he succeeded in persuading Austria and Russia that the partition of Poland would prove an acceptable alternative to aggrandizement in the Balkans.[12]

Compensation in Poland made Catherine less anxious to prolong her expensive Turkish war, particularly as she was now distracted by the Pugachev rebellion at home.[13] A change of Sultan in January 1774 paved the way for peace negotiations, which were concluded at Kutchuk Kainardji in July 1774. The Treaty gave Russia, in addition to Azov itself, Kertsch (commanding the straits between the Sea of Azov and the Black Sea) and Kinburn (at the mouth of the Dnieper). All her other principal conquests were returned to the Sultan, though under guarantees for better treatment of his Christian subjects. Territorially the gains seem insignificant. (Austria acquired more in 1775 when she took Bukovina from Turkey without firing a shot.) But strategically Russia's new footholds on the Black Sea coast were of great importance: the Black Sea trade was now open to her own shipping, while Russian merchants could trade in the Ottoman dominions 'by land as well as by water and upon the Danube in their ships . . . with all the same privileges and advantages as are enjoyed by the most friendly nations whom the Sublime Porte favours most in trade, such as the French and English.'[14]

The Bavarian Succession War, 1778–79

Frederick the Great had been content to avert an Austro-Russian conflict in the Balkans by allowing Austria to take Galicia from

[12] See below, p. 208.   [13] See above, p. 136.   [14] Marriott, *op. cit.*, p. 152.

Poland in 1772,[15] and he could not prevent her from snatching Bukovina in 1775. But when the Habsburgs began to cherish ambitions inside Germany itself, Frederick was quick to interpose. By 1777 rumours reached Berlin that Austria had designs on Bavaria, whose prince was the last of the Bavarian Wittelsbach line. At his death the succession would revert to the other branch of the Wittelsbach family, represented by Karl Theodor, the Elector Palatine. Joseph II, who in any case had no wish to see Bavaria united with the Palatinate, awaited his opportunity – 'such as occurs only once in centuries' – to extend Habsburg power within the Empire. Frederick was alive to the threat. 'I have certain knowledge,' he wrote to his brother Henry in April 1777, 'that Prince Kaunitz has said: The Imperial Court will never put up with Prussian power; that we may rule it must be destroyed.'[16] Eight months later the Elector of Bavaria died of smallpox.

Joseph was, as usual, unduly optimistic: 'The attention of all the world is occupied elsewhere and I flatter myself that this stroke will succeed without a war.' Within a week of the Elector's death, Joseph had persuaded Karl Theodor to recognize Austrian claims to Lower Bavaria (about a third of the whole Electorate) in return for money and titles for his illegitimate children, whom he preferred to his nephew and heir, Karl of Zweibrücken. But the heir had to agree to the partition, and the Duke of Zweibrücken, bolstered up by Frederick, refused his consent. On 3 March 1778 Frederick wrote to Henry:

These princes of the Empire are all broken reeds, without energy or honour. The Prince of Zweibrücken has been pushed along; left to himself he would have accepted the infamy like his uncle the Elector Palatine. It is the disgrace of our century and I blush for Germany. I realize all the difficulties ahead. That is why I have to go slow and not tread before I know by soundings if the ground is firm. I know what a poor lot these princes of the Empire are, so it is not my intention to become their Don Quixote. But to let Austria usurp despotic authority in Germany is to furnish her with arms against ourselves and to make her far more formidable than she is today, which no one in my position should tolerate. The balance

---

[15] See below, p. 210.   [16] Gooch, *op. cit.*, p. 87.

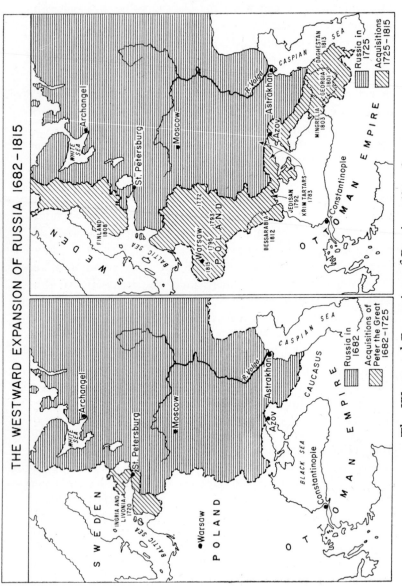

The Westward Expansion of Russia, 1682–1815

of the respective forces is the second reason which compels me to intervene, so as not to connive at her becoming so superior to us that some day we could not resist her. I regard war as inescapable; the Emperor wishes it and the armies are gathering.[17]

Henry could not believe that Joseph would risk war, but, although negotiations continued, Austrian troop movements began to confirm Frederick's predictions. In April, Joseph tried to buy Frederick's acquiescence by promising to condone Prussian annexation of Ansbach and Bayreuth on the death of their ruler. Frederick rejected Joseph's proposals as irrelevant to the Bavarian issue. By the end of June he was convinced that the Austrians were simply playing for time, and accordingly on 5 July Prussian troops invaded Bohemia. A week later Maria Theresa opened negotiations with Berlin, behind Joseph's back: 'I am acting without informing the Emperor, and I beg that it remain a secret whether or not it succeeds. I desire to renew and conclude the negotiations hitherto directed by him, and, to my great regret, broken off. Baron Thugut has full powers from myself.'[18] The Thugut mission was a failure. Maria Theresa proposed to surrender all Bavarian territory if Prussia would renounce her claims to Bayreuth and Ansbach. Frederick retorted that he would inform France and Russia of Austria's obvious insincerity.

Frederick was as suspicious of Maria Theresa as he was of Kaunitz, and set little store by rumours of a rift between the Empress and Joseph. The rift was real enough. Joseph, who told his mother that 'it would be a hundred times better to yield after several defeats than before', was furious to hear of Thugut's negotiations. Maria Theresa replied to his anger with arguments that Metternich was to re-echo a generation later: 'We were a Great Power, but we are so no longer. We must bow our head, save at least the *débris*, and render the peoples who remain to us happier than they have been during my unfortunate reign.'[19]

Her realism triumphed. During the few months that remained of the 1778 campaigning season the rival armies avoided a pitched battle, though the Prussians suffered heavy losses from

[17] *Ibid.*, p. 89.   [18] *Ibid.*, p. 95.   [19] Cf. p. 337 below.

disease and desertion. Winter brought a fresh round of negotiations. France had stayed neutral, in spite of Frederick's appeal to
her as the guarantor of German liberties[20] and despite Joseph's
attempt to bribe her support with hints of compensation in
Flanders; but she agreed to mediate. Russia, who had little to
gain from supporting either side, was also ready to act as medi-
ator, and backed up her offer with a threat to make war on
Austria if hostilities did not cease. By the time that peace was
signed at Teschen in May 1779, France was embroiled in the
American war, so that Russian influence proved paramount.
The Bavarian succession passed to the Elector Palatine and his
heir; Austria's face was saved by the cession of thirty-four
square miles of Bavarian territory. France and Russia were the
guarantors of the settlement, so that Russia had now followed
France in gaining a voice in the affairs of the Empire.

The Second Turkish War, 1787-92

The War of the Bavarian Succession had prepared the way for
Catherine II's second major war against the Turks. Joseph II,
frustrated in his German ambitions, turned East. Within a few
months of Teschen, Catherine wrote to Joseph inviting him to
visit Russia. In May 1780 she met Joseph in Lithuania and
escorted him to Smolensk, from where he went on to visit
Moscow; in June he paid a state visit to St Petersburg. Maria
Theresa's death later in the year left Joseph with a free hand, and
by June 1781 Catherine and Joseph had privately promised to
support each other in the Near East. The specific proposals
formulated by Catherine in 1782 provided for the partition of
all Turkish territory in Europe.[21] Russia would take little in
outright annexation, but the Greek Empire, including Constantinople, was to be reserved for Catherine's second grandson,
significantly named Constantine. The agreement was never
signed, partly, it is said, because neither Habsburg Emperor nor
Russian Empress would concede precedence to the other, even
on paper. But Catherine felt sure enough of Austrian support

[20] Under the Peace of Westphalia (1648). See above, p. 24.
[21] See Marriott, *op. cit.*, p. 155.

to move against the Turks. Her objective was the Crimea.

By the Treaty of Kutchuk Kainardji[22] the Sultan had renounced his political suzerainty over the Tartars of the Crimea while retaining his religious supremacy. In 1783 Catherine resolved the contradiction by annexing the Crimea. Potemkin was put in charge of developing the new province. The fortified port of Sebastopol (within two days' sail of Constantinople) was the symbol of his success in strategic terms, though evidence on the economic development of the region is more equivocal. There was probably a good deal of window-dressing when Catherine took Joseph on a conducted tour of the province in 1787, but the Emperor seems to have been impressed.[23] The Sultan looked somewhat more sourly on Potemkin's pageantry, particularly as Catherine now demanded the cession of Georgia and Bessarabia to Russia and the establishment of hereditary Russian governors in Moldavia and Wallachia. In August 1787 Turkey declared war. The following February brought Joseph II to the aid of his new ally; but the Turks twice defeated Austrian troops under the personal command of the Emperor, and Joseph, leaving Loudon in charge, returned to Vienna to die. Austria's half-hearted help was more than offset by Gustavus III's menacing advance on St Petersburg.[24]

Catherine blamed William Pitt for Sweden's untimely aggression. She gave him too much credit. The Triple Alliance between England, Prussia and Holland in 1788 had been directed against French designs on the Channel ports rather than Russian designs on Constantinople. It was Prussia's new king, Frederick William II (1786-97), who was now most anxious to use the alliance to check Austria in the Balkans. Joseph II's death in 1790 made Prussian pressure more effective, and by the Convention of Reichenbach the new Emperor Leopold promised Frederick William to make peace with the Turks; he did so in 1791. Meanwhile Pitt's demands that Russia should also make peace and return Oczakov to the Turks found little support even in the English Parliament, where Burke applauded Russia's

---

[22] See above, p. 202.

[23] For a description of the tour see G. S. Thomson, *op. cit.*, pp. 190-93.

[24] See above, p. 168.

attack on a nation of 'destructive savages', while Fox supported her 'plans for raising her aggrandizement on the ruins of the Turkish Empire'.

Russia kept Oczakov. She advanced her frontier to the Dniester, while the annexation of the Crimea was recognized and the provisions of Kutchuk Kainardji confirmed. These terms were embodied in a 'treaty of perpetual peace', signed at Jassy in January 1792. It had taken Catherine almost thirty years to establish Russia firmly on the shores of the Black Sea, but her success was now unquestionable. In the four years that remained of her life, she sought solace in the destruction of Poland.

The Partitions of Poland

Stanislas Poniatowski, whom Russia and Prussia had imposed on the Poles in 1764 as King Stanislas Augustus,[25] tried to be an enlightened monarch. He patronized artists and men of letters, he built up a royal picture gallery and library, he corresponded with Madame Geoffrin[26] and imitated the French court. In contrast to Augustus III, he took a personal interest in adminis-tration and worked at his correspondence until late at night. But nothing could hide the fact that he was the prisoner of a con-stitution designed to frustrate royal initiative and, for that very reason, guaranteed by Russia and Prussia. Frederick the Great's poor opinion of the Poles is conveyed in his letter to d'Alembert in January 1772:

I pity philosophers who interest themselves in this people, so con-temptible in every way. Their only excuse is their ignorance. Poland has neither laws nor liberty; the government has degenerated into licence and anarchy; the nobility exercise the most cruel tyranny over their slaves. In a word, it is the worst government in Europe except that of the Turks.[27]

No doubt Frederick was trying to rationalize his desire for some Polish territory. There was nothing new in the idea of partition. It had been discussed as early as 1656 by Charles X of Sweden and the Great Elector. Frederick himself did not formally

[25] See above, p. 200.   [26] See below, p. 222.   [27] Gooch, *op. cit.*, p. 83.

propose it until 1769, but it seems probable that he regarded the constitutional arrangement of 1764 as likely to provoke internal disorder and so provide a pretext for territorial confiscation.

The Russian attitude was different. Catherine wanted a peaceful Poland, docile enough to follow Russia's lead. Russian troops remained in Poland, while the Russian ambassador Repnin behaved like a 'Roman proconsul in the period of subjugation of a province after the Punic Wars'.[28] But Repnin overplayed his hand. The members of the Diet needed little persuasion to defend the *liberum veto*,[29] which they saw as a guarantee of their own privileges, but they resisted the Russian demand for the restoration of rights to the dissident religious minorities, Protestant and Orthodox. Frederick was prepared to champion the Protestant cause when opportunity offered, but he seems to have sensed the dangers of direct intervention. Not so Catherine, who within a month of her coronation had reminded her envoy in Warsaw that the rights of the Orthodox minority in Poland must be protected. In 1768 Repnin bullied the Polish Diet into promising the Dissidents not only freedom of worship but equality of civil rights, including access to the Diet, the Senate, the bench and the public service. This was to grant more toleration than Dissenters enjoyed in eighteenth-century England.

Polish resistance to Russia's interference in religious matters embroiled Catherine in war with the Turks.[30] The war resulted in the First Partition of Poland. Frederick's purpose in suggesting partition was chiefly to prevent Russia and Austria outbidding one another in the Balkans, but he was also alive to the attractions of Polish territory from the Prussian point of view. The acquisition of West Prussia would close the gap between eastern Pomerania and East Prussia, and so unite the whole of Prussia with the central Brandenburg bloc; and even if Danzig were denied him, Elbing would provide a useful port. Russia was at first less interested in partition: in reply to Frederick's overtures in 1769, Panin hinted that if Prussia and Austria would assist Russian expansion in the Balkans, Catherine would not object

---

[28] Ed. Reddaway, *The Cambridge History of Poland*, Cambridge 1941, p. 117.
[29] See above, p. 29.
[30] See above, p. 201.

to Prussian compensation in Poland. In January 1771, however, when Frederick's brother Henry was in St Petersburg still trying to sell the partition project, the Austrians changed the situation by seizing Zips, a small enclave of Polish territory on the northern border of Hungary. Frederick was quick to regard this as a precedent for general partition. As he wrote to Count Solms, Prussian ambassador in St Petersburg, there was 'no longer any question of preserving Poland intact'.

But Prussia could not move without Russia, and it was not until the end of 1771 that Catherine agreed to send troops to Poland. The Russian decision made Frederick optimistic. He told Henry that he now hoped to get Danzig:

If we do not get it now we never shall. Now is the moment to conclude our treaties with Russia since Austrian armaments are exercising their minds. The arrival of fifty thousand Russians in Poland will probably make the Austrians more circumspect and therefore diminish Russia's apprehensions. I have added to the draft convention that each party should occupy his sphere directly the treaty is signed in order that, having our bird in the hand, we run no risks, possession being as a rule the deciding factor in such acquisitions.[31]

In January 1772 Catherine and Frederick formally agreed on partition. Austria alone held back, embarrassed by her recent treaty with the Turks.[32] Only when it became clear that Austria could not expect territorial compensation elsewhere and that Prussia and Russia would if necessary act without her could Kaunitz and Joseph II at last succeed in overcoming Maria Theresa's scruples.

The First Treaty of Partition, signed at St Petersburg in August 1772 'in the name of the Most Sacred Trinity', gave Catherine White Russia with two million inhabitants, while the Habsburg share (Zips and Galicia) was scarcely less in area. Frederick did not get Thorn or Danzig, but he received the rest of West Prussia with its 600,000 inhabitants and a strategic importance out of all proportion to its size. Frederick had visited his new territory in June 1772, while the negotiations were still in progress. He wrote to Henry:

[31] Gooch, *op. cit.*, p. 81.   [32] See above, p. 202.

The Partitions of Poland, 1772–95

It is an excellent and most advantageous acquisition both politically and financially, but, to incur less envy, I tell people I saw nothing but sand, fir-trees, heath and Jews. True, it will mean a lot of work, for I imagine Canada is as well policed as this Pomerelia. No order; no system; the towns are in a deplorable condition. For instance, Culm should have 800 houses; only 100 are standing, and their inmates are Jews or monks. We come off best from a commercial point of view. We become the masters of all Poland's products and imports which are considerable. The greatest score is that our control of the wheat trade will always save us from famine.[33]

[33] Gooch, *op. cit.*, p. 84.

The inhabitants of West Prussia were probably better off under their new ruler, but for Stanislas Augustus the First Partition was a disaster. Although he bravely declared, 'I do not consider the nation as being near its fall, I rather consider it as a nation not yet mature', his kingdom had lost nearly five million subjects. It had also lost its natural frontier in the south (the Carpathians) and the salt mines of Galicia, while the value of Danzig was impaired now that the lower Vistula was in Prussian hands. The establishment of a Permanent Council of thirty-six members made government more effective in the interval between Diets, but the constitution was guaranteed by the three despoiling powers, and the Russian ambassador remained the real ruler of Poland. The period between the First and Second Partitions nevertheless brought signs of greater prosperity to Poland: the population increased by at least a million, the royal revenue rapidly doubled, and an effective army of 18,000 was built up. The disciples of the Enlightenment were heard if not heeded: an Educational Commission was established in 1773, a university was founded at Vilna, Rousseau wrote *A New Education for Poland* and *Considerations on the Government of Poland*, the Diet of 1778 authorized the codification of Polish laws (though the next Diet rejected it), while Stanislas Staszic, the friend of Buffon, called on the 1788 Diet to reform the constitution before it was too late.

By the time the Diet of 1788 was summoned, Russia and Turkey were again at war.[34] The Polish king favoured an alliance with Russia, but the Patriot party proved too strong, and in October 1788 the Diet, encouraged by the Prussian envoy, authorized the raising of a Polish army of 100,000 and the negotiation of an alliance with Prussia. The treaty was not signed until March 1790: Danzig and Thorn were promised to Prussia in return for a favourable commercial treaty and 18,000 Prussian troops. Within four months Frederick had abandoned the Poles by concluding with Austria the Convention of Reichenbach.[35] Meanwhile the 1788 Diet had been revising the Polish constitution. By the end of 1790 it had abolished the *liberum veto* and excluded landless nobles from the regional assemblies;

[34] See above, p. 207.   [35] See above, p. 207.

in 1791, through the King's initiative, there emerged the Constitution of the Third of May.[36] The privileges of the nobles were not disturbed, but a hereditary monarchy was provided for and the right of the King to control the army, veto legislation and appoint his ministers was established. Burghers of the royal cities were to be represented in the Diet, which was to meet every two years, and religious toleration was guaranteed. It was a constitution in the spirit of Montesquieu.

The Diet had prefaced its work with an expression of its desire 'to make use of the present juncture in Europe and of that moment of impending catastrophe which has restored us to ourselves, free from the shameful commands of foreign violence'.[37] Such exultation was somewhat premature. In 1792 Catherine made peace with the Turks at Jassy.[38] In May she imposed on the leading members of the Polish opposition (the so-called Targowica Confederation) an agreement nullifying the 1791 constitution. Russian armies invaded Poland to support the men of Targowica, and by July Stanislas had had to submit. In September the Austro-Prussian offensive against France was repulsed at Valmy, and Prussia demanded compensation in Poland as the price of remaining Austria's ally. Thus Prussia and Russia were able to divide the spoils between them. By the Second Partition Treaty of January 1793, Prussia took Danzig, Posen, Thorn and the upper Vistula, while Russia moved her frontier some 200 miles further west.

Poland, deprived of the 1791 constitution, was now reduced to some 80,000 square miles and about four million people. In March 1794 the Patriots rose in desperate protest under Kosciuszko, a general who had fought in the American War of Independence and who in January 1793 had secured a promise of French help in the cause of Polish liberty. By the spring of 1794, however, the French were too preoccupied in the west, and Kosciuszko had to rely on an appeal to the Polish peasantry and to the remnants of the Polish army. In April he managed to defeat a Russian army near Cracow, but the intervention of the

---

[36] Extracts are printed in R. R. Palmer, *The Age of the Democratic Revolution*, vol. I, Oxford 1959, p. 513.
[37] *Cambridge History of Poland*, p. 133.   [38] See above, p. 208.

Prussians made ultimate failure inevitable. While the Prussian army took Cracow, the Russians defeated and captured Kosciuszko at Maciejowice; and in November Warsaw capitulated.

In July 1794 Catherine had written to Vienna that 'the moment has arrived when the three neighbouring courts ought to occupy themselves not only with extinguishing, to its smallest spark, the fire which has burst out in their neighbourhood, but also to prevent once for all the possibility of its flaring up anew from the ashes'.[39] Her purpose was achieved in January 1795 when an Austro-Russian convention divided Poland without consulting Prussia. It looked for a moment as if Prussia might fight, but the rival claims had been reconciled by the end of the year. Prussia gained Warsaw and the surrounding district, Austria took the rest of Galicia including Cracow and Lublin, while Russia now embraced the Baltic duchy of Kurland and all that was left of Lithuania. Apart from the brief interlude of Napoleon's Grand Duchy,[40] Poland would not reappear as a sovereign state until 1919.

Frederick the Great had written that the First Partition 'so far from ending the jealousy between the Powers gave it something to feed on. Russia wanted to expand towards Europe, Prussia to consolidate, Austria to swell out so as not to be stifled. The "civilizing" mission of Russia, the "historical" mission of Austria and the "political" mission of Prussia, all led to annexation and conquest.'[41] These missions would continue to conflict. The disappearance of Poland meant that the three rival powers were now next-door neighbours. The Partitions had provided a peaceful solution to eighteenth-century disputes only at the expense of posing new problems for the nineteenth century.

[39] *Cambridge History of Poland*, p. 173.   [40] See below, p. 31.
[41] Quoted in R. M. Rayner, *European History, 1648-1789*, Longmans 1949, p. 319.

V

THE *ANCIEN RÉGIME*
IN FRANCE

Enlightened Absolutism suffered its most conspicuous setback in the France of the *philosophes*. Theoretically it was here that it had the greatest chance of success, for the machinery of Louis XIV's absolutism was handed down intact to his successors. But Louis XV and Louis XVI were not men of the same stamp as Frederick the Great or Joseph II, and it was in the country in which the nobles had suffered their heaviest defeat in the seventeenth century that they achieved their greatest victory in the eighteenth. It is true that the French aristocracy, by their very victory, provoked the Revolution and so ensured their ultimate destruction, but this outcome seemed much less inevitable to eighteenth-century observers than it seems to modern historians. The Revolution, which had been talked about for half a century, was unexpected when it came.

It occurred in the most prosperous country on the continent. While Versailles was attacked by the *philosophes* as the symbol of unenlightened government, it was admired by foreign authors and artists as the cultural centre of Europe. London and Washington might provide the political models for the new age, but Paris still set the tone in aesthetic matters. French literary and artistic achievements in the eighteenth century, besides being important in their own right, are of interest to the historian as an index of social change. Fashions in both literature and art became less aristocratic and more *bourgeois*, and, although the monopoly of the privileged orders in matters of taste was scarcely shaken, it had at least been challenged even before the Third Estate made its bid for political power.

15

The Age of Louis XV

The Court

When Louis XIV at length died in 1715, amid scenes of considerable jubilation,[1] he was succeeded by his great-grandson, aged
five. The Dauphin had died in 1711, '*sans vice ni vertu*', to quote
Saint-Simon's acid phrase. His son, the popular Duc de Bourgogne, pupil of Fénelon, died within the year, together with his
wife and elder son. 'We have been burying France,' commented
Saint-Simon sadly.

Philip, Duc d'Orléans, who, in defiance of Louis XIV's will,[2]
ruled as regent from 1715 to 1723, was perhaps the closest
approximation to an enlightened despot that eighteenth-century
France produced. Notorious for his mistresses, his drunkenness,
his atheism, and his licentious talk, he nevertheless had com-
pensating qualities. His mother at least spoke well of him: 'He
has the best intentions, and he loves his country more than his
life. He works all day and wears himself out. He would like to
see everyone happy. For tradition he cares nothing.'[3] He
succeeded in retaining the friendship of Saint Simon, and was
described by Duclos as possessing 'a fair acquaintance with
painting and music, chemistry and mechanics'.

It was at Saint-Simon's instigation that Orleans tried to bring
the nobles back into politics: seven councils composed of nobles
were created, and the president of each attended the meetings
of the Council of Regency. But the experiment was not a
success, and within three years most of the councils were replaced by secretaries of state. It was the last attempt under the
ancien régime to bring the nobles back into government until,

[1] For a description see G. P. Gooch, *Louis XV*, Longmans 1956, p. 30.
[2] This had provided for a Regency Council of fourteen and had entrusted the education of the heir and the command of the household troops to the Duc de Maine, Louis
XIV's illegitimate son.
[3] Gooch, *op. cit.*, p. 32.

seventy years later, the nobles themselves made a bid for political power and so precipitated the Revolution.[4]

In 1723 Louis XV came of age, and in the same year both the Regent and the dissolute Abbé Dubois, who had controlled the successful diplomacy of the Regency,[5] died. For the next three years the Duc de Bourbon, thirty-one-year-old great-grandson of the Duc de Condé, ostensibly presided over France's fortunes. 'So M. le Duc is First Minister,' recorded Barbier in his journal. 'He is very limited, knows nothing, loves nothing but pleasure and sport.' In his tastes at least the Duke resembled his master. In April 1730 Barbier was to record: 'Today the King went for six weeks to Fontainebleau to hunt stags, which is his only occupation.'

Louis was physically precocious and by the time he was fifteen was ready for marriage. Like Louis XIII and Louis XIV before him, he was engaged to his Spanish cousin, but, since the Infanta was only seven, the wedding was postponed for ten years. Louis, however, was eager for a wife, and France was anxious for an heir, so that a search was made for a more suitable consort. The outcome surprised Europe: in 1725 Louis married Maria Leszczynska, daughter of the ex-king of Poland.[6] This astonishing choice had been contrived by Madame de Prie, the Duc de Bourbon's mistress, but when the incautious pair tried to exploit their advantage, they were exiled from court. It was as a result of their disgrace that in 1726 Fleury became First Minister and for the next fourteen years pursued his Walpolean policy of peace and retrenchment.[7]

Meanwhile the new Queen applied herself to the task of providing France with an heir. Her first two children were boys, though the second son, born in 1730, survived for only three years. Thereafter she bore only daughters – five between 1732 and 1737. The King showed no marked interest in his family, and, by the time his third daughter was born, Louis had taken his first mistress, Madame de Mailly, eldest daughter of the Marquis de Nesle. For the next ten years the de Nesle family provided a succession of royal favourites: at least two of Madame

---

4 See Chapter 18 below.   5 See above, p. 17.
6 See above, p. 35.   7 See below, p. 243.

218

de Mailly's three sisters subsequently became the King's mistress. Their rule was interrupted by the King's sudden illness at Metz in 1744 when his priests persuaded him to promise amendment of life. Louis quickly recovered sufficiently to retract his confession; but Madame de Châteauroux, the last and worst of the de Nesle mistresses, was now struck down, probably with pneumonia though contemporaries said poison, and died at the age of twenty-seven.

The stage was now set for the entry of the favourite who was to dominate the Versailles scene for nearly twenty years. Jeanne Poisson, Madame d'Étioles since her marriage in 1741, secured her place in the King's affections (he had already noticed her when out hunting) at the masked ball given in honour of the Dauphin's marriage in February 1745. In April she began to appear at small supper parties given by the King; in September she was given an apartment at Versailles and presented to the Queen. Madame de Pompadour, as she quickly became, was the most painted woman of her day, and it is from her portraits that we can capture something of the magic she exercised over her contemporaries. Boucher's[8] portrait in the National Gallery of Scotland at Edinburgh shows her with an open book on her lap and a writing-table at her side, while La Tour's[9] pastel in the Louvre depicts her with a musical score in her hand, and at her elbow a globe and a collection of books that includes volume III of *Spirit of Laws*, volume IV of the *Encyclopaedia*, and a portfolio containing 'The Engraved Works of Madame de Pompadour'.[10]

The new favourite had scarcely settled at Versailles before she became the patron of artists and writers. Her numerous houses were exquisitely decorated and furnished, and at her death she left, besides a library of 3,525 volumes, so many *objets d'art* that the inventory took two lawyers more than a year to compile. The *philosophes*[11] enjoyed her patronage. Voltaire and Montesquieu had been her guests in earlier days, and soon after her arrival at Versailles she commissioned Voltaire to write an

[8] See below, p. 227.   [9] See below, p. 228.
[10] Reproduced in Edmond and Jules de Goncourt, *French XVIII Century Painters*, Phaidon 1957, plate 47.
[11] See Chapter 5 above.

opera in celebration of the victory of Fontenoy. Quesnay, the physiocrat,[12] was her physician and his *Tableau économique* (1758) was printed at the royal press. It was Quesnay who introduced Buffon the naturalist to Madame de Pompadour, and so well did Buffon get on with the King, who was a great lover of animals, that he stopped contributing to the *Encyclopaedia* rather than forfeit Louis' friendship. Madame de Pompadour did her best to support the Encyclopaedists: she secured a pension for d'Alembert and persuaded the King to lift the ban on the private (though not the public) sale of the *Encyclopaedia*.

The miniature theatre at Versailles was Madame de Pompadour's creation. The *Théâtre des Petits Cabinets*, with seats for fourteen spectators, was built in one of the galleries of the palace and decorated by Boucher. Each play was carefully rehearsed, and the first of a list of ten rules devised by the Favourite laid down that 'nobody may join the society who is not an experienced actor'. The first performance, Molière's *Tartuffe* in January 1747, was well received, and a series of plays followed in which Madame de Pompadour took the leading female part. The seal of success was set on the venture when the Queen herself was persuaded to attend, and during its five years of existence the theatre saw 122 performances of sixty-one plays, operas and ballets.

The death of Madame de Pompadour in 1764 left Louis, in his fifties, to seek consolation among the young girls of the *Parc aux Cerfs* whom Madame de Pompadour had so thoughtfully procured for him. After the Queen's death in 1768 the last of the royal favourites was installed at Versailles. Madame du Barry won over most of the court, was saluted in verse by Voltaire and painted by Drouais.[13] She was fond of jewels and of gambling, she was not insensitive to the *objets d'art* which she found around her, and she learned to appreciate Shakespeare. But she was no second Pompadour, and an air of dull domesticity characterized the last five years of Louis' life. Choiseul fell foul of the new favourite and was dismissed, but political questions did not much

[12] See above, p. 78.
[13] Reproduced in Gooch, *op. cit.*, facing p. 224.

220

obtrude themselves into the royal bedchamber. *Après moi le déluge* may not have been Louis XV's own phrase, but it aptly epitomizes the attitude of his last years.

The 'Salons'

For all the patronage accorded to artists and writers by Madame de Pompadour, the *salons* rather than the court remained the arbiters of taste and the channels of literary influence. The *salon* system had originated in the seventeenth century with the Marquise de Rambouillet, whose 'Blue Room' in the rue Saint Thomas du Louvre provided a forum where nobles and men of letters met on a footing of complete equality, and women conversed on equal terms with men. From the beginning great stress was laid upon propriety of demeanour and diction, so that the marquise earned the enviable reputation of having 'taught good manners to a whole generation'.

In the eighteenth century the tradition was carried on by Madame de Lambert in her rooms in the Hôtel Colbert. Her guests met at noon and, after a light luncheon, read their manuscripts to one another until suppertime. Card games and discussion of politics were forbidden, solemnity was a solecism, preciosity was the order of the day. Archaisms, latinisms and colloquialisms were banished from the vocabulary of the *salons* to such an extent that Fénelon accused them of impoverishing the language. Even the progressive Mademoiselle de Lespinasse was shocked when Buffon used a word that did not occur in Racine. Diderot defended the *salons* on the grounds that 'women accustom us to discuss with charm and clarity the driest and thorniest subjects. We talk to them unceasingly; we wish them to listen; we are afraid of tiring or boring them; hence we develop a particular method of explaining ourselves easily and this passses from conversation into style'. More recently the activities of the *salons* have been described less charitably as 'a method of wasting time in perfect French'.[14]

It was not until the sixties that the *philosophes* began to

[14] Kingsley Martin, *French Liberal Thought in the Eighteenth Century*, Turnstile Press 1954, p. 106.

dominate the *salons* and to impart a more philosophical flavour to their discussions. Madame Geoffrin, who on Mondays held dinners where artists could meet patrons and clients, on Wednesdays held literary dinners attended by most of the *philosophes* – though not Voltaire or Montesquieu. Hume was a frequent guest; Gustavus III of Sweden and Joseph II of Austria called on Madame Geoffrin, though she had never been presented at Versailles; her correspondents included Catherine II of Russia and Maria Theresa. Madame Geoffrin's financial support helped to keep the *Encyclopaedia* going during Diderot's darkest days, and, as mother of the Encyclopaedists, she set her own mark upon the Age of Reason. Favourable reception in the *salons* was essential for the success of any new book or play, and it was in the *salons* that many aspiring academicians won their chairs. It was through Madame du Deffand, Madame Geoffrin's greatest rival, that d'Alembert gained his secretaryship of the Academy, though this did not prevent him from deserting her for the *salon* established by Mademoiselle de Lespinasse, his lover and Madame du Deffand's niece.

The Lespinasse *salon* was more to the taste of the *philosophes*, and when Madame du Deffand died in 1780 the traditional *salon* as a school of manners died with her. Henceforth the new fashion was set by Baron d'Holbach's dinner parties, which attracted those who were seldom seen in the *salons*: Turgot, and Condorcet, Hume, Wilkes, Shelburne, Garrick, Franklin and Priestley, all enjoyed the hospitality of d'Holbach's house, which soon became known as the 'Café de l'Europe'. It was here that Rousseau revealed just how ill at ease he was in the company of the other *philosophes*. One day when d'Holbach's circle was discussing the defects of the Deity, Rousseau burst out: 'If it is a fault to allow evil to be spoken of an absent friend, it is a crime to allow anyone to speak evil of his God who is present. And for my part gentlemen, I believe in God.'[15] In the violence of his reaction against the flippancy and social artificiality of the *salon*, Rousseau spoke with the sentimental voice of the age of Romanticism. This was not, however, the language of the age of Louis XV.

[15] *Ibid.*, p. 111.

Literature

The preciosity of the *salons* pervaded the literature of the period. In poetry the reverence paid to the *style noble*, with its studied avoidance of all common words, led to such extravagant euphemisms as *feuilles de Canton* for tea and *grains du Levant* for coffee. Voltaire censured Corneille for having used expressions too colloquial for tragedy, and, in a letter to the future Frederick the Great in 1737, gave examples of the different usages demanded by poetry and prose.[16] The conventions of the *salons* were reinforced by the French Academy which laid down strict rules not only for vocabulary but also for metre.

Voltaire himself acquired a considerable reputation as a poet among his contemporaries, but whereas they hailed his *Henriade* as a great epic poem and applauded the poetry of his tragedies, posterity is inclined to notice only his 'Poem on the Lisbon Disaster':

> . . . Aux cris demi-formés de leurs voix expirantes,
> Au spectacle effrayant de leurs cendres fumantes,
> Direz-vous: 'C'est l'effet des éternelles lois,
> Qui d'un Dieu libre et bon nécessitent le choix?'
> Direz-vous, en voyant cet amas de victimes:
> 'Dieu s'est vengé, leur mort est le prix de leurs crimes?'
> Quel crime, quelle faute ont commis ces enfants
> Sur le sein maternel écrasés et sanglants?
> Lisbonne qui n'est plus eut-elle plus de vices
> Que Londres, que Paris, plongés dans les délices?
> Lisbonne est abîmée, et l'on danse à Paris. . . .

The poetic conventions of the eighteenth century were less suited to epic than to epigram, to those transient, topical and malicious exercises in verse that afforded so much amusement to the Paris *salons*.[17] Later in the century, however, there was a gradual retreat from artificiality. In the preface to his translation of the *Georgics* in 1770, Abbé Delille defended a poetry devoted to agrarian scenes, and his own poem *Les Jardins* (1782)

---

[16] J. Lough, *An Introduction to Eighteenth-century France*, Longmans 1960, p. 280.
[17] Examples are given in Lough, *op. cit.*, pp. 295–97.

did not hesitate to call a cow *une vache* – a word that in Voltaire's eyes was fit only for prose. In Saint-Lambert's *Saisons*, published in the late 1760s, the poet went so far as to devote more than a dozen lines to celebrating the agricultural improvements of 'Turnip Townshend'. This new interest in rural life no doubt owed something to Rousseau, who has been described as the only poet of eighteenth-century France, though he wrote in prose. But even Saint-Lambert shrank from introducing the peasants into his poetry: he turned rather to the smaller provincial noblemen, who, he claimed, had been neglected by the poets – those nobles who 'live in small commodious houses and cultivate several fields'. The Romantics' enthusiasm for the rustic was as yet only foreshadowed.

The novels of the period also showed signs of some weakening of aristocratic dominance. As early as 1734, when Marivaux published the second part of his novel *The Life of Marianne*, he sneered at the snobbishness of his readers; but Marivaux needed his public, and even if his heroes and heroines *started* life as peasants or apprentices, they rose to the ranks of the wealthy by the end. Lesage's *Gil Blas* was criticized for displaying a lack of knowledge of the upper classes, while in Madame Riccoboni's French adaptation of Fielding's *Amelia* the heroine's penniless young officer was transformed into a son of the aristocracy, while Sergeant Atkinson, his onetime orderly, became a lieutenant. That such an adaptation should have been made at all is an indication not only of the taste of the novel-reading public but also of its size. But it was Rousseau[18] who produced the bestseller of the century: *La Nouvelle Héloïse* (1762), a simple, sentimental love story, enjoyed a vogue that the modern reader finds inexplicable. Even Arthur Wellesley, the future Duke of Wellington, took a copy with him to India in 1796.

The hero in *La Nouvelle Héloïse* remarks, on his visit to Paris, that contemporary comedy confines itself to reproducing 'the conversations of about a hundred Paris houses', in spite of the fact that there lived in the city 'five or six hundred thousand souls who are never dealt with on the stage'. The theatre, he complains, seems able to depict men only when they are dressed

[18] See above, p. 85.

in gold brocade. Rousseau's complaint that tragedy treated subjects too remote from the experience of the man-in-the-street was reinforced by Beaumarchais (1732–99) when he argued, in an essay on serious drama in 1767, that the insistence of dramatists in choosing their tragic heroes from the ranks of royalty merely diminished the impact of the tragedy on the ordinary spectator. Before turning to write his more famous comedies, Beaumarchais wrote two *drames, Eugénie* and *The Two Friends*. The *drame*, a new *genre* defended by Diderot, was meant to occupy a place midway between tragedy and comedy, and to depict characters and situations closer to the experience of everyday. It was, said Diderot, a 'picture of the misfortunes that surround us', while Beaumarchais claimed that his second *drame*, dealing with the commercial life of Lyons, was intended 'to honour people of the third estate'.

The third estate figured equally prominently in Beaumarchais' comedies. Molière had employed the device of the 'knowing servant', the man of the people who outwits his master; but Molière's masters were *bourgeois*, and therefore fair game in an aristocratic society, while Beaumarchais' servant won his triumphs at the expense of the aristocrats themselves. *The Marriage of Figaro*, completed in 1778 but not staged until 1784 because of censorship troubles, voiced such subversive views as: 'Parce que vous êtes un grand Seigneur, vous vous croyez un grand génie! . . . Noblesse, fortune, un rang, des places: tout cela rend si fier! Qu'avez-vous fait pour tant de biens? Vous vous êtes donné la peine de naître, et rien de plus.'[19] The *bourgeoisie* applauded: at a time when a Paris play that attracted 15,000 to 20,000 spectators was regarded as a success, *The Marriage of Figaro* drew nearly 100,000. (In 1775 Beaumarchais' *The Barber of Seville* had attracted 24,000.) The survival of these *bourgeois* comedies was assured when they were turned into operas: Mozart's *Figaro* was completed in 1786, while Rossini's version of *The Barber of Seville*, first performed in Rome in 1816, marked the opening of the era of Italian grand opera.

[19] Act V Scene 3. Even Joseph II would not allow the play to be performed in Vienna until this passage was omitted.

Painting

The influence of Italy persisted in painting, but Italian artists no longer set the European fashion as they had done in the sixteenth and seventeenth centuries. Venice rather than Rome was now the artistic capital of Italy, and it was Venetian artists who visited England in the second decade of the eighteenth century to embellish the Whig country houses and to compete (unsuccessfully) for the commission to decorate the dome of St Paul's.[20] Rome continued to attract foreign artists, but they came to learn not from living Italian masters but from the masterpieces of the past. In 1677 Louis XIV had founded an Academy of Fine Arts in Rome, to which French artists, chosen by competition, were sent to study at state expense.

Watteau (1684–1721), the greatest artist of the Age of Louis XV, did not visit Rome, however; he encountered Italy at second hand through the collection of the French connoisseur Crozat, in whose house he stayed for a time. Watteau's works reflect both Italian and Flemish influences (he was Flemish by birth), but they also exhibit a refinement of spirit that is wholly French: battles are depicted without bloodshed and war is reduced to the art of 'flirting between cannon shots and killing between drinks'. The Wallace Collection in London is the best visual commentary on Watteau, but the Goncourts, writing in the 1850s, have come closest to capturing the essence of Watteau in words:

Contemplate them as they sit beneath the trees, magnetic spirits garmented in satin, clothed and christened by the poets. Linda and Gulboé, Hero and Rosaline, Viola and Olivia, and all the heroines of *As You Like It* are present here. And flower-girls pass gently from one to another, decorating with blossoms the dresses and the dark clusters of curls knotted at the top of the head. The only noise is that of the games of little children with large black eyes who patter about like birds at the feet of the lovers – miniature genii tossed by the poet on to the threshold of this dream. It is a dream in which there is nothing to do but listen to one's heart and leave free

[20] In 1715 the commission was awarded to Sir James Thornhill (1676–1734).

utterance to one's mood; to wait for refreshments to be brought, to let the sun move and the world go by; and suffer little dogs, who never bark, to be teased by little girls.[21]

If Watteau set the fashion for a century, the more substantial style of Boucher (1703–70) was perhaps more typical of the taste of Louis XV's court. If Watteau's figures are ethereal, Boucher's are voluptuous. If Watteau's landscapes are a mixture of natural and operatic scenery, Boucher's portray a nature that is picturesque but tumultuous: moss-covered marble ruins, thatched roofs sprouting flowers, mill wheels, dovecotes, and all the confusion of rustic objects that the eighteenth century, in its more romantic moments, came to love. Boucher was nothing if not versatile: he was the first French artist to make drawing an art in its own right and a source of profit to the artist, but he could also paint on a grandiose scale. In 1753 he exhibited the large canvases 'Sunrise' and 'Sunset'. They were bought by Madame de Pompadour whose patronage ensured the permanence of Boucher's fame. As early as 1747 she had placed his 'Vulcan's Forge' in Louis XV's bedroom at Marly, and it was Boucher who was most frequently commissioned to paint her portrait. In 1765, after the Favourite's death, Boucher was appointed to succeed Vanloo as First Court Painter.

Diderot was almost the only influential critic to condemn Boucher's art. In his view it was 'nothing but beauty spots, rouge, gew-gaws ... frivolous women, libidinous satyrs, bastard infants of Bacchus and Silenus.'[22] The editor of the *Encyclopaedia* demanded from art a moral or didactic purpose that was remote from the taste of the court. Yet even when the voluptuousness of Boucher's art is at its most full-blooded, it retains something of an anaemic appearance. This refinement of the grosser passions is even more marked in his pupil Fragonard (1732–1806). After five years at the Academy in Rome, Fragonard returned to secure associate membership of the Paris Academy[23] while he was still in his twenties. But he never troubled to become a full member of the Academy, and this apparent casualness is perhaps borne out by his customary

[21] Goncourt, *op. cit.*, p. 6.   [22] *Ibid.*, p. 84.
[23] Royal Academy of Fine Arts, founded 1648.

abbreviation of his signature to 'Frago'. He frequently worked with great speed: a portrait of M de la Breche painted in 1769 seems to have been done in an hour, while his landscapes have an air of impressionistic haste, as if the artist were struggling to capture the fleeting emotion of a moment. It is perhaps no accident that the theme of love, which dominates Fragonard's painting, should so often be represented at its most transient: 'The Clandestine Kiss', 'The Amorous Kiss', 'The Dangerous Kiss'. And even in 'Cupid Stealing a Nightgown',[24] the most sensuous of Fragonard's bedroom scenes, he avoids eroticism by sheer delicacy of treatment. Fragonard, like Watteau, depicted a dream world – a world of aristocratic love-making and nights at the opera.

With La Tour (1704–88) we return from the boudoir to the court. The greatest of the French portraitists, though working only in pastel, he began to exhibit in 1737. Seventeen-forty-five saw his first court portraits, and in the following year he secured full membership of the Academy. In 1753 he surprised Paris by exhibiting no fewer than eighteen portraits; in 1755 he exhibited only one. This was his famous portrait of Madame de Pompadour, which was intended to be his masterpiece, but fell short of some of his earlier work. Perhaps this was because he had begun to theorize too much. In his conversations with Diderot he deplored the tendency to 'exhort the young at too early an age to adorn nature, instead of urging them to render it with scrupulous accuracy'. But in his attempt to strike a balance between nature and art his own work lost much of its spontaneity. He spent his last years retouching his earlier works and spoiling them.

The most naturalistic of the great French masters was Chardin (1699–1779), who made his reputation as a painter of still life. A middle-class artist painting for the middle class, Chardin chose his subjects from the home and even the kitchen. Chardin did for painting what Beaumarchais did for the drama, and, like the subversive *Marriage of Figaro*,[25] his paintings were surprisingly fashionable. The Prince of Liechtenstein included four of Chardin's pictures in his gallery at Vienna, the Comte de

[24] Goncourt, *op. cit.*, plate 94.   [25] See above, p. 225.

228

Tessin bought four others for the Swedish royal palace at Drottningholm, while Catherine the Great commissioned works for the Hermitage.

With the notable exception of Chardin, the artists of Louis XV's reign depicted an aristocratic world. The air of wistful refinement and mild amusement – the Rococo mood – that pervades French painting from Watteau to Fragonard has much of the atmosphere of the *salon* about it. The painters portrayed what the *philosophes* lampooned: a society placidly awaiting the deluge.

Sculpture and Architecture

The Age of Louis XV saw the twilight of the Baroque. The style had evolved in the Rome of Bernini (1598–1680) and Borromini (1599–1667), though the Jesuit Church, the first of the Baroque churches of Rome, had been completed as early as 1584. A Baroque building was conceived as a cooperative enterprise in which painting and sculpture were treated as aspects of architecture, and the Italian artists of the eighteenth century remained superb interior decorators rather than painters or sculptors in their own right. G. B. Tiepolo (1696–1770) owed his fame to his frescoes, while if the townscapes of Canaletto (1697–1768) and Guardi (1712–93) represent a new departure in Italian painting, they also reflect a nostalgic veneration for the architectural triumphs of the high Baroque. In architecture, as in painting, the eighteenth century saw the subtle transmutation of the monumental Baroque into the more refined and whimsical Rococo. Preoccupied with decoration rather than with structure, Rococo was the style of the *salon* and the opera rather than of the piazza and the palace.

Eighteenth-century palaces were inspired by Paris rather than by Rome. In 1665 Bernini had visited Paris to submit his plans for the extension of the Louvre, which Colbert hoped to make the most majestic palace in Europe. The eventual discarding of Bernini's grand design was probably prompted by economic rather than aesthetic considerations, and it is probably misleading to regard the rejection as a symbol of the triumph of French classicism over Italian Baroque.[26] Versailles, completed in 1680, was Baroque in conception and scale, if more strictly classical in decorative detail, and it became the model for monarchs and princes throughout Europe. Marlborough's Blenheim; the Belvedere in Vienna completed in 1724 for Marlborough's ally, Prince Eugene of Savoy; Drottningholm, built near Stockholm in the last years of the seventeenth century with a French garden and French terraces; the Palazzo Reale at Caserta, begun in 1752 for Charles III of Naples – all these owed as much to Louis XIV's Versailles as to Bernini's Italian master-pieces.

But if Baroque and Rococo were the architectural styles of absolute monarchy, the classical orders were preferred by the architects of the Age of Reason. In England the Baroque had always been regarded as an alien style, the style of superstition, and most of the wealthy English gentry in the first half of the eighteenth century copied the Palladian[27] of Burlington House rather than the Baroque of Blenheim. The conventional eighteenth-century English portrait of more or less ordinary mortals was another indication of a preference for a more human scale. La Tour[28] was not perhaps the equal of Reynolds or Gainsborough, but in the sculptor Houdon (1740–1828) France was to find a portraitist of genius: his bust of Voltaire recalls the Renaissance cult of the individual rather than the Baroque devotion to grandeur. Not for nothing has the age of Louis XV been called 'the age of Louis XIV in undress'.

But the new artistic movement of the mid-eighteenth century harked back beyond the Renaissance. A novel enthusiasm for archaeology, stimulated by the writings of Winckelmann and the first systematic excavations at Herculaneum and Pompeii,[29] led to an intensified respect for antique sculpture and an attempt to use Greek architectural forms as it was thought the Greeks

[26] For a discussion of the importance of the Bernini visit see V. L. Tapié, *The Age of Grandeur*, Weidenfeld and Nicolson 1960, Chapter 6.

[27] Named after Andrea Palladio (1518–80), the Italian architect whose chief works are at Vicenza and Venice.

[28] See above, p. 228.

[29] J. J. Winckelmann's *Observations on the Architecture of the Ancients*, published in 1762, included an account of the Doric temples at Paestum near Naples. For the excavations at Herculaneum and Pompeii, see above, p. 156.

had themselves used them, and not merely as decorative features. This attempt to build in accordance with the structural and stylistic principles of the Greeks was well in tune with the thought of the Age of Reason. Symbolically enough the neo-classical style was chosen not only by Thomas Jefferson for his Virginian home, but also for most of the public buildings in the new city of Washington.

In Europe the style developed earlier but more slowly. James Stuart's Doric Temple built at Hagley Park in Worcestershire in the late 1750s and Soufflot's Sainte-Geneviève in Paris, started at the same time though not completed until 1790, may perhaps be regarded as the pioneers of neo-classicism. But this, the so-called *Louis seize* style, was really a transitional hybrid, and, although some of the Paris customs houses[30] designed by Ledoux in the 1780s were certainly classical, the triumph of neo-classicism in France had to wait for Napoleon. In sculpture the most important exponent of the new style was probably the Italian Canova (1757–1822), who sought to base his work on antique models and was hailed as the equal of the ancients by his contemporaries. But Canova's chief works also belong to the period of the Napoleonic Empire, when classical postures were also fashionable in politics.

The appearance of a Gothic revival at the same time as the classical revival was not merely a paradoxical coincidence. The two seemingly antithetical movements were related by the common impetus of archaeology. In 1742 Batty Langley introduced his *Gothic Architecture improved by Rules and Proportions In many Grand Designs* with the words:

The Rules by which the Ancient Buildings of this Kingdom were erected and adorned, having been entirely lost for many centuries, I have, therefore, for upwards of twenty years, in order to restore and publish them for the good of posterity, assiduously employed myself, as opportunities have happened, in making researches into many of the most ancient buildings now standing in this kingdom: and thence have extracted rules for forming such designs and

---

[30] Cf. above, p. 271. An illustration appears in H. R. Hitchcock, *Architecture: Nineteenth and Twentieth Centuries* (*The Pelican History of Art* series), Penguin 1958, plate 2a.

ornaments in the ancient mode which will be exceedingly beautiful in all parts of private building.[31]

Such aims would not have displeased the Encyclopaedists,[32] but Batty Langley's book did not live up to its preface: the work ends with designs for summer-houses. Horace Walpole's Strawberry Hill, built about 1770, was the first neo-Gothic building based on serious archaeological research. (The designs of fireplaces were copied from medieval tombs and altars.) Strawberry Hill looked like the mere whim of an eccentric, but it was the herald of the Romantic age in architecture – the age of Sir Walter Scott's medieval romances and of Sir George Gilbert Scott's St Pancras Station.[33]

If the Baroque style itself represents a struggle between classical rules and romantic restlessness, the simultaneous development of the neo-classical and the neo-Gothic, both owing much to the new enthusiasm for archaeology, reminds us of the tension between thought and feeling that makes the eighteenth century, in art as in politics and philosophy, so bewildering a complex of contradictions.

[31] Sir K. Clark, *The Gothic Revival*, Murray 1962, p. 52.

[32] Cf. D. Diderot's preface to the *Encyclopaedia*, p. 71 above.

[33] The Gothic Revival was not quite as parochial as this: in 1844 Gilbert Scott won the international competition for the Nikolaikirche in Hamburg, which he completed between 1845 and 1863.

16

Absolutism in Decline

The Economic Situation

The economic condition of France in 1715 was more grievous than in 1789. The indictment framed in Fénelon's famous letter to Louis XIV in 1691[1] was substantiated by the reports of *intendants* even before the Spanish Succession War broke out. Contemporaries were inclined to blame the Revocation of the Edict of Nantes, which, according to Saint Simon had 'depopulated a fourth of the realm, ruined its trade, weakened the country in all fields, . . . caused foreign states to flourish and wax wealthy at our expense'.[2] The Duke of Burgundy made a sounder diagnosis in 1710 when he contrasted the losses due to Huguenot emigration with the far greater damage caused by war. And of the thirty years between 1685 and 1715 France spent twenty-three at war.

Even after 1715, Frenchmen continued to speak of economic stagnation and even of decline. The nineteenth-century historian Michelet, who thought that the Revolution was the product of poverty, described eighteenth-century France as a nation 'organized so as to go on producing less and less, and paying more and more';[3] and although De Tocqueville wrote, 'Personally I do not believe in this continuous decline of France during the first half of the eighteenth century', he had no evidence to reinforce his scepticism. More recently E. Labrousse has revealed the pattern of prices under the *ancien régime*: between 1730 and 1770 agricultural prices rose, slowly at first,

---

[1] See above, p. 10.

[2] For a new assessment of the effect of the expulsion of the Huguenots on the French economy see W. C. Scoville, *The Persecution of the Huguenots and French Economic Development 1680–1720*, University of California Press 1960.

[3] The historiography of this dispute is traced in *The Economic Origins of the French Revolution*, 'Problems in European Civilization' series, D. C. Heath, Boston 1958.

but with spectacular speed after the end of the Seven Years War.[4] Labrousse's figures conceal regional and temporary fluctuations, and are scarcely proof of a prosperous peasantry since the peasant was seldom in a position to sell his produce. But the figures do suggest that the economy was far from stagnating, even if the *fall* in prices between 1778 and 1790 reflects the undeniably less prosperous decade immediately before the Revolution.

There is evidence of commercial, if not strictly industrial expansion in the size of towns: London was much larger than Paris, but Lyon and Marseille, each with 100,000 inhabitants, were larger than any English provincial town, while France had fifteen provincial towns of over 30,000 against England's eleven.[5] Urban prosperity was reflected in architecture as much as in population, and the second half of the century in particular saw a building boom. The establishment of a school of civil engineering in 1747 showed that the French government was scarcely behind the British in taking steps to improve the roads. Arthur Young, famous for his strictures on the condition of English roads, was full of praise for the main highways of France.

But if the cities were linked by good roads, village was still cut off from village, and bad communications could still result in pockets of local famine in a period of general plenty. More important, perhaps, was the fact that France was not a single fiscal unit. Colbert had created a customs union (the *Cinq grosses fermes*) comprising most of the northern provinces, but beyond these there were the *provinces réputés étrangères* (for example, Brittany, Flanders, Artois in the north, and Lyonnais, Provence and Languedoc in the south), each of which had separate tariff barriers, while the even more recently acquired provinces (the *provinces d'étranger effectif*) such as Alsace and Franche-Comté were treated like foreign territories from a customs point of view.

Although fiscal confusion might cramp internal trade, the prosperity of the ports bears witness to a flourishing external

---

[4] For a summary of Labrousse's findings see J. Lough, *An Introduction to Eighteenth-century France*, Longmans 1960, p.8.

[5] Lough, *op. cit.*, p. 64.

trade. In 1787 Arthur Young, while asserting the pre-eminence of London, admitted that Bordeaux did a larger trade than Liverpool, and in the following year he was mightily impressed by the evident prosperity of Le Havre and Nantes.[6] His contemporary, Arnould, estimated that between 1716 and 1788 the annual volume of France's trade with other European countries rose from 171 million to 656 million livres. The increase in colonial trade was even more striking, rising from some forty million to 204 million livres between 1716 and 1756. The Seven Years War deprived France of Canada and most of her trading posts in India,[7] but left her with her valuable islands in the West Indies, to which between four and five hundred French ships sailed each year.

The industrialization of France had to await the stimulus of the revolutionary wars, but the foundations had been laid by 1789. British inventions found their way to France and stimulated the development of the cotton industry, though by 1789 there were less than 1,000 spinning jennies in France compared with 20,000 in England. 'Iron-mad' Wilkinson's younger brother became manager of a new iron foundry on the Loire in 1777, and had a hand in the royal foundry (in which Louis XVI had some 300 shares) established near Le Creusot. The coal-mining industry, encouraged by the government's setting up of the School of Mines in 1783, greatly increased its output, but by 1789 this was still only about one-twentieth of the total British production.

In 1744 the government had issued a code to regulate the coal industry: all unworked coal was crown property, no new mine could be opened without the Controller-General's permission, and safety regulations were rigorously laid down – though less rigorously enforced. The spirit of Colbert[8] still guided government policy towards industry, and the intervention not only of inspectors responsible to the central Council of Commerce but also of the *intendants* themselves hindered rather than helped industrial development.

It was a Colbertian faith in government control that had led

---

[6] Young's remarks are quoted in Lough, *op. cit.*, pp. 74–75.
[7] See above, p. 196.   [8] See above, p. 5.

to the fiasco of John Law's 'system' under the Regency. The son of an Edinburgh goldsmith, he persuaded the French government that the clue to national wealth lay in the mobility of money, and that paper money was therefore preferable. In 1716 he was allowed to set up the *Banque Générale*, which in 1718 became a royal bank. In 1717 he secured a monopoly in the Louisiana trade for his Company of the West, which, renamed the Company of the Indies, soon absorbed the old Senegal, East Indies, China and Africa companies. In 1720 Law was appointed Controller-General, and his company, now formally united with his bank, took over not only the coveted right of farming taxes, but also responsibility for the national debt. Law's system suffered the same fate as the contemporary British South Sea Company: in 1720 the bubble burst, and in December Law finally fled to Brussels, a ruined man.

Perhaps it was the memory of 1720 that helped to keep France short of industrial capital. In England the industrialists provided much of their own capital by ploughing back their profits into the family firm. In France the profits of industry were more often devoted to purchasing administrative posts for sons or were invested in land or government stock so that the successful manufacturer could escape from the ranks of the *bourgeoisie* and 'live nobly'. Conversely, no eighteenth-century French aristocrat was prepared to turn industrialist in the manner of his English counterpart.

Yet in spite of such equivocal evidence, France seems to have prospered economically. Her economic growth was matched, and perhaps assisted, by the increase of her population from not more than nineteen millions in 1715 to twenty-five or twenty-six millions by 1789; although there had been a general European increase during this period,[9] Russia and the Austrian Empire were the only nations of comparable size before the Revolution. This rise in population certainly brought hardship to the peasantry and the urban working classes, but it did not necessarily create a penurious nation. The Revolution began not because of the misery of the peasants, but because of the poverty of the Crown.

[9] See above, p. 110.

The Administrative Machinery

The system of absolute monarchy bequeathed by Louis XIV to his successors had every appearance of unity and coherence. The King was the head of the legislative, executive and judicial powers, and all officials were theoretically appointed by and responsible to him. At the centre stood the Council, which was, in De Tocqueville's phrase, 'everything at once': it was the supreme court of justice, the highest administrative tribunal, and, subject to the King's approval, proposed laws and apportioned taxes. The functions of the Council were somewhat differentiated by division into five sections, home affairs, foreign affairs, commerce, justice and finance, but final decisions rested with the Council of State or King's Council which comprised the chief ministers of state and met two or three times a week in the King's presence. There was no titular prime minister: Fleury fulfilled the role in all but name, but after his death in 1743 Louis XV decided to be his own chief minister.

Louis XV lacked his great-grandfather's zest for administration, and in the absence of firm direction from the monarch the machinery of absolutism proved to be far more disjointed than it appeared. The edicts of the Council required the King's consent before they became law; they also required to be registered by the *parlements*, thirteen courts of appeal of which the oldest and most powerful was the *Parlement* of Paris. The *parlements*, formerly *bourgeois* in composition and the allies of the Crown in the struggle against the feudal nobility, had by the eighteenth century themselves become aristocratic in outlook. This was largely the fault of the Crown, since Louis XIV had raised money by selling judicial posts and with them the privilege of hereditary nobility, so that his successors were faced with judges whom they could not dismiss or even transfer, who bequeathed their posts to sons, nephews and sons-in-law, and who married into the ranks of the ancient nobility. The *parlements*, though theoretically subject to the King, had secured a position of virtual independence. In 1715 they had persuaded the Regent to recognize their right to present a remonstrance before registering a royal edict. Two years later the Paris *parlement* refused to register a financial edict until it had seen a statement of account, and its obstruction of further financial edicts led in 1720 to the exile of the whole Paris *parlement* to Pontoise, outside Paris. This was the only sanction that the Crown could impose on a recalcitrant *parlement*, though it could quash a refusal to register a royal edict by means of the cumbrous ceremony of a *lit de justice*, a special session at which the King presided.

If the judges were independent of the Crown, the King's ministers often acted without consulting him. In spite of the theoretical supremacy of the King's Council, the six ministers, chancellor, controller-general, and the secretaries of state for war, the navy, foreign affairs and the royal household, carried on an increasing volume of public business through their individual ministries. Although they often worked through the Council, they could short-circuit its deliberations by issuing a ministerial letter, which did not require the endorsement of the *parlements* and which had the effect of making the ministers independent not only of the council but also of each other. The Controller-General was responsible for raising revenue, but had no say in the expenditure of the other departments. Louis XV, unable to control his ministers in council, was content to control them indirectly through court intrigue: Choiseul was dismissed through the influence of Madame du Barry[10] while one controller-general after another was victim of the vested interests at Versailles. Louis XV had no fewer than eighteen foreign secretaries and fourteen controllers-general during the course of his reign.

In spite of this confusion at the centre, which led Sorel to speak of 'the most intolerable incoherence in despotism, irresolution in omnipotence, anarchy in centralization', administration at a provincial level was surprisingly energetic. In a quarter of the French provinces, the *pays d'état*, the traditional Estates, assemblies of nobles, clergy and commons corresponding to the provincial estates or diets elsewhere in Europe, preserved a nominal existence. But only in five provinces did they still meet, and only in Brittany and Languedoc did they enjoy any

[10] See above, p. 220.

administrative powers.[11] In the remaining three-quarters of the country, the provinces of the *pays d'élection*, the responsibility for local taxation and administration had been transferred by Richelieu to his newly-created *Intendants*. After their temporary eclipse during the *frondes*, the *intendants* greatly increased in importance until John Law was able to tell the Marquis d'Argenson that France was governed by thirty *intendants* 'on whom depend the happiness or the unhappiness, the plenty or the barrenness of these provinces'.

The *intendant* was the King's commissioner – the Crown never made the mistake of putting this office up for sale – and was supposed to refer all important matters to the Council. But while ministers changed with bewildering rapidity, the *intendant* remained in his *généralité* for fifteen, twenty or even thirty years, and this strengthened his hand in his dealings with his masters. The *intendant* was left with wide scope for individual initiative. While the Council fixed the provincial quotas, the *intendant* apportioned the *taille* among the parishes and supervised its collection, and controlled the recruitment of the militia. Outside the *pays d'état*, it was left to the *intendant* to supervise the maintenance of roads, to organize poor relief, to control the mounted police who were dispersed in small brigades throughout the country, and, in the towns, to nominate the members of the civic guard. The Council usually consulted the *intendants* before taking any major decision affecting their provinces, and in this way the advice of the *intendants* often shaped government policy.

The Council demanded constant information from the *intendants*. They were asked such searching questions as 'Do the nobles of your province prefer to remain at home or to live away?' In 1761 a circular addressed to all *intendants* asked for items of news suitable for inclusion in the state-controlled *Gazette de France*: 'You should send me an account of anything that happens in your generality of a nature to interest public curiosity, particularly anything connected with physical science, natural history and any singular or interesting facts.'[12]

[11] For a good summary see R. R. Palmer, *The Age of the Democratic Revolution*, vol. I., Oxford 1959, pp. 41–2.

[12] A. de Tocqueville, *L'Ancien Régime*, translated M. W. Patterson, Blackwell 1949, p. 70.

Of course, the *intendants* trod on too many toes to escape violent criticism, and their *bourgeois* origin made their intervention doubly resented: under Louis XVI all the *intendants* were noblemen, but very few of them belonged to the old nobility. The *intendant* was doubtless hampered by the fact that he had to work with countless minor officials who had purchased their posts, while the inadequate salary paid to the sub-delegate, the *intendant*'s deputy, meant that he was usually a man of meagre abilities. The *intendant* would often try to escape from these disadvantages by recruiting a team of experts (engineers, architects, medical advisers) thus creating a civil service in miniature.

Eighteenth-century France, in Gooch's phrase, 'possessed institutions but no constitution'.[13] The institutions were nevertheless capable of governing: in spite of confusion at the centre, and the survival of conflicting and overlapping jurisdictions at a local level, France had an administrative machinery that could function even without royal control. The revolutionaries captured the machine; they did not destroy it. The chief obstacle to its effective functioning under the *ancien régime* was a lack of money, and this was a problem that no *intendant*, however energetic, could hope to solve.

The 'Parlements' and Religion

The French *parlements*, though strikingly unlike the English Parliament, played a part in the events leading to revolution not unlike the role of the parliaments of the early Stuarts; and, like the parliaments of James I and Charles I, they clashed with the Crown over taxation and religion. Of the religious problems that had faced Louis XIV[14] only Jansenism survived to trouble his successors. The Jansenists,[15] a strict sect within the Catholic Church but regarded as heretics because of their emphasis on personal conversion and a theory of predestination, had apparently been extinguished in 1709 with the dispersal of the community of Port Royal, the Jansenist stronghold. But Louis

[13] G. P. Gooch, *Louis XV*, Longmans 1956, p. 76.
[14] See above, pp. 7–8.
[15] Named after Cornelius Jansen, Bishop of Ypres, d. 1638.

XIV had reopened the Jansenist controversy by attempting to close it for ever: in 1713 he persuaded the Pope to issue the Bull *Unigenitus* condemning 101 propositions from the *Réflexions* of the Jansenist Quesnel, published forty years earlier. The *parlements* did not love Jansenism, but they saw in the condemnation of Quesnel's ninety-first proposition – 'The fear of an unjust excommunication must never prevent us from doing our duty' – a fresh attack on Gallican liberties. In defending Jansenism, the *parlements* could thus claim to be more royalist than the King.

In 1720 the Regent clashed with the *parlements* over Jansenism as well as over taxation,[16] and ten years later Louis XV revived their resistence by employing a *lit de justice* to force the Paris *parlement* to register an edict requiring all clergy to accept the Bull *Unigenitus* without reservation. The *parlements* retorted by decreeing that all priests who had been suspended for Jansenist views should be reinstated. When in 1732 the Chancellor made clear to the judges that the King would not admit that Jansenism had anything to do with Gallican liberties, the *parlements* simply suspended the administration of justice. The episode ended when the King exiled 139 of the judges to the provinces where they stayed for two months.

In 1731, at the height of this particular crisis, miracles were reported at the tomb of François de Pâris, a pious Jansenist deacon. The alleged miracles of healing attracted so many spectators and gave Jansenism so much publicity at a time when the government least wanted it that the cemetery was closed. This attempt by absolute monarchy to curtail the activities of the Almighty did not escape satirical comment.

Further conflict was deferred until the 1750s when bishops began to instruct their clergy to refuse the sacraments to suspected Jansenists who could not produce a *billet de confession* certifying that they had confessed to a priest who accepted the Bull *Unigenitus*. The *parlements* were quick to intervene: they ordered the arrest of priests who had withheld the sacraments and even started proceedings against the Archbishop of Paris himself. The King's order, early in 1753, to stop all such

[16] See above, p. 238.

proceedings was met by a long and arrogant remonstrance. The King again exiled the Paris judges to the provinces. They were recalled after two months, but continued to take action against priests who withheld the sacraments from suspected Jansenists. In 1756 the outbreak of the Seven Years War persuaded the *parlements* to shift the focus of opposition from religion to taxation.[17]

The war had scarcely ended before the Paris *parlement* forced upon a reluctant government the dissolution of the Society of Jesus in France (1764). The Jesuits had been the bitterest foes of the Jansenists, and the dissolution seemed to mark the final triumph of the *parlements* in the *Unigenitus* controversy. But when in 1765 the Assembly of Clergy, by reviving the *billets de confession* issue, provoked the Paris *parlement* into declaring all acts of the assembly null and void, the King intervened. This time it was the *parlement* that was defeated.

The 'Parlements' and Taxation

The *cause célèbre* in the conflict between King and *parlements* was the Brittany affair in the 1760s. In order to carry out an ambitious road-building scheme in the province, the governor, the Duc d'Aiguillon, had enforced the *corvée* and tried to increase peace-time taxation. The Estates of Brittany protested, and were supported by the *Parlement* of Rennes, which drew up a remonstrance asserting the ominous principle that only the Estates-General could ratify new taxation. The Rennes judges defied the King by forbidding the levying of the extra taxes and suspending the administration of justice. In 1765 Louis ordered the trial of their leader, La Chalotais, and a few others before a special tribunal, and set up a new court to replace the Rennes *parlement*. When the Paris judges expressed sympathy with their colleagues at Rennes, Louis went to the Palais de Justice in person. He condemned as unhistorical their claims to be 'the assembly, the tribunal, the organ of the nation' and to be 'judge between the King and his people'. Against these claims Louis asserted: 'It is from me alone that my courts derive their

[17] See opposite page.

existence and their authority; ... the rights and interests of the Nation, which some dare to set up as a body distinct from the Monarch, are necessarily united with mine and rest only in my hands.'[18] Thus did Louis XV, only twenty-three years before the Revolution, speak with the voice of Louis XIV.

Archaic though the language may sound today, the King was within his constitutional rights, and it was the *parlements* that were being unreasonable in preventing the monarchy from modernizing itself into solvency. Fleury, who was in power from 1726 to 1743, had sought to solve the financial problem by preserving peace, and Orry, who set a record by remaining Controller-General from 1730 to 1745, contented himself with reviving old expedients: the *dixième* (a war tax abolished by the Regent) was levied in peace-time, loans were raised and offices sold, and the *corvée* was systematized. Orry succeeded in securing a small surplus, but this was the result not of bold reforms but of Fleury's foreign policy.

Machault, who succeeded Orry in 1745, had to foot the bill for the Austrian Succession War.[19] Louis had promised not to retain the *dixième*, and so Machault had to look elsewhere. In 1749 he sought by two edicts to raise a loan to pay off the war debt and simultaneously to introduce a new permanent tax, the *vingtième*, which was to be paid by all, irrespective of rank. The intention was to place the burden of taxation where it could best be borne, and the claim of the *Parlement* of Paris to be protecting the poor, therefore, carried little conviction. It eventually registered the two edicts, but the Estates of Brittany and Languedoc, and the Assembly of Clergy put up a stiffer resistance. In 1754 Louis transferred Machault to the Ministry of Marine: the privileged orders remained exempt from the *vingtième*, and the Estates of Brittany preserved their independence by compounding for a lump sum.

The Seven Years War brought a further clash over taxation. In 1756 Louis resorted to a *lit de justice* for the first time since 1732 in order to force the Paris *Parlement* to register taxation

[18] Quoted more fully in French in J. Lough, *op. cit.*, pp. 184–85, and in English in R. R. Palmer, *op. cit.*, pp. 95–96.
[19] See Chapter 12 above.

edicts. The *parlements* replied, for the first time, with the astonishing claim that all the *parlements* were part of a single body. As the *Parlement* of Rouen put it: 'By the fundamental laws of the Monarchy the *Parlement* of France, the one and only public, legal and necessary council of the Sovereign, is essentially ONE.'[20] And in 1760 the Rouen *Parlement* denounced all new taxes introduced since the last meeting of the Estates-General in 1614.

The King's assertion of sovereignty in the Aiguillon dispute (1766) did not cow the *parlements*, and the Aiguillon affair dragged on. But with the appointment of Maupeou as Chancellor in 1768 and Terray as Controller-General in 1769 the royal threats were translated into action. Early in 1771 the Paris judges were exiled and their area of jurisdiction was divided between a number of new courts. The sale of judicial posts was abolished and the new judges were appointed by the Crown. When the provincial *parlements* protested they were similarly treated. Meanwhile Terray tried to obtain more up-to-date assessments on landed incomes, and, in those districts where new assessments were made, the yield of the *vingtième* increased by a half.

The reforms were unpopular not only with the privileged orders, who stood to suffer, but also with the public at large. The new courts were dubbed 'Maupeou parlements', and even the *philosophes*, apart from Voltaire who applauded the change, mourned the *parlements* as the guardians of liberty. It was particularly unfortunate for Maupeou that no less a figure than Beaumarchais fell foul of the new Paris *Parlement*.[21] The judge in charge of his case had accepted bribes from Beaumarchais, but, as Beaumarchais had lost his case, he was able to win public sympathy for his brilliant literary crusade against the judge and the whole Maupeou system.

When Louis XV died in 1774 Maupeou's reforms died with him. Louis may not have realized what he was doing in appointing Maupeou, but it is odd that he was given so little credit for this belated attempt at reform. Louis XVI's restoration

---

[20] Palmer, *op. cit.*, p. 95.
[21] For an account of the episode see Lough, *op. cit.*, pp. 192-3.

of the *parlements* in 1774 was probably the most popular act of his reign, but it was the restoration of the institution that was to contrive the final crisis of the *ancien régime*.[22]

[22] For attempts to solve the financial problem during Louis XVI's reign, see Chapter 18.

17

Revolutionary Influences

The Example of England

The English government is not a monarchy; it is a mixed republic where the supreme power is equally divided amongst the three estates. The executive power of the laws is the King, the power of making laws in the people or their representatives, the Lords and Commons. . . . I am as zealous for prerogative as you, but a king of England has no prerogative but to do good by supplying the deficiencies of the laws, the most honourable and glorious of all prerogatives. . . .

The words are those of William Johnson Temple in a letter written to James Boswell[1] from Cambridge in 1764. His evident pride in the eighteenth-century British constitution, the product of the Glorious Revolution of 1688, is typical of his time. In his *Commentaries*, the first volume of which appeared in 1765, Sir William Blackstone wrote in eulogistic terms of the supremacy of Parliament, and quoted with approval Burghley's maxim that 'England could never be ruined but by a Parliament'.[2] Bentham would shortly pour scorn on Blackstone's praise of English law, but in 1765, when the Stamp Act was barely on the statute book and Wilkes had not yet stood for Middlesex, it was still possible for Englishmen to admire what George III called 'the beauty, excellence and perfection of the British constitution as by law established'.

It was equally admired on the continent, where it was fashionable to attribute Britain's startling success in the Seven Years War to the harmony of her political institutions. In 1760 the Marquis

---

[1] *Boswell in Holland 1763–1764*, Heinemann 1952, p. 146.
[2] R. R. Palmer, *The Age of the Democratic Revolution*, Oxford 1959, vol. i, p. 142. See also pp. 143–44 for further examples of Englishmen's pride in their constitution.

d'Argenson had written: 'Fifty years ago the public was wholly uninterested in the news. Today all read the *Gazette de Paris* even in the provinces. They talk a great deal of nonsense about political matters, but they take an interest in them. English liberty has conquered us.'[3] Voltaire and Montesquieu both praised British parliamentary government,[4] and in 1771 Delolme's *Constitution of England* first appeared in a French edition. A London edition followed in 1775, and it was Delolme's work even more than Montesquieu's that popularized the notion of the separation of powers.[5]

It is easy to smile at Delolme, the former Genevan democrat, dedicating later editions of his book to George III, and to notice with Namier that the presence of a hundred placemen in the House of Commons makes nonsense of the separation of powers. But George III was trying to raise politics above the level of family factions, and Wilkes not only won the right to represent Middlesex but also established the illegality of general warrants by dragging an under-secretary of state into court.[6] Chatham might defend an electoral system that gave two seats to Old Sarum, but he also boasted that 'the poorest man may in his cottage bid defiance to all the forces of the Crown'. That was what Frenchmen meant by 'English liberty' – *limited* government rather than representative government – and it helps to explain why Corsica, in revolt against the Genoese,[7] looked to Chatham's England for deliverance, and perhaps why the principal inn at The Hague in the 1760s was named 'The Parliament of England'.

Certainly England was regarded as a suitable asylum for political exiles. In 1726 Voltaire had been released from the Bastille on condition that he went to live in England; he stayed for nearly three years. He spent part of his time in London at the home of Bolingbroke, whom he hed met in France in 1722, and then withdrew to Wandsworth to learn English. His *Philosophical Letters*[8] were published in English in London a year

[3] G. Salvemini, *The French Revolution*, Cape 1954, p. 52.
[4] See above, p. 79.
[5] For a fuller discussion of Delolme's importance see Palmer, *op. cit.* pp. 145–48.
[6] On Wilkes see article by G. Rudé in *History Today*, September 1957.
[7] See below, p. 249.   [8] See above, p. 74.

before they appeared in French. Nine months after Voltaire's departure, Montesquieu arrived on the last stage of his comparative tour of European governments. He attended debates in the House of Commons, was granted an audience with the King and Queen, and was elected a member of the Royal Society. He stayed for eighteen months, a little longer than Rousseau, who lived in England from 1766 to 1767 as the guest of David Hume.[9] In spite of receiving a pension of £100 a year from George III, Rousseau felt himself persecuted in England, and, by the time he left, he and Hume were enemies. England did not, of course, always play the host. Bolingbroke and Wilkes both sought refuge in France, John Kay, the ill-treated inventor of the flying shuttle, actually died there, while every young British nobleman whose family could afford it acquired at least a superficial acquaintance with the continent through the Grand Tour.

The best-documented Grand Tour of the century is that made by Boswell in his early twenties. Boswell is scarcely typical, but his *Journal* is nevertheless revealing. Within six months of leaving London in 1763, he was reading a paper on 'Poverty', in French, to a literary society at Utrecht. Six months later he was inspecting Frederick the Great's library at Potsdam. In Berlin he attended a meeting of the Prussian Academy; at Leipzig he discussed dictionaries with a German professor and was shown the university library. In all the principal libraries he visited on the continent he noticed a collection of books 'bound in red morocco, and adorned with gilded stamps of the cap of liberty, pitchforks, swords and I know not what other terrible instruments of fury', which had been presented by 'a certain unknown whimsical Englishman ... no doubt a most prodigious Whig'.[10] In October 1764, while visiting the court of the Duke of Bavaria, Boswell records that he is reading Rousseau's *Nouvelle Héloïse*,[11] and by the following spring he has started a correspondence with Wilkes.[12]

[9] On Rousseau's stay in England see article by M. Cranston in *History Today*, September 1961.

[10] *Boswell on the Grand Tour: Germany and Switzerland 1764*, Heinemann 1953, p. 209.

[11] See above, p. 224.

[12] *Boswell on the Grand Tour: Italy, Corsica and France 1765–1766*, Heinemann 1955, pp. 55 ff.

Boswell's meetings with Rosseau and Voltaire are even more remarkable. In December 1764 he invited himself to stay with Voltaire, who seems to have received him civilly; before leaving Ferney, Boswell gave Voltaire copies of his poem *Parliament* and of his *Ode to Ambition*. Perhaps Voltaire was amused by this presumption, but, if so, he concealed his amusement. Rousseau, whom Boswell had visited three weeks earlier, seems to have taken a liking to him,[13] and in May 1765 Boswell was writing to Rosseau, describing his Italian tour. Later in the year he wrote again from Corsica.

Corsica was in 1765 almost clear of Genoese troops, except for the fortified coastal towns, which were garrisoned by the French. The Corsicans appealed to the imagination of contemporary European liberals as an example of a primitive people living happily under a republican constitution. In fact General Paoli's revolutionary government was a benevolent dictatorship – what Boswell called 'a species of despotism founded . . . on the affection of love'. But Rousseau had commended Corsica in his *Social Contract,* and in 1764 had received a request to draw up a constitution for Paoli's republic. Boswell therefore saw himself as an unofficial ambassador in Corsica both for Rousseau and for the British government, who in 1763 had forbidden British subjects to aid the Corsican 'rebels'. Despite this disappointing decree, Boswell found Paoli very sympathetic towards things English. His library contained copies of the *Spectator*, Pope's *Essay on Man*,[14] *Gulliver's Travels*, and Barclay's *Apology for Quakers*, and he had not only read many of the parliamentary debates, but had apparently seen Wilkes' *North Briton*. Boswell was captivated: he wore Corsican costume, played Scottish airs to his hosts on a German flute, and sang them Garrick's 'Heart of Oak',[15] to be received with cries of *bravo Inglese!*

When Boswell returned to England, he not only published his *Account of Corsica* (1768), but in 1766 obtained an interview with the future Lord Chatham. Pitt was not yet back in office, and, to Boswell's pleas on behalf of Corsica, merely replied:

---

[13] *Germany and Switzerland*, pp. 211 ff.   [14] See above, p. 92.
[15] Written to celebrate the Year of Glorious Victories, 1759.

'Sir, I should be sorry that in any corner of the world, however distant or however small, it should be suspected that I could ever be indifferent to the cause of liberty.' Lord Holland expressed the official view when he remarked: 'We cannot be so foolish as to go to war because Mr Boswell has been to Corsica.' Thirty years later a British cabinet would decide to allow Russia to have Corsica. It was never done, but the decision is a reminder of the way in which British governments set their faces against revolutionary movements in the last three decades of the century: America, Ireland, the Belgian revolt of 1789 and the French Revolution itself.[16]

Yet in spite of the attitude of the British government, the revolutionary influence of England persisted. The Masonic lodges that spread throughout Europe during the century and played their part in the diffusion of revolutionary ideas[17] had originated in the Grand Lodge founded in London in 1717. More obvious in their effects were the political societies that arose in England in the last quarter of the century. The Wilkes episode had given rise to a number of societies devoted to constitutional reform, like Cartwright's 'Society for Promoting Constitutional Information' founded in 1780. But the centenary of the Glorious Revolution was marked by the formation of a number of ambiguously named 'Revolution Societies'. In November 1789 the London Revolution Society, presided over by the Nonconformist minister Dr Price, unanimously adopted an address of congratulation to the French National Assembly. The Assembly replied with a warm message of thanks, while the Patriotic Society of Dijon wrote: 'In securing their own happiness, Englishmen have prepared the way for that of the Universe.' During the next three years more than forty popular societies in France corresponded with the London Revolution Society. When the French Jacobins commissioned David to paint his 'Tennis Court Oath', the London society was invited

[16] See R. C. Cobb, 'The English Jacobins and the French Revolution' in *The Eighteenth Century Revolution*, D. C. Heath, Boston, 1963.

[17] It now seems unlikely that the Masons were behind the *Encyclopaedia*, as used to be believed, but the Masonic lodges certainly spread the new cult of Deism throughout France, and in 1787 a lodge founded at Toulouse took the name of the *Encyclopaedia*.

to subscribe; and when Dr Price died in 1791 the French societies went into mourning.[18]

It was Price's address to the London Revolution Society in November 1789 that prompted Burke's *Reflections on the Late Revolution in France* (1790). Burke, in dismissing the members of the revolutionary societies as 'little, shrivelled, meagre, hopping, though loud and troublesome, insects of the hour',[19] implied that they were untypical of British opinion and therefore unimportant. Burke's fear was rather that the French political clubs would influence their British counterparts. With reason, it seems, for in 1792 the London Corresponding Society was writing, 'Frenchmen you are already free, and Britons are preparing to become so'. Yet the French themselves continued to acknowledge a debt to England: in August 1792 French citizenship was conferred on Joseph Priestley, Jeremy Bentham, Thomas Clarkson and Tom Paine.

The Impact of America

Tom Paine (1737–1809), perhaps more than any other of his contemporaries, personifies the interaction between England, France and America at this time. Born at Thetford, the son of a Quaker, he went to America in 1774 after meeting Benjamin Franklin in London. Through his *Common Sense*, Paine became the chief propagandist of the colonists' cause and seems to have invented the term 'the United States'. For two years during the War of Independence he served as secretary of the Congress Committee on Foreign Affairs. In 1790 he settled in Paris where he wrote his *Rights of Man* (1791) as a reply to Burke; in 1792 he showed that his acceptance of French citizenship was no mere formality, when he took his seat in the National Convention, and, though he spoke no French, served on the committee appointed to consider Condorcet's constitution.[20] *Common Sense*, published in January 1776, had ended with the words:

[18] For a detailed study of the relationship between the British and French political societies see G. S. Veitch, *Genesis of Parliamentary Reform*, Constable 1913.

[19] E. Burke, *Reflections on the Late Revolution in France*, Dent (Everyman's Library), p. 82.

[20] See below, p. 300. Paine and Sieyès were the only members of the committee who survived the Revolution.

O ye that love mankind! Ye that dare oppose not only tyranny but the tyrant, stand forth! Every spot of the old world is overrun with oppression. Freedom hath been hunted round the Globe. Asia and Africa have long expelled her. Europe regards her as a stranger and England hath given her warning to depart. O! receive the fugitive and prepare in time an asylum for mankind.

And when in 1790 Lafayette entrusted him with the key of the Bastille to deliver to George Washington, Paine wrote in a covering letter to the President: 'The key is the symbol of the first ripe fruits of American principles translated into Europe.... That the principles of America opened the Bastille is not to be doubted and therefore the Key comes to its right place.'

No such revolutionary expectations could have been in Lafayette's mind when, at the age of nineteen, he escaped from France to serve in America. It is true that on arrival he quickly fell under Washington's spell and became an ardent champion of the political ideals underlying the rebellion, but his original motives were probably a desire for adventure and a wish to fight against England. Certainly the unofficial support given to the colonists by the French government before 1778[21] was not intended to hasten a revolution at home. Vergennes saw the war as a way of destroying British supremacy in North America won during the Seven Years War, and, when France formally declared war on England in 1778, she did not confine hostilities to the American continent. The war also involved Holland and Spain as active combatants and most of the other major European powers as members of the League of Armed Neutrality directed against England (1780–83).[22] The terms of the Treaty of Versailles (1783) show how global the scope of the war had been. Besides recognizing American independence, England surrendered Minorca to Spain, but retrieved her West Indian possessions and gained the right to trade with the Dutch East Indies; France recovered St Lucia and Tobago in the West Indies, her African territories (Senegal and Gorée), and her

[21] Vergennes, the French foreign minister, authorized Beaumarchais to set up a company to send aid to the rebels, and in 1777 alone 30,000 muskets and a good deal of gunpowder were sent from French sources.

[22] The members were: Russia, Prussia, the Empire, Denmark, Sweden, Portugal and the Two Sicilies.

fishing rights off Newfoundland, but finally relinquished her ambitions in India; Spain had failed to take Gibraltar, but gained Florida in addition to Minorca.

The financial cost of the war had disastrous consequences for Louis XVI's government,[23] and it was by inflating the French national debt rather than by inspiring the French nation that America hastened the downfall of the *ancien régime*. But propaganda also played its part. If the American Revolution had started over the mundane matter of taxation, so would the French Revolution, while the universal language of the American Declaration of Independence[24] awoke echoes in the country of the Encyclopaedists. French admiration for the eighteenth-century British constitution was an admiration for the political theories of John Locke as much as for the constitutional practice of Hanoverian government. Montesquieu's writings were a development and popularization of Locke's arguments: to Locke's doctrine of the justifiability of curbing arbitrary government by means of rebellion Montesquieu added the principle of limitation by separation and balance of powers.[25] The *Spirit of Laws* was widely read in America in the 1750s and 1760s, although the first American edition did not appear until 1802. Franklin had his own copy, John Adams annotated his with 'a sort of index to every paragraph', while James Madison had been a student of Montesquieu since his days at Princeton, where by the 1760s *Spirit of Laws* was already a textbook. Thus the Declaration of Independence, embodying a description of the social contract that reads like a paraphrase of Locke, was couched in terms familiar to the French. It had, of course, been drawn up with the deliberate intention of enlisting European sympathy in the colonists' causes, and it succeeded triumphantly.

Frenchmen, who until 1776 had regarded the American struggle as a colonial rebellion against England, now saw it as the birth-pangs of a nation. Locke's theories had previously seemed admirable but abstract; they justified the English Revolution of 1688 but were not self-evidently practicable elsewhere. Now, by using Locke's arguments against Englishmen

---

[23] See below, p. 263.   [24] See Appendix 6.
[25] On Locke, see above, p. 65. On Montesquieu, see above, p. 79, and Appendix 5.

and by creating a confederation which seemed, from the distance of Europe, to enshrine both the social contract and the separation of powers, the Americans had apparently vindicated the armchair politicians of the *Encylopaedia*. The Constitution of the United States was not ratified until 1788, but by 1777 all the thirteen states had independently adopted constitutions, and all but three of these were new documents. In 1778 these constitutions, together with the Declaration of Independence, were published in France in a single volume dedicated to Franklin. Five years later a more ambitious collection, including various other documents relating to American independence and called *The Constitutions of the Thirteen States of America*, was actually published by the King's printer. For an avowedly absolutist government, this was a dangerous way of trying to stimulate patriotism.

Even without government encouragement, a pro-American mood was sweeping French intellectual circles. In his *Charles XI*, written in 1787 though not performed until 1789, the dramatist Marie-Joseph Chénier[26] spoke thus of America:

> Ce vaste Continent, qu'environnent les mers,
> Va tout-à-coup changer l'Europe et l'Univers.
> Il s'élève pour nous, aux champs de l'Amérique
> De nouveaux intérêts, une autre politique.

Earlier in the 1780s learned societies introduced competitions for the best papers on the effects of America on the world, while in 1785 the publication of Turgot's criticisms of the American constitutions started a heated pamphlet warfare in which John Adams' *Defence of the Constitutions of the United States* occupied a central position and in which Mirabeau, the Abbé Mably and Condorcet were all involved. French views on America were often somewhat fanciful. In *Historical and Political Essays on the Anglo-Americans*, published in French at Brussels in 1782, the following picture is painted of the American democratic process: 'They say that in Virginia the members chosen to establish the new government assembled in a peaceful wood removed from the sight of the people, in an enclosure prepared by nature

---

[26] Brother of the poet André who was to die on the guillotine.

with banks of grass; and that in this sylvan spot they deliberated on who should preside over them.'[27]

There were some who knew better. Apart from Lafayette, at least three dozen Frenchmen who served the revolutionary cause in America were later to play a leading part in the early stages of the French Revolution. There were also those who did not take part in the war but visited America soon afterwards. Brissot, founder of the Gallo-American Society in France and the future leader of the Girondins,[28] arrived in the United States in 1788 while the new constitution was still being debated. On his return to France he published his 'Plan of Conduct', which was intended to guide the members of the newly summoned Estates-General. He proposed a constitutional convention, and expressed the hope that 'this device or method of the Free Americans can perhaps be very easily adapted to the circumstances in which France now finds itself'.

Some impressive representatives of Free America had already visited France. Benjamin Franklin (1706–90) arrived in Paris in December 1776 as ambassador of the new American government. He had been a member of the French *Académie des Sciences* since 1772, on the strength of his scientific experiments. Now, Turgot saluted him with the famous epigram *Eripuit caelo fulmen sceptrumque tyrannis*, while the Countess d'Houdetot welcomed him as 'legislator of one world and benefactor of two'. He met Turgot and Condorcet; he publicly embraced Voltaire at the *Académie*; he served with Lavoisier on a committee appointed by the *Académie* to investigate Mesmerism; he arranged for the American constitutions to be translated into French. And he procured the Treaty of Alliance by which France formally entered the American war. When Franklin returned home in triumph in 1783, he was replaced as United States ambassador by Thomas Jefferson (1743–1826), his partner in drafting the Declaration of Independence. Jefferson was less of a social success in Paris, but his *Notes on Virginia* (1789) appeared first in French, and in 1789 he helped Lafayette with the draft of a French Declaration of Rights. And it was Jefferson who wrote to Dr Price from France:

[27] Palmer, *op. cit.*, p. 254.   [28] See below, p. 293.

Though celebrated writers of this and other countries had already sketched good principles on the subject of government, yet the American war seems first to have awakened the thinking part of this nation in general from the sleep of despotism in which they were sunk. The officers too who had been to America were mostly young men, less shackled by habit and prejudice, and more ready to assent to the dictates of common sense and common right. They came back impressed with these. The press, notwithstanding its shackles, began to disseminate them; conversation too assumed new freedom; politics became the theme of all societies, male and female, and a very extensive and zealous party was formed, which may be called the Patriotic party, who, sensible of the abusive government under which they lived, longed for occasions of reforming it.[29]

The Writings of the 'Philosophes'

Did the writings of the *philosophes* cause the French Revolution? Stated as baldly as that, the question looks absurd even to the non-Marxist historian who refuses to attribute revolutions to the high price of bread. If one asks rather whether ideas played a larger part in directing events than is usual in political up-heavals, the question makes sense, but historians will not agree on an answer.[30] Contemporaries were expecting a revolution of some kind from at least the 1750s onwards, though not the kind of revolution that eventually came. Arthur Young expected an *increase* in privilege, while in 1751 the Marquis d'Argenson, commenting on the general unrest, wrote that 'a riot might lead to a rising, and a rising to a general revolution in which there would be tribunes elected by the people, legislative assemblies and independent communes, and in which kings and ministers would be deprived of excessive power'.[31] D'Argenson was not alone in thinking that the disturbances which accompanied the revival of the Jansenist quarrel in the 1750s[32] might start just such a chain-reaction.

[29] L. Gottschalk, 'The Place of the American Revolution in the Causal Pattern of the French Revolution' in *The Eighteenth Century Revolution*, D. C. Heath, Boston, 1963.
[30] For the historiography of the dispute see *French Liberal Thought in the Eighteenth Century*, Turnstile Press 1954, pp. 66 ff.
[31] Salvemini, *op. cit.*, p. 52.
[32] See above, p. 241.

But the Revolution did not come in the 1750s. Why? Some historians argue that it was precisely because the bulk of the *philosophes'* writings had only just begun to appear. De Tocqueville regarded the influence of the *philosophes* as self-evident:

The writers furnished not merely their ideas to the people who made [the Revolution], but also their temperament and disposition. As the result of their long education, in the absence of any other instructors, coupled with their profound ignorance of practice, all Frenchmen from reading their books finally contracted the instincts, the turn of mind, the tastes and even the eccentricities of those who write. To such an extent was this the case that, when finally they had to act, they transported into politics all the habits of literature.[33]

The writers in question were not, of course, a compact group with a coherent philosophy: Montesquieu, Voltaire and Rousseau represent widely different points of the political compass.[34] But they would all have acknowledged the aim which the British essayist Joseph Addison (1672–1719) had set himself in an early issue of the *Spectator*:

It was said of Socrates that he brought philosophy down from heaven, to inhabit among men: and I shall be ambitious to have it said of me, that I have brought philosophy out of closets and libraries, schools and colleges, to dwell in clubs and assemblies, at tea-tables and in coffee-houses.

The *philosophes*, however much they differed among themselves, set people talking about political principles and accustomed them to the idea that any change must be for the better.

Particularly change in the Church. Catholicism in France was attacked both as a dogma and as an institution. Newtonianism in the eighteenth century, no less than Darwinism in the nineteenth, led to a demand for the 'de-mythologizing' of religion. The 'natural religion' of Deism, expounded by Voltaire and diffused by the Freemasons, was thought to be firmly grounded in observed facts, while Catholicism demanded blind obedience to authority. (It was not until 1757 that the Congregation of the

---

[33] A. de Tocqueville, *L'Ancien Régime*, trans. M. W. Patterson, Blackwell 1949, p. 156.
[34] See Chapters 5 and 6 above.

Holy Office decided not to enforce the decree against books that taught the movement of the earth.) But if the Church invited criticism by its hostility to Newtonian science, it provoked abuse by its policy of persecution. As late as 1762 a Huguenot pastor and three Protestant noblemen were executed at Toulouse, where, in the same year, Jean Calas was broken on the wheel for allegedly killing his son to prevent him from embracing Catholicism. In taking up the cause of Calas, Voltaire was striking at religious intolerance as a whole. No sooner had he vindicated Calas in 1765, than he turned to defend Chevalier de la Barre, who was tortured and executed for showing irreverence to a religious procession. Voltaire's *Philosophical Dictionary* was burned with La Barre's body, but, from the safety of Switzerland Voltaire replied by denouncing the execution in *The Cry of Innocent Blood*.

The campaign against persecution had some success even before the Revolution. In 1787 freedom of conscience, though not of worship, was granted to 'those who do not profess the Catholic religion'. But progress was slow because the Church controlled censorship. In 1767, in its condemnation of *Belisarius*, Marmontel's plea for toleration, the Sorbonne asserted that it was the duty of the state 'to repress every publication, in whatever manner it is produced, of false maxims of atheism, deism, materialism, etc., which cut all the bonds of society, destroy the rein of conscience, cause the distinction between good and evil to disappear, and open the door to every sort of crime'.[35] In theory, no book could be published without the consent of the Director of Publications, who was liable to withdraw his permission at a later date if the clergy, or the Sorbonne, or the *Parlement* of Paris objected. As Beaumarchais made Figaro say:

Provided I neither spoke of the Wealth of Nations in my writings, nor of the Government, nor of Religion, nor of any Corporate Companies, nor offended the favourite Mistress of the Minister's Favourite Footman, nor said any one thing which could be twisted into a reference, or hint, derogatory to any one Individual who had more powerful friends than I had, I was at liberty to write freely, all

[35] Quoted in French in J. Lough, *Introduction to Eighteenth Century France*, Longmans 1960, p. 305.

and whatever I pleased, under the inspection of some two or three
Censors![36]

Most of the *philosophes* spent short spells in prison or in exile
as the result of their writings, but on the whole the system of
censorship seems to have been extraordinarily inefficient. In
1754 a decree imposed the death penalty on the distributors as
well as the authors of subversive literature, at a time when the
Encyclopaedia was still being published under royal sanction.
When in 1759 the publication and sale of the *Encyclopaedia* were
forbidden, nothing was done to prevent its private circulation.
Beaumarchais' *Marriage of Figaro* perhaps provides the most
striking example of halfhearted censorship. When performance
of the play was forbidden, Beaumarchais gave a series of well-
attended private readings. Marie Antoinette asked for a copy,
but when Louis XVI discovered its contents he is reputed to have
predicted that its performance would bring down the Bastille.[37]
A public performance was nevertheless advertised in 1783, and
the government waited until the day of the show before stepping
in to forbid it. Meanwhile the master of court pleasures, the
Comte de Vaudreuil, arranged for a private showing at his
country home. Beaumarchais insisted on resubmitting the play
to the censor, who now authorized it for private performance.
Seven months later, in April 1784, the play was at last publicly
staged by the Comédie-Française and played to packed houses.[38]
In the last resort, censorship had bowed to popular demand
rather than to royal wish. In more ways than one *The Marriage
of Figaro* was, as Napoleon said, 'the Revolution already in
action'.

The popularity of Beaumarchais' masterpiece showed how
fashionable it had become to laugh at the *ancien régime*, even
among the aristocracy themselves. The theories of the *philosophes*
were freely discussed in the *salons,* and, as the Comte de Ségur
wrote in retrospect, 'Liberty delighted us by its daring and
equality by its agreeableness. . . . We never dreamed that this
wordy warfare might threaten the exalted life that was ours

[36] Act V, Scene 3. The translation is from an eighteenth-century English edition.
[37] G. R. Havens, *The Age of Ideas*, Peter Owen 1957, p. 377.
[38] See above, p. 225.

and that for so many centuries we had regarded as unassailable.'[39] Of course, some of the *philosophes* were themselves aristocrats by birth, and most were aristocrats at heart. Montesquieu had been a president of the *Parlement* of Bordeaux, and this may help to explain the tendency of the *philosophes* to regard the *parlements* as bulwarks against despotism. It was, admittedly, largely for selfish reasons that the *parlements* opposed all royal attempts to reform taxation, but they also objected to the persecution of the Jansenists, and their remonstrances used the language of natural law, the social contract and even of popular sovereignty.[40] In Louis XV's reign Barbier had written in his journal: 'If the Government succeeds in diminishing the authority and accepted rights of the *Parlements* there will no longer be an obstacle in the way of assured despotism. If, on the contrary, the *Parlements* unite to oppose this move with strong measures, nothing can follow but a general revolution.'[41]

In siding with the *parlements* against Maupeou at the end of Louis XV's reign,[42] the *philosophes* made the second of Barbier's alternatives more probable. They may thus be said to have influenced the early stages of the Revolution in at least three ways. Their support of the *parlements* smoothed the path for the aristocratic revolt of 1787; but when the *parlements* showed that they had demanded the Estates-General only in order to preserve privilege, the *philosophe* propaganda ensured that there was an articulate and politically conscious *bourgeoisie* to challenge them; and, when that challenge came, the forces of conservatism, for so long exposed to ridicule, were too discredited and demoralized to resist. The *philosophes* had created a revolutionary climate of thought, and, when the storm broke, the amateur politicians of the successive assemblies turned to the theories of the *philosophes* in search of a constitutional programme. As Condorcet himself put it: 'Incompetence in government precipitated this revolution, philosophy guided its principles, and popular force destroyed the obstacles capable of obstructing change.'

[39] Salvemini, *op. cit.*, p. 56. It is only fair to add that Beaumarchais himself was taken by surprise: when the Revolution came he was having a new house built – opposite the Bastille.

[40] Palmer *op. cit.*, p. 95, and K. Martin, *op. cit.*, p. 85.

[41] K. Martin, *op. cit.*, p. 81. [42] See above, p. 244.

18

Revolutionary Agents

The King

The lesson of Louis XV's last years had been that only a monarch who was bold enough to attempt a frontal assault on the privileges of clergy and nobility could hope to save his government from bankruptcy. 'Events had reached the point at which there had to be either a great king or a great revolution,' wrote Sorel. But there was bound to be a revolution in any case, for the only way in which the Bourbons could have imposed equality of taxation and so restored solvency was by an alliance with the Third Estate against the privileged orders; and, in the context of the *ancien régime*, that was to ask the King himself to become a revolutionary.

Louis XVI, who was barely twenty when he came to the throne, desired nothing more than a quiet life that left plenty of time for his daily mass, meals and hunting. His first question on rising seems usually to have been to ask what there was for dinner, and on 20 June 1789, when the representatives of the Third Estate took their famous 'Tennis Court Oath', the word *rien* in the King's diary indicated that there had been no hunting. His wife, on the other hand, perhaps took too much interest in politics,[1] and even if her political influence has probably been exaggerated, she was a splendid symbol of all that was most reactionary at Versailles. Although Marie Antoinette may never in fact have suggested cake as a substitute for bread, the story is psychologically true, if not historically so, while the famous affair of the diamond necklace in 1785 left the public with the impression that the Queen had used the court jewels to reward her lovers.

[1] Her brother, Joseph II of Austria, clearly disapproved of her political intrigues. See G. Salvemini, *The French Revolution*, Cape 1954, pp. 89–90.

It was, however, the extravagance rather than the immorality of the monarchy that excited criticism. Louis XVI's daughter, when only one month old, had no less than eighty persons in her service, and in the last years of the reign some 15,000 courtiers consumed, in salaries, pensions and gratuities, forty million *livres* a year – a twelfth of the public revenue. Contemporaries grossly exaggerated the cost of Versailles, but, as James I had found in England, it was difficult to persuade the taxpayer that the government was bankrupt while so much conspicuous waste was tolerated at court. France in 1788 devoted one quarter of her annual expenditure to the armed forces, and about half to paying the interest on the national debt. This distribution was about the same as in contemporary England, while the French debt of 4,000 million *livres* was only about two-thirds of the English debt and less than that of Holland. The trouble was not the size of the debt, but the fact that the budget did not balance. In 1774 there had been a deficit of nearly fifty million in spite of the unpopular measures of Terray.[2]

By recalling the *parlements* in 1774, Louis XVI showed that he was prepared to postpone the struggle with the privileged orders on the question of taxation. Yet so little did he understand the issues at stake that he simultaneously appointed a reforming controller-general. 'No greater fortune could befall France or the mind of man,' exclaimed Voltaire at the news of Turgot's appointment, and Paris was scarcely less jubilant. Turgot's programme – 'No bankruptcy, no increase in taxes, no loans' – could be implemented only by reducing expenditure. He made a saving of six million *livres* in the cost of tax-collection by curbing the profits of the tax-farmers; he commuted the *corvée* to a tax on all landowners, irrespective of class; in accordance with his physiocratic principles,[3] he abolished the guilds, still active in France, and established a free trade in corn. Unluckily for Turgot, the bad harvest of 1774 pushed up the price of bread, and his free trade scheme was inevitably blamed.

But it was the *parlements* who defeated Turgot. When the *Parlement* of Paris objected to the new land tax on the grounds that it would 'overturn civil society, whose harmony rests only

[2] See above, p. 244.   [3] See above, p. 77.

on that gradation of powers, authorities, pre-eminences and distinctions which holds each man in his place and guarantees all tations against confusion',[4] the King supported Turgot in a *lit de justice*. But the opposition at court proved too strong for Louis, and in May 1776 Turgot was dismissed.

The rule of Necker[5] from 1777 to 1781 embraced the period of French intervention in the American War.[6] Turgot had predicted that 'the first cannon shot would force the state into bankruptcy'. Necker avoided increasing taxes by resorting to loans (which in his own conservative estimate amounted to 530 million *livres*) and won applause for his cleverness. The climax of the confidence trick came with his famous *Compte rendu* for 1781, which purported to show a surplus of ten million *livres*. What it did not show was that the additional war expenditure of some 2,000 million *livres* had been met by loans of 8 or 10 per cent. It was due chiefly to Necker that the total interest on the national debt rose from 93 million in 1774 to over 300 million by 1789.[7]

Calonne, who became Controller-General in 1783, at first pursued Necker's principles, even to the extent of arguing that lavish and ostentatious expenditure made it easier for the government to borrow. It also made it more difficult for Calonne to win support for the policy of retrenchment that he abruptly announced in 1786, particularly as Necker was waiting in the wings and claiming that the financial crisis was due solely to Calonne's mismanagement. Calonne did not risk suggesting complete equality of taxation, but he did propose a general tax on all land to replace the existing *vingtième*, a reform of the *gabelle*, the *taille* and the *corvée* (though not in such a way as to affect the privileged orders), and the setting up of provincial assemblies, under the control of the *intendants* but chosen without distinction from all three orders. Calonne sought to avoid a

[4] R. R. Palmer, *The Age of the Democratic Revolution*, vol i, p. 451. It is only fair to add that the majority of an eighteenth-century English parliament might have expressed themselves in much the same terms on the question of the extension of the franchise.

[5] As a Protestant he could not hold the office of Controller-General, and so bore the title of General Director of Finance. The job was the same.

[6] See above, p. 252.

[7] A. Cobban, *A History of Modern France*, Penguin 1961, vol. i, p. 121.

head-on clash with the *parlements* by resorting to an 'Assembly of Notables', last convened in the reign of Louis XIII (1610–43).

The summoning of the 'Assembly of Notables' was a tactical defeat for the Crown: an absolute monarch had taken the remarkable step of consulting not merely his council, but a representative body of the nation.[8] When this assembly at length met in February 1787, it revealed that it had a programme of its own.

The Nobles

The nobles who dominated Calonne's 'Assembly of Notables' were not the representatives of an easily definable class. Montesquieu's famous definition of a noble 'as a man who sees the King, speaks with ministers, and possesses ancestors, debts and pensions' is hardly very precise, while Talleyrand was later to say that there were seven or eight different categories of noble.[9] The main division in the nobility was between *noblesse d'épée* and *noblesse de robe*. The nobility of the sword were the descendants of the old feudal families. The Marquis de Bouillé thought that of about 80,000 noble families that still survived up to 1789, perhaps a thousand had their origins lost in antiquity, and that of these scarcely two or three hundred remained at all prosperous.[10]

The *noblesse d'épée* were a class in decline and conscious of it. Sources of wealth other than land, the Church, or the army were denied to them, since to take part in trade or industry was a mark of *bourgeois* status. The law of primogeniture helped to preserve the family estates for the eldest sons, but left the younger sons with no means of livelihood and (unlike their English counterparts) with the additional handicap of a noble title. It is perhaps not surprising, then, to find that in 1789 the French army of 135,000 other ranks had 35,000 officers, of whom 1,171 were generals.[11] Those nobles who had estates did not live on them, but lodged at Versailles: they did not know precisely

---

[8] For the composition of this body see J. Lough, *An Introduction to Eighteenth Century France*, p. 217.

[9] *Ibid.*, p. 110.   [10] *Ibid.*, p. 111.

[11] Only 3,500 officers were on the active list, but the total cost of officers' pay to the state was nevertheless forty-six million livres a year.

what their incomes were and even affected not to know whether they were in debt. Of course, they were. The Comte d'Artois had to devote his large income to paying the interest on his debts, the Duc de Choiseul had property worth fourteen million *livres* and debts amounting to ten million, while the Duc d'Orléans owed seventy-four million. When the revolutionaries confiscated the estates of the *émigré* nobles, they found that the richest were all mortgaged.[12]

The economic decline of the *noblesse d'épée* was matched by loss of political and even administrative power. Three hundred and fifty dukes, princes, counts and marquises still drew four and a half million *livres* from the treasury in salaries, but their former judicial, administrative and military functions had been transferred to *intendants*. Louis XIV had deliberately excluded the nobility from his councils, and although nobles returned to politics under his successors, they were nearly all *noblesse de robe* rather than *noblesse d'épée*. Many of the former feudal nobility had even surrendered their seigneurial rights: all that remained of feudalism in France were the feudal dues and *banalités*,[13] and many nobles had actually sold the right of collecting these to wealthy *bourgeoisie*.

Many of the *bourgeoisie* had bought their way into the ranks of the nobility either by purchasing *lettres de noblesse* or by acquiring judicial or administrative posts. These were the *noblesse de robe*. In 1784 Necker listed some 4,000 posts which carried the status of hereditary nobility,[14] although of these some of the judicial posts were in practice closed to candidates who were not nobles already. It was the *noblesse de robe* who dominated the council and the *parlements*, and, far from being a class in decline, they were very much a class on the make. The claims that they advanced in the *parlements*,[15] with increasing vehemence as the century progressed, were not merely a last-ditch defence of antiquated privileges, but an aggressive assertion of their right to play a fuller part in the business of government. In this sense the Revolution was a clash between a rising *bourgeoisie* and a rising nobility.

[12] Salvemini, *op. cit.*, p. 21   [13] See below, p. 271.
[14] The list appears in Lough, *op. cit.*, p. 117.   [15] See Chapter 16 above.

The privileges in question were, of course, antiquated. Immunity from taxation was a relic from feudal times when the nobles had given military service instead. The nobles were wholly exempt from the most burdensome tax of all, the *taille*, a property tax, levied in some provinces on land only and in others on all personal wealth. They were not supposed to escape the *capitation* or the *vingtième* (both more recently introduced taxes on income), but the nobles and clergy between them seem to have paid only a half of their fair share of the *vingtième* and as little as an eighth of what they should have paid in *capitation*.[15a] In addition the nobles enjoyed a number of legal privileges and had a monopoly of hunting rights, the *droit de chasse*.

In 1787 the 'Assembly of Notables' did not dare to defend such privileges openly. Instead they condemned government extravagance and, reasonably enough, demanded a statement of account. Brienne, who replaced Calonne as Controller-General in April 1787, agreed to submit the treasury accounts to them and modified the proposed provincial assemblies in the interests of the privileged orders; but he insisted on retaining Calonne's land tax, and added to it an increase in stamp duty. The Marquis de Lafayette, doubtless remembering his recent service under Washington,[16] took the lead in demanding the summoning of the Estates-General to ratify the new taxes. Brienne dismissed the 'Notables' in May 1787, but the demand for the calling of the Estates-General was taken up by the *parlements*. The slogan that had ushered in the American Revolution was to herald the French Revolution also.

The Clergy

The French Church, divided by Jansenism and derided by the *philosophes*, was still economically powerful in 1789. The clergy numbered between 100,000 and 140,000, of whom about 60,000 were in monasteries and convents. This was a comparatively modest figure: Spain, with a smaller population than France,

---

[15a] Miss Behrens thinks that the extent of evasion by the privileged orders has been exaggerated and reminds us that, in any case, the wealthier *bourgeoisie* evaded taxes too. See *Economic History Review*, April 1963, p. 463.

[16] See above, p. 252.

had nearly 190,000. But the clergy, though numerically small, owned between 5 and 10 per cent of all the land in France. They were exempt from *taille*, *capitation* and *vingtième* by virtue of their traditional 'free gift', which was voted at the quinquennial Assembly of the Clergy. The 'free gift' amounted to rather less than a fair share of their wealth. In 1750 Machault[17] had calculated that, after allowing for stipends, schools, hospitals and charitable activities, the French Church had a taxable income of 114 million *livres*. Machault wanted to levy the *vingtième* on this figure, which would have raised five and a half million *livres* annually, whereas the annual average from 'free gifts' since the beginning of the century amounted to little more than three and a half million; in the event he merely asked for an extra one and a half million a year for five years to help pay off the national debt. Even this was denied him; and the very last Assembly of the Clergy in 1788 not only secured a confirmation of its immunity from taxation, but voted only one quarter of the 'free gift' for which it had been asked.

The wealth of the clergy was, however, very unevenly spread. The highest posts of the Church, although the preserves of the nobility, were probably no wealthier than their counterparts in England, where Canterbury carried £7,000 a year, Durham £6,000, and Winchester £5,000.[18] But the lower clergy, unlike their English equivalents, were recruited from the peasant class and were pitifully paid. In 1775 the *curés* and *vicaires* had petitioned the King on the inadequacy of their stipends, which were then 500 and 300 *livres* a year respectively; in 1786 they were raised to 700 and 350 *livres*, but even this was well below the 1,200 *livres* mentioned as a minimum for a *curé* in many of the *cahiers* presented to the Estates-General in 1789.

The clergy of the *ancien régime* were probably no more corrupt than elsewhere in Europe, but the French Church had become so identified with the defence of privilege and the resistance to new ideas that it was attacked on political rather than on doctrinal grounds. It also represented censorship: the

---

[17] See above, p. 243.

[18] It is difficult to be certain for the figures given in the 'Royal Almanac' are probably too low. Pluralism was in any case somewhat more gross than in England.

Archbishop of Paris, who persecuted Jansenists in the 1750s, had Rousseau's *Émile* burned in the 1760s. De Tocqueville thought that complete freedom of publication would have been less harmful to the Church than the ineffective censorship that it imposed on the *philosophes*.

The clergy who sat in the 'Assembly of Notables' were nearly all bishops or archbishops, but when the Estates-General eventually met, it became clear that not all the clergy were in favour of privilege: the poverty of the lower clergy persuaded them to side with the *bourgeoisie* against the privileged classes, thereby transforming the rebellious deputies of the Third Estate into a National Assembly.[19]

The 'Bourgeoisie'

In theory the Third Estate comprised all those who did not belong to either of the privileged orders; in fact all the representatives of the Third Estate who sat in the Estates-General were drawn from the *bourgeoisie*. But the *bourgeoisie* was even less homogeneous as a class than the other two orders, and the only generalization that it is safe to make about the class as a whole is that it had increased in prosperity to a point where it began to resent its lack of social privileges and political power. The resentment was reflected in the middle-class *drames* of Beaumarchais[20] and in the popularity of the writings of the *philosophes*.[21] In 1789 the burghers of La Rochelle even complained of legal discrimination in the death penalty, whereby a noble was beheaded and a commoner hanged.

The wealthiest *bourgeoisie*, the big merchants and financiers, were the richest men in the realm. They could afford to purchase nobility, and the merchants often did so; but those families who made their fortunes as government contractors or tax-farmers tended to prefer power to privilege. The Pâris brothers owed their wealth to war contracts, and through their influence at court[22] could break generals or even ministers: they secured the dismissal of Orry[23] in 1745 and the removal of d'Estrées from

---

[19] See below, p. 278. [20] See above, p. 225. [21] See Chapters 5 and 17.
[22] Madame de Pompadour's father had been steward to the Pâris brothers.
[23] See above, p. 243.

his command in 1757. The forty Farmers General, who every six years bought the right to collect indirect taxes, profited so much at the taxpayer's expense that during the Revolution they were rounded up and executed: Lavoisier was among them.

It was not, of course, the wealthiest *bourgeoisie* who led the revolt of the Third Estate. Of the 648 *bourgeois* deputies who sat in the Constituent Assembly,[24] eighty-four were merchants or manufacturers, 166 were practising lawyers, and no fewer than 278 held minor administrative posts in local or central government.[25] This surprisingly large proportion of municipal and government officials is in itself an index of *bourgeois* discontent. The point is that they were *minor* officials. The major political posts were reserved for the nobility: all Louis XVI's bishops were noblemen, while, of his ministers, Necker alone was a commoner. As Cobban reminds us, before the Revolution neither Robespierre nor Danton could have risen above the rank of petty attorney (so despised by Dr Johnson), whereas in England the highest judicial official would have been open to them. Thiers, who knew some of the revolutionaries personally, thought that if Louis XVI had promised greater equality in official appointments, the chief *bourgeois* grievance would have been removed.

De Tocqueville described the *bourgeois* administrative officials as 'the aristocracy of the new society which was already formed and living; it only waited for the Revolution to clear a place for it'.[26] It is true that these venal public offices were abolished by the revolutionaries, but their holders were given monetary compensation which they were able to reinvest in the newly confiscated church lands.[27] Nor did the successive revolutionary assemblies ever consider repudiating the national debt in order to solve the government's financial difficulties, since the *bourgeoisie* were the biggest holders of government bonds. The *bourgeoisie* in 1789 wanted equality of opportunity – but particularly for the *bourgeoisie*.

[24] See below, p. 279.
[25] A detailed analysis appears in A. Cobban's inaugural lecture, *The Myth of the French Revolution*, published for University College, London, by M. K. Lewis, 1955.
[26] A. de Tocqueville, *L'Ancien Régime*, trans. M. W. Patterson, Blackwell 1949, p. 69.
[27] See below, p. 285.

The Town Crowd

If the *bourgeoisie* were not much interested in the needs of the lower orders, the *bourgeois* revolt nevertheless depended on the support of the urban working-classes, particularly the people of Paris. The population of Paris was a little over half a million. A mid-eighteenth-century estimate put the number of clergy at 10,000, nobility at 5,000, and *bourgeoisie* of the financial, commercial and professional classes at 40,000. The remainder were the *sansculottes*, ranging from small shopkeepers, through craftsmen and journeymen, to the vagrants and city poor. There were as yet no distinctive working-class districts in Paris: masters, craftsmen and journeymen lived side by side and would join together in protests against farmers, millers, bakers and the city authorities.

By eighteenth-century standards Paris was well policed. The lieutenant of police and the forty-eight commissioners of the Châtelet had 1,500 men under their direct command and could call on a military reserve of between 5,000 and 6,000 *gardes*. In 1780 the dramatist Sebastien Mercier wrote that such disturbances as the recent Gordon Riots in London would be inconceivable in a city as well policed as Paris.

But the police could not control the price of corn. The eighteenth-century Paris worker probably spent as much as half his income on bread, and whenever the price rose above two *sous* a pound he began to feel the pinch. Seventeen-eighty-eight saw a bad harvest throughout Europe, and by the end of the year bread in Paris cost three *sous* a pound. In April 1789 workers of the *faubourg* Saint-Antoine sacked the factories of Réveillon and Henriot, and broke into food shops. By now the price of bread was almost four *sous* in Paris and nearly double that in some provinces. The harvest of 1789 was a good one, but the shortage continued because a drought prevented millers from grinding their corn.

The wage-earners began to suspect a conspiracy. Government officials were accused of hoarding, and tolls and duties were blamed for hindering the free movement of food. Two days before the storming of the Bastille, attacks had started on the ring of fifty-four customs posts which Calonne had erected around Paris in 1785. In four days of rioting forty of these posts or *barrières* were burned down. In August there were disturbances in the public workshops, while various trades from wigmakers to domestic servants began to demand higher wages. Meanwhile demonstrations against bakers became more frequent and more violent.

This was the background against which the National Assembly held its deliberations, and throughout the Revolution the price of bread was to remain the chief political preoccupation of the wage-earners. The relationship between the *bourgeoisie* and the Paris crowd is neatly illustrated by the March to Versailles in October 1789: the *bourgeoisie*, fearing an aristocratic coup, used the demonstration to persuade the King and Assembly to move from Versailles to Paris, but it had begun as a bread march.[28]

The Peasants

The peasants did not profit from the high price of bread. They comprised four-fifths of the population, yet held on average little more than one-third of the land. The French peasant was better off than his other continental counterparts,[29] but his advantages were purely relative. Serfdom had all but disappeared in France, though it had been abolished on crown lands as recently as 1779 and still survived in provinces such as Burgundy and France-Comté and on some Church estates. But if the majority of peasants had shaken off serfdom, relics of feudalism remained. In addition to feudal dues and manorial courts, the peasant was still confronted with the seigneurial monopoly of manorial mill, bakery and winepress. These *banalités* had made sense when the feudal lord was the peasant's protector, but by 1789 the peasant had surrendered the benefits of feudalism without losing the burdens. It was precisely because he was no longer a serf that he so keenly resented the relics of serfdom; and the tendency of manorial lords to sell their *banalités* to wealthy *bourgeoisie*, who were intent on exploiting them to the full, served to increase the peasant's resentment.

Although most peasants were free, they were not all land-owners. The wealthier peasants were tenant-farmers who sold their produce and could profit from high prices. Below them were the *métayers* or share-croppers, who held land, stock and even seed from their lord in return for rent in kind; since half their crops went in rent, the *métayers* farmed for subsistence rather than for market. But the majority of peasants were poorer still, having no land at all, or insufficient for subsistence even in good years. Unlike England, where enclosure was already well advanced, eighteenth-century France was a country of small peasant proprietors, who clung to the open-field system (based on what Arthur Young called 'the execrable system of fallow-ing') because it at least guaranteed grazing rights after the harvest and a local grain supply. Young thought that French arable land yielded less than half as much per acre as its English equivalent.

But archaic feudal dues and a wasteful agrarian system were not the peasant's only handicaps. He had to pay tithes to the Church and taxes to the state. Of the direct taxes the *taille*, the *capitation* and the *vingtième* all bore heavily on the peasant. Of the indirect taxes the *gabelle* was the most burdensome, though it varied greatly from region to region: in some pro-vinces salt cost as much as sixty-two *livres* a hundredweight, in others as little as sixteen *livres*.

No doubt the peasants, like the family described by Rousseau in his *Confessions*, [30] exaggerated their poverty in order to deceive the tax-collectors, but it is difficult to avoid the conclusion that more than half the peasantry lived barely above starvation point even in good years; and the eighteenth century saw a succession of grain shortages. It is true that there was nothing quite as serious as the famine of 1709; but there were periods of bad harvests in 1738–41, 1751–53, and 1768–70. In 1778 began a decade of agricultural depression, particularly in the wine-growing districts, until the bad harvest of 1788 brought a return to famine prices. Tithes and feudal dues that were burdensome at

[30] Lough, *op. cit.*, p. 57

best became intolerable in such conditions. The countryside was already in revolt when the events of July 1789 in Paris stampeded the peasants into panic.[31]

[31] For an account of 'the Great Fear' and the part played by the peasants in the Revolution, see the next chapter.

VI

THE FRENCH REVOLUTION

The summoning of the Estates-General for the first time since 1614 was a measure of the dissatisfaction for the existing political system felt by all sections of French society from the King down. But an analysis of the discordant aims of the various classes is not enough: the Revolution must also be studied as a narrative of events portraying what H. A. L. Fisher called 'the play of the contingent and the unforeseen'. The historian is in the position of a man trying to follow a symphony from an orchestral score: the part of the first violin or the second clarinet when studied in isolation may give no clue to the surprising impact of each instrument when heard in the context of the full orchestra. There is nothing inevitable about the march to the scaffold.

However, there are certain themes that may be traced throughout the greater part of the revolutionary symphony and which serve to give some semblance of continuity to its complex pattern. Of these perhaps the most important are: the economic situation, the pressures of war, the personalities of the men in power for the time being, and the intervention of the people of Paris. And it is these very elements that give meaning to the grand finale – the entry of Napoleon Bonaparte.

19

The Experiment in Constitutional Monarchy

From Estates-General to Constituent Assembly

The representatives of the three estates who sat in the Estates-General were elected in the provinces and could therefore claim to speak for the nation while Versailles spoke only for the court. The *cahiers* of grievances submitted by the respresentatives were surprisingly unanimous on some points: all three estates demanded security of person and property, the guaranteeing of the national debt, the reduction of court extravagance, full ministerial responsibility, and periodic sessions of the Estates-General for fiscal and legislative purposes. But beyond this agreement on the need to restrict absolute monarchy, the *cahiers* revealed wide differences, even between the privileged orders. Broadly speaking, the nobles were in favour of curtailing clerical privileges, and the clergy of curtailing the privileges of the nobles; but the nobles jealously defended their own feudal rights, while the clergy insisted on keeping their control over education and censorship. The Third Estate was divided within itself, but since almost all its representatives came from the professional *bourgeoisie*,[1] and since its *cahiers* largely ignored the grievances of the urban artisans and of all but the most prosperous peasants,[2] the Third Estate at first exhibited more outward harmony than did the privileged orders.

The method of voting in the Estates-General was therefore of crucial significance. The Paris *parlement*, which had resumed its functions in September 1788 amid popular approval, at once

---

[1] See above, p. 269.
[2] The *laboureurs*, whose grievances appeared in the parish *cahiers*, were not labourers but the better-off farmers.

declared in favour of privilege by demanding that the Estates-General should be constituted as in 1614 (that is, three roughly equal chambers sitting separately). In the face of the vigorous pamphlet warfare that this decision provoked, the Crown agreed to double the representation of the Third Estate so that it numbered as many as the other two orders combined; but the question of whether voting was to be by head or by chamber was not explicitly settled. The Third Estate assumed that voting would be by head: voting by chamber would still give a two to one majority in favour of privilege.

The question of voting was still undecided when the Estates-General was formally opened on 5 May 1789, with faithful adherence to seventeenth-century precedent in matters of ceremony and even of dress.[3] From the very first session the Third Estate refused to accept the principle of sitting as separate chambers, and since the Third Estate had been allotted the hall that was also to be used for combined sittings of all three orders, its claim to represent the general assembly of the nation seemed more plausible. For five weeks the Third Estate sat and waited. On 12 June it sent a final invitation to the other orders to attend its meetings, and the next day the clergy began to come over. On 17 June it declared itself the National Assembly by 491 votes to eighty-nine. Two days later more than half the remaining clergy, including six prelates, voted to join the Third Estate. Their arrival was inauspicious: on the 20th the members of the National Assembly were left standing in the rain because their hall had been closed, ostensibly for alterations in readiness for the royal session. They adjourned to the nearby indoor tennis court where they took their famous oath not to disband until France had been given a constitution.

At the royal session on 23 June the King conceded joint meetings of all three orders to discuss matters of common interest, including taxation, but insisted on separate sessions for such matters as 'the ancient and constitutional rights of the three orders, the powers to be awarded to the Estates-General, questions concerning feudal property, and the ancient rights and

[3] The somewhat comic opera quality of the opening session is well described in A. Cobban, *A History of Modern France*, Penguin 1961, vol. i, p. 140.

prerogatives of office reserved to the first two orders'. These were, of course, precisely the questions that the Third Estate wanted to discuss. The King repudiated the decisions of the Third Estate since 17 June and ordered a reversion to separate sittings. But at the end of the royal session the National Assembly (including the lower clergy) continued to sit, justifying its action in the astonishing words of its president, Bailly: 'The assembled nation cannot receive orders.' Louis' reaction was characteristic: 'They want to stay? Then let them stay.' Four days later he commanded the other orders to join the National Assembly, which on 2 July renamed itself the Constituent Assembly and turned to constitutional reform.

The royal session had not revealed a royal programme, but rather the absence of a royal programme. Necker, who had been recalled as Controller-General in August 1788, had stayed away from the royal session in protest against the rejection of his own compromise scheme. The death of the Dauphin on 4 June had not only distracted Louis from political issues, but had brought him under the influence of his more reactionary relatives. The dismissal of Necker on 11 July and his replacement by the Queen's favourite Breteuil were indications that Louis had again capitulated to the Queen's party.

To the people of Paris the dismissal of Necker looked like the prelude to a *coup d'état*. Louis had started to concentrate troops at Versailles, but they made no move against the assembly, so that the King's explanation that they were there to *protect* the assembly may well have been the true one. There was some need for protection. The prolonged inactivity of the Estates-General had led to trouble in the provinces where the delay was interpreted as evidence of an aristocratic plot to thwart the King's benevolent intentions. The peasants did not actually blame the privileged orders for the bad weather, but they attributed the grain shortage to conspiracy rather than to natural hazards. Bread riots and attacks on grain convoys, apparently on their way to the ports, had started in the spring of 1789. By the summer the countryside was swept by fear of brigands. Nobody knew who the brigands were or why there were so many of them, but at Montpellier in 1789 they were expected to arrive by sea.[4]

The Great Fear reached its height after the fall of the Bastille, but the decision of the Paris electors[5] to create a civic guard was prompted by fear of working-class panic as much as by fear of royal troops. No doubt the panic in Paris was partly stimulated by supporters of the Duke of Orleans, who hoped that the younger Bourbon line might seize the succession, but their headquarters at the Palais Royal can hardly be credited with having inspired all the sporadic and unconcerted riots of mid-July. The attack on the customs posts[6] began on the 12th. That night the monastery of the St Lazare brotherhood was broken into in search of grain, while gunsmiths, armourers and harness-makers throughout the city were raided for arms. On the 13th enrolment of the National Guard began. This was a *bourgeois* body: in most districts a property qualification was required for membership, the unemployed were expressly excluded, and all citizens not in the guard were forbidden to carry arms.

The attack on the Bastille seems to have been inspired by a desire to capture the powder and shot in its arsenal rather than to free the political prisoners who were believed to be in its dungeons. The electors, who had established a permanent committee at the Hôtel de Ville, had intended to negotiate with Governor de Launay for the surrender of the fortress, but events quickly passed out of their control. To describe those events, Carlyle himself confessed, 'perhaps transcends the power of mortals' – though his own account probably comes closest to conveying the confusion and clamour of the assault.[7] The attackers surged through the outer courtyard of the Bastille and penetrated as far as the inner courtyard, but had come no nearer to forcing an entry into the fortress itself when they were fired on by the garrison of Swiss Guards and Invalides. The crowd became infuriated, but fury and mere musketry could accom-

---

[4] For a description of the Great Fear see G. Lefebvre, *The French Revolution*, Routledge and Kegan Paul 1962, pp. 127–8, and C. Brinton *A Decade of Revolution*, Harper 1934, pp. 35–7.

[5] Elections to the Estate-General were indirect. The electors who had been appointed to choose representatives for Paris in the Estates-General now assumed to themselves the role of municipal government.

[6] See above, p. 271.

[7] See also article by G. Rudé in *History Today*, July 1954.

plish little until a detachment of regular Gardes Françaises arrived with five cannon taken from the Hôtel des Invalides. De Launay now finally lost his nerve. He agreed to lower the draw-bridge in return for a promise of safe-conduct. Rather sur-prisingly amid so much turmoil, most of his troops were safely escorted to the Hôtel de Ville, but de Launay himself was less lucky. His head was struck off with a butcher's knife and carried through the streets on a pike. Meanwhile the dungeons of the Bastille were made to disgorge their victims: there were seven, none of them a political prisoner and two of them insane.

The capture of the Bastille was a military operation: without the intervention of the Gardes Françaises and their cannon, the attack could scarcely have succeeded, while on the list of *vainqueurs de la Bastille* later drawn up by the secretary of the *vainqueurs*, six out of every seven were enrolled members of the National Guard.[8] The importance of the fall of the Bastille was, of course, political rather than military. The King agreed to dismiss the troops at Versailles – their loyalty was in any case now somewhat suspect – and rather courageously came to Paris to recognize the new municipal government and to confirm Lafayette as commander of the National Guard. Louis had already recognized the revolutionary National Assembly; he had now surrendered a second time in the face of force. The success of the municipal revolution in Paris encouraged imitators in provincial towns. Where bread prices were high, municipal officers were chased out with the cry of 'bread at two *sous*', and new officials appointed; elsewhere the burghers contented themselves with creating a militia. In the countryside the news from Paris intensified the Great Fear: at Visargent on 23 July even members of the National Guard were mistaken at a distance for brigands.[9]

The Great Fear stimulated but did not inspire the peasant revolution. Since the spring there had been scattered risings against feudal lords. After 14 July such riots became more widespread: manorial archives were burned, walls and fences

[8] See G. Rudé, *The Crowd in the French Revolution*, Oxford 1959, chapter 4, for an analysis of the stormers of the Bastille.
[9] G. Lefebvre, *The Coming of the French Revolution*, Vintage 1957, p. 129.

pulled down, and seigneurial hunting and fishing rights ignored. The peasants were doing what they expected the Assembly to sanction. On the night of 4 August 1789 the Vicomte de Noailles, not himself a landowner, persuaded the privileged orders to vote away their privileges. The decree of 11 August announced: 'The National Assembly destroys the feudal régime in its entirety.' This was inexact. Although tithes were abolished without compensation, most of the feudal dues were to be redeemed by a cash payment. But the distinction was academic, for the peasant refused to pay any dues. The abolition of feudalism, the most lasting achievement of the Revolution, was accomplished not by the Assembly but by the peasants themselves.

The Reforms of the Constituent Assembly

Before turning to constitutional reform, the Constituent Assembly drew up the Declaration of Rights of Man and Citizen (20–26 August 1789). The extent to which the declaration reflected the ideas of the *philosophes* and the influence of its American prototype[10] is clear from the words of the preamble:

> The representatives of the French people, constituted as a National Assembly, believing that ignorance, forgetfulness, or contempt of the rights of man are the only causes of public misfortunes and of the corruptions of governments, have resolved to set forth in a solemn declaration the natural, inalienable and sacred rights of man; in order that this declaration being constantly before all members of the social body may always recall to them their rights and their duties; in order that the acts of the legislative and executive powers being constantly capable of comparison with the objects of all political institutions may on that account be the more respected; in order that the demands of citizens being founded henceforth on simple and incontestable principles may be always directed to the maintenance of the constitution and the happiness of all. Consequently the National Assembly recognizes and declares in the presence and under the auspices of the Supreme Being the following rights of man and citizen.[11]

[10] See Chapter 17. Lafayette submitted the draft to Jefferson, who was representing his government at Versailles.
[11] All the articles are quoted in G. Salvemini, *The French Revolution*, Cape 1954, pp. 144–46, and the preamble and some of the articles in A. J. Grant and H. Temperley, *Europe in the Nineteenth and Twentieth Centuries*, Longmans 1932, Chapter 2.

The actual articles were less woolly: although framed in abstract terms they dealt with concrete political issues and, no less than the English Declaration of Rights in 1689, were directed against specific abuses. The absence of any article explicitly providing for freedom of worship is a reminder that the reformers were hard-headed enough to see that they could not yet afford to alienate the lower clergy. But if there was nothing particularly new about the drawing up of a declaration of rights, some of the rights claimed had novel implications. Perhaps the most striking was in the third article: 'The principle of sovereignty is vested in the nation. No form of collective power and no individual can exercise authority that does not directly emanate from the nation.' This sounds like Rousseau, although Sieyès's famous *What is the Third Estate?* had used similar language.[12] As yet, however, the revolutionaries regarded Montesquieu[13] as their model: the separation of powers rather than the sovereignty of the people was the basis on which the constitution-makers began to build.

The Constituent Assembly was dominated by the 'Patriot' party, a somewhat uneasy partnership between the Lafayette–Sieyès–Talleyrand wing and the more radical triumvirate of Barnave, Duport and Alexandre de Lameth. Lafayette was no orator, but the Society of '89 gave him a rudimentary political organization, while his American experience entitled him to pose as the interpreter of Montesquieu. Montesquieu was misinterpreted: the rigid separation of powers eventually embodied in the constitution of 1791 put effective power squarely in the hands of the assembly. Mirabeau, the shrewdest politician of the day, saw the danger and insisted that the King should be allowed an absolute veto. He also opposed the exclusion of ministers from the assembly, which the strict separation of powers would entail. Mirabeau's advice on both matters was disregarded: quite apart from his scandalous private life, he was thought to be in the pay of the court and known to be an ambitious politician. And so ministers were forbidden to be deputies and the King was allowed only a suspensive veto. If Lafayette and Mirabeau could have worked together, they might have controlled the

[12] Cobban, *op. cit.*, p. 161.   [13] See above, pp. 79 and 253.

Assembly, but Lafayette was uncompromising: 'I have resisted the King of England in his power, the King of France in his authority, the people in its rage; I am not going to yield to Mirabeau.'[14]

On 3 September a journeyman roofmaker was arrested for publicly accusing Lafayette of deliberately helping to cause a bread shortage. A fortnight later the Hôtel de Ville was besieged by angry women protesting against bakers. On 5 October, after a similar demonstration outside the Hôtel de Ville, several thousand women marched to Versailles – in pouring rain. It is not known who organized this march, or whether it was as spontaneous as it seemed, though the Orleanist press had recently been clamouring for the return of the King to Paris.[15] In any case, Lafayette hesitated for several hours before dispatching some 20,000 National Guardsmen to Versailles. Their eventual arrival late that night helped to calm the crowd and probably prevented a wholesale massacre of the royal bodyguard when the palace was invaded in the early hours of the next morning. That afternoon, in the midst of a motley and by now somewhat muddy crowd, the royal family was escorted back to Paris and lodged in the Tuileries. The Assembly followed. Now both king and legislature were exposed to the pressure of the people of Paris.

Not all the sovereign people were allowed to vote. Only those who paid taxes equal to the value of three days' wages qualified as 'active' citizens entitled to vote in the election of electors, who in turn elected the deputies; only those who paid taxes equal to ten days' wages could be electors; and only those who paid a tax of fifty days' wages (the so-called silver mark) could sit as deputies.[16] Marat denounced 'this aristocracy of rich men'; but about two-thirds of all Frenchmen over twenty-five were given the vote, and, if only 50,000 could serve as electors at any one time, about three million (or three-quarters of the 'active' citizens) were qualified to do so. Even if this was a narrower franchise than the Declaration of Rights had seemed to promise,

[14] Mirabeau died in April 1791; Lafayette lived long enough to play a part in the second French revolution of 1830.

[15] See Rudé, *op. cit.*, Chapter 5.

[16] The silver mark was dropped before the constitution became law.

it was rather more democratic than the British franchise even after the Reform Act of 1832.[17]

'Active' citizens voted also in local government elections. The *intendants* and the tradition of centralized bureaucracy that they were supposed to symbolize[18] had not survived the summer of 1789. The new system carried the principle of decentralization to extremes: the 41,000 communes or municipalities were grouped into some 4,000 cantons, the cantons into 550 odd districts, and the districts into the eighty-three departments which replaced the thirty old *généralités* of the *intendants*. At each level there were elected councils, but there was no unifying bureaucracy and therefore no effective integration between the various layers of the administrative pyramid. And it was the friction between commune and department in particular that the Jacobins were later to exploit in their bid for power.[19]

The breakdown in local government was matched by a final failure of the fiscal system. The Estates-General had been called to redistribute taxation, but the result of the disorders of July 1789 was simply that taxes were no longer paid. In March 1790 the Assembly agreed to abolish indirect taxes, while the old direct taxes, *taille*, *capitation*, *vingtième*, were replaced by a single property tax. But the new units of local government were not particularly zealous in the assessment and collection of the new tax, and in order to reduce the growing deficit the Assembly had either to repudiate the national debt or find new sources of revenue. It was perhaps natural that a *bourgeois* assembly should shrink from the first alternative and prefer to confiscate Church lands. In December 1789 the first *assignats* were issued on the security of the confiscated lands. The *assignats* were not as absurd an expedient as they are sometimes made to appear. They were not at first legal tender: they could be used only to purchase Church lands, and incoming *assignats* were to be destroyed. But since the Church lands could be paid for by instalments, the amount of *assignats* in circulation soon exceeded the amount of

---

[17] For a discussion of the democratic and *bourgeois* features of the franchise of 1791 see R. R. Palmer, *The Age of the Democratic Revolution*, Oxford 1959, vol. i, pp. 522–8.

[18] For the reality see Chapter 16 above.

[19] See Chapter 20 below.

FRANCE BEFORE 1789

France before 1789

land on the market, and later assemblies were content to ac-
centuate this inflationary trend by further issues.[20]

The nationalization of Church property left the clergy
dependent on a state stipend. The Civil Constitution of the
Clergy (July 1790) defined their obligations to the state. It
also attempted to rationalize ecclesiastical organization, no
doubt with one eye on economy. The religious orders were
dissolved, archbishoprics abolished, and bishoprics reduced to
one for each department; bishops and priests were to be elected
by the councils of departments and districts respectively;

[20] See below, p. 295.

REVOLUTIONARY FRANCE
(Showing the departments
created in 1789)

Revolutionary France

salaries were fixed, ranging from 50,000 francs for the bishop
of Paris to 1,200 francs for the parish priest. In November the
Assembly decreed that all clergy must take an oath of allegiance
to the new constitution, including the Civil Constitution of the
Clergy.[21] About half the clergy and all but seven of the bishops
refused.

The Civil Constitution, promulgated without reference to
the Pope, probably owed as much to Gallicanism as to rationalism: most of the jurists and canon lawyers who framed it were

---

[21] In 1791 the Civil Constitution was separated from the constitution as a whole and
was therefore itself no longer subject to the oath.

Jansenists.[22] But the anti-clerical propaganda of the *philosophes* probably helped to conceal from the members of the Assembly the political implications of a divided Church. Louis signed the November decree, but when in the spring of 1791 the Pope at last condemned the Civil Constitution and the Revolution as a whole, the experiment in constitutional monarchy was doomed. Louis XVI, like Charles I of England, would not forsake his Church; he preferred to forsake his throne. On the night of 20 June 1791 (the second anniversary of the Tennis Court Oath) the King and Queen, their two children, Madame Elizabeth, and a governess escaped in disguise from the Tuileries and set out, two hours behind schedule and in a cumbersome coach, on the road to Metz. They were recognized more than once, but they travelled for twenty-four hours before they were stopped and surrounded by a hostile crowd at Varennes. The Marquis de Bouillé had stationed troops on the Varennes road in order to meet the coach and escort it to Montmédy, beyond the Meuse; but the troops had dispersed before the royal party arrived, and, by the time Bouillé had found fresh troops, it was too late to attempt a rescue. On the morning of 22 June the royal carriage began its melancholy return journey to Paris.

After the flight to Varennes, the new constitution on which the Assembly had worked for nearly two years could be preserved only by the fiction that the King had been kidnapped against his will. In July a demonstration of 50,000 in the *Champ de Mars* to demand the King's abdication was broken up by Lafayette and the National Guard. In September the King signed the completed constitution, and the Constituent Assembly gave place to the Legislative Assembly, which met on 1 October.

The constitution was obsolete before it became law, but the Constituent Assembly had not concerned itself solely with constitution-making. All internal customs duties were removed, guilds and restrictions on manufactured goods were suppressed, and some monopolies were abolished; trial by jury was established; torture, flogging, mutilation and branding were expunged from the penal code; life sentences were limited to

[22] See above, p. 240.

twenty-four years and the privilege of decapitation extended to all ranks; the *parlements* were replaced by a new system of courts with elected magistrates. Slavery was not abolished in the colonies, and the Le Chapelier law of 1791 maintained the ban on trade unions, but the reforms of the Constituent Assembly were to survive long after the Constitution of 1791 and the Constitutional Church had perished, and they help to explain the enthusiastic response which the first phase of the Revolution evoked in Europe.

The Revolution and Europe

It was not only in the England of Fox and Wordsworth that the early achievements of the Revolution were hailed with enthusiasm. Of the leading figures of the *Aufklärung*,[23] Goethe and Schiller were non-committal, but Herder, Kant and Fichte quickly voiced their approval. At Göttingen university the undergraduate Hegel helped to plant a tree to commemorate 14 July. Many foreign writers made the pilgrimage to France to experience the miracle at first hand; among them came Wilhelm von Humboldt, the Russian historian Karamzin, and the Italian tragic dramatist Alfieri, who dedicated an ode to the fall of the Bastille. At Milan the economist and liberal reformer Pietro Verri wrote: 'France will give a sense of freedom to all Europe. . . . Oppression will no longer be tolerated. The people, aware of their strength, will sooner or later follow the example of the French'.[24]

His prediction was soon fulfilled. Throughout 1790 the Habsburg Empire was in a ferment: the 'United States of Belgium' was proclaimed in Brussels, the Bohemian Diet demanded an 'indestructible constitution', the county assemblies of Hungary claimed the right to make a new contract with each new king at his coronation because 'by the social contract which creates the state, sovereignty lies in the hands of the people', and even the Tyrol said it should crown its ruler in return for a confirmation of liberties.[25] But as the Emperor Leopold II was quick to point out, the Estates of the Empire were aristocratic assemblies.

---

[23] See Chapter 6 above.   [24] Salvemini, *op. cit.*, p. 190.
[25] Palmer, *op. cit.*, p. 388.

The mood of 'the people' was more accurately mirrored in the Decretum of the Peasants which circulated in Hungary in May 1790: 'Let us advance . . . raise up our sticks, pitchforks and axes against the cruel, parasitic, time-stealing, country-ruining, king-robbing lords.'[26] The troubles in Ireland and Poland, Holland and Switzerland were due mainly to constitutional grievances, but in the Palatinate and along the Rhine, on the island of Rügen and in Saxony, in Tuscany and in Savoy, agrarian disturbances were the rule.

As if these manifestations were not enough to frighten European monarchs, the Constituent Assembly had embarked on an aggressive foreign policy. The German princes who held lands in Alsace, which since 1648 had been a French possession though within the Empire, had lost their feudal privileges as a result of the decree of August 1789. This was a breach of the Treaty of Ryswick (1697) and, although the Assembly offered compensation, the German princes, prompted by Louis XVI, refused it; they could hardly accept such reforms in Alsace while denying them to their own subjects. The French plea was that the people of Alsace wanted to be French citizens. The same argument was used in September 1791 to justify French annexation of the papal enclaves of Avignon and the Comtat Venaissin. This was to state a new principle in international law: diplomacy was to be conducted not between princes but between peoples. If the Constituent Assembly had begun as a champion of liberalism, it ended as a champion of nationalism.

There were also good, old-fashioned dynastic interests at stake. The Emperor Leopold II was Marie Antoinette's brother; another brother was Archbishop of Cologne, while her sisters ruled in the Netherlands and in Naples. But the Emperor already had his hands full: Joseph II had bequeathed to him not only disturbances throughout his Empire, but a war, in alliance with Russia, against the Turks.[27] Prussia was pleased to see Austria and Russia at war in the east since it gave her a chance to foment trouble in the Netherlands and in Poland, but when Russia was attacked by the Swedes under Gustavus III, Prussia and Austria came to terms at Reichenbach (July 1790). Even in

---

[26] *Ibid.*, p. 393. [27] See above, p. 207.

1791, however, when Austria had made peace with the Turks, and Russia with the Swedes, the European powers were reluctant to intervene in France. Indeed it looked much more likely that they would intervene in Poland.[28] The truth is that, however determined they were to avert revolution in their own territories, the European powers were delighted that France had temporarily ceased to count diplomatically. Pitt in particular was able to exploit Spanish isolation in the Nootka Sound dispute of 1790, and his contempt for French finances confirmed him in his belief that France was powerless. Only Gustavus III of Sweden, deprived of the subsidy of one and a half million *livres* that he had enjoyed under the *ancien régime*, favoured a monarchist crusade – with himself at the head. But in March 1792 he was assassinated at a masked ball in Stockholm.

Meanwhile, from the comfort of the small German courts of the Rhineland and from the extravagant entourage of the Comte d'Artois, first at Turin and then in the territories of his uncle the Elector of Trèves, the *émigrés* did their utmost by propaganda and diplomatic pressure to persuade the European monarchs to act. But it was Louis XVI himself who forced Leopold's hand. The flight to Varennes meant that the Emperor could no longer pretend that the royal family was not under duress. In August 1791 Leopold and Frederick William II of Prussia issued from Pillnitz their joint declaration pledging themselves to intervene in France if the other powers would collaborate. Since England's attitude made it certain that the condition would not be fulfilled, the Declaration of Pillnitz, for all the panic it provoked in Paris, was purely a piece of bluff. Louis XVI's acceptance of the constitution in September confirmed Leopold in his strenuous inactivity, and when in December the Legislative Assembly summoned the Elector of Trèves to disperse the *émigrés*, the Emperor would guarantee Trèves no help unless the summons was obeyed. Yet in the same month Leopold promised imperial protection to the Alsatian princes and continued to canvass the idea of a coalition.

The Legislative Assembly replied with the decree of 25 January 1792 calling on the Emperor to 'renounce every treaty and

[28] See above, p. 213.

convention directed against the sovereignty, independence and safety of the French nation'. A fortnight later the property of the *émigrés* was sequestrated. Leopold, still suspicious of Russian intentions in Poland, concluded a defensive alliance with Prussia in February. On 1 March Leopold died. Under his more bellicose son Francis II the Prussian alliance soon became offensive: war was to begin early in April. But the revolutionaries stole the initiative. On 27 March a final ultimatum was sent to Austria, while Marie Antoinette's message to Vienna that an attack on the Netherlands was imminent disrupted Austro-Prussian invasion plans. On 20 April the Legislative Assembly declared war, prefacing its motion with the words:

> In accordance with the sacred principles of the Constitution, which do not permit France to take part in a war of conquest or to use her forces against the liberties of other peoples, the French nation is taking up arms solely in defence of its own independence: it is fighting not in a war between nation and nation, but in rightful defence of a free people against the unjust aggression of a King.[29]

These noble words did not, of course, deter Revolutionary France from setting out to acquire the 'natural frontiers' claimed by Louis XIV.

[29] Salvemini, *op. cit.*, p. 260.

20

The Republican Phase

The Legislative Assembly and the Fall of the Monarchy

The Legislative Assembly's declaration of war against 'the King of Hungary and Bohemia' on 20 April 1792 was the result of internal stresses as well as of external threats. The centre party of the Constituent Assembly, the party of Lafayette and the triumvirate,[1] became the right wing of the new assembly. But it comprised different men, for, by the 'Self-Denying Ordinance' of May 1791, deputies who had sat in the Constituent were excluded from the Legislative Assembly. About one-third of the 745 deputies in the new assembly were enrolled as Feuillants (the new club whose members had seceded from the Jacobins in July), 136 were members of the Jacobin and Cordeliers clubs, while over 300 remained uncommitted, ready to vote as prudence rather than principle dictated. Thanks to its superior organization, the numerically inferior left wing was able to dominate the Assembly. In the absence of the leading Paris Jacobins, disqualified by the Self-Denying Ordinance, the initiative passed to Brissot and the Jacobin deputies from the Gironde Department, of whom Vergniaud was the chief orator. These were the new men of the Revolution: born in the middle ranks of the *bourgeoisie* and entering politics from the lower ranks of the legal profession, they had no vested interest in preserving the monarchy and every reason for pressing the attack on privilege still farther.

The Brissotins, or Girondins as they are now more usually called, worked for war in order to confirm their power. Denunciation of the *émigrés* was a good rallying cry: Brissot opened the campaign in October 1791, and in November the Assembly decreed that all prominent *émigrés* who did not return

[1] See above, p. 283.

293

by 1 January 1792 should be held guilty of treason. 'Either we shall conquer the *émigrés* and priests,' declared Brissot, 'and establish the country's credit upon a solid basis, or we shall be betrayed and defeated, the traitors will be unmasked at last and punished, and we shall then sweep away everything that stands in the way of the nation's greatness.' The implication seems to be that war would provide a welcome excuse for taking tougher measures at home, but Brissotin propaganda naturally laid more stress on the attractions of victory. 'When the light of philosophy flashes upon the enemy armies,' predicted Isnard, 'the peoples will defy their tyrants and embrace one another in a land restored to peace beneath the propitious heavens.'[2]

Others saw a different vision. Narbonne, a noble who had sided with the patriots and was now Minister of War, thought that a successful war was the best means of saving the monarchy. In March 1792 he was replaced by Dumouriez who pursued the same aim with more energy: a bold bid to seize the 'natural frontiers' of France would be followed by diversion of the army to suppress the revolutionaries at home. Robespierre, who opposed the war, seems to have sensed this danger. In January he predicted: 'The victories of our generals would be more disastrous for us than our defeats.' Meanwhile Marie Antoinette revealed Dumouriez's war plans to the Austrians in an attempt to hasten her deliverance.

The war was to seal the fate of the monarchy. The Constituent Assembly had refrained from deposing the King for fear of provoking war, but once the war had begun the monarchy became a dangerous liability. As Verginaud was to claim so eloquently that summer:

It is in the King's name that the French princes have tried to rouse every court in Europe against the French nation. It is to vindicate the King's dignity that the Treaty of Pillnitz and the monstrous alliance between the courts of Vienna and Berlin has been concluded. . . . It is to overcome the French nation and the National Assembly and to maintain the splendour of the throne that the Emperor makes war on us and the King of Prussia marches towards our frontiers. . . . O man unmoved by the generosity of

[2] Quoted in G. Salvemini. *The French Revolution*, p. 252.

the French people, O man conscious only of a love for despotism, you have not fulfilled that which the Constitution enjoined upon you. You are nothing now to this Constitution which you have so unworthily betrayed, and to this people that you have so vilely deceived.[3]

To Girondin and Jacobin alike the logic behind the rhetoric seemed irrefutable.

But for the moment, the war effort took priority. The army, far from achieving Dumouriez's dashing designs, could scarcely defend France's existing frontiers. Two-thirds of the infantry officers had deserted, the high command was divided by jealousies, and the 169 new volunteer battalions were not yet trained or equipped. When at the end of April French troops got their first sight of the Austrians near Tournai, they retreated in disorder and murdered their commander. But France's enemies failed to exploit their advantage, for Catherine II chose this moment to invade Poland.[4] Austria and Prussia spent three months in extracting guarantees from Russia, and it was not until 19 August that the first Prussian troops crossed the French frontier. By then the French Army was fit to fight. The gaps at the various levels of command had been filled by promotions; the new battalions, instructed in the tactical techniques of Guibert current since the 1770s, were all the better for being volunteers; and the artillery, trained on Gribeauval's gunnery manual of 1776, was the best in Europe.

If the military situation had improved, the economic situation had deteriorated. In June 1792, by which time the total number of *assignats* issued amounted to 2,400 million *livres*, the *assignat* in Paris had fallen to 57 per cent of its face value. Prices were inevitably affected, particularly where scarcity aggravated the effects of inflation. In January 1792 there were riots in Paris when the disruption of sugar supplies by the revolt of slaves in the West Indies caused the price to rise rapidly from twenty-five *sous* to three or three and a half *livres* a pound.[5] In February a shortage of soap led to further riots, and in March the mayor of

3 3 July 1792. For a fuller version see Salvemini, *op. cit.*, p. 286.
4 See above, p. 213.
5 For an explanation of currency values see Appendix 4.

Étampes was killed by a mob who believed he had profiteered in foodstuffs. While the deputies decreed that a monument should be raised to the murdered mayor, Robespierre at the Jacobin Club demanded a reprieve for the murderers.

Meanwhile the Jacobins of Marseille marched on Aix-en-Provence, disarmed its troops and set up a new municipal government; they then did the same for Arles and Avignon. The Girondins, misconstruing the drift of events, decided to exploit the revolutionary zeal of the provinces to strengthen their own position in Paris: 25,000 provincial National Guardsmen (*fédérés*) were summoned to defend the capital. The 4,500 who obeyed the summons began to arrive on 8 July. Three weeks earlier the King had vetoed two decrees. As a result, the anniversary of the Tennis Court Oath was celebrated by an invasion of the Tuileries, led by men of the *faubourg* Sainte-Antoine and supported by women and members of the National Guard. For two hours the King submitted to their insults, wore the red 'cap of liberty' which they offered to him, and drank their health. The episode passed off without bloodshed, but it should have been a warning to the Girondins of where the appeal to popular revolutionary fervour might lead.

Yet the Assembly proceeded to authorize the distribution of pikes to all citizens and the admission of 'passive' citizens to the hitherto *bourgeois* National Guard. The Jacobins may not have directed the 'June Days', but they did their utmost to excite popular feeling against the Girondins. In his *Ami du peuple* Marat castigated Brissot as a 'faithless representative of the people, abettor of the ministerial faction and henchman of the despot', while at the end of July Robespierre demanded the replacement of the Legislative Assembly by a National Convention elected by universal suffrage. But it was Danton, deputy *procureur* of the Paris commune, who has best claim to be regarded as the leader of the popular movement at this stage. He may not have played as dominant a role as he later claimed at his trial, but his *section* of Paris, the Théâtre Français, seems to have given the lead in the confused events of late July and early August.

By the end of July, forty-seven of the forty-eight *sections* had declared in favour of the King's abdication and set up a 'Central Office of Coordination'. Most of the *fédérés* had moved to their camp at Soissons, but a couple of thousand, including the Marseillais contingent, remained in Paris, centred on the Jacobin Club and in contact with the coordinating office of the *sections*. On 1 August the Brunswick Manifesto was published in Paris. By promising the city 'complete military subjection and martial law' if the 'least violence' were inflicted on the royal family, Brunswick provoked the very event he had meant to avoid. On 6 August the *faubourg* Sainte-Antoine warned the Assembly that, unless the King had abdicated by 9 August, the *sections* would act. On the 9th a revolutionary commune was set up, with the mayor of Paris as its prisoner. On the 10th a force of perhaps 20,000 from forty-four *sections*, led by National Guard and *fédérés*, attacked the Tuileries. It was a motley crowd composed of fifty or sixty trades from shoemakers and wigmakers to clerks and domestic servants.[6] Through a combination of accident and treachery the Tuileries fell, the Swiss guards were butchered, and the King sought refuge with the Assembly. The Assembly, with only 285 deputies present, suspended the King from his functions, dismissed the King's ministers, set up a provisional executive council with Danton as Minister of Justice, and approved the election of a National Convention by universal suffrage to 'pronounce upon measures for assuring the sovereignty of the people and the reign of liberty and equality'.

The National Convention and the Fall of the Girondins

The attack on the Tuileries of August 1792 was a logical consequence of the flight to Varennes. The King and Queen were now imprisoned in the Temple to await the verdict of the National Convention. The final collapse of the experiment in constitutional monarchy was signalized by the defection of Lafayette: having failed to persuade the troops of Sedan to march on Paris and avenge the August Days, he deserted with his staff to the Austrians, who promptly imprisoned him as a dangerous revolutionary.

[6] See J. M. Thompson, *The French Revolution*, Blackwell 1943, p. 288.

The Austrians were now on the way to Paris. Longwy fell on 23 August, Verdun a week later. On 2 September, when rumours of the fall of Verdun were already current in Paris, the church bells summoned the city to arms. Meanwhile there were rumours of a counter-revolutionary plot and demands for reprisals against suspected royalists. This was the atmosphere in which the 'September massacres' were planned. As early as 23 August the leaders of the revolutionary commune seem to have agreed in principle to a general massacre of prisoners before the Paris volunteers left for the front. On Sunday 2 September twenty priests on their way to the Abbaye prison in Marat's *section* were murdered at the prison gates. Exhilarated by their work, the crowd moved on to other prisons where they set up tribunals and summarily executed all prisoners adjudged guilty. By the end of the following day nearly half of the 2,800 prisoners in the nine prisons involved had been massacred. Only about a quarter of the victims were priests, nobles or political prisoners; the rest were common criminals.[7]

The Republic had been baptized in blood. No group ventured to claim credit for the massacres, but the Jacobins were the chief beneficiaries. In the National Convention, which met for the first time on 20 September 1792, the Girondins outnumbered the Jacobins, for although Paris was solidly Jacobin, the provinces preferred Brissot's supporters. But in the struggle to dominate the Convention, which contained as many as 400 neutrals in a chamber of 765, control of the capital was likely to prove more decisive than support in the country. Robespierre, who had been excluded from the Legislative Assembly, was now able to take his seat in the Convention together with Marat, while Danton resigned his ministerial post in order to sit as a deputy. The Jacobins, occupying the higher seats at the back of the chamber, became known as the Mountain. It was an apt name, for the Jacobins stood for a broadly based but pyramid-shaped governmental structure with firm centralized regulation of food supplies, prices and wages – a system of controls. The Girondins, the party of the provinces, wanted to preserve the decentralization introduced by the Constituent Assembly,[8]

[7] G. Rudé, *The Crowd in the French Revolution*, p. 110.   [8] See above, p. 285.

thinking, perhaps, that this provided a better safeguard for
private property. In twentieth-century eyes there can be little
doubt as to which system was better suited to waging war.

For the time being, however, the war seemed to be going
well after all. On the very day that the Convention met, the
revolutionary army won its first victory at Valmy: Dumouriez
surprised Brunswick by standing firm when he was expected
to retreat, and the French artillery, aided by bad weather, forced
the Prussians to withdraw. It was just the kind of fillip the
National Convention needed. Dumouriez was given a hero's
welcome in Paris before being dispatched to invade the Netherlands. At the beginning of November he defeated the Austrians
at Jemappes and proceeded to overrun Belgium. Meanwhile
other French forces occupied Mainz on the Rhine, Nice and
Savoy. In an ebullient mood the Convention declared the
Scheldt estuary open to shipping, thus violating the treaty of
Westphalia (1648), and issued the famous Edict of Fraternity,
offering armed help to all other nations who attempted to overthrow their kings. A week later Brissot admitted: 'We cannot
be calm until Europe, all Europe is in flames.' The Revolution
had taken the offensive.

Now that Paris was no longer in danger the Convention
could decide what to do with the King. The monarchy had been
formally abolished on 21 September, but the ensuing discussions
on the fate of the King occupied seven hours a day for two
months. They were conducted in a mood of high seriousness:
the trial of Charles I of England was carefully studied and the
competence of the Convention to try the King was patiently
argued. A new urgency was given to the discussions when a
secret iron chest was discovered at the Tuileries containing royal
correspondence of a treasonable nature. Robespierre was quick
to point the moral. He argued that a trial was unnecessary and
the appeal to the Constitution irrelevant: 'If the King is not
guilty, then those who have deposed him are. . . . The Constitution prohibited everything you have done.' Yet the Girondins clung to legal forms, and the King appeared before the
Convention in December. Given the assumptions on which
the Convention had been elected, there could be no defence.

The King was declared guilty by a unanimous vote; a motion recommending a reprieve was defeated by 380 votes to 310. On 21 January 1793 Louis was executed.

On 15 February Condorcet presented to the Convention the constitution on which the drafting committee (including Danton, Vergniaud, Sieyès, and even Tom Paine) had been working since September. But events had overtaken the polite political principles of the *philosophes,* and after three months' discussion the Convention had dealt with only six of Condorcet's 368 articles. Five Jacobins were now appointed to the committee and a new draft constitution was produced in a week.

The rejection of Condorcet's constitution was a measure of Girondin failure to control the Convention. They had also failed to control the country. The declaration of war against England and Holland (1 February 1793) and against Spain (7 March) had been followed by Dumouriez's defeat by the Austrians at Neerwinden in mid-March and his desertion to the enemy. Other French forces were driven back from the Rhine, while the Vendée[9] rose in protest against the selective conscription which had been decreed in February. In Paris, where the prices of sugar and soap were double their 1790 level, food riots broke out at the end of February. This time the chief troublemakers were the so-called *enragés,* who demanded a return to economic controls. While Marat exhorted the rioters to hang some grocers, the Commune fixed the price of bread at three *sous* a pound. This did not prevent the 'March Days' when a number of pro-Girondin newspaper offices were sacked by a crowd. The demonstrators were deterred from marching on the Convention only by the action of the National Guard, which for once did its job.

In this explosive atmosphere the Convention passed a series of emergency measures directed not against rioters but against counter-revolutionaries: harsher penalties were imposed on *émigrés* and non-juror priests, watch committees were set up in every commune, commissioners were appointed to bolster up the loyalty of the provinces, the famous Revolutionary Tribunal

9 For a study of the role of the Vendée in the revolution see H. Kurtz in *History To-day,* January and March 1963.

300

was created to deal swiftly with suspected traitors, and, on 6 April, the Committee of Public Safety was established. The Girondins had thus acquiesced in the creation of the machinery of the Terror. They had little choice, for they were under pressure to prove their patriotism. The Jacobin press charged Brissot with complicity in Dumouriez's treason, and when in mid-April the Girondins retaliated by charging Marat before the Revolutionary Tribunal, Marat was acquitted. A week earlier, Robespierre's brother, in a speech at the Jacobin Club, had invited the help of the Paris *sections* in expelling *les députés infidèles*. By the middle of April, thirty-five of the forty-eight *sections* had agreed to demand the purging of the Convention, and a Central Revolutionary Committee was set up by the Commune to coordinate action. At the end of May this committee called on the *sections* to raise a revolutionary militia of 20,000 to augment the National Guard. The pattern of August 1792 was being repeated.

The Girondins provoked the final stroke by appointing a Commission of Twelve, all Girondins, to investigate the activities of the *sections*. On 2 June a huge crowd comprising elements of the National Guard and the new revolutionary militia surrounded the Tuileries and demanded the expulsion of the leading Girondin deputies. After ineffective protests the Convention complied: twenty-nine deputies and two ministers were arrested. The Jacobins had unseated their rivals: in the absence of constitutional provision for a dissolution, they had invoked the support of the people of Paris. In order to stay in power themselves they would have to keep that support.

The Dictatorship of Robespierre

The expulsion of the Girondin deputies did not put an end to government by Convention, but the role of the Convention was greatly reduced. The administrative failures of the Girondins had shown the futility of trying to direct a war by means of a debating society of 765 members. Under Jacobin rule there would be few debates: the main governmental decisions were now delegated to committees of the Convention, while the

Convention itself was reduced to listening to committee reports and approving committee decisions.

The committees had been set up during the period of Girondin rule. The Committee of General Security had been established in October 1792 to coordinate police measures against counter-revolutionaries. The Committee of Public Safety as first constituted in April 1793 comprised nine members (including Danton and Barère) subject to monthly re-election by the Convention. Its task was 'to supervise and speed up the administration in charge of the Provisional Executive Council'.[10] By September 1793 there were twelve members, who were henceforth re-elected without change. Robespierre did not become a member until 27 July 1793 (a fortnight after Danton left the committee) and he never became its leader in any formal sense. The committee was, in J. M. Thompson's phrase, 'a Cabinet without a Premier'. There were no chairman and no minutes, the members were individually responsible for different departments (Carnot for defence, Lindet for the Quartermaster General's department), and decrees of the committee often carried the signatures of only a few of its members. Robespierre seems to have had a roving commission: his notebook gives the impression that he dealt with matters ranging from nomination of judges and juries for the Revolutionary Tribunal to providing pensions for war widows. Perhaps this is why he appeared to be the dominant member of the committee.

Robespierre's rise to power seems indeed to have been due mainly to conscientious persistence. The little lawyer from Arras, with his spectacles, his thin voice and his provincial accent, was not a prepossessing figure, but he displayed a high degree of moral earnestness at a time when solemnity actually won votes. In contrast to Mirabeau, who had been regarded as a political opportunist with the morals of a rake, Robespierre had won his reputation for incorruptibility by apparently cutting short his political career in proposing the Self-Denying Ordinance.[11]

---

[10] The ministers of the Executive Council were in practice subordinated to the Committee, and in April 1794 were replaced by twelve commissions of civil servants who had no control over policy.

[11] See above, p. 293.

This was probably not so much a piece of cynical calculation as a patriotic excuse for devoting his energies to the Jacobin Club, where he was so much more at home. More than half of the 634 speeches Robespierre delivered between 1789 and 1794 were made at the Club. But it was not just that he spoke so often; he was so often right. He had condemned the narrow franchise of 1791, he had opposed the declaration of war in 1792, he had urged the execution of the King, and he had called for the introduction of war-time controls. By the summer of 1793, when he became the acknowledged spokesman of the Committee of Public Safety, he had already become the oracle of the Revolution.

In a memorandum,[12] apparently drawn up when he joined the Committee in July 1793, Robespierre summarized the problems facing the new Jacobin government. His objective was 'the use of the Constitution for the benefit of the people', and the chief obstacles in the way were: the moneyed classes, a corrupt press, the poverty of the working classes, and 'the war at home and abroad'. The path must be cleared 'by making a terrible example of all the traitors who have outraged liberty and spilt the blood of patriots'. This was the recipe for the Terror.

The revolts that had followed the expulsion of the Girondin deputies were certainly harshly suppressed. At Bordeaux in October 1793, 800 'rebels' were tried and nearly 300 executed; at Marseille between March and May 1794 there were 460 executions; the notorious decree against Lyon[13] led to 2,000 executions in six months; the *noyades* or wholesale drownings at Nantes probably accounted for another 2,000. The Vendée, where a royalist revolt had been raging since March 1793, was meanwhile cowed, though not finally pacified, by the brutal punitive measures of the winter of 1793–94. It was in vindictive provincial reprisals such as these, rather than through the activities of the Revolutionary Tribunal in Paris, that most of the 40,000 victims of the Terror were to meet their deaths.

While so much of France was in rebellion it is not surprising

---

[12] For the full text of this memorandum see J. M. Thompson, *Robespierre and the French Revolution*, E.U.P. 1952, p. 79.

[13] Thompson, *The French Revolution*, p. 410.

that the new constitution of 1793,[14] although approved by plebiscite in July, was shelved 'until the peace'. By the decree of 4 December 1793 the Committee of Public Safety assumed control of all subordinate authorities, except for police, which remained nominally under the Committee of General Security. The administrative powers of the departments were transferred to districts and municipalities,[15] where 'national agents' were appointed to act on the instructions of the central government. The agents were kept on their toes by 'representatives on mission', dispatched from Paris for specific purposes such as the organization of conscription. The *levée en masse* of August 1793 had called to the colours all unmarried men between 18 and 25, and the French armies now started to enjoy numerical superiority. By October 1793 a series of French victories began, and by the following summer the whole left bank of the Rhine was again French, while the victory of Fleurus prepared the way for the reconquest of Belgium.

On the home front the Jacobins had inherited economic problems inseparable from a pre-railway age: how to ensure the equitable distribution of grain in the provinces and the supply of food to the towns, particularly Paris. Girondin decentralization had made matters worse, and it was not until 4 May 1793 (a month before the Girondins fell) that the first 'Maximum' fixed the price of grain in each department. In July the Jacobins made hoarding a capital crime;[16] in September the second 'Maximum' fixed the prices of forty commodities and pegged wages at the level of 1790 plus 50 per cent; on Christmas Day 1793 bread rationing was introduced in Paris, followed by meat rationing in April 1794; the sale of white bread was forbidden, and a coarser *pain d'egalité* made of mixed flours was substituted.

Such economic controls, regarded with horror by nineteenth-century liberal historians, are now accepted as the necessary means of organizing a nation for war. Similarly the modern historian, familiar with spy trials and the bombing of cities,

---

[14] For extracts from the constitution see Thompson, *Robespierre and the French Revolution*, p. 115.

[15] See above, p. 285.

[16] This was later amended so as to retain the death penalty only for deliberately allowing foodstuffs to perish.

is perhaps better able to understand (though not necessarily to excuse) the phenomenon of the Terror. The Revolutionary Tribunal, which sent 2,795 persons to the guillotine between January 1793 and June 1795, was a war-time court to try crimes against the state. Many of its victims were not political offenders at all, but middle- and lower-class citizens who had broken the criminal law: all too easily swift justice degenerated into just swiftness. But the tribunal seems to have enjoyed a reputation for fairness in spite of its arbitrary procedure; and the Terror was accepted by normally sane and civilized men as a necessary means of meeting a national emergency. Of course, it is undeniable that the Jacobins used their emergency powers to remove their rivals: in October 1793 the Girondin deputies, their fate sealed by the murder of Marat in July, followed Marie Antoinette to the scaffold; in March 1794 it was the turn of the left-wing Hébertists, and in April of the right-wing Dantonists. Danton was scarcely a conservative, but his crime was to advocate leniency at a time when rigour was identified with patriotism; and the Dantonists or 'Indulgents' were suspected of having used the emergency to line their own pockets.

In February 1794 the Dantonist Desmoulins had protested against police attempts to curb gambling: 'Let us beware of connecting politics with moral regeneration – a thing at present impracticable. Moralism is fatal to freedom.' In Jacobin eyes this was heresy. Robespierre's 'Republic of Virtue' was to be built on Rousseau's principle that the individual must be 'forced to be free';[17] the Committee of Public Safety was the embodiment of the General Will and the Revolutionary Tribunal its executor. By an argument reminiscent of the medieval Inquisition, the traitor to the republic was held to have put himself outside the law and could not therefore invoke the 'rights of man'. The mark of the true republican was sobriety: both sexes abandoned wigs, powdered hair,[18] and personal ornaments other than the tricolour cockade or revolutionary buttons, while *Louis seize* furniture went out of fashion and plainer

[17] See above, p. 87; cf. Appendix 9.
[18] Robespierre was one of the few members of the Convention who still powdered his hair and dressed in pre-revolutionary style.

'patriotic beds' came in. The Jacobin attempt to republicanize society was nothing if not thorough. Theatres were threatened with closure if they 'tended to deprave public opinion, or to revive the shameful superstition of royalism'; town and street names were changed, so that Mont Martre became Mont Marat and Lyon became 'Ville-affranchie'; kings and queens disappeared even from playing cards, to be replaced by the Genius of War and Liberty of Worship.

Robespierre, like Rousseau, regarded religion as a bulwark of public morality, and his chief grievance against the Hébertists had been their encouragement of the dechristianizing movement which had reached its climax in the blasphemous celebration of the Feast of Reason in Notre Dame in November 1793. In December a decree reaffirmed liberty of worship, and on 7 May 1794 the Cult of the Supreme Being was decreed in fifteen articles that began with the affirmation: 'The French people recognize the existence of the Supreme Being, and the immortality of the soul.'[19] A month later Robespierre, newly elected President of the Convention, presided over the extravagant ceremonies staged in honour of the Supreme Being.[20]

However absurd Robespierre's Deism seems to modern eyes, it is essential for our understanding of the Terror to realize that Robespierre took it seriously. And in case we are tempted to think that it was merely a gimmick to distract attention from the guillotine, we may reflect that the preamble to the Declaration of Rights[21] had invoked the Supreme Being, that it was the Jacobins who abolished slavery in the French colonies, and that, at a moment when the republic was fighting for its life, the Convention decided to reform the calendar.[22]

---

[19] For the other articles see Thompson, *Robespierre and the French Revolution*, p. 126. [20] *Ibid.*, pp. 129–31. [21] See above, p. 282. [22] See Appendix 8.

21

The Return to Absolutism

The Fall of Robespierre

The celebrations in honour of the Supreme Being, held in the *Champ de la Réunion* (formerly the *Champ de Mars*) on 8 June 1794, marked the peak of Robespierre's success; but the very manner of his triumph was to hasten his downfall. The somewhat ludicrous liturgy of the Cult of the Supreme Being served to evoke a nostalgia for religious rites without providing a substitute for Catholicism, while Robespierre's own role as chief prophet of the new religion showed how far he had cut himself off from his colleagues.

The Committee of Public Safety was divided within itself. While Carnot, Lindet, Saint-André and the two Prieurs tackled the more mundane administrative matters, Robespierre, Couthon and Saint-Just quarrelled with Billaud-Varenne and Collot d'Herbois, who objected to using the machinery of the Terror to support Robespierre's programme of moral reformation and Saint-Just's plans for the redistribution of property. In mid-March Saint-Just and Robespierre had pushed through the Ventôse decrees, by which 300,000 'suspects' were to be brought to trial and the property of the guilty was to be shared out among the patriotic poor; in mid-April the *bureau de police* had been set up to keep watch on government officials, thus encroaching still further on the jurisdiction of the Committee of General Security; and now on 10 June, two days after the Feast of the Supreme Being, the Law of the 22nd Prairial was passed.

The Law of Prairial was probably intended to inaugurate a purge to end purges. In order to speed up the machinery of justice, the Revolutionary Tribunal was divided into four separate courts sitting simultaneously, while the privilege that had previously protected deputies from the jurisdiction of the

Tribunal was now withdrawn. No doubt Robespierre would have argued that not even parliamentary privilege ought to impede impartial justice, but the members of the Convention concluded that Robespierre regarded some of them as traitors.

Barère seems to have tried to preserve the unity of the Committee of Public Safety, but Robespierre, apparently blind to the precariousness of his position, pursued his uncompromising course. In the seven weeks that followed the passing of the Law of Prairial, the guillotine claimed more victims than it had done in the preceding thirteen months; and this in spite of the fact that the victory at Fleurus on 26 June seemed to mark the end of the threat of foreign invasion. Yet at the very moment when Robespierre ought to have been explaining why harsher emergency measures were needed to meet an apparently diminishing emergency, he seems to have disappeared from public life. After his fortnight as President of the Convention ended on 18 June, Robespierre appeared rarely at meetings of the Committee of Public Safety and made no speeches in the Convention. When at length he did speak in the Convention on 26 July it was already too late.

Robespierre's last speech was a forthright defence of the policy of repression: Hébert and Danton were dead, but the atheism and the 'indulgence' for which they stood had survived. Even the government was not immune and must itself be purged. And in words that must have confirmed the deputies' fears that their own names were on the proscription list, Robespierre called for measures:

... to punish traitors; to appoint new members to the Sub-Committees of the Committee of General Security; to purge this Committee itself, and put it under the Committee of Public Safety; to purge that Committee, too, and re-establish a centralized government under the supreme authority of the National Convention, its centre and its supreme court of appeal.[1]

The speech played into the hands of his enemies. When he read it again at the Jacobin Club the same evening it received a mixed reception, and the next day in the Convention Robespierre was

[1] J. M. Thompson, *Robespierre and the French Revolution*, E.U.P. 1952, p. 145.

obstructed as he tried to make a further speech. On this occasion, at least, his weak voice was a handicap: he was easily shouted down in a tumult of abuse, sufficiently concerted to suggest that it was prearranged, and amid cries of *Vive la Liberté* and *Vive la République*, he was placed under arrest, together with Couthon, Saint-Just, and his own brother.

But although he had been defeated in the Convention, Robespierre had not necessarily lost the support of Paris. The Commune still stood behind him: it met the Convention's decree of outlawry on all Robespierrists by issuing warrants for the arrest of Robespierre's opponents, and by ordering the governors of the Paris prisons to send Robespierre and his fellow prisoners to the Town Hall. It also called out the National Guard, and some 3,000 guardsmen from about a third of the Paris *sections* assembled in somewhat disorganized fashion at the Town Hall. But the *sections* as a whole did not respond, and by the time Barras and his troops arrived, early on the 28th, the Town Hall was undefended. In the ensuing scuffle Robespierre apparently tried to shoot himself; but a doctor was found to dress his injured jaw so that he was fit to face the guillotine later the same day.

The *sansculottes*, to whom Robespierre had appealed so successfully for so long, did not raise a finger in his defence. And yet it was the wage-earners of Paris who had helped the Jacobins to power in June 1793.[2] The explanation of this paradox lies in the failure of the Jacobins' economic policies. The second 'Maximum' of September 1793[3] had been interpreted as a pledge that the new government would relieve the plight of the wage-earners. But the enforcement of so complicated a piece of economic regulation was beyond the administrative resources of even the Jacobins, and by the spring of 1794 there were riots in the Paris markets. Yet at this point the Commune began to try to implement the other provision of the second 'Maximum' – the limitation of wages. When the workingmen protested, the Le Chapelier law, forbidding combinations of workmen, was invoked, and in June 1794 a number of alleged agitators among the arms workers were arrested. In June and July there were demands for higher wages from building workers and others engaged on government contracts, and even from the printing workers of the Committee of Public Safety itself.

On 23 July the Commune published the list of wages that were to apply in private industry within the capital: it stuck rigidly to the wage limits imposed by the 'Maximum', in spite of the failure to enforce the corresponding limitation of prices. It is perhaps not surprising that the wage-earners began to blame Robespierre and his cheerless Republic of Virtue, which provided neither bread nor circuses, and to regard the Commune as being in league with the Committees. This sense of betrayal, rather than the belief that the war was nearly over, probably explains the passivity of the *sansculottes* in the hour of Robespierre's disgrace. As he was led to his death, the crowds shouted not only *'À bas le tyran!'* but also *'À bas le maximum!'*[4]

Reaction

Although the execution of Robespierre on 10 Thermidor was greeted with popular acclaim, his removal from power was due not to the intervention of the Paris crowd, as the expulsion of the Girondin deputies had been in June 1793,[5] but to a *coup d'état* by members of the Convention who feared for their own skins. In disposing of Robespierre, the men of Thermidor had not intended to halt the Terror. Men like Fouché and Collot d'Herbois who had punished Lyon, Tallien who had terrorized Bordeaux, and Fréron the scourge of Toulon,[6] had no qualms about employing the guillotine; they merely wanted to ensure that it was not used against themselves.

But if the Thermidoreans were not reactionaries, they soon found that they had started a popular reaction which they were powerless to control. Robespierre had come to be regarded as the personification of all the repressive features of Jacobin rule, and four days after his death the Paris police report notes: 'People are asking for the total purification of members of the

4 G. Rudé, *The Crowd in the French Revolution*, Oxford 1959, p. 140.
5 See above, p. 301.   6 See above, p. 303.

Revolutionary Tribunal, which they are now calling the "bloody" tribunal.' And within a week the report adds that 'prostitutes are reappearing with their customary audacity'.[7] Jacobinism was attacked in the press and on the stage, the 'Reveil du Peuple' replaced the 'Marseilleise' as the battle-hymn of the republic, while Fréron organized young men of wealth (the *Jeunesse doré*) into armed gangs which went in search of suspected Jacobins. One of their first targets was the Jacobin Club, thus providing the new government with an excuse for closing it. Fashion reflected the reaction against the Republic of Virtue. Mme Tallien created a vogue for classical robes in which feminine charms were displayed with a prodigality previously thought proper only for Greek goddesses. By 1795 there was a craze for blond wigs, and English fashions were popular in spite of the war.

The anti-Robespierrists in the Convention were quick to take their cue from the public opinion of Paris. Wholesale release of suspects began (between 18 and 23 Thermidor 478 were freed in Paris alone) and in the spring of 1795 the surviving Girondins were pardoned and allowed to return to the Convention. Attempts were made to pacify the provinces, and even the Vendéans, who had fought to restore Church and King, were temporarily mollified by a measure of religious toleration. In February 1795 Catholics throughout France were granted the right to worship, though churches remained the property of the state and priests were not to wear clerical dress in public. The official justification of this conciliatory gesture was that Catholicism was more likely to thrive on persecution than on indifference.

Meanwhile the machinery of the Terror was dismantled. In August 1794, sixteen committees had been set up to take over much of the work previously done by the two great Committees. The role of the Committee of Public Safety was now reduced to the control of foreign and war policy, and a quarter of its members were to retire each month. In the provinces local government was purged of Jacobins and again reorganized, while in Paris the Commune was abolished and the forty-eight

<hr />

[7] C. Brinton, *A Decade of Revolution*, Harper 1934, p. 196.

revolutionary committees (one for each *section*) were reduced to twelve (one for each *arrondissement*). The Law of the 22nd Prairial[8] was swiftly repealed, and the Revolutionary Tribunal was reorganized. The Tribunal was finally abolished in May 1795, but not before it had been used to eliminate most of the Robespierrist 'tail', as the survivors were derisively called. Carrier, the commissioner for Nantes, was executed early in 1795. Fouquier-Tinville, the former public prosecutor, survived until March, but his plea, familiar to modern ears, that he had merely carried out the orders of his superiors, did not save him. Barère, Billaud-Varenne and Collot d'Herbois were spared for the moment; they had, after all, been in the plot against Robespierre.

But if many of the personnel and much of the procedure of the Terror had been destroyed, the economic problems remained. Saint-Just's socialistic schemes embodied in the decrees of Ventôse[9] were shelved: confiscated lands were simply sold to the highest bidder. A revised wages 'Maximum', to replace the one of 23 July,[10] was issued in August 1794, but its concessions were quickly outweighed by the rise in prices and the fall in monetary values. The value of the *assignat* had increased under the Terror: it had risen from 22 per cent of its nominal value in August 1793 to 48 per cent in December, and was still at 36 per cent in the following July. By December 1794 it was down to 20 per cent, and by May 1795 to $7\frac{1}{2}$ per cent. Meanwhile the final abolition of the 'Maximum' in December 1794 removed the last check on rising prices. Bread and meat were still rationed and their price controlled, but unrationed bread could now be sold on the open market: while the controlled price for the four-pound loaf was twelve *sous*, bread on the open market rose from twenty-five *sous* at the end of March to sixteen *livres* by the middle of May.[11]

In mid-March deputations from two *faubourgs* had complained to the Convention: 'We lack bread and are beginning to regret all the sacrifices we have made for the Revolution.'[12] And the

---

8 See above, p. 307.
9 See above, p. 307.   10 See above, p. 310.
11 G. Rudé, *op. cit.*, p. 144.   12 *Ibid.*, p. 148.

swelling volume of protests about the shortage of rationed bread culminated on 1 April (12 Germinal) in an invasion of the Convention by demonstrators from the *sections* demanding 'bread and the Constitution of 1793'. The insurgents, lacking leaders, were easily dispersed, and the immediate outcome of the disturbances was the deportation to Guiana of Collot d'Herbois, Billaud-Varenne and Barère. But the shortage of bread continued, and seven weeks later, on 20 May (1 Prairial), men of the *faubourg* Saint Antoine invaded the Convention. This time some of the deputies were bold enough to voice their demands: the safeguarding of the food supply, the implementation of the Constitution of 1793, and the release of Jacobin prisoners. But again the demonstrators failed to exploit their advantage, and, on the 22nd, regular army units frightened the *faubourg* Saint Antoine into surrender, without a shot being fired.

Reprisals were harsh. A special Military Commission sentenced nineteen to death, including six deputies, and the number of suspected sympathizers who were arrested and disarmed ran into thousands. The hunting out of Jacobins in the provinces was now intensified: in the Lyonnais the so-called Company of Jesus avenged the earlier repression of Fouché, while further south the campaign of assassination was carried on by Companies of the Sun. The agents of the 'White' Terror had little to learn from the Jacobin commissioners of the 'Red'.

The internal troubles of the republic were partly offset by external triumphs. By the spring of 1795 the revolutionary armies had passed beyond France's 'natural frontiers', and some at least of her enemies were thinking of peace. Prussia came to terms in April, doubtless hoping to get her hands free in time to seize a fair share in the third partition of Poland.[13] The treaty of Basel publicly recognized France's right to keep the left bank of the Rhine until a general peace and secretly permitted her to annex it in return for the promise of a territorial compensation for Prussia elsewhere. Three months later, also at Basel, Spain made peace: France withdrew from Spain in return for the cession of St Domingo. Meanwhile the Dutch admitted defeat and Holland became a French satellite.

[13] See above, p. 214.

At home the Convention received little credit for these trans-actions. In August there were demands in Paris for a return to economic controls, and in September some even spoke of the need to revive the Terror.[14] There were also some signs of royalism: in August the refrain in the streets was said to have been 'a king or bread'. But it is doubtful whether there was any real risk of a royalist revival. Louis XVI's son had died in June, leaving Louis's *émigré* brother, the Comte de Provence, as Louis XVIII. Provence, scarcely a popular candidate, at once ruined the royalist cause by his Declaration of Verona, which promised the full restoration of the *ancien régime* and full retri-bution to the regicides.

Yet, as the Convention at length turned to the task of con-triving a new constitution, the threat of a royalist reaction seems to have been taken seriously enough. The constitution-makers tried to steer a course between Jacobinism and monarchy. Indirect elections on a limited franchise replaced Robespierre's universal male suffrage; the executive power was vested in five 'directors', chosen by the two legislative chambers, the 'Council of Five Hundred' and the 'Council of Ancients';[15] and in the preface to the new constitution there appeared at last a declara-tion of *duties* as well as of rights. In its determination to escape from the fatal discontinuity that the 'Self-Denying Ordinance' had imposed in 1791, the Convention ruled that two-thirds of its members must sit in the new legislative chambers. The 'Constitution of the Year III' was approved by plebiscite, but the two-thirds decree was voted down in Paris, and the Con-vention's attempt to falsify the returns provoked the insurrection of Vendémiaire (4–6 October 1795).

Vendémiaire, the last great 'day' of the Revolution, took place against the familiar economic background: only about one-third of the bread rations (nominally one to one and a half pounds a head) was being issued, and meat was practically unob-tainable at its controlled price. But, unlike the abortive risings of Germinal and Prairial, the motive now seems to have been

---

[14] Rudé, *op. cit.*, p. 164.

[15] The 'Council of Ancients' consisted of men over 40 and had a suspensive veto of one year.

primarily political. Certainly the rioters were drawn from the professional classes (journalists, civil servants, deputies, stock-jobbers) rather than from the *sansculottes*, and most of them were members of the National Guard.[16] But National Guardsmen were no match for artillery. Barras had called in the army and put the gunners under the command of Napoleon Bonaparte. Napoleon's 'whiff of grapeshot'[17] was decisive, but it merely dramatized a political fact that had been true since Robespierre's execution: the revolutionary government no longer rested on popular support but on military force.

The Rise of Bonaparte

Napoleon Bonaparte's role in the events of Vendémiaire did not make his rise to supreme power inevitable. Banished from his native Corsica in 1793, he had first served the revolutionary cause by helping to recapture Toulon from the British in December 1793, thus frustrating their attempt to aid the Girondin rebels of Marseille.[18] But his part in the siege of Toulon, as in the suppression of the insurrection of Vendémiaire, has probably been exaggerated by the hindsight of historians. Perhaps more significant at the time was his marriage in March 1796 to Josephine de Beauharnais, a leading figure in the newly revived Paris *salons*[19] and a former mistress of Barras. Bonaparte rightly described the match as 'an additional pledge of my fixed resolve to entrust all my fortunes to the Republic'.[20]

Barras alone of the five Directors was a representative of the more decadent features of Thermidorean society. The others, Reubell, Larévellière-Lépeaux, Carnot and Letourneur, were stolid *bourgeois* republicans, unimaginative, but hardworking. They hardly deserve the bad press that they have generally received from historians.[21] The constitution of the Directory did, of course, have obvious defects. Only those who paid direct

---

[16] Rudé, *op. cit.*, p. 175.   [17] The famous phrase is Carlyle's.
[18] See above, p. 303.   [19] See above, p. 221.
[20] J. M. Thompson, *Napoleon Bonaparte: His Rise and Fall*, Blackwell 1951, p. 56.
[21] Even A. Cobban in his *History of Modern France*, Penguin 1961, dismisses the Directory briefly and derisively.

taxes or who had fought for the republic were entitled to vote, and then only for 'electors', who chose the deputies of the two councils. The property qualification for electors was higher than in 1791, and only about 20,000 were eligible. Even so, some five million qualified for the indirect franchise, as against the seven million who would have done so under universal male suffrage. Perhaps a more serious flaw was the rift between legislature and executive produced by the rigid separation of powers: one-third of the assemblies retired each year, but only one of the Directors, so that the Directors were likely to find themselves faced with hostile chambers. But although such deadlocks were, true to the revolutionary tradition, resolved by force, the *coups d'état* of the Directory were mild and almost gentlemanly affairs compared with the 'days' of the early 1790s.

Nor were the economic policies of the Directory as futile as they are often portrayed. It is true that the attempt to replace the *assignats* (now down to one-three-hundredth of their face value) by *mandats*, issued on the security of conquered as well as confiscated lands, proved a failure, since the *mandats* themselves quickly depreciated. But the Directory then proceeded to repudiate the paper currency altogether – an unpopular but necessary measure from which Napoleon would later profit.[22] Meanwhile government expenditure was reduced by a third, chiefly by suspending interest on two-thirds of the national debt, and the revised taxation system worked better than that of either the *ancien régime* or the Jacobins.

Opposition to the Directory came from two sides. In a frankly capitalistic society, Babeuf's plans for the abolition of private property and the running of production and distribution on cooperative lines attracted some support; but the government knew all about the plot, and Babeuf was arrested in the spring of 1796 and sent to the guillotine. He scarcely seems to merit his fame as a Marxist before Marx. The revolt from the right came from within the government itself. The elections of April 1797 returned a large number of constitutional monarchists, who, in spite of the intransigence of the *émigrés*, now commanded a majority in both chambers and the support of two of the

[22] See below, p. 324.

Directors, Carnot and the recently elected Barthélemy. The three republican Directors appealed to Bonaparte, who, knowing that the monarchists would probably end the war, sent his lieutenant Augereau to Paris. Carnot fled, and Barthélemy, together with a number of deputies, was deported to Guiana. A specially appointed commission amended the election results in the government's favour, and all opposition journals were banned. This was the *coup d'état* of Fructidor (September 1797).

There was to be one more government reshuffle (the so-called *coup d'état* of Prairial) before Bonaparte seized power himself. In 1799 the government was again defeated in the elections, but this time the assemblies succeeded in ousting the Directors of Fructidor and replacing them with a new quintet: Barras, Sieyès, Gohier, Roger Ducos and Moulin. Within less than six months they had given way to Bonaparte.

For the time being, however, Bonaparte was busy conducting his Italian campaign which has so impressed military historians ever since. In a matter of months he drove a wedge between the Austrian and Sardinian armies, defeated them both separately, drove the Austrians back to the Alps, and, without consulting Paris, forced Sardinia to make peace at Leoben (April 1797). Yet the campaign was a triumph of logistics as much as of tactics. Masséna later described how unprepossessing Bonaparte had seemed to his generals when he took over the Italian command in 1796. 'But a moment afterwards,' added Masséna, 'he put on his general's hat and seemed to have grown two feet. He questioned us on the position of our divisions, on the spirit and effective force of each corps, prescribed the course which we were to follow, announced that he would hold an inspection on the morrow, and on the following day attack the enemy.'[23] A month later Bonaparte wrote to the Directors:

You can have no idea of the military and administrative condition of the army. When I got here it was under the influence of disaffected agitators, without bread, without discipline and without order. I made some examples, I took every step I could to reorganize the commissariat; and victory did the rest. All the same, our lack of wagons,

[23] H. A. L. Fisher, *Napoleon*, Williams & Norgate 1924, p. 36.

the badness of our horses, and the greed of contractors keep us in a state of absolute penury.[24]

That was on 24 April 1796. By 9 May he was able to report: 'We are all getting fat: the men eat none but the best bread, plenty of good fresh meat, excellent wine and so forth. Discipline is improving every day, though we still have to shoot a good many men, for there are some intractable characters incapable of self-restraint.'[25]

The *coup d'état* of Fructidor had ensured the final break-down of the peace negotiations with England, opened at Lille in the summer of 1797; but in October the peace of Campo Formio was signed. Austria was allowed to annex the Venetian Republic, but was required to recognize France's 'natural frontiers'; the Cisalpine Republic was created in North Italy and the Republic of Genoa was replaced by the Ligurian Republic. This redrawing of the map of Italy was Bonaparte's own work; the choice of names from Rome's classical past was typical of him, as was the zeal with which he sent convoys of captured art treasures to Paris. Before handing Venice over to the Austrians, he removed the four bronze horses from the front of St Mark's, and as early as May 1796 he had promised the Directory: 'I will send you as soon as possible Corregio's finest pictures, including a St Jerome which is said to be his *chef d'oeuvre*.'[26] Another pledge of devotion to the Republic?

Bonaparte continued to combine the roles of conqueror and connoisseur in his Egyptian expedition of 1798. The Directors regarded this as a substitute for the proposed invasion of England, which had to be called off because of British naval supremacy.[27] Instead, England was to be weakened by an attack on the route to India. Bonaparte's instructions required him 'to drive the English from all their possessions in the East', and he himself told his troops that they were 'going to strike a blow against England more effective and more deeply felt than any other; a preliminary to her death blow'. Yet he was not con-

[24] Thompson, *Napoleon Bonaparte*, p. 63.
[25] *Ibid*, p. 68.   [26] *Ibid.*, p. 68.
[27] In 1799 the French were to show that even a successful invasion of Ireland was beyond them, Brinton, *op. cit.*, p. 242.

cerned solely with strategy. An Egyptian expedition had been recommended by Leibnitz to Louis XIV in 1672,[28] and no fewer than 167 representatives of the arts and sciences landed with Bonaparte's army. 'For the first time since the Roman Empire,' Bonaparte wrote of the expedition to Upper Egypt, 'a civilized nation, cultivating the arts and sciences, was about to visit, measure and explore those superb ruins which for so many centuries have engaged the curiosity of the learned world.'[29] The result of this research was the encyclopaedic *Description of Egypt*. But perhaps more symbolic of the whole enterprise was the fact that Bonaparte's surveyors working on the project for a Suez canal reported that the difference in level between the Red Sea and the Mediterranean would necessitate locks.

Militarily too, the expedition was a miscalculation. Malta was captured en route, and the Mamelukes, outnumbered four to one, were easily defeated at the Battle of the Pyramids. But Nelson's destruction of the French fleet in Aboukir Bay (August 1798) dissolved Bonaparte's dreams. A sortie into the Holy Land, checked by Sir Sidney Smith's famous defence of Acre, could not disguise failure, and Bonaparte, leaving his army, slipped back to France. The series of French reverses, culminating in the loss of Italy in the summer of 1799, had been countered by Masséna's successes in Switzerland before Bonaparte reached Paris; France no longer needed saving. But the *coup d'état* of Prairial had carried the Directory too far to the left for some tastes, and Sieyès, the incorrigible constitution-maker, called in Bonaparte to redress the balance.

With the collusion of Barras and Roger Ducos, the chambers were summoned to Saint-Cloud to discuss measures for dealing with an alleged Jacobin plot. The real plot was rather different: on 18 Brumaire (10 November) the deputies met to find that Sieyès, Barras and Roger Ducos had resigned, and the other Directors had been arrested. Bonaparte offered to step into the breach, but he found that the deputies were less gullible than his armies, and it was only his brother Lucien, President of the

---

[28] Thompson, *op. cit.*, p. 107.
[29] Fisher, *op. cit.*, p. 76.

Council of Five Hundred, who saved the day by persuading the waiting troops that their general was in danger of assassination. No doubt Napoleon had intended to rely on rhetoric, but the *coup d'état* of Brumaire owed its success to bayonets.

22

Napoleonic Europe

Napoleon in France

During the seven weeks that elapsed between the *coup d'état* of Brumaire and the promulgation of the Constitution of the Year VIII, Bonaparte was careful to conceal the military basis of the new regime. He took pains to appear in civilian clothes, and opposition to the events of Brumaire was met not by a purge, but by sending a propaganda team of twenty-four deputies to tour the provinces and circulate the official version of what had happened. Two days after the *coup d'état* a proclamation *Aux Français* had asserted: 'To make the Republic loved by its own citizens, respected abroad and feared by its enemies – such are the duties we have assumed in accepting the First Consulship. Its citizens will love it if the laws and authoritative acts of Government are always marked by the spirit of order, justice and moderation.'[1] This was hardly the slogan of 1789, and the implication that Frenchmen were now expected to accept good government as a substitute for representative government was borne out in the Constitution of the Year VIII, Sieyès' third attempt at constitution-making. Voters were allowed a direct choice of candidates only for posts at a local level: the deputies for the two legislative assemblies (the Tribunate and the Legislative Body) were chosen by the Senate from a national list of up to 10,000 candidates nominated by the departments. The Senate (*Sénat Conservateur*), for which the lower age limit was forty, was evidently intended by Sieyès to combine the functions of Supreme Court and Senate in the American constitution. But since the majority of its sixty members were nominated by the consuls, Bonaparte was soon able to use the Senate as a means of bypassing the two legislative assemblies. The real centre of

[1] J. M. Thompson, *Napoleon Bonaparte: His Rise and Fall*, Blackwell 1958, p. 146.

government was the Council of State, presided over by the First Consul.

The new constitution was endorsed by plebiscite: 3,011,007 voted in favour and 1,562 against. These votes were really votes for Bonaparte, and his popularity was further enhanced by an attempt on his life in December 1800. The conclusion of peace treaties with the Austrians at Lunéville (1801) and with the British at Amiens (1802), together with the enthusiasm evoked by the signing of the Concordat with the Papacy,[2] enabled him in 1802 to secure a majority of three and a half million to 8,000 for his appointment as First Consul for life. Even Jeremy Bentham voted in favour. Bonaparte's head now appeared for the first time on the coinage, though the reverse face still bore the legend *République Française*. As F. A. Simpson remarked of a later Bonaparte, 'The superscription remained the Republic's, but the image was already Caesar's.'[3] The discovery of a second plot to assassinate Bonaparte – the Cadoudal conspiracy of 1803 – was used to usher in the Empire in 1804. This time the plebiscite figures were 3,572,329 for and 2,579 against.

The proclamation of the Empire merely gave constitutional recognition to a system of government that had been already in existence under the Consulate. As Sieyès himself is supposed to have said after Brumaire: 'Gentlemen, you have got a master – a man who knows everything, wants everything, and can do everything.' Napoleon's personal dominance in the government is perhaps nowhere more clearly revealed than in the introduction of the five new legal codes: the civil code (*Code Napoléon*) (1804), the code of civil procedure (1806), the commercial code (1807), the code of criminal procedure (1808) and the penal code (1810). The *Code Napoléon* as printed in 1810 contained less than 120,000 words (about the length of this textbook) and could be carried in the pocket. It followed the French armies into the Netherlands, Bavaria, Baden, Westphalia and Switzerland, and it was translated into Portuguese and Spanish. It remains the

---

[2] See below, p. 324.
[3] F. A. Simpson, *Louis Napoleon and the Recovery of France 1848–56*, Longmans 1923, p. 191.

greatest monument to Napoleon's rule in Europe.[4] How far did Napoleon himself influence its compilation? His role is much debated, but of the fifty-five sessions of the drafting committee that he attended, thirty-five were concerned with the discussion of civil rights, marriage and divorce, paternity and adoption. On all these issues the Code reflected the Roman Law principles that Napoleon was known to favour: marriage must be preceded by parental approval and the production of birth certificates, divorce was to be much more difficult than under the Directory, the authority of parents over the persons and property of their children was strengthened. Yet much of the work of the Revolution was preserved: seigneurial privileges and dues were not restored, equality at law and freedom of worship were retained, property rights were protected and there was no return to the principle of primogeniture. Napoleon's codes were a fusion of old and new. 'From Clovis to the Committee of Public Safety,' he boasted in 1809, 'I embrace it all.'

Napoleon's skill in clothing old institutions in new dress may be seen in the prefects, appointed by the central government, who wielded administrative authority in the departments in place of the popularly elected councils of the period of Girondin and Jacobin rule. The prefects were put into a dignified uniform and armed with a sword, but their functions were essentially those of the old *intendants*.[5] They were probably allowed less initiative. In a circular of the year VIII Lucien Bonaparte issued this warning: 'General ideas must come from the centre. I note with regret that some of you, with praiseworthy intentions doubtless, concern yourselves with the interpretation of the laws. It is not this that the government expects of its administration.'[6] It was largely the energy and efficiency of the prefects, nevertheless, that restored economic prosperity to the provinces, though in the later years of the Empire their activities became increasingly concentrated on the problem of raising men and money for the war. Although Revolutionary governments had abolished tax exemption and had put tax-collection into the

[4] The best account of the Codes is still H. A. L. Fisher's chapter in *Cambridge Modern History*, ix, 1907.

[5] See above, p. 239.

[6] A. Cobban, *A History of Modern France*, vol. ii, Penguin 1961, p. 24.

hands of paid officials, the Napoleonic administration brought about an important innovation: the taxes were actually collected, and in 1802 the budget balanced. Napoleon's newly achieved financial stability was symbolized in a new institution: the *Banque de France*, established in 1800 and one of the most permanent of Napoleon's creations.

The colourful dress of the prefects was matched by the 'baubles' of the new orders of chivalry. The Legion of Honour had been established in 1802. With the advent of the Empire came a series of sonorous titles ranging from 'grand imperial dignitaries' such as the 'Arch-Chancellor of the Empire' down to Grand Officers of the Empire like the 'Grand Chamberlain' and the 'Grand Huntsman'. In 1807 Marshal Lefebvre was created Duke of Danzig, and in the following year an hierarchy of hereditary titles – Prince, Duke, Count, Baron and Knight – was introduced. Many of the highest dignities were reserved for the princes of the imperial family, but the Napoleonic peerage, like the Napoleonic army, was open to talent, irrespective of birth.

Napoleon was well aware of the importance of pomp as a prop of government and was alive to the power of historical memories. By persuading Pope Pius VII to come to Paris for the imperial coronation in December 1802 and then insisting on crowning himself, Napoleon not only invoked the aura of the Catholic liturgy, but also challenged comparison with Charlemagne. The way in which the coronation was stage-managed[7] symbolized the role in which Napoleon had cast the Church. 'In religion,' he remarked, 'I do not see the mystery of the Incarnation but the mystery of the social order.' And as he told the Council of State in August 1799:

My policy is to govern men as the great majority wish to be governed. That I believe is the way to recognize the sovereignty of the people. It was as a Catholic that I won the war in the Vendée, as a Moslem that I established myself in Egypt, and as an Ultramontane that I won the confidence of the Italians. If I were governing Jews, I should rebuild the temple of Solomon.[8]

[7] For an account see Hales, *Napoleon and the Pope*, Eyre & Spottiswoode 1962, pp. 69 ff.

[8] J. M. Thompson, *op. cit.*, p. 172.

The attack on the Catholic Church in France had perhaps been the revolutionaries' biggest tactical error. In Boulay's famous words, it was 'worse than a crime, it was a mistake'. He saw that, as the Concordat itself put it, Catholicism was 'the religion of the majority of Frenchmen'. The Concordat, signed in July 1801, besides recognizing Catholicism according to this formula, though not as the state religion, provided for the deposition of all existing French bishops by the Pope. This made it look as if the Pope was being given an opportunity to deny the principle of Gallicanism. Pius was, however, reluctant to demand the resignation of those 'refractory' bishops who had remained loyal to Rome, and he at first refused to recognize the 'constitutional' bishops even to the extent of asking them to resign. His instinct was sound, for the remaining articles of the Concordat made clear that it was Napoleon who gained most. He had obtained the removal of all bishops who could be regarded as in any sense schismatic and gained the right to nominate their successors. (The Pope could refuse to consecrate them only on grounds of heresy or immorality.) The Republic received papal recognition; the Vatican agreed to drop the question of Church lands and tithes, and to renounce her claims to Avignon;[9] Catholic clergy were to receive a state stipend, but so were Protestant ministers, so that the principle of toleration was admitted.

When the Concordat was promulgated in April 1802, the Pope found that a number of 'Organic Articles' had been added, without his permission. Ostensibly these merely regulated the French Church in minor matters relating to the public peace; in fact they reinforced still further the traditional Gallican position. No papal bulls were to be applicable to France without government consent; no synod of French clergy could meet without the First Consul's permission; no bishop could be absent from his diocese without leave, even if summoned by the Pope; and the declaration of Gallican liberties (as embodied in Bossuet's Articles of 1682)[10] was to be taught to all ordinands. Well might the proclamation accompanying the publication of the Concordat claim that 'the Head of the church has, in his wisdom, and in the interests of the Church, considered proposals dictated by the interests of the State'; though it was a little premature in adding that 'thus there is an end of all elements of discord'.

In restoring the Catholic religion to France, Napoleon had perhaps restored more than he intended. The Pope may have been denied his rightful role in the coronation of the Emperor, but the people of Paris gave him a tumultuous welcome. As Pius himself told Fouché, 'We passed through France in the midst of a people on their knees'. Later, in 1809, after French armies had overrun the Papal States and Napoleon had declared the Pope's temporal sovereignty abolished, the same Pius replied by excommunicating the Emperor. Napoleon kept him in custody for five years, first at Savona and then at Fontainebleau, but it was Pius who won in the end. Although he had said to his agents before the Concordat, 'Treat the Pope as if he had 200,000 men', Napoleon was perhaps too much a man of the eighteenth century to understand the tenacity of religious faith.[11]

Certainly Napoleon would have won the applause of the *philosophes* by refusing to restore clerical control of education. His new school system of four grades (primary, secondary, semi-military *lycées*, and technical schools), all under the supervision of the Imperial University established in 1808, was never brought completely into force, but by 1813 the French secondary education was the best in Europe. By contrast, primary education remained much as it had been under the *ancien régime*. But as a safeguard against a reading public, press censorship was rigorously enforced. At the time of Brumaire there had been seventy-three political journals in Paris; in January 1800, sixty of them were suppressed; by the end of 1800 only nine such papers survived; by 1810 the number had been reduced to four. The circulation of non-political journals increased, but even these were subject to an elaborate system of censorship. Madame de Staël and Chateaubriand both fell foul of the censors, while the plays of Racine and Voltaire were purged of references that might be construed as critical allusions to the régime. Artists and architects were more fortunate. Between 1804 and 1813 Napo-

---

[11] Cf. his miscalculation in Spain, p. 336 below.

leon spent some £12 million on imperial arches, pillars and palaces in the neo-classical style[12] (now *le style Empire*), while even before he became Emperor the Tuileries had been adorned with a score of statues from Demosthenes and Alexander to Washington and Frederick the Great. But perhaps more than any other artist, Jacques Louis David, painter of 'The Tennis Court Oath',[13] earned official gratitude by pointing the parallels between Napoleon's Grand Empire and the Empire of the Caesars.

The Grand Empire

Napoleon's own account of his imperial aims and ambitions, recollected as they were in the tranquillity of his St Helena exile, is notoriously unreliable as a guide to his motives and intentions at the time. In the St Helena memoirs he poses as the representative of the Revolution who must fulfil the ideas of 1789, as the champion of nationality, as the friend of religion and protector of the Pope. But above all he appears as the man of peace who defended Europe from British war-mongering:

All my victories and all my conquests were won in self-defence. This is a truth which time will render every day more evident. Europe never ceased from warring against France, against French principles, and against me, so we had to strike down in order not to be struck down. The coalition continued without interruption, be it open or in secret, admitted or denied; it was there in permanence. It depended solely on the allies to give us peace.[14]

It is thus no surprise to find Napoleon claiming that the resumption of hostilities in 1803 was totally unexpected:

At Amiens I imagined in all good faith that I had settled France's destiny and my own. . . . I was planning to devote myself exclusively to the administration of France, and I believe that I could have worked wonders. I might have achieved the moral conquest of Europe, just as I have been on the verge of accomplishing it by arms.[15]

Napoleon held England responsible for breaking the Peace of

[12] See above, p. 231.   [13] See above, p. 278.
[14] P. Geyl, *Napoleon: For and Against*, Cape 1957, p. 252.   [15] *Ibid.*, p. 274.

Amiens (1802),[16] since the British had, in defiance of the treaty, refused to evacuate Malta. The British retorted that the terms of the treaty had been agreed on in the light of the European situation in 1802, and that by 1803 Napoleon had so tipped the balance in his favour that England deserved compensation. The Treaty of Lunéville (1801) had recognized four new independent republics in Europe. Napoleon had promptly treated them as satellites. The Cisalpine Republic became the Italian Republic, with Napoleon as its President; Switzerland (the Helvetic Republic) was compelled to contribute troops; French garrisons remained in the Ligurian Republic (Genoa) and in the Batavian Republic of Holland. England was bound to react violently to the prospect of France in control of the Dutch ports, and, if Napoleon's annexation of Elba, Parma, Piacenza and Piedmont in 1802 concerned England less closely, she nevertheless demanded that Sardinia and Switzerland should be compensated. The French missions dispatched to India and the Levant were seen as a revival of Napoleon's dreams of conquest in the East – hence the British determination to keep Malta. Of course, from Napoleon's point of view, British naval supremacy provided a permanent threat to the security of French gains. As early as October 1797 Napoleon had written: 'Our government must destroy the English monarchy, or it must expect itself to be destroyed by these active islanders. Let us concentrate our energies on the navy and annihilate England. That done Europe is at our feet.'[17]

When war was resumed in March 1803 Napoleon reoccupied Naples, poured more troops into Holland, and seized Hanover as a hostage for Malta. By the autumn the Grand Army was starting to assemble at Boulogne, where it waited for enough barges to convey it to England. While the French tried vainly to build up their invasion flotilla, Pitt returned to power in England and set about constructing the Third Coalition.[18] By the summer of 1805 Sweden, Austria and Russia had allied with England. Pitt's task had been made easier by the provocation

[16] England had agreed to restore most of her recent colonial conquests in return for French evacuation of the Papal States, Naples and Egypt.
[17] H. A. L. Fisher, *Napoleon*, Williams & Norgate 1924, p. 59.
[18] For a summary of the various coalitions see Appendix 12.

that Napoleon had given to Russia and Austria in Italy. The occupation of Naples, and of Tarento in particular, had seemed to threaten Russian interests in the eastern Mediterranean, while the conversion of the Italian Republic into the Kingdom of Italy and the annexation of the Ligurian Republic, both in the early summer of 1805, presented a challenge to Austria. With such ample evidence of Napoleon's aggressive intentions, it seems almost superfluous to add that the coldblooded execution of the Duc d'Enghien in March 1804, on the completely un-substantiated charge of complicity in the Cadoudal conspiracy, had caused a shock in European capitals. Only the Russian court made a formal protest, but Beethoven's angry decision to delete the dedication to Napoleon from his *Eroica* Symphony was symbolic of a more general indignation when the execution of Enghien was followed by the proclamation of the Empire.

The formation of the Third Coalition did not at once dissuade Napoleon from the invasion of England. He later claimed that the invasion plan was a piece of bluff and that the Boulogne camp had really been directed against his enemies on the conti-nent. If so, it was an elaborate piece of bluff. In March 1805 Villeneuve's squadron escaped from Toulon and made for Martinique, picking up the Cadiz squadron on the way. The other French and Spanish squadrons were supposed to slip out of their blockaded ports as best they could, elude the blockading British squadrons and persuade them to give chase. The com-bined Franco-Spanish fleets were then to race back from their rendezvous in the West Indies, so as to give Napoleon the tem-porary command of the English Channel that he so sorely needed. But the British Admiralty had forbidden the blockading squadrons to pursue ships that eluded their blockade: instead they were to reinforce Cornwallis' Channel fleet. Nelson, with characteristic independence, sailed for the West Indies, thus turning the French plan into a double fiasco: Villeneuve left the West Indies before the squadrons he was supposed to meet had arrived, and he returned to the Spanish coast to find that the rest of the British fleet was still guarding the Channel. Yet as late as 22 August 1805 Napoleon sent the following message to Villeneuve:

I hope you have arrived at Brest. Start, without losing a moment and sail up the Channel with all the ships you have. England is ours. We are all ready: every man is on board. Appear for 24 hours, and the thing is done.[19]

But Villeneuve had put into Cadiz. Napoleon had no choice but to break up the Boulogne camp and march against Austria.

When Villeneuve eventually emerged from Cadiz, it was to meet defeat at Trafalgar (21 October). Two days before Nelson's victory, Mack surrendered with 33,000 Austrians at Ulm. The road to Vienna was thus left open, and the city was occupied in November. The Austrians and Russians joined forces north of Vienna, and on 2 December were defeated at Austerlitz. Austerlitz marked the end of Austrian resistance, though the Russians withdrew to regroup their forces, and Napoleon was provided with a chance to redraw the map of Germany.

By the Treaty of Pressburg (December 1805) the Habsburgs were excluded from Italy and deprived of their authority in Germany: Venetia was given to the Kingdom of Italy, while slices of Habsburg territories in Germany went to Baden, Bavaria and Württemberg. The last two states, together with Saxony, were promoted to the status of kingdom. The Holy Roman Empire had disappeared at last.[20] In July 1806 all German territories, apart from Austria and Prussia and those lands already annexed by France, were joined in the Confederation of the Rhine. The Treaty of Lunéville had confirmed the French seizure of the left bank of the Rhine, and in 1803 Napoleon had compensated the Rhineland states by allowing them to absorb many of the smaller German states, ecclesiastical principalities and imperial cities. Now the Confederation of the Rhine was to embrace sixteen states, nominally independent, but with the Emperor of the French as their 'Protector'. A Diet was to meet at Frankfurt; it never did. And the true purpose of the Con-federation was made clear in the article that empowered the 'Protector' to fix the size of the contingents that each member state should supply in the event of war.

---

[19] *Letters of Napoleon*, ed. Thompson, Blackwell 1934, p. 127.

[20] Francis II surrendered the title of Holy Roman Emperor, but retained that of 'Emperor of Austria' (which he had adopted in 1804) as Francis I.

The chain of events that ended in the creation of the Confederation of the Rhine had begun with the formation of the Third Coalition, which Napoleon had brought into being by his own provocative acts. He could hardly have foreseen the outcome, but he was quick to exploit opportunities as they arose. He displayed the same opportunism in the events of 1806–7. In September 1806, on hearing that Prussia was mobilizing, he wrote to Talleyrand:

The idea that Prussia can take me on singlehanded is too absurd to merit discussion. ... Her cabinet is so contemptible, her king so weak, and her court so dominated by young officers in search of adventure that no one can depend on her. She will go on acting as she has acted – arming today, disarming tomorrow; standing by, sword in hand, while the battle is fought, and then making terms with the conqueror.[21]

Within the month the Prussian army took the field and marched to humiliation at Jena (14 October) and the French occupied Prussia without even the formality of a peace treaty. The Prussian attack had taken Napoleon by surprise; he was also surprised by the Tsar's refusal to ratify the Franco-Russian treaty concluded by his representative in July, by which Russia had approved the proposed incorporation of Sicily into Napoleon's Kingdom of Naples.[22] After Jena therefore Napoleon turned his armies against the Russians in Poland. A costly and indecisive defeat of the Russo-Prussian forces at Eylau in February 1807 was followed by the convincing French victory at Friedland in June. By the Treaty of Tilsit in July, Russia and France became allies. Russia was to have Finland (if she could seize it) and part of Prussian Poland, while the rest of Prussian Poland was to form the independent Grand Duchy of Warsaw; the Prussian provinces on the Rhine were to become the new Kingdom of Westphalia. Prussia, whose king was not consulted about her fate, thus lost all her territory west of the Elbe, together with half her population.

Perhaps the chief importance of Tilsit was that it seemed to

[21] Ed. Thompson, *Letters*, p. 159.
[22] Napoleon never achieved the union of the Two Sicilies; they were joined by the Congress of Vienna in 1815.

have brought Napoleon's 'Continental System' within sight of completion. The notion of a commercial blockade went back as far as the policy of the National Convention, and in 1796 the Directory had decreed that any ship carrying British goods might be seized in any French port. From 1803 onwards Napoleon forced those states either defeated by or allied with France to close their ports to British ships – the Italian Republic and Holland, Spain and Naples, the Confederation of the Rhine, Prussia. Now, by the Treaty of Tilsit, Napoleon not only gained Russian adhesion to the Continental System, but extracted a promise of her support in compelling Denmark, Sweden and Portugal to join too. The British bombardment of Copenhagen and capture of the Danish fleet was a direct sequel.[23] In November 1806 the Berlin Decree had declared the British Isles to be 'in state of blockade'. Article 5 decreed: 'Commerce in English merchandise is forbidden, and all merchandise belonging to England, or coming from her factories or from her colonies, is declared good prize.'[24] The aim of the blockade was not, in the manner of Hitler's U-boats, to starve England into surrender. It was rather to cut England off from her markets and so, according to Mercantilist theory, provoke a financial crisis by causing a glut of goods on the home market. Similarly the British Orders in Council of 1807 were designed not to deprive Europe of food and raw materials – an impossible task, since Europe was self-supporting – but to stop those states which had closed their ports to British goods from trading with neutrals or with one another.

Did the system work? The total value of British exports actually increased from £41 million in 1805 to £50 million in 1810; the value of colonial goods re-exported rose during the same period from £10 million to £12¾ million. This was accounted for partly by the development of new markets outside Europe and by increased trade with European countries outside the blockade, and partly by effective smuggling. Even so 1811 was a critical year for England, and the situation became even more grave when in the winter of 1811–12 the United

---

[23] The second bombardment; the first had been in 1801.
[24] R. B. Mowat, *The Diplomacy of Napoleon*, Arnold 1924, p. 202.

States suspended trade with England. It is probable that the continental states suffered even more. The Continental System was, in Mowat's phrase, 'a blockade of the French Empire by itself'. But exclusion of British goods was not Napoleon's only aim: he wanted to capture European markets for French goods. The Milan Decree of December 1807 forbade ships of any country, on pain of confiscation, even to submit to search by a British vessel. Yet as early as 1809 Napoleon was already selling to French merchants licences permitting them to export to England, while in 1810 he did not hesitate to sell France's wheat surplus to England; the Kingdom of Italy was cut off by tariff barriers from Genoa and Piedmont (which were treated as part of France), yet was required to levy only half dues on goods admitted from France and to sell all her raw silk to French manufacturers; in 1810 King Louis of Holland was deposed and his kingdom annexed to France as a punishment for failing to enforce the blockade, while in 1811 the coastal departments of the Kingdom of Westphalia were annexed for the same reason. Well might Napoleon write to Eugène Beauharnais (Josephine's son) in 1810: 'My principle is France first.'[25]

Yet in the early days of the Continental System Napoleon had been able to count on a good deal of European hostility to British commercial and naval supremacy. The second League of Armed Neutrality was as recent as 1801.[26] But as the policy of 'France first' became more clearly exemplified, the satellite states found the French commercial monopoly even more burdensome than the British had been. And while Napoleon embarked on the disastrous Peninsular War in an attempt to close the Portuguese coast to British trade, the mounting resentment of Russia led to the first overt breach in the blockade and thus, in its turn, to the French retaliation that brought the Grand Army to the gates of Moscow.

The Defeat of Napoleon

In 1810 the Grand Empire was at its zenith. (See map, p. 340.) All the major states of Europe except Portugal were nominally

---

[25] *Letters*, ed. Thompson, p. 274.
[26] Its members were Russia, Prussia, Sweden and Denmark. Cf. p. 252 above.

in alliance with France. Austria, who had again challenged
France in 1809, had again been defeated, and now, as a pledge of
future good will, the Austrian Emperor consented to the marriage of his daughter Marie Louise to Napoleon.[27] To marry
into the Habsburgs was the ultimate mark of respectability, and
Napoleon clearly regarded it as one of his greatest triumphs. It
was the summit of his success: henceforth his fortunes would
decline. The refusal of thirteen of twenty-seven cardinals to
attend a reception given in Paris in honour of the marriage might
have been regarded as an omen. In August Marshal Bernadotte,
who was related to Napoleon by marriage, was elected Crown
Prince of Sweden and took over the government from the
ailing and childless Charles XIII (1809–18).[28] This looked like a
victory for Napoleon, but Bernadotte was to prove one of the
chief agents of his defeat. On the last day of 1810 the Tsar issued
his decree increasing the duties on goods entering Russia by
land and giving preferential treatment to American shipping,
thus letting in British goods and British ships, which were now
freely using the American flag. It was in 1810 also that Fouché's
intrigues with England were discovered and he was dismissed,
as Talleyrand had been the previous year. They were, said Metternich, like sailors eager to mutiny against a daring pilot, but
not until the ship had struck some rocks. In 1810 the rocks were
already visible, for that year saw the turning-point of the war
in Spain.

Spain had been actively allied with France since the Treaty of
Madrid in 1801. Godoy, the Queen's lover and accordingly
both chief minister and generalissimo, had alternated between
obsequious subservience to Napoleon and intrigues against him.
In 1804 Spain had declared war on England; in 1806 Godoy
summoned the Spaniards to arms, with the aim of supporting
Prussia, but Jena occurred before he had made his intentions
clear, so that he could pretend that the troops were for the
defence of France. In 1807 France and Spain secretly agreed to
partition Portugal, who had refused to close her ports to the
British, and by the end of November French troops were in

---

[27] His marriage with Josephine was annulled in 1809.
[28] Charles had succeeded his deposed nephew Gustavus IV.

Lisbon. There were also French troops in Spain, and Charles IV's son Ferdinand seized his opportunity to remove Godoy (who was now urging resistance to the French invasion) by means of a palace revolution and forced Charles to abdicate. Napoleon did not, however, give Ferdinand the support he expected and instead announced his intention of coming in person 'to besiege Gibraltar and to go to Africa, and to regulate the affairs of Spain'. By the Treaty of Bayonne (May 1808) Ferdinand was forced to renounce the crown in order 'to put an end to the anarchy of Spain, to save this brave nation from the agitation of factions and to . . . maintain its integrity, guarantee its colonies, and to enable it to unite its means to those of France in order to arrive at a maritime peace'.[29] That is how the preamble put it. Napoleon, writing to tell his brother Louis that he was thinking of offering him the Spanish crown, was more explicit: 'Convinced as I am that I shall never secure lasting peace with England until I set the whole of Europe in motion, I have determined to put a French prince on the throne of Spain.'[30]

In fact Joseph, King of Naples since 1806, became the new King of Spain. Napoleon apparently thought that 12,000 troops would be sufficient to impose his brother on the reluctant Spaniards; in the event it took half a million. The campaign went badly almost from the start: in July 1808 Dupont's division surrendered to the Spaniards at Baylen, while in August a British expeditionary force defeated Junot's Army of Portugal at Vimiero and occupied Lisbon. Napoleon sent reinforcements to Spain, and by December 1808 was himself in Madrid. The British army, now under Moore, abandoned the attempt to save Madrid and saved itself by a timely retreat to Corunna, whence it was evacuated by sea. In January 1809 Napoleon returned to France, and four months later Wellington arrived in Portugal with 40,000 men. The French had some 300,000 in the Peninsula, though, thanks to a divided command, less than half of these were entrusted to Masséna, the new commander of the Army of Portugal. Wellington was nevertheless heavily outnumbered, but his defensive tactics, so bitterly criticized at home, saved Lisbon and forced Masséna to retire for the winter. The

[29] Mowat, *op. cit.*, p. 213.   [30] *Letters*, ed. Thompson, p. 214.

Spanish forces, showing no such inhibitions, rashly challenged the French and were soundly beaten; but by the spring of 1811 Wellington had been reinforced, and he now embarked on an offensive that was to bring him ultimately as far as Toulouse. By 1812 the Spaniards had given up attempting pitched battles and had adopted the guerrilla tactics that were to prove so much more effective.

It was his undervaluing of the strength of Spanish resistance, when buttressed by the British army, that was Napoleon's greatest miscalculation. In 1808 he had written to Talleyrand: 'The Spaniards are like other peoples, and are not a class apart; they will be happy to accept the imperial institutions.'[31] But, in spite of the revolutionary *Cortes* convened at Cadiz in 1810 and the constitution of 1812, modelled on the French constitution of 1791, the Spaniards as a whole remained blind to the benefits of French rule. Catholicism rather than nationalism was at the basis of Spanish resistance. Napoleon was not altogether wrong in regarding the war as 'a war of monks', but he was mistaken in believing that the religious fervour of clergy and people could be defeated by the liberal principles of constitutional lawyers.

The Poles submitted more readily to Napoleonic rule, but the Grand Duchy of Warsaw, established at Tilsit and enlarged after the defeat of Austria in 1809, was one of the primary causes of the Russian campaign. In 1809 Napoleon had offered to set Russia's fears at rest by promising never to re-establish the Kingdom of Poland, but he had been thinking of marrying the Tsar's sister at the time: when the marriage project fell through, he withdrew his undertaking about Poland. At Erfurt in 1808 the Tsar and Napoleon had reaffirmed the alliance of Tilsit, but now the Polish question on the one hand and Russia's withdrawal from the Continental System on the other led both sides to prepare for war. What did Napoleon hope to gain from his invasion of Russia in June 1812? Did he expect a quick victory in the manner of Friedland and a peace treaty in the fashion of Tilsit? Apparently not. 'People will want to know where we are going,' he said; 'we are going to make an end of Europe, and then to throw ourselves like robbers on other robbers less daring

[31] F. M. H. Markham, *Napoleon and the Awakening of Europe*, E.U.P. 1954, p. 111.

than ourselves and become masters of India.'[32] And at Vilna at
the end of June, Caulaincourt reports Napoleon as saying:

Alexander is making fun of me. Does he suppose I have come all the
way to Vilna to negotiate commercial treaties? I have come to make
an end once and for all to the Colossus of the barbarian north. My
sword is drawn. These barbarians must be driven back into their
Arctic icefields so that for the next twenty-five years they shan't come
and interfere in the affairs of civilized Europe.[33]

Perhaps it was that, as he later told Metternich, he needed military success abroad to maintain his power at home. Perhaps he
thought that with an army of 600,000 it was impossible to fail.
He had miscalculated in Spain; this time there would be no
mistake, and the critics of his Spanish failures would be silenced.

Whatever Napoleon's motives were, his invasion of Russia
gave his enemies their opportunity. No one was quicker to see
this than Count Metternich of Austria. Metternich (1773–1859),
described by a modern historian as 'the *beau idéal* of the eighteenth-century aristocracy',[34] and previously Austrian ambassador
in Paris, was now in charge of Habsburg diplomacy. The
Austrian defeat at Wagram in 1809, her third at the hands of
Napoleon, had convinced Metternich of the folly of any
Austrian attempt to take on France again singlehanded. 'Only
one escape is left to us,' he told the Emperor Francis, 'to con-
serve our strength for better days, to work for our preservation
with gentler means – and not to look back.'[35] It was in this
spirit that he urged the marriage of Marie Louise to Napoleon:
'In the marriage with the daughter of Your Majesty Napoleon
found a guarantee which he had sought in vain . . . in the overthrow of the Austrian throne.'[36] And Napoleon does seem to
have believed that the marriage gave him security against
Austrian attack, since no father would wage war against his
son-in-law.

In 1812 Metternich put a corps of 30,000 at Napoleon's disposal for the Russian campaign, in return for a French guarantee

[32] Fisher, *op. cit.*, p. 219.   [33] Thompson, *Napoleon*, p. 324.
[34] H. A. Kissinger, *A World Restored*, Weidenfeld & Nicolson 1957, p. 9.
[35] *Ibid.*, p. 20.   [36] *Ibid.*, p. 22.

of the integrity of the Austrian Empire. But at the same time Metternich urged England to intensify her efforts in Spain, while he suggested to Russia that they should come to an understanding that would keep the Austrian corps out of the main fighting.[37] For a long time there was little fighting: the Russians preferred to retreat, burning the crops as they went. Napoleon's unwieldy Grand Army toiled through the summer heat to win a costly but indecisive victory at Borodino in September. Moscow was occupied, but the Muscovites had deliberately deserted their city, and the emissaries who were expected to bring the Tsar's peace terms never came. Instead, as is well known, Napoleon's much depleted army had to retrace its steps through the devastated Russian countryside, now made doubly inhospitable by the onset of winter. In December 1812, within a fortnight of the retreat of the French army across the Beresina, Metternich offered Napoleon Austria's good offices for the negotiation of a general peace. A month later the Russian advance was used as a pretext for withdrawing the Austrian corps to Galicia and increasing its size to 100,000.

Meanwhile Prussia was preparing to move against France. In October 1807 Baron vom Stein (1757–1831) had become chief minister of Frederick William III. Five days later serfdom was abolished. The edict of 9 October abolished the legal status of serfdom. It did not turn the serfs into peasant proprietors, but it gave them the right to leave the land and it removed the existing prohibitions on the free exchange of lands and the free choice of professions.[38] By the time he was dismissed a year later, Stein had also reorganized the central government on more efficient lines and had given the middle classes a voice in municipal government. Stein's successor Hardenberg (1750–1822) preserved and extended Stein's reforms. While Wilhelm von Humboldt overhauled the educational system, Scharnhorst, assisted by Gneisenau and Clausewitz, modernized the army, introducing conscription and, by a system of part-time training, creating a reserve army about three times as large as the 42,000 permitted

[37] *Ibid.*, p. 45.
[38] The degree of freedom corresponded roughly to that conferred by Joseph II's Edict of Emancipation (1781), see above, p. 145.

by Napoleon. The patriotic spirit that was to pervade the new army perhaps owed something to Fichte,[39] whose *Addresses to the German Nation* were delivered at Berlin in 1808, though they caused little stir at the time. German nationalism in 1808, as in 1848, was largely an affair of the intellectuals.

Nevertheless by January 1813 Frederick William felt sure enough of his army to look for allies. Metternich, anxious not to commit himself yet, politely rejected Prussian overtures, and when in February Prussia allied with Russia in the Treaty of Kalisch, Austria still held aloof. In the summer of 1813, after the allied defeats at Lützen and Bautzen, Metternich's services as a negotiator were again in demand. He persuaded Russia and Prussia to offer Napoleon merely their minimum conditions for a preliminary peace. These were stated in the Treaty of Reichenbach (24 June): the Grand Duchy of Warsaw to be dissolved, Prussia to be enlarged, Illyria to be ceded to Austria, and Hamburg and Lübeck to be restored as Free Cities. Napoleon rejected these conditions, as Metternich seems to have expected, and in the famous interview at Dresden on 26 June Napoleon made clear that he could offer no territorial concessions: 'I know how to die; but never shall I cede one inch of territory. Your sovereigns, who were born upon the throne, can allow themselves to be beaten twenty times, and will always return to their capitals; I cannot do that; I am a self-made soldier.'[40] He agreed to meet the allied representatives at Prague, but the conference never took place, and in August Austria at length declared war.

The Sixth Coalition was now complete. It achieved sudden and surprising success: in October 1813 Napoleon was defeated at Leipzig. But at their first victory the allies' newly found solidarity looked like disintegrating. Metternich, suspicious of Russian designs in Poland, began to work to prevent the total defeat of Napoleon. As he wrote to the chief of his chancery: 'I need not tell you that I am as much embarrassed by the plenitude of success as heretofore by the plenitude of disaster.'[41] In

[39] See above, p. 90.

[40] For an account of the interview (Metternich's account) see Sir H. Nicolson, *The Congress of Vienna*, Constable 1946, pp. 41–44.

[41] Kissinger, *op. cit.*, p. 111.

Europe in 1810

Territory directly under Napoleon's rule

Dependent states

Scale 0 100 200 Miles

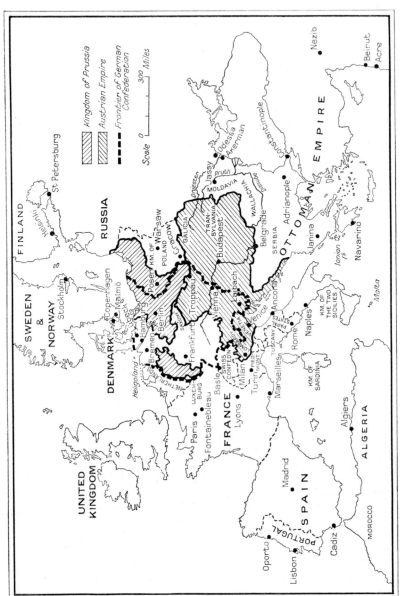

Europe in 1815

November the Frankfurt Proposals demanded a France restored to her 'natural' frontiers, an independent Holland and the restoration of the Spanish Bourbons. These terms were much more moderate than the military situation warranted, but Napoleon first returned an evasive answer, and then accepted too late. The allied armies had invaded France – from Spain, through Switzerland and across the Rhine. But even now Metternich ordered Schwarzenberg, the Austrian commander, to advance 'cautiously' and 'to utilize the desire of the French common man for peace by avoiding warlike acts', and on 16 January Schwarzenberg was told to halt the advance until further orders.

Two days later Castlereagh arrived at Basel, to find that rooms had been reserved for him in both the Austrian and the Russian sectors. He quickly began to see things from Metternich's point of view, and their agreement was reflected in the Langres Protocol, signed by the allies on 29 January. This made it clear that the only alternative to Napoleon was Louis XVIII, not Bernadotte as the Tsar had hoped. Any discussion of the Polish question was also deferred. Throughout February and much of March peace talks continued at Châtillon, their course fluctuating according to varying fortunes in the field.[42] By 18 March the conference had clearly failed and the allies resumed the march on Paris. They had by now redefined their war aims in the Treaty of Chaumont (1 March 1814): an enlarged and independent Holland, a confederated Germany, an independent Switzerland, a Bourbon Spain and the restoration of the Italian states. England's contribution in men and money was to be double that of any of the other signatories, and the four powers were to combine for twenty years after the end of hostilities in order to defend the settlement. Here was the origin of the Quadruple Alliance that was to dominate European diplomacy in the years immediately after 1814. Castlereagh reported to the Foreign Office: 'I send you my treaty which I hope you will approve. This, I trust, will put an end to any doubts as to the claim we have to an opinion on Continental matters.'[43]

---

[42] See Nicolson, *op. cit.*, p. 73.
[43] Kissinger, *op. cit.*, p. 133.

On 30 March the allies entered Paris. On 2 April a provisional government, with Talleyrand at its head, deposed Napoleon and invited Louis XVIII to return to France. On 6 April at Fontainebleau Napoleon signed his unconditional abdication.

Epilogue

The recall of the Bourbons did not restore the *ancien régime*. In terms of territorial expansion, Napoleon had achieved in a decade more than Louis XIV had done in half a century. Yet for all Napoleon's strategic and tactical genius, his military triumphs were based squarely on the social and political successes of the French Revolution: a centralized administrative system geared to the needs of war, a state where careers were open to talent, a professional army in which promotion was on merit and tradition was at a discount, and, least tangible but nonetheless important, a belief that the ideas of '89 were worth fighting for. But if Napoleon owed much to the Revolution, he could himself claim to have rescued the Revolution and restored to it a sense of direction. In 1799 the positive achievements of the Revolution had been in jeopardy; by 1815, in spite of Waterloo, they were secure.

The statesmen at Vienna hoped to undo the work not only of Napoleon's Empire but of Revolutionary France as well, to put the clock back at least to 1792, if not to 1789. Yet the very terms of the Vienna Settlement show how many of the changes of the past twenty-five years were irreversible. The Bourbons were restored in Naples, Spain and France, in accordance with Talleyrand's principle of Legitimacy, and the rulers of Central Italy, including the Pope, returned to their thrones; but elsewhere in Europe Talleyrand's formula was ignored, either in order to provide new safeguards against French aggression or to reward the conquerors. Austria gained Lombardy and Venetia; the Austrian Netherlands were joined to Holland; Norway was transferred from Denmark to Sweden; most of Poland was left in the hands of the partitioning powers, while part of central Poland (about three-quarters of Napoleon's Grand Duchy) was declared politically independent, with the Tsar as its king; Prussia gained territory at the expense of Saxony; and although the German Confederation of thirty-nine states was a fragmentation of Napoleon's Germany, it was considerably more consolidated than the 300-odd states of the Holy Roman Empire.

The Vienna Settlement ignored the principle of nationality, but it may be doubted whether in 1815 nationalism was yet very strong. In Germany it was little more than a literary movement, while Metternich's belief in the essential provincialism of the Italians – no Italian, he said, would lend money to a city of which he couldn't see the church tower – has not been altogether contradicted by subsequent history. Nor was Metternich entirely specious in arguing that, unlike the Grand Empire which had tried to make all men French, the Habsburg Empire gave due recognition to its subject nationalities: 'Never has this monarchy given the name of Germans to Hungarians, Italians or Poles.' For all his claims on St Helena to be the champion of nationality, Napoleon's chief contribution to the cause of nationalism had been to provoke it in the form of opposition to his rule. Poland was perhaps an exception, though Napoleon was more interested in conscripting an army than in restoring Polish institutions. As he told Narbonne: 'I want in Poland a camp and not a forum . . . the whole problem consists in exciting the national fibre of the Poles without awakening the liberal fibre.' Napoleon was eventually defeated not by nationalistic uprisings, but by conventional eighteenth-century-style diplomacy which held together a coalition of mutually hostile states just long enough to enable their weight of numbers to ensure victory.

Napoleon was himself very much a man of the eighteenth century. He was a firm believer in the dynastic principle, perhaps because he felt he needed it to legitimize his regime. He is said to have told Murat that he regarded the marriage of Eugène Beauharnais to Princess Augusta of Bavaria as 'a success on a level with the victory of Austerlitz', while his own marriage into the Habsburgs seems to have blinded him to the fact that Austria was still working to avenge Austerlitz. Only his attachment to the dynastic principle can explain his zeal in establishing his relatives on the thrones of Europe. By 1810 a brother (Joseph) ruled in Spain, another (Louis) in Holland, a third

(Jerome) in Westphalia; Murat was King of Naples, and Eugène was Viceroy of the Kingdom of Italy. It is difficult to believe that Napoleon would have tolerated many of them in such positions of authority if they had not been his relatives. No doubt he expected to control them all the more effectively. He deposed Louis in 1810 and deprived Jerome of part of Westphalia in 1811, while the 'Big Brotherly' tone of his correspondence is illustrated in his letter to Jerome in November 1807:

I enclose the Constitution for your Kingdom. . . . You must faithfully observe it. . . . Don't listen to those who say that your subjects are so accustomed to slavery that they will feel no gratitude for the benefits you give them. There is more intelligence in the Kingdom of Westphalia than they would have you believe; and your throne will never be firmly established except upon the trust and affection of the common people. . . . The benefits of the *Code Napoléon*, public trial, and the introduction of juries will be the leading features of your government. And to tell you the truth, I count more upon their effects for the extension and consolidation of your rule than upon the most resounding victories. . . . What people will want to return under the arbitrary Prussian rule, once it has tasted the benefits of a wise and liberal administration? In Germany, as in France, Italy and Spain, people long for equality and liberalism. I have been managing the affairs of Europe long enough now to know that the burden of the privileged classes was resented everywhere. Rule constitutionally. Even if reason, and the enlightenment of the age, were not sufficient cause, it would be good policy for one in your position; and you will find that the backing of public opinion gives you a great natural advantage over the absolute kings who are your neighbours.

If this clearly reveals Napoleon's dictatorial approach to government, it also demonstrates his belief in the power of reason. And his downfall was brought about by precisely those irrational factors that he found so hard to understand: the Russians' willingness to burn their homeland, the Russian winter itself, the persistence of British hostility, the Spaniards' attachment to their monarch and their Church, the passive resistance of the Pope.

Pius VII survived the indignities he suffered at Napoleon's hands and outlived the Emperor by two years, dying in 1823 at the age of eighty-one. It seems somehow symbolic. When his predecessor had died in 1799, his death had been hailed as the death of the *last* pope. Yet at the Congress of Vienna all the former papal territories in Italy were restored to the Church, while a bull of 1814 re-established the Society of Jesus. It looked as if the Enlightenment had been defeated after all. And although those absolute monarchs restored in 1815 remained suspicious of the Jesuits, and although Alexander I expelled them from Russia in 1820, the spirit of 'enlightened absolutism' was dead. Metternich saw to it that anti-liberal policies were pursued not only in Austria but throughout Germany and northern Italy, the French Bourbons soon illustrated the truth of the famous gibe that they 'had learned nothing and forgotten nothing', Ferdinand VII in Spain and Ferdinand I in the Kingdom of the Two Sicilies both provoked their states to rebellion in 1820 and were restored by foreign troops; only in the Sweden of Charles XIV (formerly Bernadotte) did anything resembling eighteenth-century 'enlightened absolutism' persist.

Enlightened Absolutism had demonstrated its inadequacies even before the outbreak of the French Revolution; the excesses of the French revolutionaries and the successes of Napoleon finally discredited it. Frederick the Great and his contemporaries, for all their unveiled militarism, had paid rather more than lip-service to the ideas of the Enlightenment, though doubtless for sound political reasons. Their achievements were limited by the fact that they ruled states with a largely agrarian economy and poor communications, so that they were forced to rely on the landed classes and, in the last resort, to respect their vested interests. The French Revolution showed that aristocratic privilege could best be removed not by an absolute monarch legislating from above but by an active middle class rebelling from below. Napoleon's contribution to the Enlightenment was to ensure that the ideas of 1789 remained in currency long enough for them to be recalled and refurbished when the spread of industrialization eventually undermined the political supremacy of the European aristocracy. Industrialism was to prove the greatest ally of liberalism. But the story of that revolution belongs to the Railway Age rather than to the Age of Reason.

Appendices

Royal Family Trees

N.B. The family trees have been very much simplified.
The dates beneath the Sovereigns refer to their reigns.

FRANCE: THE HOUSES OF BOURBON AND BOURBON-ORLEANS

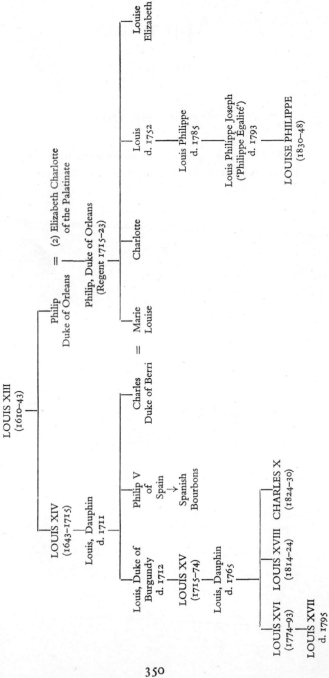

SPAIN AND NAPLES: THE HOUSE OF BOURBON

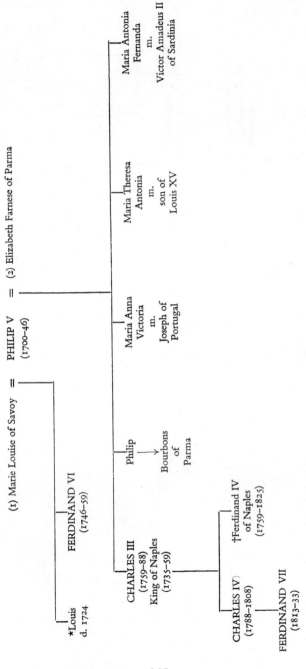

(1) Marie Louise of Savoy = PHILIP V = (2) Elizabeth Farnese of Parma
(1700–46)

★Louis
d. 1724

FERDINAND VI
(1746–59)

Philip
→ Bourbons of Parma

Maria Anna
Victoria
m.
Joseph of
Portugal

Maria Theresa
Antonia
m.
son of
Louis XV

Maria Antonia
Fernanda
m.
Victor Amadeus II
of Sardinia

CHARLES III
(1759–88)
King of Naples
(1735–59)

†Ferdinand IV
of Naples
(1759–1825)

CHARLES IV
(1788–1808)

FERDINAND VII
(1813–33)

★ Reigned as LOUIS I of Spain for a few months in 1724 when PHILIP V temporarily abdicated.
† Ferdinand I of the Kingdom of the Two Sicilies, 1814–25.

351

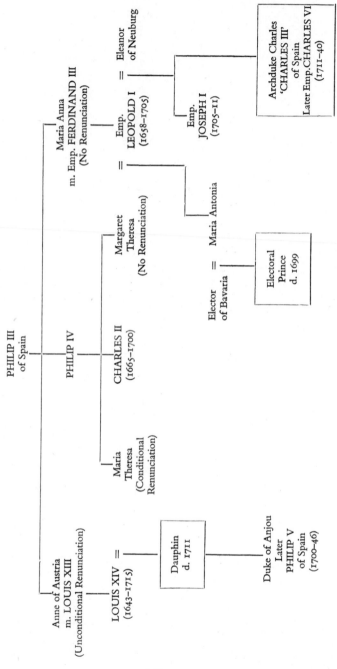

THE SPANISH SUCCESSION: THE THREE CLAIMANTS, 1698–1700

PHILIP III
of Spain

Maria Anna
m. Emp. FERDINAND III
(No Renunciation)

= Eleanor
of Neuburg

PHILIP IV

Emp.
LEOPOLD I
(1658–1705)

Archduke Charles
'CHARLES III'
of Spain
Later Emp.CHARLES VI
(1711–40)

Emp.
JOSEPH I
(1705–11)

Anne of Austria
m. LOUIS XIII
(Unconditional Renunciation)

Maria
Theresa
(Conditional
Renunciation)

CHARLES II
(1665–1700)

Margaret
Theresa
(No Renunciation)

=

Maria Antonia

Elector = Maria Antonia
of Bavaria

Electoral
Prince
d. 1699

LOUIS XIV =
(1643–1715)

Dauphin
d. 1711

Duke of Anjou
Later
PHILIP V
of Spain
(1700–46)

352

THE AUSTRIAN HABSBURGS

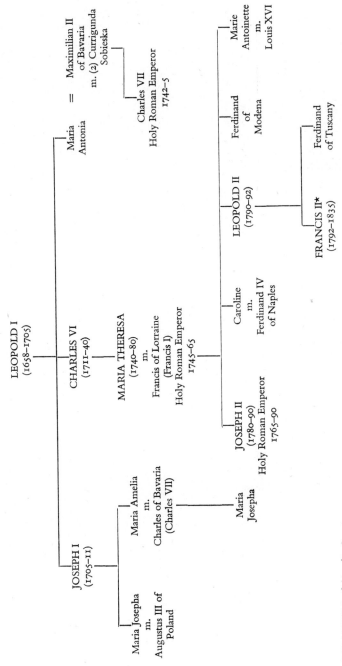

LEOPOLD I
(1658–1705)

JOSEPH I
(1705–11)

CHARLES VI
(1711–40)

Maria Antonia = Maximilian II
of Bavaria
m. (2) Currigunda
Sobieska

Charles VII
Holy Roman Emperor
1742–5

Maria Josepha
m.
Augustus III of
Poland

Maria Amelia
m.
Charles of Bavaria
(Charles VII)

MARIA THERESA
(1740–80)
m.
Francis of Lorraine
(Francis I)
Holy Roman Emperor
1745–65

Maria
Josepha

JOSEPH II
(1780–90)
Holy Roman Emperor
1765–90

Caroline
m.
Ferdinand IV
of Naples

LEOPOLD II
(1790–92)

Ferdinand
of
Modena

Marie
Antoinette
m.
Louis XVI

FRANCIS II*
(1792–1835)

Ferdinand
of Tuscany

* FRANCIS I of Austria 1804–35.

RUSSIA: HOUSE OF ROMANOV

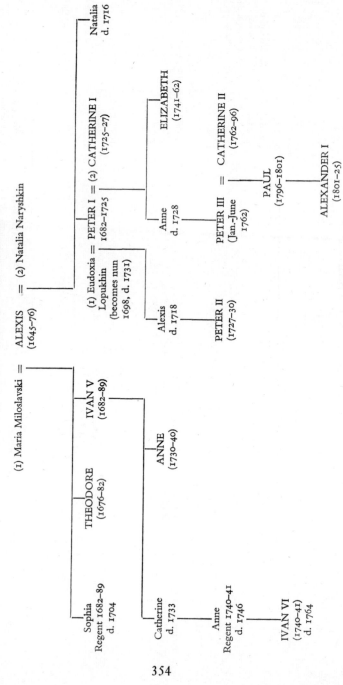

FRANCE: THE HOUSE OF BONAPARTE

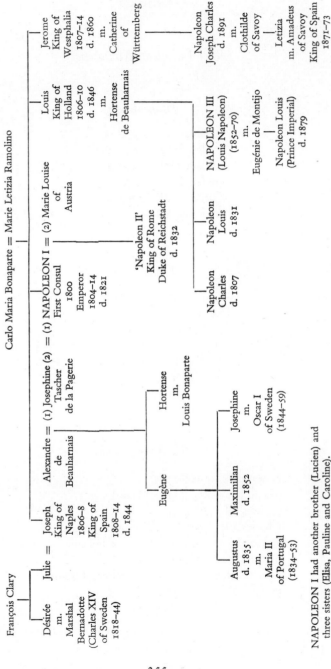

Carlo Maria Bonaparte = Marie Letizia Ramolino

NAPOLEON I had another brother (Lucien) and three sisters (Elisa, Pauline and Caroline).

Other European Monarchs

Denmark

Christian V	1670–99
Frederick IV	1699–1730
Christian VI	1730–46
Frederick V	1746–66
Christian VII	1766–1808
Frederick VI	1808–39

England

James II	1685–88
William III	1689–1702
and Mary II	1689–94
Anne	1702–14
George I	1714–27
George II	1727–60
George III	1760–1820

The Holy Roman Empire

Leopold I	1658–1705	⎫
Joseph I	1705–11	⎬ Habsburg
Charles VI	1711–40	⎭
Charles VII	1742–45	Elector of Bavaria
Francis I	1745–65	Duke of Lorraine
Joseph II	1765–90	⎫
Leopold II	1790–92	⎬ Habsburg-Lorraine
Francis II	1792–1806	⎭

The Holy Roman Empire became extinct in 1806. Francis II then kept the title of Francis I, Emperor of Austria, assumed in 1804.

Poland

John Sobieski	1674–96
Augustus II	1697–1733
Augustus III	1733–63
Stanislas Poniatowski	1764–95

Portugal

Pedro II	1668–1706
John V	1706–1750
Joseph I	1750–77
Maria Francisca	1777–1816

Prussia

Frederick William (the Great Elector)	1640–88
*Frederick III (I)	1688–1713
Frederick William I	1713–40
Frederick II (the Great)	1740–86
Frederick William II	1786–97
Frederick William III	1797–1840

*Frederick III, Elector of Brandenburg, was in 1701 given permission by the Holy Roman Emperor to take the title of King in Prussia, as Frederick I.

Sardinia

In 1720 Victor Amadeus II, Duke of Savoy, took the title of King of Sardinia.

Victor Amadeus II	1720–30
Charles Emmanuel III	1730–73
Victor Amadeus III	1773–96
Charles Emmanuel IV	1796–1802
Victor Emmanuel I	1802–21

Sweden

Charles XI	1660–97
Charles XII	1697–1718
Ulrica Eleanora	1718–20
Frederick I	1720–51
Adolphus Frederick	1751–71
Gustavus III	1771–92
Gustavus IV	1792–1809
Charles XIII	1809–18
Charles XIV (Bernadotte)	1818–44

APPENDIX 3

Popes

Innocent XI	1676–89
Alexander VIII	1689–91
Innocent XII	1691–1700
Clement XI	1700–21
Innocent XIII	1721–24
Benedict XIII	1724–30
Clement XII	1730–40
Benedict XIV	1740–58
Clement XIII	1758–69
Clement XIV	1769–74
Pius VI	1775–99
Pius VII	1800–23

APPENDIX 4

French Currency

The basic unit of money was the *livre tournois* or *franc*.

3 *livres* = 1 *écu*. 24 *livres* = 1 *louis*. The *livre* was divided into *sous* and *deniers*: 1 *livre* = 20 *sous*, 1 *sou* = 12 *deniers* (or 4 *liards*).

From 1726 onwards the pound sterling was worth approximately 24 *livres*. Reckoning the *livre* as being worth 10½d, Arthur Young, at the end of the *ancien régime*, gave a table of conversion from which the following figures are taken:

Livres	£	s	d
5		4	4½
10		8	9
50	2	3	9
100	4	7	6
500	21	17	6
1,000	43	15	0
5,000	218	15	0
10,000	437	10	0

(From John Lough, *An Introduction to Eighteenth-Century France*, Longmans 1960, p. vi.)

APPENDIX 5

Montesquieu and the Separation of Powers

From *Spirit of Laws* (*De l'Esprit des Lois*), book xi, ch. vi.

In every state there are three kinds of power: the legislative power, the executive power in matters relating to the law of nations, and the executive power in those relating to civil law.

By the first, the prince or magistrate makes laws, temporary or permanent, and amends or abrogates those which exist. By the second, he makes peace or wages war, sends or receives embassies, maintains public order, prevents invasions. By the third, he punishes crimes or judges disputes between individuals. We shall call this last the judicial power; and the other simply the executive power of the state. . . .

There is no liberty when the legislative power is combined with the executive power in the same person or the same body of magistrates, because there is a danger that the same monarch or the same senate may make tyrannical laws and execute them tyrannically.

Again there is no liberty if the judicial power is not separated from the legislative and executive powers. If it is combined with the legislative power, the power over the lives and liberty of citizens becomes arbitrary; for the judge is then the legislator. If it is combined with the executive power, the judge then has the strength of an oppressor.

All would be lost if the same man, or the same body of leading men, or of nobles, or of the people, exercised these three powers; that of making laws, that of executing public resolutions, and that of judging crimes or disputes between individuals. . . .

Since in a free state every man who is supposed to have an independent judgement ought to be governed by himself, it would be necessary for the people in a body to have the legislative power; but as this is impossible in large states, and has many disadvantages in small ones, the people must do through their representatives everything that they cannot do by themselves. . . .

In any state there are always people distinguished by birth, riches or dignities; now if they were mingled with the people, and if they had only one voice like the others, the common liberty would become their slavery, and they would have no interest in defending it, because the majority of measures would be directed against them. The share which they have in legislation must therefore be proportionate to the other advantages they enjoy in the state: which will be achieved if they form a body which has the right to halt the projects of the people, in the same way as the people have a right to halt theirs.

Thus the legislative power will be entrusted both to the body of nobles and to the body which will be chosen to represent the people, who will each have their separate assemblies and debates, as well as their separate outlook and interests. . . .

The executive power must be in the hands of a monarch, because that part of government, which almost always needs instantaneous action, is better administered by one than by several; whereas that which depends on the legislative power is often better ordered by several than by one man.

(French text in W. C. Costin and J. Steven Watson, *The Law and Working of the Constitution*, Black 1952, vol. i, pp. 378–82. A longer series of extracts, in English, appears in *From Absolutism to Revolution: 1648–1848*, ed. H. H. Rowen, Macmillan 1963, pp. 117–24.)

APPENDIX 6

The American Declaration of Independence 1776

... We hold these truths to be self-evident, that all men are created equal, that they are endowed by their Creator with certain unalienable rights, that among these are life, liberty and the pursuit of happiness. That to secure these rights, governments are instituted among men, deriving their just powers from the consent of the governed, that whenever any form of government becomes destructive of these ends, it is the right of the people to alter or abolish it, and to institute new government, laying its foundations on such principles and organizing its powers in such forms, as to them shall seem most likely to effect their safety and happiness. ...

(Full text in Henry Bragdon and Samuel McCutcheon, *History of a Free People*, Macmillan 1959.)

Arthur Young and the French Crowd

Strasbourg, 21 July 1789

I have been witness to a scene curious to a foreigner; but dreadful to Frenchmen that are considerate. Passing through the square of the *hotel de ville*, the mob were breaking the windows with stones, notwithstanding an officer and a detachment of horse was in the square. Perceiving that their numbers not only increased, but that they grew bolder and bolder every moment, I thought it worth staying to see what it would end in, and clambered on to the roof of a row of low stalls opposite the building, against which their malice was directed. Here I beheld the whole commodiously. Perceiving that the troops would not attack them, except in words and menaces, they grew more violent, and furiously attempted to beat the door in pieces with iron crows; placing ladders to the windows. In about a quarter of an hour, which gave time for the assembled magistrates to escape by a back door, they burst all open, and entered like a torrent with a universal shout of the spectators. From that minute a shower of casements, sashes, shutters, chairs, tables, sofas, books, papers, pictures, etc., rained incessantly from all the windows of the house, which is seventy or eighty feet long, and which was then succeeded by tiles, skirting boards, bannisters, framework, and every part of the building that force could detach. The troops, both horse and foot, were quiet spectators. They were at first too few to interpose, and, when they became more numerous, the mischief was too far advanced to admit of any other conduct than guarding every avenue around, permitting none to go to the scene of the action, but letting every one that pleased retire with his plunder; guards being at the same time placed at the doors of the churches and all public buildings. I was for two hours a spectator at different places of the scene, secure myself from the falling furniture, but near enough to see a fine lad of about fourteen crushed to death by something as he was handing plunder to a woman, I suppose his mother, from the horror pictured in her countenance. I remarked several common soldiers, with their white cockades, among the plunderers, and instigating the mob even in sight of the officers of the detachment. There were amongst them people so decently dressed, that I regarded them with no small surprise: they destroyed all the public archives; the streets for some way around strewed with papers; this has been a wanton mischief; for it will be the ruin of many families unconnected with the magistrates.

(Arthur Young, *Travels in France*, Bell 1892, pp. 208–9.)

The Republican Calendar

Autumn: 22 September to 21 December

Vendémiaire	Wine harvest
Brumaire	Fog
Frimaire	Frost

Winter: 22 December to 21 March

Nivôse	Snow
Pluviôse	Rain
Ventôse	Wind

Spring: 22 March to 21 June

Germinal	Seedtime
Floréal	Blossomtime
Prairial	Haymaking

Summer: 22 June to 21 September

Messidor	Honey
Thermidor	Heat
Fructidor	Fruit harvest

The twelve months were named according to their prevailing characteristic – weather, seedtime, harvest. Each month of thirty days was divided into three 'decades'. In addition there were five (six in a leap year) *fêtes* or *sansculottides*, which were public holidays. This brought the total to 365 days (366 in a leap year).

The calendar was introduced on 24 November 1793, but was back-dated to 22 September 1792, the beginning of the Year I. It was abolished by Napoleon on 1 January 1806.

The Republic of Virtue

Robespierre's speech in the National Convention, 5 February 1794

... We wish an order of things where all low and cruel passions are enchained by the laws, all beneficent and generous feelings awakened; where ambition is the desire to deserve glory and to be useful to one's country; where distinctions arise only from equality itself; where the citizen is subject to the magistrate, the magistrate to the people, the people to justice; where the country secures the welfare of each individual, and each individual proudly enjoys the prosperity and glory of his country; where all minds are enlarged by the constant interchange of republican sentiments and by the need of earning the respect of a great people; where industry is an adornment to the liberty that ennobles it, and commerce the source of public wealth, not simply of monstrous riches for a few families.

We wish to substitute in our country morality for egotism, probity for a mere sense of honour, principle for habit, duty for etiquette, the empire of reason for the tyranny of custom, contempt for vice for contempt for misfortune, pride for insolence, large-mindedness for vanity, the love of glory for the love of money, good men for good company, merit for intrigue, talent for conceit, truth for show, the charm of happiness for the tedium of pleasure, the grandeur of man for the triviality of grand society, a people magnanimous, powerful and happy for a people lovable, frivolous and wretched – that is to say, all the virtues and miracles of the Republic for all the vices and puerilities of the monarchy.

We wish in a word to fulfil the course of nature, to accomplish the destiny of mankind, to make good the promises of philosophy, to absolve Providence from the long reign of tyranny and crime. May France, illustrious formerly among peoples of slaves, eclipse the glory of all free peoples that have existed, become the model to the nations, the terror of oppressors, the consolation of the oppressed, the ornament of the universe; and in sealing our work with our blood may we ourselves see at least the dawn of universal felicity gleam before us! That is our ambition. That is our aim. . . .

We do not pretend to cast the French Republic in the mould of Sparta. We do not wish to give it either the austerity or the corruption of the cloister. We have just laid before you in all its purity the moral and political principle of popular government. . . .

If the basis of popular government in time of peace is virtue, the basis of popular government in time of revolution is both virtue and terror: virtue without which terror is murderous, terror without which virtue is powerless.

(From R. R. Palmer, *Twelve Who Ruled*, Princeton 1941, pp. 275–76.)

Joseph II's Instructions to His District Commissioners 1784

They were to observe:

Whether the censual and vital statistics registers were kept.

Whether the houses were numbered.

What was the condition of the buildings.

Whether the population was industrious or lazy; well-to-do or poor; and why.

Whether the conscription books were kept in order.

Whether the barracks were habitable.

How many men could be quartered among citizens and peasants.

Whether the army behaved properly towards the civilian population.

Whether the population had sufficient protection.

Whether the toleration edicts were observed.

Whether there was any superstition.

Whether the clergy were respected, and what their discipline was.

Whether the divine services were properly carried out and whether the churches were in good condition.

Whether the preachers delivered indiscreet sermons.

Whether anyone cared for the orphans, foundlings and homeless children.

Whether anything was being done for the blind, deaf and crippled children to make them ultimately self-supporting.

What was the condition of the schools.

Whether there were any roving clowns and jugglers on the land.

Whether the restrictions against drunkenness were carried out.

Whether there was a need for more workhouses and prisons.

Whether the laws were carried out.

Whether the judges were obedient to the superior courts.

Whether the roads were cleared.

Whether there were sufficient precautions in the sale of poisons.

Whether the sale of contraceptive methods was prohibited.

Whether the church penances and the dishonouring punishments of unfortunate girls were abolished, and whether there were institutions for the saving of such girls, and foundlings.

(From S. K. Padover. *The Revolutionary Emperor*, Cape 1934, pp. 186–87.)

APPENDIX II

Catherine the Great's Charter of the Nobility, 1785

1 The noble calling is the result, rising out of the qualities and virtues of men who held high office in the past, and distinguished themselves by their merits, by which they transformed the service itself into a dignity, and won for their descendants the noble appellation.

2 It is not only useful for the empire and the throne, but also just, to preserve and firmly establish the honourable estate of the well-born nobility; and hence the dignity of nobility shall remain inalienable from oldest times to the present, and for all time by inheritance to the descendants of those families that now enjoy it, as follows:

3 The nobleman transmits his noble status to his wife.

4 The nobleman transmits his well-born noble status by inheritance to his children.

8 Without judicial proceedings no well-born person can lose noble status.

10 Without judicial proceedings no well-born person can lose his life.

11 Without judicial proceedings no well-born person can lose his property.

12 The well-born person can be judged only by his peers.

15 Corporal punishment may not be inflicted on any well-born person.

16 Noblemen serving in the lower ranks of our Army shall be liable only to such punishments as our military regulations prescribe for higher officers.

17 We guarantee independence and freedom to the Russian nobility for all time, by inheritance in future generations.

20 [Duty of nobles to defend the state.]

26 Well-born persons are confirmed in the right to purchase villages.

27 Well-born persons are confirmed in the right to sell at wholesale what has been harvested in their villages or produced by handicraft.

28 Well-born persons are permitted to have manufactories and industrial works in their villages.

30 Well-born persons are confirmed in the right to possess, build or buy houses in the cities, and to carry on manufacturing enterprises therein.

32 Well-born persons are permitted to sell products raised on their estates at wholesale overseas or to have them exported through the designated ports. . . .

33 Well-born persons . . . are confirmed in the right to possess, not only the surface of the lands belonging to them, but also whatever minerals or plants may be present in the depths beneath the soil or waters, and likewise all metals extracted therefrom. . . .

34 Well-born persons are confirmed in the right to possess the forests on their estates, and in the right of free use of these forests. . . .

35 In the villages the house of the lord shall be exempt from military quartering.

36 The well-born person is himself freed from personal taxes.

(From R. R. Palmer, *The Age of the Democratic Revolution*, Oxford 1959, vol. i, pp. 508–9.)

The Coalitions against France, 1793–1813

The date in brackets after a country indicates the year in which that country *left* the coalition.

Number	Date of Formation	Members
1st	1793	England, Holland (1794), Prussia (1795), Spain (1795), Tuscany (1795), Sardinia (1796), Austria (1797)
2nd	1799	England (1802), Russia (1799), Austria (1801), Turkey (1801), Portugal (1801), Naples (1801).
3rd	1805	England, Austria (1805), Russia, Sweden.
4th	1806	England, Prussia (1806), Russia (1807), Sweden (1809).
5th	1809	England, Portugal, Austria (1809). England, Portugal, since 1808
6th	1813	England, Russia, Sweden, Portugal, Russia, Sweden, Portugal, since 1812 Prussia, Austria.

An alternative method of numbering is to discount the coalitions of 1806 and 1809 and to call the 1813 coalition the 4th.

Goethe and the Religion of Nature

Faust apostrophizes the Exalted Spirit:

You gave me glorious Nature for my kingdom
With power to feel her and enjoy her. . . .
Aye, you parade the ranks of living things
Before me and you teach me to know my brothers
In the quiet copse, in the water, in the air.
And when the storm growls and snarls in the forest
And the giant pine falls headlong, bearing away
And crushing its neighbours, bough and bole and all,
With whose dull fall the hollow hill resounds,
Then do you carry me off to a sheltered cave
And show me myself, and wonders of my own breast
Unveil themselves in their deep mystery.
And now that the clear moon rises on my eyes
To soften things, now floating up before me
From walls of rock and from the dripping covert
Come silver forms of the past which soothe and temper
The dour delight I find in contemplation.   (p. 104)

Faust replies to Gretchen's question whether he believes in God:

Does not the Heaven vault itself above us?
Is not the earth established fast below?
And with their friendly glances do not
Eternal stars rise over us?
Do not my eyes look into yours,
And all things thrust
Into your head, into your heart,
And weave in everlasting mystery,
Invisibly, visibly around you?
Fill your heart with *this*, great as it is,
And when this feeling grants you perfect bliss,
Then call it what you will –
Happiness! Heart! Love! God!
I have no name for it!
Feeling is all;
Name is mere sound and reek
Clouding Heaven's light.   (p. 113)

(J. W. von Goethe, *Faust*, Part I, trans. Louis MacNeice, Faber 1951.)

Select Bibliography

This bibliography is deliberately selective. I have used almost all the works listed either in the preparation of this book or in sixth-form history teaching. The edition cited is not in all cases the most recent edition, and not all the works are now in print.

GENERAL WORKS

LORD ACTON, *Lectures on Modern History*, Macmillan 1950.

J. M. THOMPSON, *Lectures on Foreign History*, Blackwell 1945.

H. H. ROWEN, ed., *From Absolutism to Revolution: 1648–1848*. Macmillan, New York, 1963. (A collection of documents.)

MAX BELOFF, *The Age of Absolutism*, Hutchinson 1954.

W. F. REDDAWAY, *A History of Europe from 1715 to 1814*, 4th ed., Methuen 1951.

R. M. RAYNER, *European History 1648–1789*, Longmans 1949.

M. S. ANDERSON, *Europe in the Eighteenth Century*, Longmans 1961.

ROBERT ERGANG, *Europe from the Renaissance to Waterloo*, Heath, Boston, 1954.

SIR HAROLD NICOLSON, *The Age of Reason*, Constable 1960. (Bedside reading.)

R. R. PALMER, *A History of the Modern World*, Knopf 1956.

P. ROBERTS, *The Quest for Security 1715–40*, Harper 1947.

WALTER L. DORN, *Competition for Empire 1740–63*, Harper 1940.

L. GERSHOY, *From Despotism to Revolution 1763–89*, Harper 1944. (The above three books published by Harper are volumes in the *Rise of Modern Europe series*, ed. WILLIAM L. LANGER and now available in paperback. They are a little too sophisticated for the average A Level candidate, but they make very stimulating reading.)

R. MOUSNIER and E. LABROUSSE, *Le XVIIIe Siècle: Révolution Intellectuelle, Technique et Politique*, Presses Universitaires de France 1955.

The Cambridge Modern History, vol. vi, Cambridge 1909.

The New Cambridge Modern History, vols. v and vii, Cambridge 1961 and 1957.

DIPLOMATIC

HERBERT BUTTERFIELD, *Man on His Past*, ch. 5, Cambridge 1955.

J. A. R. MARRIOTT, *The Eastern Question*, Oxford 1918.

R. B. MOWAT, *The Diplomacy of Napoleon*, Arnold 1924.

ALGERNON CECIL, *Metternich 1773–1859*, Eyre & Spottiswoode 1933.

HENRY KISSINGER, *A World Restored: Metternich, Castlereagh and the Problems of Peace*, Weidenfeld & Nicolson 1957.

SIR HAROLD NICOLSON, *The Congress of Vienna*, Constable 1946.

C. K. WEBSTER, *The Congress of Vienna*, Bell 1934.

A. DUFF COOPER, *Talleyrand*, Cape 1932.

COLONIAL AND ECONOMIC

The Cambridge History of the British Empire, vol. i, Cambridge 1929.

RAMSAY MUIR, *A Short History of the British Commonwealth*, 2 vols, Philips 1920.

J. A. WILLIAMSON, *A Short History of British Expansion*, Macmillan 1927.

E. M. CARUS-WILSON, ed., *Essays in Economic History*, Arnold 1954.

S. B. CLOUGH and C. W. COLE, *An Economic History of Europe*, Heath, Boston, 1952.

A. GOODWIN, ed., *The European Nobility in the Eighteenth Century*, Black 1953.

W. O. HENDERSON, *The Industrial Revolution on the Continent 1800–1914*, Cass 1961. (The first few pages only.)

J. L. and BARBARA HAMMOND, *The Rise of Modern Industry*, Methuen 1925.

E. J. HOBSBAWM, *The Age of Revolution: Europe 1789–1848*, Weidenfeld and Nicolson 1962. (Also useful as a general history of the period.)

CHARLES WILSON, *Mercantilism*, Historical Association pamphlet 1958.

RELIGIOUS

G. R. CRAGG, *The Church in the Age of Reason 1648–1789*, Hodder & Stoughton 1962; and ALEC R. VIDLER, *The Church in an Age of Revolution*, Hodder & Stoughton 1962.

R. A. KNOX, *Enthusiasm*, Oxford 1950.

E. E. Y. HALES, *Revolution and Papacy 1769–1846*, Eyre & Spottiswoode 1960.

—*Napoleon and the Pope*, Eyre & Spottiswoode 1962.

Original Writings

RENÉ DESCARTES, *Discours sur la méthode de bien conduire la raison et chercher la vérité dans les sciences.* English translation in Everyman's Library, Dent 1916.

WILLIAM HARVEY, *De Motu Cordis*, trans. Franklin, Blackwell 1957.

STUART HAMPSHIRE, ed., *The Age of Reason*, Mentor Books 1956. (An anthology of extracts.)

HUGH F. KEARNEY, *Origins of the Scientific Revolution*, Longmans 1964. (Part II contains select documents.)

Secondary Sources

BENJAMIN FARRINGTON, *Francis Bacon: Philosopher of Industrial Science*, Lawrence & Wishart 1951.

ARTHUR KOESTLER, *The Sleepwalkers*, Hutchinson 1959.

HERBERT BUTTERFIELD, *The Origins of Modern Science*, Bell 1949.

A. R. HALL, *The Scientific Revolution 1500–1800*, Longmans 1954.

F. L. NUSSBAUM, *The Triumph of Science and Reason 1660–85*, Harper 1953.

DOUGLAS MCKIE, *Antoine Lavoisier: Scientist, Economist, Social Reformer*, Constable 1952.

THE ENLIGHTENMENT

Original Writings

JOHN LOCKE, *Second Treatise of Civil Government*, Blackwell 1948.

DAVID HUME, *A Treatise of Human Nature*, Dent (Everyman's Library) 1911.

JEAN-JACQUES ROUSSEAU, *The Social Contract and Discourses*, Dent (Everyman's Library) 1947.
Émile for Today, ed. William Boyd, Heinemann 1956. (A very readable abridgement of Rousseau's *Émile*.)

JEREMY BENTHAM, *A Fragment on Government and An Introduction to the Principles of Morals and Legislation*, Blackwell 1948.

CARON DE BEAUMARCHAIS, *The Barber of Seville and the Marriage of Figaro*, Penguin 1964.

JAMES BOSWELL, *Boswell on the Grand Tour: Germany and Switzerland 1764*, Heinemann 1953.

J. W. VON GOETHE, *Faust: Part I*, trans. L. MacNeice, Faber 1951.

ANDRÉ LAGARDE et LAURENT MICHARD, eds, *XVIIIe Siècle*,

Bordas 1962. (*Collection Textes et Littérature.*) (An anthology of extracts from eighteenth-century French literature.)

VOLTAIRE, *Candide*, Hamish Hamilton 1947.

Secondary Sources

BASIL WILLEY, *The Eighteenth Century Background*, Chatto & Windus 1946.

ERNST CASSIRER, *The Philosophy of the Enlightenment*, English trans., Beacon Press, Boston, 1955.

PAUL HAZARD, *The European Mind 1680–1715*, English trans., Penguin 1964.

KINGSLEY MARTIN, *French Liberal Thought in the Eighteenth Century*, Turnstile Press 1954.

GEORGE R. HAVENS, *The Age of Ideas*, Peter Owen 1957.

PETER AMANN, *The Eighteenth Century Revolution*, Heath, Boston, 1963.

T. D. KENDRICK, *The Lisbon Earthquake*, Methuen 1956.

CYNTHIA COX, *The Real Figaro*, Longmans 1962. (A life of Beaumarchais.)

ALFRED COBBAN, *In Search of Humanity*, Cape 1960.

J. H. BROOME, *Rousseau: a Study of his Thought*, Arnold 1963.

W. H. BRUFORD, *Germany in the Eighteenth Century: the Social Background of the Literary Revival*, Cambridge 1935.

THE ARTS

E. H. GOMBRICH, *The Story of Art*, chs. 21–24, Phaidon 1960.

EDMOND and JULES GONCOURT, *French XVIII Century Painters*, Phaidon 1957.

VICTOR-L. TAPIÉ, *The Age of Grandeur*, Weidenfeld & Nicolson 1960. (A Study of the Baroque.)

HARALD BUSCH and BERNARD LOHSE, eds, *Baroque Europe*, Batsford 1962 (*Buildings of Europe series*). (Illustrations.)

HENRY A. MILLON, *Baroque and Rococo Architecture*, Prentice Hall 1961 (*Great Ages of World Architecture series*). (Illustrations.)

JAMES LEES-MILNE, *Baroque in Italy*, Batsford 1959.

—*Baroque in Spain and Portugal*, Batsford 1960.

—*Earls of Creation: Five Great Patrons of Eighteenth Century Art*, Hamish Hamilton 1962.

FRANCIS HASKELL, *Patrons and Painters*, Chatto & Windus 1963.

MARCEL BRION, *Pompeii and Herculaneum*, Elek Books 1960.

JOHN FLEMING, *Robert Adam and his Circle*, Murray 1962.
SIR KENNETH CLARK, *The Gothic Revival*, new edn, Murray 1962.
The Pelican History of Art, when fully published, will have at least four volumes on the eighteenth century.

NATIONAL HISTORIES
FRANCE

General
JOHN LOUGH, *An Introduction to Eighteenth Century France*, Longmans 1960.
J. M. WALLACE-HADRILL and J. MCMANNERS, eds, *France: Government and Society*, Methuen 1957.
GORDON WRIGHT, *France in Modern Times*, Murray 1962.
HERBERT BUTTERFIELD and others, *A Short History of France*, Cambridge 1959.
ALFRED COBBAN, *A History of Modern France*, 2 vols, Penguin 1961.

Louis XIV
ARTHUR TILLEY, ed., *Selections from Saint-Simon* (in French), Cambridge 1920.
—*The Decline of the Age of Louis XIV*, Cambridge 1929.
DAVID OGG, *Louis XIV*, Oxford 1933.
MAURICE ASHLEY, *Louis XIV and the Greatness of France*, E.U.P. 1946.
JOHN LOUGH, *An Introduction to Seventeenth Century France*, Longmans 1954.
WILLIAM F. CHURCH, ed., *The Greatness of Louis XIV*, Heath, Boston, 1959.
H. G. JUDGE, *Louis XIV*, Longmans 1965 (*Problems and Perspectives in History series*).
W. J. STANKIEWICZ, *Politics and Religion in Seventeenth Century France*, University of California Press 1960.
WARREN C. SCOVILLE, *The Persecution of the Huguenots and French Economic Development 1680–1720*, University of California Press 1960.

Louis XV
G. P. GOOCH, *Louis XV*, Longmans 1956.

SELECT BIBLIOGRAPHY

PIERRE GAXOTTE, *Louis XV and His Times*, trans. J. L. May, Cape 1934.

NANCY MITFORD, *Madame Pompadour*, Penguin 1958. (Bedside reading.)

—JACQUES LEVRON, *Pompadour*, trans. C. E. Engel, Allen & Unwin 1963. (Bedside reading.)

Louis XVI and the French Revolution

ALEXIS DE TOCQUEVILLE, *L'Ancien Régime*, trans. M. W. Patterson, Blackwell 1949.

ARTHUR YOUNG, *Travels in France*, Bell 1892, and Dent (Everyman's Library).

EDMUND BURKE, *Reflections on the Late Revolution in France*, Dent (Everyman's Library) 1953.

TOM PAINE, *The Rights of Man*, Dent (Everyman's Library) 1958.

A. MATHIEZ, *The French Revolution*, trans. C. A. Phillips, Williams & Norgate 1928.

THOMAS CARLYLE, *The French Revolution*, Chapman & Hall 1837, and Dent (Everyman's Library), 3 vols.

G. SALVEMINI, *The French Revolution 1788–92*, trans. I. M. Rawson, Cape 1954.

G. LEFEBVRE, *The Coming of the French Revolution*, Vintage 1957.

—*The French Revolution*, Routledge & Kegan Paul 1962.

CRANE BRINTON, *A Decade of Revolution, 1789–99*, Harper 1934.

ALFRED COBBAN, *The Myth of the French Revolution*, University of London pamphlet, M. K. Lewis 1955.

RALPH W. GREENLAW, ed., *The Economic Origins of the French Revolution*, Heath, Boston, 1958.

G. RUDÉ, *The Crowd in the French Revolution*, Oxford 1959.

G. PERNOUD and S. FLAISSIER, *The French Revolution*, trans. Richard Graves, Secker & Warburg 1960. (Eye-witness accounts.)

J. M. THOMPSON, *The French Revolution*, Blackwell 1943.

—*Leaders of the French Revolution*, Blackwell 1929.

—*Robespierre and the French Revolution*, E.U.P. 1952.

R. R. PALMER, *Twelve Who Ruled: The Year of the Terror in the French Revolution*, Princeton 1941.

N. HAMPSON, *A Social History of the French Revolution*, Routledge & Kegan Paul 1963.

E. L. WOODWARD, *French Revolutions*, Oxford 1934.

GODFREY ELTON, *The Revolutionary Idea in France*, Arnold 1923.

Napoleon

J. M. THOMPSON, ed., *Letters of Napoleon*, Blackwell 1934.

J. M. THOMPSON, *Napoleon Bonaparte: His Rise and Fall*, Blackwell 1951.

H. A. L. FISHER, *Napoleon*, Williams & Norgate 1924.

—*Bonapartism*, Oxford 1908.

GEOFFREY BRUUN, *Europe and the French Imperium 1799–1814*, Harper 1938.

HERBERT BUTTERFIELD, *Napoleon*, Duckworth 1939.

PIETER GEYL, *Napoleon: For and Against*, Cape 1957.

LOUIS MADELIN, *The Consulate and Empire*, trans. E. F. Buckley, Heinemann 1934.

F. M. H. MARKHAM, *Napoleon and the Awakening of Europe*, E.U.P. 1954.

—*Napoleon*, Weidenfeld & Nicolson 1963.

J. C. HEROLD, *Bonaparte in Egypt*, Hamish Hamilton 1963.

The Cambridge Modern History, vol. ix, Cambridge 1907.

GERMANY AND EASTERN EUROPE

MARSHALL DILL, *Germany*, University of Michigan 1961.

A. J. P. TAYLOR, *The Course of German History*, Hamish Hamilton 1945.

KOPPEL S. PINSON, *Modern Germany*, Macmillan, New York, 1955.

J. A. R. MARRIOTT and C. GRANT ROBERTSON, *The Evolution of Prussia*, Oxford 1915.

CONSTANTIN DE GRUNWALD, *Baron Stein*, Cape 1936.

The Cambridge History of Poland 1697–1935, Cambridge 1941.

DENIS SINOR, *A History of Hungary*, Allen & Unwin 1959.

ITALY

JAMES BOSWELL, *Boswell on the Grand Tour: Italy, Corsica and France 1765–66*, Heinemann 1955.

J. W. VON GOETHE, *Italian Journey 1786–88*, trans. W. H. Auden and Elizabeth Mayer, Collins 1962.

MAURICE VAUSSARD, *Daily Life in Eighteenth Century Italy*, trans. Michael Heron, Allen & Unwin 1962.

J. P. TREVELYAN, *A Short History of the Italian People*, Putnam 1920.

A. J. WHYTE, *The Evolution of Modern Italy*, Blackwell 1959 (ch. 1 only).

SPAIN

J. H. ELLIOTT, *Imperial Spain 1469–1716*, Arnold 1963 (last chapter only).

CHARLES E. CHAPMAN, *A History of Spain*, Macmillan, New York, 1938.

HAROLD LIVERMORE, *A History of Spain*, Allen & Unwin 1958.

R. TREVOR DAVIES, *Spain in Decline 1621–1700*, Macmillan 1957 (last two chapters only).

RUSSIA

RICHARD CHARQUES, *A Short History of Russia*, 2nd edn., Phoenix House 1962.

BERNARD PARES, *A History of Russia*, Cape 1937. (Also in Methuen 'University' Paperbacks.)

B. H. SUMNER, *Peter the Great and the Emergence of Russia*, E.U.P. 1950.

IAN GREY, *Peter the Great*, Hodder & Stoughton 1961. (Bedside reading.)

VASILI KLYUCHEVSKY, *Peter the Great*, trans. L. Archibald, Macmillan 1958.

WARREN B. WALSH, *Russia and the Soviet Union*, University of Michigan 1958.

SWEDEN

R. SVANSTRÖM and C. F. PALMSTIERNA, *A Short History of Sweden*, trans. J. Bulman, Oxford 1934.

C. HALLENDORFF and A. SCHÜCK, *History of Sweden*, trans. Lajla Yapp, C. E. Fritze, Stockholm, 1938.

R. NISBET BAIN, *Charles XII and the Collapse of the Swedish Empire*, Putnam 1907.

F. G. BENGTSSON, *The Life of Charles XII*, trans. N. Walford, Macmillan 1960.

ENLIGHTENED ABSOLUTISM
(*See also national histories above*)

General

R. R. PALMER, *The Age of the Democratic Revolution*, vol. 1, Oxford 1959.

GEOFFREY BRUUN, *The Enlightened Despots*, Holt, New York, 1947.

FRITZ HARTUNG, *Enlightened Despotism*, Historical Association pamphlet 1957. (Chiefly a discussion of the historiography of the term.)

PRUSSIA

W. F. REDDAWAY, *Frederick the Great and the Rise of Prussia*, Putnam 1908.

G. P. GOOCH, *Frederick the Great*, Longmans 1947.

EDITH SIMON, *The Making of Frederick the Great*, Cassell 1963. (Ends with Frederick's accession.)

SIR J. WILLIAM WHITTALL, *Frederick the Great on Kingcraft*, Longmans 1901. (French text of extracts from Frederick's writings, with English translation.)

LORD MACAULAY, 'Frederick the Great' in *Essays and Lays of Ancient Rome*, Longmans 1886.

RUSSIA

G. P. GOOCH, *Catherine the Great and Other Studies*, Longmans 1954.

GLADYS SCOTT THOMSON, *Catherine the Great and the Expansion of Russia*, E.U.P. 1947.

IAN GREY, *Catherine the Great*, Hodder & Stoughton 1961. (Bedside reading.)

AUSTRIA AND THE EMPIRE

G. P. GOOCH, *Maria Theresa and Other Studies*, Longmans 1951.

S. K. PADOVER, *The Revolutionary Emperor*, Cape 1934

ERNST WANGERMANN, *From Joseph II to the Jacobin Trials*, Oxford 1959.

A. FAUCHIER MAGNAN, *The Small German Courts in the Eighteenth Century*, trans. M. Savill, Methuen 1958.

SPAIN AND NAPLES

RICHARD HERR, *The Eighteenth Century Revolution in Spain*, Princeton 1958.

HAROLD ACTON, *The Bourbons of Naples*, Methuen 1957.

Index

Dates after rulers' names refer to their reigns

Aachen, 169
Abercrombie, James, British commander-in-chief in America, 194
Aboukir Bay, battle of (1798), 319
Académie des Sciences, Paris, 54, 111, 113, 114, 255
Acadia: *see* Nova Scotia
Aché, Admiral d', 196
Acre, 319
Adams, John (1735–1826), 253, 254
Addison, Joseph (1672–1719), 75, 257
Adolphus Frederick, King of Sweden (1751–71), 165
Adrian, Patriarch of Moscow, 42
Africa, 105
Agriculture: in Europe, 110–11; in Sicily, 110; in Prussia, 122; in the Austrian territories, 148; in Spain, 162; in France, 271–2
Aiguillon, Duc d', Governor of Brittany, 242, 244
Aix-la-Chapelle, treaty of (1748), 182, 184, 185, 186, 193
Aix-en-Provence, 296
Alberoni, Giulio, Cardinal (1664–1752), 18; reforms in Spain, 22–23
Alberti, Leone Battista (1404–72), 68
Alcabala, 163
Alembert, Jean le Rond d' (1717–83), 129, 161, 220; co-editor of the *Encyclopaedia*, 70–72; writes against Rousseau, 85; relations with Frederick the Great, 116, 117, 208; and the *salons*, 222
Alexander I, Tsar of Russia (1801–25), 139, 334, 336, 337, 338, 342, 348
Alexis, Tsar of Russia (1645–76), 38
Alfieri, Vittorio, Count (1749–1803), 289
Algeria, 31
Alicante, 23
Alleghanies, 194
Alps, 317
Alsace, 16, 234, 290, 291
Altranstädt, 35
Alxinger, Johann Baptist von, 150
America, American Colonies: and the slave trade, 107; War of Independence, 213, 251–3, 263; Tom Paine and, 251; Declaration of Independence, 253, 254, 361; Constitution of the United States, 254; and the French Revolution, 253–6, 263, 282; and Napoleon's Continental System, 332, 334

Amherst, Field-Marshal Lord, 194
Amiens, treaty of (1802), 322, 327–8
Amsterdam, 39, 108
Anjou, 10
Anjou, Duc d', 14
Anna, Empress of Russia (1730–40), 131, 173
Anne, Queen of England (1702–14), 14
Ansbach, 205
Anson, Admiral Lord, 183
Antwerp, 181,
Aragon, 22
Aranda, Pedro Pablo Abarca de Bolea, Count of (1719–98), 159, 161
Archaeology, 156–7, 230–2, 319
Archangel, 38, 40, 134, 137
Arcot, 184
Argenson, René Louis de Voyer de Paulmy, Marquis d' (1694–1757), 181, 239, 247, 256
Aristocracy: in the Holy Roman Empire, 99, 100–1; in Sweden, 99–100; in Hungary, 99, 100, 102, 111, 143–4, 145–6, 289–90; in Prussia, 101, 102–3, 121; in Russia, 101–2, 103, 131, 132–4, 366–7; in Austria, 143–4, 145–6, 148, 151; in Naples, 155; in Spain, 161–2; in Portugal, 165; in France, 236, 237, 240–5, 259–60, 262–6, 279, 281–2
Aristotle, 64, 79, 164; Aristotelian astronomy, 59–60
Arles, 296
Armed Neutrality, League of (1780–3): 168, 252; (1801): 333
Arnould, author of *De la balance du Commerce et des relations commerciales de la France dans toutes les parties du monde* (1788), 235
Artois, 234; Comte d', later Charles X, King of France (1824–30), 265, 291
Asiento, 14, 16, 17, 19, 49, 107, 182, 184
Assembly of Clergy, 242, 243, 267
Assembly of Notables, 264, 266, 268
Assignats, 285, 295, 312, 316
Athens, 32
Aufklärung: *see* Enlightenment
Augereau, Marshal, 317
Augsburg, War of the League of (1688–97), 9
Augusta, Princess of Bavaria, 346
Augustus II, King of Poland (1697–1733); Frederick Augustus I ('the Strong'),

Augustus II—*cont.*
  Elector of Saxony (1694–1733), elected to the Polish throne, 29; struggle with Charles XII of Sweden, 35; restored to Polish throne, 37; death, 30
Augustus III, King of Poland (1733–63), Frederick Augustus II, Elector of Saxony (1733–63), 155n.; Polish succession war, 30–31, 47; Seven Years War, 189; death, 200
Austerlitz, battle of (1805), 330, 346
Austria: under Charles VI (1711–40), 45–47; aristocracy, 143–4, 145–6, 148, 151; commercial treaty with Russia (1785), 136; under Maria Theresa and Joseph II (1740–90), 140–52; Austrian succession war, 173–82; treaty of Aix-la-Chapelle (1748), 184; Diplomatic Revolution, 185–90; Seven Years War, 190–3; treaty of Hubertusburg, 197–8; Turkish war (1768–74), 199–202; seizes Bukovina, 202; Bavarian succession war, 202–6; Turkish war (1787–92), 206–8; Partitions of Poland, 208–14; and the French Revolution, 290–92, 294–5, 299; Napoleonic wars, 317–18, 328–9, 330, 334, 336; treaty of Campo Formio (1797), 318; treaty of Lunéville (1801), 328; Metternich and the defeat of Napoleon, 337–8, 339–43; gains at Congress of Vienna, 345. *See also* Holy Roman Empire
Austrian Succession, War of (1740–48), 142, 154, 165, 173–84, 185, 186, 193
Avignon, 290, 296, 325
Azov, 32, 36, 39–40, 199

Babeuf, François Noel ('Gracchus') (1760–97), 316
Bacon, Francis (1561–1626), 64, 69, 160; pioneer of experimental method, 53–56; influence on Royal Society, 54–55; connexion with *philosophes*, 53, 56
Baden, 322, 330
Baiardi, Ottavio, 156
Bailly, Jean Sylvain (1736–93), 279
Ballooning, 113–14
Baltic Sea, 37, 40, 168, 191, 199, 201, 214
Banque de France, 324
Banque Générale, 236
Barbados, 49
Barbier, the French lawyer and diarist, 218, 260
Barbon, Nicholas (1640–98), 104
Barcelona, 163
Barclay, Robert (1648–90), 249

Barère de Vieuzac, Bertrand (1755–1841), 302, 308, 312, 313
Barnave, Antoine Pierre Joseph Marie (1761–93), 283
Barnett, Commodore, 183
Baroque: in Italy, 229; elsewhere in Europe, 229–30, 232
Barras, Paul François Nicholas, Comte de (1755–1829), 315, 317, 319
Barthélemy, Marquis de, 317
Basel, treaty of (1795), 313
Bassignano, 181
Bastille, 74, 247, 252, 289; storming of, 271, 280–81
Batavian Republic: *see* Holland
Bautzen, battle of (1813), 339
Bavaria, 27, 34, 248, 322; Spanish succession war, 14; Austrian succession war, 173–81; Bavarian succession war, 126, 202–6
Bayle, Pierre (1647–1706), exile in Holland, 8; *Historical and Critical Dictionary*, 71, 73–74; defence of toleration, 74
Baylen, battle of (1808), 335
Bayonne, treaty of (1808), 335
Bayreuth, 205
Beauharnais: Eugène de, 333, 347; Josephine de, first wife of Napoleon I, 315, 334n.
Beaumarchais, Pierre Augustin Caron de (1732–99), 252n., 260n.; *drames*, 225, 268; and the *parlements*, 244; *Marriage of Figaro*, 225, 259
Beccaria, Cesare Bonesana, Marquis de (1738–94), 76, 133, 158, 160
Beethoven, Ludwig van (1770–1827), 329
Belgium: *see* Netherlands
Belgrade: captured from Turks (1717), 32; treaty of (1739), 33, 178, 199
Belle-Isle, Comte (later Duc) de, 178, 179, 181
Belvedere Palace, Vienna, 230
Benedict XIV, Pope (1740–58), 155
Bengal, Nawab of, 195
Bentham, Jeremy (1748–1832), 76–77, 137, 246, 251, 322
Beresina, river, 338
Berg, 34, 175
Berlin, 42, 45, 115, 116, 118, 125, 192, 339; effect of Thirty Years War on, 26; treaty of (1745), 179, 181; Academy, 116–17, 125, 133, 248; Decree (1806), 332
Bernadotte, Marshal, later Charles XIV, King of Sweden (1818–44), 334, 342, 348
Bernini, Giovanni Lorenzo (1598–1680), 229–30
Bernis, Cardinal de, 196

Bernstorff, Andreas Peter, Count von (1735–97), 170; Johann Hartwig Ernst Count von (1712–72), 170
Bessarabia, 207
Bestuzhev-Ryumin, Alexius Petrovich, Count (1693–1768), 187, 189
Bialystok, 103
Bibikov, General Vasili, 136
Billet de confession, 241–2
Billaud-Varenne, Jacques Nicolas (1756–1819), 307, 312, 313
Biscay, bay of, 18, 201
Black Sea, 136, 199, 202, 208
Blackstone, Sir William (1723–80), 246
Blenheim, battle of (1704), 15; Palace, 230
Bohemia, 46, 47, 102, 142, 143, 144, 145, 146, 147, 148, 178, 179, 190, 191, 192, 205, 289
Boisguilbert, Pierre le Pesant (1676–1714), 105
Bolingbroke, Henry St John (1678–1751), 247
Bombay, 49, 196
Bonaparte: Lucien, 319, 323; Louis, King of Holland, 333, 335, 346; Jerome, King of Westphalia, 333, 347; Joseph, King of Spain, 335, 346. *See also* Napoleon
Bordeaux, 235, 260, 303, 310
Borelli, Giovanni Alfonso (1608–79), 63
Borodino, battle of (1812), 338
Borromini, Francesco (1599–1667), 229
Boscawen, Admiral, 184, 194, 195
Bosporus, 136
Bossuet, Jacques Bénigne (1627–1704), views on divine right, 7; the Four Articles (1682), 7, 325; views on persecution, 7–8
Boswell, James (1740–95), on bombardment of Dresden, 192–3; letter to, 246; on the Grand Tour, 248–9; *Account of Corsica*, 249; interview with Pitt, 249–50
Boucher, François (1703–70), 219, 220, 227
Bouillé, François Claude Amour, Marquis de (1739–1800), 264, 288
Boulay de la Meurthe, Antoine Jacques Claude Joseph, Comte (1761–1840), author of the phrase '*C'est pire qu'un crime, c'est une faute*' (on hearing of the Duc d'Enghien's execution), 325
Boulogne, 328–30
Bourbon, Duc de, 218
Bourgeoisie (in France): tastes in literature, 224–5; painted by Chardin, 228; buy up seigneurial rights, 265, 272; purchase nobility, 265; economic position and aims in 1789, 268–9. For part in French Revolution *see* Chs. 19–21

Bourgogne (Burgundy), Duc de, grandson of Louis XIV, 217, 233
Boyle, Robert (1627–91), 54n., 64
Brahe, Tycho (1546–1601), 60–61
Brandenburg, 14n., 16, 24, 43–4, 192, 197, 209; effect of Thirty Years War on, 26; battle of Fehrbellin (1675), 33; Elector of, 16, 43; textile industries of, 123. *See also* Prussia
Branicki family, 103
Brazil, 164
Brest, 330
Breteuil, Louis Charles Auguste le Tonnelier, Baron de (1730–1807), 279
Brienne, Étienne Charles de Loménie de, Cardinal (1727–94), 266
Brissot, Jacques Pierre (1754–93), 255; in Legislative Assembly, 293–4, 296; in National Convention, 299–301; and Dumouriez, 301; guillotined, 305. *See also* Girondins
Brittany, 234, 238, 242, 243
Brumaire, *coup d'état* of (1799), 319, 321, 322
Bruno, Giordano (1548–1600), 62
Brunswick, Ferdinand, Duke of, 191; his nephew Karl Wilhelm Ferdinand, 299; Manifesto (1792), 297
Brussels, 144, 181, 236, 254, 289
Bucharest, 201
Budapest, 32, 33, 144
Buffon, George Louis Leclerc, Comte de (1707–88), 70, 212, 221; contributes to *Encyclopaedia*, 71; relations with Louis XV, 220
Bukovina, 202
Burgoyne, General, 197
Burgundy, 271. *See also* Bourgogne
Burke, Edmund (1729–97), 207, 251
Burlington House, 230
Bute, John Stuart, 3rd Earl of Bute (1713–92), 193, 197
Butler, Joseph, Bishop (1692–1752), 75
Byng, Admiral, 18, 23

Cadiz, 23, 163, 164, 329, 330, 336
Cadoudal, Georges (1771–1804), 322, 329
Cahiers, 133, 267, 277
Calcutta, 49, 183, 195
Calas, Jean, 258
Calonne, Charles Alexandre de (1734–1802), 263–4, 266, 271
Cambrai, Congress of (1721), 19
Campo Formio, treaty of (1797), 318
Canada, 107, 183, 190, 194–5, 197, 235
Canaletto, Antonio (1697–1768), 229
Canals, 41, 123, 136, 163
Canova, Antonio (1757–1822), 231
Cape Breton Island, 48

Capodimonte, 156
'Caps', party in Swedish *Riksdag*, 165, 167
Carinthia, 46, 142
Carlos, Don, 19, 153. *See also* Charles III, King of Naples
Carlowitz (Karlowitz), treaty of (1699), 32
Carmer, Johann von (1721–1801), 120–1
Carniola, 46
Carnot, Lazare Nicolas Marguerite (1753–1823), 302, 307, 315, 317
Carpathians, 212
Carrier, Jean Baptiste (1756–94), 312
Cartagena, 183
Carteret, John, 2nd Baron Carteret, later Earl Granville (1690–1763), 180
Cartwright, John (1740–1824), 250
Caserta, 156, 230
Castile, 22, 162
Castlereagh, Robert Stewart, Viscount, later Marquess of Londonderry (1769–1822), 342
Catalonia, 20, 22, 163
Catherine I, Empress of Russia (1725–27), 130
Catherine II, Empress of Russia (1762–96), 38, 40, 147, 168, 171, 295; and Poland, 30, 200–202, 209–14; dependence on the nobles, 101, 103; Legislative Commission, 101, 133–4, 136; Charter of Nobility, 101, 103, 135, 366–7; serfdom, 101–2, 103; relations with the *philosophes*, 128–30, 139; centralization in government, 130–2; favourites, 131; law reform, 132–5; economic policy, 135–7; religious policy, 137–8; educational policy, 138–9; 1st Turkish War, 134, 199–202; 2nd Turkish War, 206–8; mediation in Bavarian succession war, 206; corresponds with Mme Geoffrin, 222; patron of Chardin, 229; and the French Revolution, 139, 295
Caulaincourt, Armand Augustin Louis, Marquis de (1772–1827), 337
Celsius, Anders (1701–44), 166
Censorship: in France, 72–73, 258–60, 267–8, 326; in Prussia, 125; in Russia, 139; in Habsburg Empire, 141, 150, 151; in Naples, 155; in Spain, 160–1 in Sweden, 167
Cerdagne, 20
Ceuta, 20
Chambers, Ephraim (d. 1740), 71
Champ de Mars, Massacre of (1791), 288
Chandernagore, 183
Chardin, Jean Siméon (1699–1779), 228–9

Charles, Archduke of Austria, later Holy Roman Emperor, 11, 15, 22. *See also* Charles VI
Charles I, King of England (1625–49), 67n., 240, 288, 299
Charles II King of Spain (1665–1700), 23; Spanish Succession question, 11–12
Charles III, King of Naples (1735–59): accession, 153; control of government, 154; law reform, 154–5; dealings with nobles, 155; religious policy, 155; patronage of the arts, 155–7; and of education, 157; economic policy, 157; foreign policy, 154, 180. *See also* Don Carlos and Charles III of Spain
Charles III, King of Spain (1759–88), accession, 158; centralization in government, 158; religious policy, 158–60; and the Enlightenment, 160; treatment of nobles, 161–2; economic policies, 162–3; educational reform, 163–4; patronage of the arts, 164; foreign policy, 196–7
Charles IV, King of Spain (1788–1808), 335
Charles VI, Holy Roman Emperor (1711–40), 140, 173; treaty of Rastatt (1714), 16, 45; war *v.* Spain, 1717–19, 18; alliance with Spain, 19; Hungary, 46, 100; Pragmatic Sanction, 47, 140, 142, 173–4; administrative reforms, 47; Ostend Company, 19, 47, 147
Charles X, King of Sweden (1654–60), 33, 208
Charles XI, King of Sweden (1660–97), 33–34, 168
Charles XII, King of Sweden (1697–1718), accession, 34; campaigns: *v.* Denmark, 33–34; *v.* Augustus I of Saxony, 29, 35–36; *v.* Peter II of Russia, 34–36, 40; seeks refuge in Turkey, 36, 199; death, 36–37
Charles Albert, Elector of Bavaria, later Charles VII, Holy Roman Emperor (1742–5), 140, 173, 175, 178
Charles-Emmanuel III of Savoy, King of Sardinia (1730–73), 180–1, 184
Charles Frederick, Duke of Holstein-Gottorp, 34, 36
Châteauroux, Mme de, 219
Chatham, Lord: see William Pitt the Elder
Châtillon, Conference of (1814), 342
Chaumont, treaty of (1814), 342
Chauvelin, Germain-Louis de, 175
Chénier, André de (1762–94), poet, 254
Chénier, Marie-Joseph Blaise de (1764–1811), dramatist, 254

China, 107

Chios, 202

Chkalov (Orenburg), 136

Choiseul, Étienne François, Duc de (1719–85), 195, 196–7, 201, 220, 238, 265

Chotusitz, battle of (1742), 178

Christian VII, King of Denmark (1766–1808), 170

Cinq grosses fermes, 234

Cirillo, the Neapolitan lawyer, 155

Cisalpine Republic, 318, 328

Clarendon, George William Frederick Villiers, 4th Earl of Clarendon (1800–70), 24

Clarkson, Thomas (1760–1846), 251

Clausewitz, Karl von (1780–1831), 338

Classicism: Goethe and Schiller, 93–94; in French literature, 223–4; in sculpture and architecture, 230–1

Clement XII, Pope (1730–40), 156

Clement XIV, Pope (1769–74), 124, 148

Cleves, 26, 34, 43

Clive, Robert (1725–74), 195

Coal industry, 109, 235

Coalitions: 3rd, 328–30, 331; 6th, 339–43. *See also* Appendix 12

Cocceji, Samuel von (1679–1755), 120

Coimbra, university of, 165

Colbert, Jean Baptiste (1619–83), 3, 160, 163, 229, 235; advice on government, 4–5; economic policies, 5–6, 104, 105, 106, 234; and the navy, 6, 106; objects to cost of Versailles, 9

Collot d'Herbois, Jean Marie (1750–96), 310, 312, 313

Cologne, 290

Committee of General Security, 302, 304, 307, 308, 311

Committee of Public Safety, 301–2, 304, 305, 307–10, 311, 323

Commune of Paris, 296–7, 298, 300, 301, 309–10

Comtat Venaissin, 290

Concordat of 1802, 322, 325–6

Condillac, Étienne Bonnot de (1715–80), 70

Condorcet, Marie Jean Antoine Nicolas Caritat, Marquis de (1743–94), 71, 222, 251, 254, 255, 260, 300

Confederation of the Bar, 201

Constantine Pavlovich (1779–1831), Grand Duke and Tsarevitch of Russia and grandson of Catherine the Great, 206

Constantinople, 32, 178, 199, 206, 207

Constituent Assembly, 269, 294; replaces National Assembly (in name only), 279; composition, 283–4; formal abolition of feudalism, 282; other

reforms, 282–9; Declaration of Rights, 282–3; foreign policy, 290–91; Self-denying Ordinance (1791), 293; replaced by Legislative Assembly, 288

Consulate, 321–6. *See also* Napoleon I

Continental System, 331–3

Coote, Sir Eyre, 196

Copenhagen, 34, 60, 332

Copernicus, Nicolaus (1473–1543), 59–60, 61, 62, 65, 90

Cordeliers Club, 293

Coresio, Giorgio, professor of natural philosophy at the university of Pisa, 61n.

Corneille, Thomas (1625–1709), 223

Cornwallis, Admiral Sir William (1744–1819), 329

Coromandel, 182

Corsica, 247, 249–50, 315

Cortes of Spain, 22n., 336

Corunna, 335

Cossacks, 133, 135–6

Couthon, Georges (1755–94), 307, 309

Cowley, Abraham (1618–67), 55

Cracow, 32, 35, 213, 214

Crimea, 137, 199, 202, 207, 208

Croatia, 33

Crozat, Pierre (1661–1740), art connoisseur, 226

Cuba, 49

Cumberland, William Augustus, Duke of (1721–65), 181, 191

Czartoryski family, 100

Danton, Georges Jacques (1759–94), 269, 308; and the 'Days of August' (1792), 296–7; in National Convention, 298; on Committee of Public Safety, 302; trial and execution, 305

Danube, river, 15, 202

Danzig, 30, 209, 210, 212, 213; Duke of, 324

Dardanelles, 136

Darwinism, 257

Daschkov, Catherina Romanovna Vorontsov (1744–1810), 139

Daun, Field-Marshal Count, 191, 192

David, Jacques Louis (1748–1825), painter, 250, 327

Davy, Sir Humphry (1778–1829), 111, 114

Declaration of Independence (American), 1776, 253, 255; quoted, 361

Declaration of Rights (English), 1689, 283

Declaration of the Rights of Man and Citizen (French), 1789, 255, 284; quoted, 282

Deffand, Marquise du (1697–1780), 222

Defoe, Daniel (1659–1731), 108; *Robinson Crusoe* put on the Index, 161

Denain, 16

Deism, Deists: connexion with Descartes, 58, 74–75; attacked by Hume, 84; persecuted by Joseph II, 149, 150; and Freemasonry, 250; and the French Revolution, 282, 306, 307; Goethe and the religion of nature, 369–70

Dekker, Sir Matthew, 182

De la Gardie, Magnus Gabriel, Count (1622-86), 33

Delille, Jacques, Abbé (1738-1813), 223

Delolme, Jean Louis, Swiss jurist (1740-1806), 247

Denmark, 33, 125, 193; Alliance of Hanover (1725), 19; war with Sweden (1700), 34; commercial treaty with Russia (1782), 136; enlightened absolutism in, 170; League of Armed Neutrality (1780–83), 168, 252n.; (1801), 333n.; and Napoleon, 332; and Vienna Settlement, 345

Descartes, René (1596–1650), 160; importance of mathematics, 56; principle of 'systematic doubt', 56–57; Cartesian dualism, 57–58; physical theories, 58; connexion with the Enlightenment, 58, 68, 74; eclipsed by Newton, 64; defended by Fontenelle, 111

Desmoulins, Lucie Simplice Camille Benoist (1760–94), 305

Dettingen, battle of (1743), 180

Diderot, Denis (1713–84), 161; debt to Bacon, 53; edits *Encyclopaedia*, 70–73; relations with Rousseau, 72, 85, 88; religious views, 75; political views, 80; relations with Catherine II, 129–130; and the *salons*, 221–2; defends *drames*, 225; condemns Boucher's painting, 227

Diet: Imperial, 24, 26; Polish, 28–30, 100, 201, 209, 212–13; Swedish (*Riksdag*), 33, 99–100, 165–6, 167, 168–9; Hungarian, 46–47, 100, 143–4

Dijon: Academy of, 85; Patriotic Society of, 250

Diplomatic Revolution, 185–90

Directory, 323, 332; replaces National Convention, 314–15; Constitution of the Year III (1795), 314, 315–16; the Directors, 315; economic policies, 316; opposition to, 316–17; and Bonaparte, 317–20; *coups d'état* of Fructidor and Prairial, 317; foreign policy, 318–19; *coup d'état* of Brumaire, 319–20

Dnieper, river, 202

Dniester, river, 201, 202, 208

Dominica, 197

Don, river, 32, 135

Dresden: treaty of (1745), 179, 181; in Seven Years War, 190; bombardment of, 192–3; Napoleon and Metternich at, 339

Drottningholm, 166, 229, 230

Drouais, François Hubert (1727–75), court painter to Louis XV, 220

Du Barry, Marie Jeanne Bécu, Comtesse (1746–93), 220, 238

Dubois, Guillaume, Abbé, later Cardinal (1656–1723), 218

Duclos, Charles, eighteenth-century French historian, 217

Ducos, Roger, one of the Directors, 317, 319

Duma (Russia), 41

Dumouriez, Charles François du Perier (1739–1823), 294, 295, 299, 300, 301

Dupleix, Joseph François (1697–1763), 105, 183–4, 195

Dupont de l'Étang, Pierre Antoine, Comte (1765–1840), French marshal, 335

Duport, Adrien, one of the triumvirate, 283

Duquesne, Governor of Canada, 194; Fort Duquesne, 194

Dvina, river, 35

East India Company: British, 48, 107, 183, 195–6; French, 107, 183, 195–6, 236; Dutch, 107; Danish, 107; Austrian, 147

East Indies, 107, 252

Edict of Fraternity (1792), 299

Edinburgh, 82, 139, 219, 236

Education: Rousseau's theories, 87–88; Prussia, 125–6; Russia, 138–9; Habsburg Empire, 151–2; Naples, 157; Spain, 163–4; Poland, 212; Egypt, 318–19, 328n.

Elba, island of, 328

Elbe, river, 102, 331

Elbeuf, Prince d', 156

Elbing, 209

Electors, Imperial, 26n.

Electricity, 114

Elizabeth, Empress of Russia (1741–62), 131, 132, 136, 173, 181, 187, 189, 193

Élizabeth, Philippine Marie Hélène of France ('Madame Elizabeth'), sister of Louis XVI, 288

Elphinstone, Admiral John, 201n.

Émigrés, 265, 291–2, 293–4, 300, 316

Émile, 87–88, 161, 268

Empire, British: 1689–1740, 48–50; Anglo-French colonial rivalry, 1740–89, 105–7, 183–4, 193–7

Empire, Holy Roman: Spanish succession war, 11-17; war v. Spain, 1717-19, 18-19; alliance with Spain, 19; political organization, 24-28; effects of Thirty Years War on, 24-26; military resources, 27; judicial organization, 27; under Charles VI, 45-47; the imperial court and the aristocracy, 100-1; under Joseph II, 140-52; League of Armed Neutrality (1780-83), 252n.; final abolition of, 330. See also Austria and Germany

Encyclopaedia, 51, 70; debt to Bacon, 53; edited by Diderot and d'Alembert, 71-73; debt to Bayle, 71; chief contributors, 71; and censorship, 72-73, 259; and Catherine the Great and Mme de Pompadour, 219-20

Encyclopaedia Britannica, 72

Enghien, Duc d', 329

England: William III's Grand Alliance, 9n., 14n.; Spanish succession war, 14-16; asiento, 16, 19, 49, 182, 184; gains at Treaty of Utrecht, 16-17; Triple Alliance (1717), 18; Alliance of Hanover (1725), 19; Pragmatic Sanction, 47, 180; War of Jenkins' Ear, 49, 182-3; colonial and commercial rivalry with France, 48-50, 105-7, 182-4, 194-7; industrial development, 108-110, 114; Austrian succession war, 180-4; Diplomatic Revolution, 185-90; Seven Years War, 190-8; Triple Alliance (1788), 207; admiration for British constitution, 246-8; political societies, 250-1; War of American Independence, 252-3; war with Revolutionary France, 300, 317-19; French plans for invasion, 318, 328-30; Treaty of Amiens, 322; and its rupture, 327-8; 3rd Coalition, 328-30; Trafalgar campaign, 329-30; Continental System, 331-3; Peninsular War, 334-6; 6th Coalition, 339-43; other coalitions, 368

Enlightened Absolutism: general characteristics of, 97-98, 152; Frederick the Great, 115-27 (cf. Stein's reforms, 338); Catherine the Great, 128-39; Maria Theresa and Joseph II, 140-52; Charles III of Naples and Spain, 153-64; Leopold of Tuscany, 158; Pombal in Portugal, 164-5; Gustavus III of Sweden, 165-70; Struensee in Denmark, 170; Stanislas Augustus in Poland, 208, 212-13; influence of philosophes on, 115-17, 128-30, 140-42; centralization in government, 117-20, 130-32, 142-4, 169; law reform, 120-1, 132-5, 144-6, 154-5, 158, 167; economic policies, 122-4, 135-7,

147-8, 157, 161-3; religious policies, 124-5, 137-8, 148-50, 155, 158-60, 164-5; educational reform, 125-7, 138-9, 151-2, 157, 163-4; obstruction of nobles, 99-103, 133-5, 143, 146, 162, 169, 240-5; military motives for reforms, 97-98, 118, 126-7, 141, 142, 168; foreign policy, 171-214; failure in France, 215-45; Napoleon I and, 321-7, 346-7; effect of French Revolution on, 139, 348

Enlightenment, 51, 58, 84, 97-98, 121; in France, 68-80, 85-89; in Germany, 89-95; in Spain, 160-1; in Sweden, 166-7; in Poland, 212; and the French Revolution, 256-60; Napoleon I and, 318-19, 322-3, 326-7, 336, 346-7, 348. See also Enlightened Absolutism

Enragés, 300

Escurial, treaty of (1733) (1st Family Compact), 153, 196n.

Estates-General, 255, 260, 266, 267, 268, 275; method of voting, 277-8; becomes National Assembly, 278

Esterházy family, 102

Estonia, 34

Estrées d', Marshal, 268

Étampes, 296

Etherege, Sir George (1635-91), quoted, 26

Eudoxia Lopukhina (1669-1731), wife of Peter the Great, 40

Eugene of Savoy, Prince (1663-1736), 230; Spanish succession war, 14-16; drives Turks from Hungary, 32

Evelyn, John (1620-1706), diarist, 39, 55

Experimental method: in science, 53-56, 59-64, 81-83, 111-14; in psychology and sociology, 65-67, 82; in archaeology, 231-2; in other branches of knowledge, 68-71

Eylau, battle of (1807), 331

Family Compact: 1st (1733) Treaty of Escurial, 153, 196n.; 2nd (1743) Treaty of Fontainebleau, 196n.; 3rd (1761), 196

Faraday, Michael (1791-1867), 114

Farnese, Elizabeth (1692-1766), 19, 20, 22, 23, 153-4; war of 1717, 18; Austrian succession war, 181

Faust, 93-94, 369-70

Fédérés, 296-7

Fehrbellin, battle of (1675), 33

Fénelon, François de Salignac de la Mothe (1651-1715), Archbishop of Cambrai, 217, 221; letter to Louis XIV, 10, 233

Ferdinand IV of Naples and I of the Two Sicilies (1759–1825), 348
Ferdinand VI, King of Spain (1746–59), 154, 158, 160, 163, 181, 196
Ferdinand VII, King of Spain (1813–33), 335, 348
Feudalism: as an obstacle to Enlightened Absolutism in: Prussia, 101, 102, 121, 338; Poland, 100, 102; Austria and Hungary, 100, 102–3, 143–4, 145–6, 148, 289–90; Russia, 101–2, 103, 132–5, 366–7; Spain, 161–2; Denmark, 170; relics of in France, 264–6, 271–3; formal abolition of in France, 281–2, 323
Feuillants, 293
Feyjóo y Montenegro, Benito Gerónimo, 160
Fichte, Johann Gottlieb (1762–1814), 90, 289, 339
Fielding, Henry (1707–54), 224
Finck, Friedrich August von, Prussian general, 192
Finland, 34, 40, 168, 331
Flanders: see Netherlands
Fleury, André Hercule de (1653–1743), Cardinal, 19, 175–8, 179, 218, 237, 243
Fleurus, battle of (1794), 304, 308
Florence, 153
Florida, 197–253
Floridablanca, Don Jose Monino y Redondo, Count of (1728–1808), 164
Fogliani, Marchese Giovanni, 154, 156
Fontainebleau, 326; treaty of, 343
Fontenelle, Bernard le Bovier de (1657–1757), 111
Fontenoy, battle of (1745), 220
Fouché, Joseph, Duke of Otranto (1763–1820), 310, 313, 326, 334
Fouquier-Tinville, Antoine Quentin (1746–95), 312
Fox, Charles James (1749–1806), 208, 289
Fragonard, Jean-Honoré (1732–1806), 227–8, 229
France: under Louis XIV, 3–10; Spanish succession war, 11–17; economic effects of, 233; war v. Spain, 1718–19, 18; Polish succession war, 30, 199; colonial and commercial rivalry with England, 48–50, 105–7, 182–4, 194–7; industrial and commercial development, 108–11, 234–6; population, 110, 236; agriculture, 233–4; fiscal confusion, 234; Austrian succession war, 173–84; Diplomatic Revolution, 185–90; Seven Years War, 190–8; Family Compact with Spain (1761), 196; neutrality during Bavarian succession war, 206; and Poland, 213; under Louis XV, 217–45; literature,

68–80, 85–89, 223–5; painting, 226–9; sculpture and architecture, 229–31; the *philosophes*, 68–80, 85–89, 256–60; the *salons*, 221–2; the *parlements* under Louis XV, 240–45; War of American Independence and its effects, 252–6, 263; attack on the Catholic Church in, 257–8, 285–8, 306, 311; under Louis XVI, 261–300; the army, 264, 295, 304; economic position of the clergy, 266–8, 286–7; and of the *bourgeoisie*, 268–9; and of the peasants, 271–3. See *also* the French Revolution and Napoleon
Franche-Comté, 234, 271; ceded to France by Spain, 20
Francis II, Holy Roman Emperor (1792–1806), later Francis I, Emperor of Austria (1806–35), 222, 292, 330, 334, 337
Francis Stephen, Duke of Lorraine, later Francis I, Holy Roman Emperor (1745–65), 47, 140, 178, 179
Franklin, Benjamin (1706–90), 114, 222, 253, 254, 255
Frankfurt-on-Main, 330; Frankfurt Proposals, 342
Frederick I, King of Sweden (1720–51), formerly Frederick of Hesse, 37
Frederick I of Prussia and III of Brandenburg (1688–1713), 44, 116n.
Frederick II, King of Prussia (1740–86), 80, 91, 97, 133, 141, 147, 166, 168, 171, 215, 248, 484; and Poland, 30, 200–2, 208–14; relations with *philosophes*, 115–17, 125, 208, 223; centralization in government, 117–20; views on government, 119–20; and the *Junkers*, 101, 120–1; law reform, 120–1; and the army, 121, 127; economic policies, 122–4; religious policy, 124–5; educational reforms, 125–7; meets Joseph II (1769), 141; seizes Silesia, 173–9; Austrian succession war, 179–82; Treaty of Aix-la-Chapelle, 184; Diplomatic Revolution, 185–90; Seven Years War, 190–3; Treaty of Hubertusburg, 197–8; Bavarian succession war, 126, 202–6
Frederick III of Brandenburg and I of Prussia (1688–1713), 44, 116n.
Frederick IV, King of Denmark (1699–1730), 34
Frederick V, King of Denmark (1746–66), 170
Frederick, Crown Prince of Denmark, later Frederick VI (1808–39), 170
Frederick William of Brandenburg-Prussia, 'The Great Elector' (1640–88), 43–44, 208

Frederick William I, King of Prussia (1713–40), 97, 101, 115, 116n., 173; military and administrative reforms, 44–45, 118; law reform, 20

Frederick William II, King of Prussia (1786–97), 207, 291

Frederick William III, King of Prussia (1797–1840), 338–9

Fredrikshall, 36–37

Freemasons, 250, 257

Free Trade: see *laissez-faire*

French Revolution, 99, 348; influence of America on, 251–6, 263; and of *philosophes* on, 256–60; demands of the various social classes, 264–73; Estates-General, 277–8; Tennis Court Oath and National Assembly, 278–9; Constituent Assembly, 279–89; Great Fear, 279–81; fall of the Bastille, 280–1; abolition of feudalism, 281–2; Declaration of Rights of Man and Citizen, 282–3; Constitution of 1791, 283–5; franchise (1791), 284; (1792), 297; (1795), 314; (1799), 321; march of the women to Versailles, 284; attack on the Church, 285–8; reforms of local government, 285; and of taxation, 285; Civil Constitution of the Clergy, 286–8; other reforms of Constituent Assembly, 288–9; flight to Varennes, 288; massacre of the Champ de Mars, 288; and Europe, 213, 289–92; Legislative Assembly, 288–9, 291–2, 293–7; war *v.* Austria and Prussia, 292, 294–5, 297–9, 300; economic consequences, 295; Days of August and suspension of Louis XVI, 296–7; September Massacres, 298; National Convention, 298–314; trial and execution of Louis, 299–300; war *v.* England, Holland and Spain, 300; March Days (1793), 300; Revolutionary Tribunal, 300–301, 302, 303, 305; Committee of Public Safety, 301, 302–3, 304, 305; expulsion of Girondin deputies, 301; period of Jacobin rule, 301–10; Girondin revolts in provinces, 303; Constitution of 1793, 304; 1st 'Maximum', 304; 2nd, 304, 309–10; 3rd, 312; the Terror, 303–12; Republic of Virtue, 305–10, 364–5; reform of the calendar, 306, 363; Cult of the Supreme Being, 306–7; Ventôse decrees, 307, 312; Law of 22nd Prairial, 307–8, 312; fall of Robespierre, 307–10 Thermidorian Reaction, 310–15; peace with Prussia, Spain, Holland, 313; Constitution of the Year III, 314; insurrection of Vendémiaire, 314–15; *coups d'état* of Fructidor and Prairial, 317; foreign policy of the Directory, 317–19; *coup d'état* of Brumaire, 319–20. *See also* Napoleon I

Fréron, Louis Marie Stanislas (1765–1802), 310, 311

Friedland, battle of (1807), 331, 336

Froebel, Friedrich Wilhelm August (1782–1852), 88

Fructidor, *coup d'état* of (1797), 317

Gages, Jean Bonaventure Dumont, Count, Spanish general, 181

Gainsborough, Thomas (1727–88), 230

Galicia, 202, 210, 214, 338

Galileo Galilei (1564–1642), 56, 60, 61–63, 112

Galitzin (Golitsyn), Vasili Vasilevich (1643–1714), 39

Gallicanism: Four Articles (1682), 7, 325; and Jansenism, 240–1; and Civil Constitution of the Clergy (1790), 287; and Concordat (1802), 325

Galvani, Luigi (1737–98), 114

Garrick, David, the actor, 222, 249

Gazette de France, 239

General Directory of Prussia, 44, 118

Geneva, 72, 88

Genoa, 181, 247, 249, 318, 328, 329, 333

Genovesi, Abbé Antonio (1712–69), 157

Geoffrin, Marie Therese (1699–1777), 208, 222

George I, King of England (1714–27), 18

George II of England (1727–60), 80, 174, 180, 186, 187

George III of England (1760–1820), 246, 247, 248

Georgia (North America), 48

Georgia (Asia Minor), 207

Germany: Enlightenment in, 89–95; serfdom, 100–1, 102; industrial development, 109; population, 110; and the French Revolution, 289; and Napoleon I, 330–1, 347; and Vienna Settlement, 346, 348. *See also*: Holy Roman Empire, Austria, Prussia, Confederation of the Rhine, Bavaria, Saxony, Westphalia

Gibraltar, 16, 19, 181, 182, 197, 253, 335

Gilbert, William (1544–1603), 63

Girondins, 255; in Legislative Assembly, 293–5; and the *fédérés*, 296; and the Days of August, 297; in National Convention, 298–301; trial of Marat, 301; Commission of Twelve, 301; expulsion from Convention, 301; provincial revolts, 303; executions, 305; return to Convention, 311

Gluck, Christoph Willibald (1714–87), 155

Gneisenau, August Wilhelm Anton, Count Neithardt von (1760–1831), 338
Gobelin tapestry works, 5
Godoy, Manuel de, Duke of Alcudia (1767–1851), 334–5
Goertz (Görtz), Georg Heinrich von (1668–1719), 55, 56
Goethe, Johann Wolfgang von (1749–1832), 129; *Sturm und Drang* period, 91–92; scientific interests, 92–93; dramatic writings, 94; travels in Italy, 94; and Sicily, 111; nationalism, 94–95; attitude to French Revolution, 289; and the religion of nature, 369–70
Gohier, Louis Jerome (1746–1830), one of the Directors, 317
Gorée, island of, 195, 197, 252
Göteborg, 168
Gothic Revival, 91, 231–2
Göttingen, 289
Gournay, Vincent de (1712–59), 105
Goya y Lucientes, Francisco (1746–1828), 164
Granada, university of, 249
Grand Alliance: 1689, 9n., 14n.; 1701, 14
Grand Empire, 327–43, 346. See Napoleon I
Grand Tour, 248–9
Gravesande, William Jacobs' (1688–1742), 82
Gray, Thomas (1716–71), 91
Great Britain: see England
Great Elector, the: see Frederick William I
Grenada, 197
Gribeauval, Jean Baptiste de (1715–89), French artillery general, 295
Grimaldi, Marqués de, 159, 164
Grimm, Friedrich Melchior, Baron von (1723–1807), 129–30, 137
Grosley, author of *Observations on Italy and the Italians made in 1764 by Two Swedish Gentlemen* (1770), 110
Guadalajara, 22
Guadeloupe, 107, 195, 197
Guardi, Francesco (1712–93), 229
Guiana, 313, 317
Guibert, Jacques Antoine Hippolyte, Comte de (1743–90), author of *Défense du systeme de guerre moderne* (1779), 295
Gustavus III, King of Sweden (1771–92): accession and *coup d'état* of 1772, 165–6; patronage of the arts, 166–7; economic policies, 167; Constitution of 1772, 167; law reform, 167; military reforms, 167–8; foreign policy, 168, 169, 207, 290–1; defeats the nobles (1789), 169; visits Mme Geoffrin, 222;

and the French Revolution, 290–1; assassination, 169
Gustavus IV, King of Sweden (1792–1809), 334n.

Hagley Park, 231
Hague, The, 15, 22, 247
Halberstadt, 43
Halifax, 194
Hamburg, 26, 91, 232n., 339
Hanover, 26n., 37, 180, 186, 187, 190, 191, 328; Alliance of (1725), 19
Harvey, William (1578–1657), 64
'Hats', party in Swedish *Riksdag*, 165
Haugwitz, Ludwig, Count, chancellor of Bohemia and Austria, 142–3, 144–5
Havana, 195
Hawke, Admiral, 195
Hébert, Jacques René (1757–94) and Hébertists, 305, 306, 308
Hegel, Georg Wilhelm Friedrich (1770–1831), 89, 289
Helvetic Republic: see Switzerland
Helvétius, Claude Adrien (1715–71), 70, 76–77, 161
Hennersdorf, battle of (1745), 179
Henry, Prince, brother of Frederick the Great, 203, 205, 210
Herculaneum, 156–7, 230; Academy, 157
Herder, Johann Gottfried von (1744–1803), 91–92, 289
Hobbes, Thomas (1588–1679), 76, 86
Hochkirk, battle of (1758), 192
Hohenfriedberg, battle of (1745), 179
Holbach, Paul Heinrich Dietrich, Baron d' (1723–89), 70, 76, 222
Holland, 180, 181, 290, 342; separates from Spain, 20; Spanish succession war, 11–17; Triple Alliance (1717), 18; Pragmatic Sanction; 47, trade 104–5, 107–8; economic decline, 107–8; agriculture, 110; Austrian succession war, 180, 181; Triple Alliance (1788), 207; War of American Independence, 252; war with Revolutionary France, 300, 313; and with Napoleon, 328; and Continental System, 332, 333; and Vienna Settlement, 345
Holland, Henry Fox, 1st Baron Holland (1705–74), 250
Holstein, 34, 36–37
Holy Synod (Russia), 42
Hooke, Robert (1635–1703), 63
Horn, Arvid Bernhard, Count (1664–1742), 165

Houdetot, Elisabeth Françoise Sophie de la Live de Bellegarde, Comtesse de (1730–1813), 255

Houdon, Jean Antoine (1740–1828), French Sculptor, 129, 230

Howe, William, Viscount (1729–1814), British general, 295

Hubertusburg, treaty of (1763), 197, 200

Hudson's Bay, 16, 48

Huguenots, 258; numbers and position in 1660, 7; *caisse de conversions*, 7; *dragonnades*, 8; Revocation of Edict of Nantes, 8, 73

Humboldt, Karl Wilhelm von (1767–1835), 289, 339

Hume, David (1711–76), 51, 75, 222; quoted on Germany, 28; principal writings, 82; exposes limitations of experimental method, 82–83; views on morality, 83–84; political theories, 83–84; religious scepticism, 84; and Rousseau, 248

Hungary: under Turkish rule, 31–32; civil war in, 46; Diet of Pozsony, 46; aristocracy, 100, 111, 143–4; serfdom, 102–3, 146; under Maria Theresa, 143–4; under Joseph II, 144, 146, 148; rebellion (1789), 144, 289–90

Huygens, Christiaan (1629–95), 63, 82

Illyria, 339

Index of prohibited books, 58, 60, 150, 161

India, 48–49, 105, 107, 253, 318, 328, 337; Austrian succession war, 183–4; Seven Years War, 195–7, 235

Industry, 98, 348; Spain, 22, 23, 162–3; Russia, 42, 103, 137; England, 108–10, 114; France, 108–10, 235–6; Prussia, 123; Austria, 147; Sweden, 167

Ingria, 34

Intendants, 215, 239–40, 263, 265, 285, 323

Inquisition, 258; Naples, 155; Tuscany, 158; Spain, 159, 160; Portugal, 164

Ireland, 290, 318n.

Iron industry, 42, 103, 109, 235

Italy: Spanish succession war, 14, 15; agriculture, 110–11; painting, 226, 229; sculpture and architecture, 229–30; Austrian succession war, 180–1; French Revolution and, 289; Napoleon and, 317–18, 319, 328, 329, 330, 331, 332, 333, 347; and the Continental System, 332–3; and the Vienna Settlement, 345, 346, 347. *See also* Naples and Tuscany

Ivan the Terrible, Tsar of Russia (1533–85), 199

Ivan V, Tsar of Russia (1682–9), dies 1696, 39, 131

Ivan VI, Tsar of Russia (1740–41), 131, 173

Jacobins, Jacobin Club, 285, 303, 316, 319; in Legislative Assembly, 293; in the provinces, 296; and the Days of August, 297; in National Convention, 298–310; acquittal of Marat, 301; oust Girondins, 301; suppress Girondin revolts in provinces, 303; The Terror, 303, 305; administrative reforms of, 304; economic policies, 304, 309–10; Republic of Virtue, 305–6; Cult of the Supreme Being, 306–7; fall of Robespierre, 307–10; closing of Jacobin Club, 311; exclusion from political power, 311–12; victims of the 'White' Terror, 313

Jamaica, 49

James I, King of England (1603–25), 103, 240, 262

James II of England (1685–89), 11, 14, 67n.

James Edward (the 'Old Pretender') d. 1766, 14, 18

James, Robert, author of *Medicinal Dictionary*, 71

Jansenism: in France, 8, 240–2, 256, 260, 288; in Spain, 159

Jassy, 201; treaty of (1792), 208, 213

Jefferson, Thomas (1743–1826), 231, 255–6, 282n.

Jemappes, battle of (1792), 299

Jena, battle of (1806), 331, 334

Jenkins, Captain Robert, and the 'War of Jenkins' Ear', 49, 182

Jesuits: and Frederick the Great, 124–5; and Catherine the Great, 138; expelled by Maria Theresa, 148; in Naples, 155; expelled from Spain, 159; and from Portugal, 165; and from France, 242; dissolved by Clement XIV (1773), 148; re-established by Pius VII (1814), 348; their church in Rome, 229

Jeunesse doré, 311

Jews: Prussia, 125, 211; Russia, 138; Habsburg Empire, 148–9; Naples, 155

John V, King of Portugal (1706–50), 196

Johnson, Dr Samuel (1709–84), 82, 269

Joseph I, Holy Roman Emperor (1705–11), 15, 46

Joseph I, King of Portugal (1750–77), 164

Joseph II, Holy Roman Emperor (1765–90), 140, 158, 161n., 186, 197, 222, 225, 290, 338; memorandum of 1765, 141; attitude to *philosophes*, 141–2,

Joseph II—*cont.*
147; centralization in government, 144, 365–6; serfdom, 102–3, 145–6, 148; law reform, 145–6; economic policies, 147–8; religious policies ('Josephism') 149–50; educational reforms, 151; Bavarian succession war, 202–6; visits Russia, 207; the army, 141, 144, 148; the nobles, 144, 146, 148; 1st Turkish War (1768–74), 202; 2nd Turkish War (1787–92), 148, 207; 1st partition of Poland, 210
Joseph Ferdinand, Electoral Prince of Bavaria, d. 1699, 11
Josephine, Empress of France: *see* Beauharnais
Junkers, 44, 101, 102, 103, 118, 121
Junot, Andache, Duc d'Abrantes, French general, 335
Jurieu, Pierre (1637–1713), 73

Kalisch, treaty of (1813), 339
Kant, Immanuel (1724–1804), 51, 85; defines Enlightenment, 89; astronomy, 89–90; ethics, 90; and the French Revolution, 289
Kara, Mustapha Pasha, Grand Vizier, 32
Karamzin, Nikolai Mikhailovich (1765–1826), 289
Karelia, 34
Karlowitz (Carlowitz), treaty of (1699), 32
Kaunitz, Wenzel Anton, Prince von (1711–94), 142, 145, 149, 191, 203, 205, 210; and the Diplomatic Revolution, 185–90
Kay, John (1704–78?), British inventor, 248
Kempenfelt, Richard, British rear-admiral, 196
Kepler, Johann (1571–1630), 61, 62, 63
Keppel, Augustus, Viscount, British admiral, 195
Kertsch, 202
Kesseldorf, battle of (1745), 179
Kiev (Kief), 129
Kinburn, 202
Kiuprili, Mohammed, Grand Vizier, 31; Fazil Ahmed, his son and successor as Grand Vizier, 31, 32
Kleinschnellendorf, Convention of (1741), 178
Klinger, Friedrich Maximilian von (1752–1831), 91
Klosterseven, Convention of (1757), 191
Knobelsdorff, Hans Georg Wenceslaus, Baron von (1699–1753), 115
Kochowski Vespazian (1633–99), 29
Kolin, battle of (1757), 191

Kollowrat Count, Supreme Chancellor under Joseph II, 150
Königsberg, 44
Kosciuszko, Tadeusz Andrzej Bonawentura (1746–1817), 213–14
Kunersdorf, battle of (1759), 192
Kurland, 214
Kutchuk Kainardji, treaty of (1774), 136, 202, 207, 208

La Barre, Jean-François Lefebvre, Chevalier de, 258
La Bourdonnais, Bertrand François, Count Mahé de, French naval commander, 183–4
La Chalotais, Louis René de Caradeuc de (1701–85), French jurist, 242
Lacy, Franz Moritz, Count, Austrian general
Lafayette, Marie Joseph Paul Yves Roch Guilbert du Motier, Marquis de (1757–1834); in America, 252, 255; and Jefferson, 255; in Assembly of Notables, 266; commands National Guard, 281; hostility to Mirabeau, 283–4; the March to Versailles, 284; massacre of the Champ de Mars, 288; defects to Austrians, 297
Lagos (Portugal), battle of (1759), 195
La Harpe, Jean François de (1739–1803), 139
Laissez-faire, 77–78, 105; free trade under Catherine the Great, 136; and Joseph II, 147; and Gustavus III, 167; and Turgot, 262; during the French Revolution, 288
Lally-Tollendal, Thomas Arthur Lally, Baron de Tollendal (1702–66), French general, 195–6
Lamarck, Jean Baptiste Pierre Antoine de Monet, Chevalier de (1744–1829), 112
Lambert, Mme de, 221
Lameth, Alexandre Theodore Victor, Comte de (1760–1829), 283
La Mettrie, Julien Offray de (1709–51), 70
La Mothe, Vallin de, French architect, 130
Landrecht (1791), 101, 120–1
Langley, Batty (1696–1751), 231–2
Langres, 71; Protocol, 342
Languedoc, 234, 238, 243
Laplace, Pierre Simon, Marquis de (1749–1827), 112
Larévellière-Lépeaux, Louis Marie de (1753–1824), 315
La Rochelle, 268
La Salle, René Robert Cavelier (1643–87), French explorer, 48

La Tour, Maurice Quentin de (1704–88), 219, 228, 230
Lau, T. L., 104
Laufeldt, battle of (1747), 181
Launay, Jourdan Marquis de, Governor of the Bastille, 280–1
Lavoisier, Antoine Laurent (1743–94), 112–14, 255, 269
Law, John (1671–1729), 106, 236
Law reform: demanded by *philosophes*, 76–77; France, 6, 288–9, 322–3; Prussia, 120–1; Russia, 133–5; Habsburg Empire, 144–6; Naples, 154–5; Tuscany, 158; Sweden, 167; Denmark, 170
Le Breton, publisher of the *Encyclopaedia*, 71, 72
Le Chapelier law, 289, 309
Le Creusot, 235
Ledoux, Claude-Nicolas (1736–1806), 231
Leeuwenhoek, Antony van (1632–1723), 112
Lefebvre, Pierre François Joseph (1755–1820), Duke of Danzig, French marshal, 324
Legion of Honour, 324
Legislative Assembly: replaces Constituent Assembly, 288; declares war on Austria, 292; composition, 293; campaign against *émigrés*, 293–4; conduct of the war, 295; economic situation, 295–6; suspension of Louis XVI, 297; replaced by National Convention, 297. *See also* French Revolution
Legislative Commission of Catherine the Great, 101, 132–5, 136
Le Havre, 235
Leibnitz, Gottfried Wilhelm (1646–1716), 63, 92, 116n., 319
Leipzig, 26, 35, 91, 150; battle of (1813), 339
Lemberg, 35
Lenz, Jacob Michael Reinhold (1751–92), 91
Leoben, treaty of (1797), 317
Leopold I, Holy Roman Emperor (1658–1705), 45; and Spanish succession war, 11–14
Leopold II, Holy Roman Emperor (1790–92), formerly Grand-Duke of Tuscany, 144, 146, 148; enlightened absolutism in Tuscany, 158; revolt of 1789 in Hungary, 289; and the French Revolution, 290–2; Declaration of Pillnitz, 291
Lesage, Alain-René (1668–1747), French novelist and dramatist, 224
Lespinasse, Julie de (1732–76), 221, 222
Lessing, Gotthold Ephraim (1729–81), 93–94, 116, 125

Leszczynska, Marie (1703–68), wife of Louis XV, 19, 218
Leszczynski, Stanislas, King of Poland (1704–9 and 1733–5; d. 1766), 29–30, 35–36, 47, 175–6, 199
Letourneur, Honoré (de la Manche), one of the Directors, 315
Leuthen, battle of (1757), 191
Levant Company (Prussian), 123
Levée en masse, 304
Leyden, University of, 82
Leyden jar, 114
Liberum veto, 29, 30, 100, 201, 209, 212
Liechtenstein, Prince of, 228
Liegnitz, battle of (1760), 192
Ligne, Charles Joseph, Prince de (1735–1814), 116
Ligurian Republic: *see* Genoa
Liljencratz, Johan, Swedish physiocrat and finance minister of Gustavus III, 167
Lille, 15, 318
Lindet, Robert, member of Committee of Public Safety, 302, 307
Linnaeus [Carl von Linné] (1707–78), 112, 166
Lisbon: treaty of (1668), 20; earthquake, 75; Voltaire's poem on, 223; Peninsular War, 335
Lit de justice, 238, 241, 243, 263
Lithuania, 28, 206, 214
Liverpool, 235
Livonia, 34, 40, 187, 189
Locke, John (1632–1704), 56, 74; psychology, 65–66; natural law, 66, 81; politics, 66–67; social contract, 66–67; *Letter Concerning Toleration*, 73; regarded with suspicion in Spain, 164; influence in America, 253
Lodigiano, 110
Loire, river, 235
Lombardy, 146, 345
London, 110, 215, 234, 270; Corresponding Society, 251; Revolution Society, 250
Longwy, battle of (1792), 298
Lorraine, Duchy of, 30, 47, 179
Loudon, Ernst Gideon von (1717–90), Austrian general, 192, 207
Louis XIV, King of France (1643–1715), 115, 116, 215, 217, 218, 292, 319; judgement of historians, 3–4; and Mme de Maintenon, 3, 8–9; Voltaire's view of, 4; and Enlightened Absolutism, 4; views on kingship, 4; system of government, 4–5, 237–8; economic policies, 5–6; legal system, 6; religious policy, 7–8, 240–1; revocation of Edict of Nantes, 8; War of the League of Augsburg, 9; financial situation,

Louis XIV—*cont.*
9–10; criticized in letter by Fénelon, 10; Spanish succession war, 11–17
Louis XV of France (1715–74), 215, 261; engagement to Marie Leszczynska, 19, 218; Austrian succession war, 175–84; Diplomatic Revolution, 185–90; Seven Years War, 190–8; Family Compact with Spain (1761), 196; illness at Metz (1744), 219; and Mme de Pompadour, 219–20; and Mme Du Barry, 220–21; the Paris *salons* during his reign, 221–2; literature, 223–5; painting, 226–9; sculpture and architecture, 229–32; industrial and commercial development, 109–10, 234–6; system of government, 237–40; struggle with the *parlements*, 240–45
Louis XVI of France (1774–93), 215; interest in agriculture, 111; lack of interest in politics, 261; restores the *parlements*, 262–3; War of American Independence, 252–3, 263; the financial problem, 263–4; the Estates-General, 277–9; concentrates troops at Versailles, 279; and dismisses them, 281; recognizes National Guard, 281; powers under Constitution of 1791, 283; leaves Versailles for Tuileries, 284; flight to Varennes, 288; suspended, 297; imprisoned in the Temple, 297; trial and execution, 299–300
Louis XVII of France, d. 1795, 314
Louis XVIII of France (1814–24), formerly Comte de Provence, 314, 343
Louisbourg, 48, 183, 184, 194
Louisiana, 48, 197, 236
Louvois, François Michel le Tellier, Marquis de (1641–91), military reforms, 6; and the Huguenots, 7–8
Louvre, the, 219, 229
Lübeck, 339
Lublin, 214
Lunéville, treaty of (1801), 322, 328, 330
Luther, Martin, 60, 91
Lützen, battle of (1813), 339
Lyon, 234, 303, 306, 310
Lyonnais, 234

Maastricht, 181
Mably, Gabriel Bonnot de, Abbé (1709–85), 254
Machault d'Arnouville, Jean Baptiste de (1701–94), 243, 267
Maciejowice, battle of (1794), 214
Mack von Leiberich, Charles, Baron, Austrian general, 330
Madison, James (1751–1836), 253

Madras, 49, 183, 184, 196
Madrid, 18, 24, 154, 156, 159, 161, 163, 164; treaty of (1801), 334; in Peninsular War, 335
Magdeburg, 43
Mailly-Nesle, Louise-Julie, Comtesse de (1710–51), 218
Maine, Duc de, 17, 217n.
Maintenon, Françoise d'Aubigné, Marquise de (1635–1719), 3, 8, 9
Mainz, 299
Malplaquet, battle of (1709), 15
Malta, 319
Mamelukes, the, 319, 328
Manchester, 109
Mandeville, Bernard de (1670–1733), 105
Manila, 197
Marat, Jean Paul (1743–93), 139, 298, 300; attacks Constitution of 1791, 284; attacks Brissot, 296; in National Convention, 298; acquitted by Revolutionary Tribunal, 301; murdered by Charlotte Corday, 305
Margaret Theresa, daughter of Philip IV of Spain, 11
Maria Antonia, daughter of Emperor Leopold I, 11
Marianne, daughter of Emperor Charles VI, 46
Maria Theresa, daughter of Philip IV of Spain, 11
Maria Theresa, Empress of Austria (1740–80), 46, 47, 101, 206; accession, 140; and the *philosophes*, 140–1; centralization in government, 142–4; serfdom, 102, 145–6; the army, 142; the nobles, 143–4, 145, 151; law reform, 144–6; economic policies, 147–8; religious policy, 148–50; educational reforms, 151; Austrian succession war, 173–81; Treaty of Aix-la-Chapelle, 184; Diplomatic Revolution, 185–90; Seven Years War, 190–93; treaty of Hubertusburg, 197–8; Bavarian succession war, 202–6; 1st partition of Poland, 208–10; corresponds with Mme Geoffrin, 222
Marie-Antoinette (1755–93), wife of Louis XVI, 259, 290; interest in politics, 261; and dismissal of Necker (1789), 279; flight to Varennes, 288; interferes in diplomacy, 292, 294; executed, 305
Marie Louise (1791–1847), 2nd wife of Napoleon I, 334, 337
Marivaux, Pierre Carlet de Chamblain de (1688–1763), 224
Marlborough, John Churchill, Duke of (1650–1722), 230; and Spanish succession war, 14, 15

Marmontel, Jean François (1723–99), historian and contributor to the *Encyclopaedia*, 258
Marriage of Figaro, 225, 258–9
Marseille, 234, 296, 297, 303
Martinet, Jean, d. 1672, inspector-general of infantry under Louis XIV, 6
Martinique, 195, 197, 329
Massachusetts, 183
Masséna, André, Duke of Rivoli (1756–1817), 317, 319, 335
Matviev, Artamon Sergyeevich, d. 1682, 38
Maupeou, René Nicolas Charles Augustin (1714–92), 244, 260
Maupertuis, Pierre Louis Moreau de (1698–1759), 116
Mauritius, 183, 196
Mauvillon, author of *Lettres françaises et germaniques* (1740), 90
Maxen, battle of (1759), 192
'Maximum': 1st, 304; 2nd, 309–10; 3rd, 312
Mazarin, Jules (1602–61), Cardinal, 3, 4
Mecklenburg, 18
Medicine: William Harvey, 64; vaccination against smallpox, 138
Mediterranean, 163, 194, 200, 319, 329
Mehmed II, Sultan of Turkey (1648–87), 32
Meikle, Andrew, Scottish industrialist, 111
Mengs, Antony Raphael (1728–79), German painter, 164
Mercantilism, 78; under Colbert, 5, 104, 106; Thomas Mun's theories, 104; adopted by enlightened despots, 105; Anglo-French commercial rivalry, 106–8; under Frederick the Great, 123; under Catherine the Great, 136; under Austrian Habsburgs, 147; under Charles III of Spain, 160, 163; under Gustavus III of Sweden, 167; Napoleon I's Continental System, 331–3
Mercier, Sebastien (1740–1814), French dramatist, 270
Mesmerism, 255
Metastasio, Pietro (1698–1782), Italian poet, 155
Methodism, 51
Methuen Treaties (1703), 15
Metternich-Winneburg, Clemens Wenzel Lothar, Count (later Prince) (1773–1859), 205, 334; and the defeat of Napoleon, 337–43; and Vienna Settlement, 346, 348
Metz, 219, 288
Meuse, river, 288
Mexico, 14, 21, 23n., 163

Michael Romanov, Tsar of Russia (1613–45), 38
Michelet, Jules (1798–1874), French historian, 233
Michelson, General, 136
Microscope, 112
Milan, 14, 45, 110, 143, 180, 289; Decree (1807), 333
Minden, 43, 191
Minorca, 15, 16, 181, 182, 194, 197, 252, 253
Minsk, 35
Mirabeau, Honoré Gabriel Riqueti, Comte de (1749–91), 120, 151; opposes separation of powers in Constitution of 1791, 283–4; contrasted with Robespierre, 302
Mississipi, river, 48, 194, 197
Mitchell, Sir Andrew, British ambassador in Berlin, 124
Moldavia, 31, 199, 202, 207
Molière [Jean Baptiste Poquelin] (1622–73), 220, 225
Mollwitz, battle of (1741), 175
Moltke, Count Adam Gottlob (1710–92), Danish courtier, 170
Monceau, Duhamel du, French writer on agriculture, 111
Mons, 15
Montaigne, Michel de (1533–92), 81
Montcalm, Louis-Joseph de Montcalm-Gozon, Marquis de (1712–59), French general, 195
Montealegre, Marquis of, Neapolitan minister, 154
Montemar, Count of, Spanish general, 154
Montesquieu, Charles-Louis de Secondat, Baron de (1689–1755), 70, 128, 140, 145, 199, 213, 219, 248, 260; contributes to *Encyclopaedia*, 71; scientific interests, 78; political theories, 79–80, 247, 253, 359–61; natural law, 81, 88; influence on Catherine the Great, 133; and in Spain, 160; and in America, 253; and on the French Revolution, 257, 283
Montgolfier brothers, Joseph Michel (1740–1810) and Jacques Étienne (1745–99), 113–14
Montmédy, 288
Montpellier, 280
Montreal, 48, 195
Moore, Sir John (1761–1809), British general, 335
Moravia, 46, 149, 175
Moravians, 149
Moscow, 35, 39, 110, 133, 136, 137, 206, 333, 338
Moulin, Jean-François-Auguste, Baron, 317

Mozart, Wolfgang Amadeus (1756–91), 225

Mun, Thomas (1571–1641), 104

Murad IV, Sultan of Turkey (1623–40), 31

Murat, Joachim (1767–1815), King of Naples, 347

Munich, 26

Münnich, Burkhard Christoph, Count (1683–1767), Russian general, 200

Nakaz (Catherine II's *Instructions*), 133, 139

Namur, 15

Nantes, 235, 312; revocation of Edict of Nantes, 8; and economic effects of, 233; *noyades* at, 303

Naples, 16, 19, 45, 47, 159; commercial treaty with Russia (1787), 136; under Charles III, 153–8; Austrian succession war, 180–1; League of Armed Neutrality (1780–3), 252n.; and Napoleon, 328, 329, 331, 335, 347, 368; and Continental System, 332; restoration of Bourbons, 345

Napoleon I, Emperor of the French (1804–14), 94, 259; at Toulon, 315; insurrection of Vendémiaire, 315; *coup d'état* of Fructidor (1797), 317; in Italy, 317–18, 328; in Egypt, 319, 328n.; *coup d'état* of Brumaire, 319–20; Constitution of the Year VIII (1799), 321–2; the Consulate, 321–7; treaty of Amiens, 322, 327–8; Concordat and relations with the Papacy, 322, 324–6; Cadoudal conspiracy, 322, 329; proclamation of the Empire, 322; coronation, 324; the Codes, 322–3, 347; administrative reforms, 323–4; new orders of chivalry, 324; educational reforms, 326; censorship, 326; patronage of the arts, 326–7; St Helena memoirs, 327, 346; breach of Treaty of Amiens, 328; proposed invasion of England, 328–30; execution of Duc d'Enghien, 329; Trafalgar campaign, 329–30; Austerlitz, 330; Jena, 331; Tilsit, 331; Continental System, 331–3; and Poland, 331, 336, 346; marriage to Marie Louise, 334; Peninsular War, 334–6; invasion of Russia, 336–8; and the 6th Coalition, 339–43; abdication, 343; and the Enlightenment, 319, 322–3, 336, 347, 348; and nationalism, 336, 338–9, 347; his family on European thrones, 333, 335, 346–7; summary of achievements, 345–8

Napoleon III, Emperor of the French (1852–70), 97, 322

Narbonne, Comte de, French war minister, 294, 346

Narva, battle of (1700), 34, 36, 40, 42

Naryshkin, Natalia, d. 1694, mother of Peter the Great, 38

National Assembly, 268; proclaimed, 278; and the British political societies, 250; re-named Constituent Assembly, 279

National Convention, 251, 296, 332; replaces Legislative Assembly, 297; composition, 298; trial and execution of Louis XVI, 299–300; March Days (1793), 300; expulsion of Girondin deputies from, 301; under Jacobin rule, 301–10; reform of the calendar, 306, 363; Law of Prairial, 307–8; fall of Robespierre, 307–10; Thermidorian Reaction, 310–13; invaded (days of Germinal and Prairial), 313; foreign policy, 313; replaced by Directory, 315. *See also* French Revolution

National Guard: and storming of Bastille, 280–1; mistaken for brigands, 281; march to Versailles, 284; massacre of Champ de Mars, 288; in the provinces (*fédérés*), 296; invasion of Tuileries, 296–7; protects Convention during March Days, 300; forces expulsion of Girondin deputies, 301; fails to support Robespierre, 309; insurrection of Vendémiaire, 314

Nationalism: in Germany, 91–95, 338–9; in Poland, 212–14; and the French Revolution, 289–90; in Spain, 335–6; and the Vienna Settlement, 346

Natural law: Locke, 65–67; Montesquieu, 81, 88; Rousseau, 86; Kant, 90; Goethe, 92–93

Natural Religion: *see* Deism

Navigation Acts, 106–7, 108

Necker, Jacques (1732–1804), 263, 265, 279

Neerwinden, battle of (1793), 300

Neisse, Silesian town, 141, 378

Nelson, Horatio, Viscount (1758–1805), 319, 329–30

Nesle, Marquis de, 218

Netherlands, 14, 20, 186, 187, 188, 206, 322; Spanish succession war, 15; ceded to Austria, 16, 45, 47; industrial development, 109; under Maria Theresa, 143; under Joseph II, 144, 146; Austrian succession war, 180, 181, 184, 185; Seven Years War, 190, 192; revolt of (1789), 144, 250, 289; invaded by Revolutionary France, 292, 295, 299, 304

Newcastle, Thomas Pelham, Duke of (1693–1768), 186–90

New England, 107
Newfoundland, 16, 48, 197, 253
New Orleans, 194, 197
Newton, Sir Isaac (1642–1727), 53, 55n., 61, 69; law of universal gravitation, 62–64; optics, 64; influence on *philosophes*, 65, 66, 68–69, 74, 81, 257–8; and on Kant, 89–90; popularization of Newton's ideas, 111–12, 160
Nice, 299
Niemen, river, 35, 175
Nieuport, 188
Nikon [Nikita Minin] (1605–81), Patriarch of Moscow, 42
Noailles, Louis Marie, Vicomte de (1756–1804), 282
Nobility: *see* aristocracy
Nootka Sound, 291
Northern War, Great (1700–21), 34–37, 40, 45
Norway, 168, 170; Charles XII's invasion of, 36; transferred from Denmark to Sweden, 345
Nova Kydne, 147
Novara, 47
Nova Scotia, 16, 48, 183
Novikov, Nikolai Ivanovich (1744–1818), 139
Nymegen, treaty of (1678), 20
Nymphenburg, treaty of (1741), 180
Nystadt, treaty of (1721), 37, 40

Oczakov, 199, 208
Oder, river, 122
Oglethorpe, James Edward (1696–1785), 48
Ohio, river, 194
'Old Believers' in Russia, 138
Olmütz, 192
Opera: Berlin, 115; Naples, 155; Stockholm, 166; Mozart and Rossini, 225
Oran, 23
Orders in Council, British (1807), 332
Orenburg (Chkalov), 136
'Organic Articles' (1802), 325
Orleans, Philip, Duke of, Regent of France, 1715–23, 17, 217, 237, 241; Louis-Philippe Joseph ('Philippe Égalité') Duke of (1747–93), 280
Orlov, Alexis Grigorievich, Count (1737–1808), 128, 131, 201; Gregory Grigorievich, Count (1734–83), 131; Theodore Grigorievich, Count (1741–90), 131
Oropesa, Count of, Spanish minister, 21
Orry, Jean (1652–1719), reforms in Spain, 22
Orry de Fulvy, Jean-Henri-Louis (1703–51), Controller-General of France, 243, 268

Osiander, Andreas (1498–1552), 60n.
Ossian, 91
Ostend, 188; Company, 19, 47, 147
Ottoman Empire: *see* Turkey
Oudenarde, battle of (1708), 15
Oviedo, university of, 164

Padua, 62n., 64
Paine, Tom (1737–1809), 251–2, 300
Palais Royal, 280
Palatinate, Elector Palatine, 24, 26n., 186, 203, 206
Paley, William (1743–1805), 75
Palladian architecture, 230
Panin, Nikita Ivanovich, Count (1718–83): Russian minister, 209; Peter, Russian general, brother of Nikita, 136
Paoli, Pasquale (1725–1807), Corsican general, 249
Papal States, 326, 328n., 345, 348
Paris, 91, 110, 117, 130, 161, 224, 234, 262, 273, 319; treaty of (1763), 197; the *salons*, 129, 221–2, 223, 259, 315; Bernini's design for the Louvre, 229; Franklin's visit, 114, 255; price of food, 270–1, 295–96, 300, 304–5, 312, 314; population, 270; Commune of, 296–7, 301; visit of Pius VII (1804), 324; occupied by the Allies (1814), 343. *See also* French Revolution
Pâris, François de, Jansenist deacon, 241; Pâris brothers, 268
Parlements, 237–8, 265; disputes over religion, 240–2; and over taxation, 242–5, 262–3, 266; suspended by Louis XV, 244; restored by Louis XVI, 262; contribution to French Revolution, 258–60, 262–4, 266, 277; abolition, 289
Parma, Duchy of, 18, 19, 47, 153, 156, 184, 328
Pascal, Blaise (1623–62), 74
Passarowitz, treaty of (1718), 32
Patiño, Jose (1666–1736), 23
Paul, Tsar of Russia, 128
Paul III, Pope (1534–49), 60
Pays d'état, 238–9
Pays d'élection, 239
Peasants: *see* serfdom *and* feudalism
Peninsular War (1808–14), 333, 335–6
Peru, 21
Pestalozzi, Johann Heinrich (1746–1827), 88
Peter I ('the Great'), Tsar of Russia (1682–1725), 18, 129, 130, 131, 132, 133, 137, 138, 199; rise to power, 38–39; travels in Europe, 39; war *v.* Turkey, 39–40; Great Northern War, 34–36, 40; military reforms, 40–41; administrative reforms, 41; economic

Peter I—*cont.*
policies, 41–42, 109; religious policy, 42; treatment of nobles, 42–43, 101; and of serfs, 43, 101–2
Peter II, Tsar of Russia (1727–30), 130
Peter III, Tsar of Russia (Jan.–June 1762), 128, 131, 135, 136, 193, 200
Petty, Sir William (1623–87), 55, 104
Philip II, King of Spain (1556–98), 5
Philip IV of Spain (1621–65), 11
Philip V of Spain (1700–46), 153; Spanish succession war, 15–16; war *v.* France (1717), 17–18; Spain during his reign, 22–23, 163, 181
Philip, Don, younger son of Philip V and Elizabeth Farnese, 181, 184, 188
Philippines, 163
Philosophes, 38, 51, 89, 97–98, 215, 229, 268; debt to Bacon, 53; influence of Newton, 65, 68–69, 74, 81; list of principal writings, 69–70; *Encyclopaedia*, 71–73; scepticism and Deism, 73–76, 257–58; Utilitarianism and *laissez-faire*, 76–78; political attitudes, 78–80; and Rousseau, 88–89; and censorship, 72–73, 258–59, 268; and Frederick the Great, 115–17, 125, 223; and Catherine the Great, 128–30, 139; and Maria Theresa, 140–1; and Joseph II, 141, 147; influence in Naples under Charles III, 157; and in Spain, 160–1; attitude to foreign policy, 171; patronized by Mme de Pompadour, 219–20; the *salons* and, 221–2; the *parlements* and, 244, 259–60; influence on the French Revolution, 256–60, 268, 287–88, 300, 305–6; and Napoleon I, 326, 347
Physiocrats, 77–78, 105, 147, 160, 167, 220, 262
Piacenza, 18, 19, 47, 153, 184, 328
Piedmont, 110, 328, 333. *See also* Sardinia
Pillnitz, Declaration of (1791), 291, 294
Pisa, 61
Pistoia, Bishop of, 158
Pitt, William the Elder, later Lord Chatham (1708–78), 190, 191, 193, 194, 195, 196–7, 247, 249–50
Pitt, William the Younger (1759–1806), 77, 105, 207, 291, 328
Pius VI, Pope (1775–99), 150, 348
Pius VII, Pope (1800–23), 324–6, 348–9
Plassey, battle of (1757), 195
Plato, 59
Pocock, Sir George, British Admiral, 196
Poland, 103, 136, 138, 191–2, 199, 290; extent, 28; political organization, 28–29; population, 34; invaded by Charles XII, 35; Polish succession war,

30; *szlachta*, 28; serfdom, 102; Rousseau and, 87–88, 212; Partitions: 1st, 200–2, 208–11; 2nd, 213; 3rd, 214; reforms of Stanislas Augustus, 212–13; Constitution of 1791, 213; and the French Revolution, 213, 291, 295; and Napoleon, 331, 336, 346; and Vienna Settlement, 345
Polish Succession, War of (1733–5), 30, 47, 153, 199
Poltava, battle of (1709), 29, 36, 40
Pombal, Sebastião Jose de Carvalho e Mello, Marquess of (1699–1782), 164–5
Pomerania, 34, 43, 45, 120, 189, 191, 209
Pomerelia, 211
Pompadour, Jeanne Antoinette Poisson le Normant d'Étioles, Marquise de (1721–64), 268n.; influence on foreign policy, 188; introduction at court, 219; portraits of, 219; patron of the *philosophes*, 219–20; and of the arts, 220, 227, 228
Pompeii, 156, 230
Pondicherry, 183, 184, 196
Pontoise, 238
Pope, Alexander (1688–1744), 65, 66, 92n., 249
Population: European increase in, 110
Porcelain industry, 123, 157
Portici, 156, 157
Portobello, 182
Port Royal, 240
Portugal, 160; revolt *v.* Spain, 20; Spanish succession war, 11–16; Methuen Treaties (1703), 15; commercial treaty with Russia (1787), 136; enlightened absolutism in, 164–5; Seven Years War, 197; League of Armed Neutrality (1780–3), 252n.; and Napoleon, 332, 333, 368; Peninsular War, 334–5
Posen, 213
Potemkin, Grigory Aleksandrovich, Prince (1739–91), 131, 137, 207
Potsdam: effect of Thirty Years War on, 26; court of Frederick the Great at, 115–16, 118, 248
Pozsony, 46
Pragmatic Sanction, 19, 47, 140, 142, 173–5, 180
Prague, 60, 61, 145, 191
Prairial, *coup d'état* of (1799), 317, 319
Prato, 158
Prefects, 323
Pressburg: Diet of (1741), 143; Treaty of (1805), 330
Price, Richard (1723–91), 250–1, 255
Prie, Mme de, mistress of Duc de Bourbon, 218

Priestley, Joseph (1733–1804), 222, 251
Prieur of the Marne [Pierre Louis Prieur] (1756–1827), 307; of the Côte d'Or [Comte Claude Antoine Prieur-Duvernois] (1763–1832), 307
Provence, 181, 234; Comte de: see Louis XVIII
Prussia, 16, 19, 37; territorial extent (1688), 43–44; population, 44, 110; under Frederick I, 44; under Frederick William I, 44–45; the army, 44–45, 126; Great Northern War, 45; Pragmatic Sanction, 47, 173–4; junkers, 101, 103, 121; serfdom, 102–3; Berlin Academy, 116–17, 125, 133, 248; under Frederick II, 115–27; seizure of Silesia, 173–9; Austrian succession war, 179–81; Treaty of Aix-le-Chapelle, 184; Diplomatic Revolution, 185–90; Seven Years War, 190–3; Treaty of Hubertusburg, 197–8; partitions of Poland, 200–2, 208–14; League of Armed Neutrality (1780–83), 252n. (1801), 333; and French Revolution, 289–92, 295, 313; and Napoleon, 331–2, 338–43, 368; and Continental System, 332; reforms of Stein and Hardenberg, 338–9; and Vienna Settlement, 345
Ptolemy, 59–60
Pufendorf, Samuel (1632–94), German jurist, 24
Pugachev, Emel'yan Ivanovich (1741?–75), 132, 134, 136, 202
Pyrenees, 14, 18; Treaty of (1759), 20
Pyramids, battle of (1798), 319

Quadruple Alliance: 1718 (England, France, Holland, Empire), 18; 1814 (England, Austria, Prussia, Russia), 342
Quakers, 74, 249
Quebec, 48, 195
Quesnay, François (1694–1744), 70, 78, 220
Quesnel, Pasquier (1634–1719), 241
Quiberon Bay, battle of (1759), 195

Racine, Jean (1639–99), 221
Raditchev (Radishchev), Alexander, 139
Radziwill, Karol, Prince of Poland, 102
Rakoczy, Francis, Prince of Transylvania (1676–1735), 46
Rambouillet, 111; Marquise de, 221
Ramillies, battle of (1706), 15
Rastadt, treaty of (1714), 16, 45
Ratisbon, 26
Red Sea, 319
Reichenbach: Convention of (1790), 207, 212, 290; Proposals (1813), 339

Religion: in France under Louis XIV, 7–8; attacked by philosophes, 73–76, 257–8; Hume's attack on Deism, 84; Kant and, 90; Goethe and, 369; in Prussia under Frederick the Great, 124–5; in Russia under Catherine the Great, 137–8; under the Austrian Habsburgs, 148–49; in Naples, 155, 157; in Tuscany, 158; in Spain, 158–60, 161, 266, 336; in Portugal, 164–5; in France during the Revolution, 266–8, 285–8, 306, 307; and under Napoleon I, 322, 324–6
Renaissance of the 15th and 16th centuries, 68
Repnin, Anikita-Ivanovich, Prince, Russian ambassador in Poland, 209, 212
Reubell, one of the Directors, 315
Revolutionary Tribunal (Paris), 302, 303; set up, 300; in action, 305; and the Law of Prairial, 307; abolished, 312
Reynolds, Sir Joshua (1723–92), 130, 230
Rheinsberg, 115
Rhine, Rhineland, 15, 27, 175, 191, 291, 299, 300, 313, 342; Confederation of, 330, 332
Riccobini, Marie Jeanne (1714–92), 224
Richelieu, Armand Jean du Plessis de (1585–1642), Cardinal, 117, 187
Riga, 35, 40
Riksdag (Swedish Diet); deprived of control over finance, 33; regains power under Constitution of 1720, 37, 99–100, 165; after Constitution of 1772, 167; and Gustavus III's coup of 1789, 169
Ripperda, Johann Willem, Baron (1680–1737), 22, 23
Robespierre, Maximilien François Marie Isidore de (1758–94), 88, 269, 296, 310, 312, 314; Self-denying Ordinance, 293, 302; opposes war, 294; calls for National Convention, 296; in National Convention, 298–310; on execution of Louis XVI, 299; member of Committee of Public Safety, 302; reasons for rise to power, 302–3; views on government, 303; and the Terror, 303, 305, 308; Republic of Virtue, 305–6, 364–5; president of Convention, 308; and the Law of Prairial, 308; fall, 308–10
Robot, 102, 145–6
Rocco, Father, 157
Rococo, 229, 230
Romanticism: influence of Hume, 83, 84; and of Rousseau, 85–89, 224–5; and of Kant, 89–90; Sturm und Drang movement, 91–92; Goethe and Schiller, 93–94; in poetry, 223–4;

INDEX

Romanticism—*cont.*
in architecture, 231–2; in politics, 249, 254–5
Rome, 153; Royal Academy of Fine Arts founded by Louis XIV, 226, 227; painting in, 229; sculpture and architecture in, 229–30
Rossbach, battle of (1757), 191
Rossini, Gioachino Antonio (1792–1868), 225
Rostov, Archbishop of, 137
Rotterdam, 73
Rousseau, Jean-Jacques (1712–78), 70, 80, 272; contributes to *Encyclopaedia*, 71; *Discourse on the Arts and the Sciences*, 85; *Discourse on the Origin and Foundation of Inequality*, 86; *Social Contract*, 85–87, 88, 249; on education, 87–88; works banned in Spain, 160–1; and burned in France, 268; influence in Poland, 212; and Corsica, 249; in the *salons*, 222; *La Nouvelle Héloïse*, 224, 248; link with Romanticism, 85–89, 224–5; visits Hume, 248; meets and corresponds with Boswell, 249; influence on the French Revolution, 257, 283, 305; and on Robespierre, 305–6
Roussillon, 20
Royal Institution (London), 114
Royal Society (London), 54–55, 63, 166, 248
Rügen, island of, 290
Ruhr, 109
Russia: Great Northern War, 34–37, 40; under Peter the Great, 38–43; under Catherine the Great, 128–39; serfdom, 43, 101–2, 103, 134–5; industrial development, 42, 109; aristocracy, 42–43, 101, 103, 132–5, 366–7; population, 110; army, 135; and Poland, 29–30, 136, 200–2, 208–14; Austrian succession war, 173, 181; Diplomatic Revolution, 185–90; Seven Years War, 190–3; 1st Turkish War (1768–74), 199–202; 2nd Turkish War (1787–92), 206–8; mediation in Bavarian succession war, 206; League of Armed Neutrality (1780–3), 252n.; (1801), 333; attacked by Gustavus III, 168; campaigns *v.* Napoleon, 328–9, 331, 336–8, 339–43, 368; and the Continental System, 331–3, 336
Russia Company: British, 38; Prussian, 123
Ryswick, treaty of (1697), 9, 20, 48, 290

Saint-André, Jeanbon (1749–1813), member of Committee of Public Safety, 307

Saint-Cloud, 319
St Domingo, French (Haiti), 49, 107; Spanish (Santo Domingo), 313
Sainte-Geneviève, Paris, 231
St Helena, 327, 346
St Janarius, 157
Saint-Just, Antoine Louis Léon de Richebourg de (1767–94), 307, 309, 312
Saint-Lambert, Jean François (1716–1803), 224
St Lawrence, river, 48, 194
St Lucia, 197, 252
St Petersburg, 40, 42, 128, 129, 130, 168, 188, 189, 206, 207, 210; Convention of (1757), 190
St Vincent, 197
Saint-Simon, Louis de Rouvroy, Duc de (1675–1755), 8, 9, 217
Salamanca, university of, 164
Salons, 129, 221–2, 223, 315
Saltikov, Peter Semyonovich, Count, 192
Saltikov, Serge, Count, 131
San Carlo Opera House, Naples, 155
San Ildefonso, 23
Sansculottes, 270, 309–10, 315
Sans Souci, 115
Santiago (Spain), university of, 164
Santiago de Cuba, 183
Santo Stefano, Count of, Neapolitan minister, 153
Saragossa, 163, 164
Sardinia, 16, 17, 18, 45, 47, 175, 180, 181, 317, 328, 368. *See also* Savoy
Savona, 326
Savoy, 16, 18, 180, 184, 290, 299. *See also* Sardinia
Saxe, Maurice, Comte de (1696–1750), 181–2
Saxony, 26, 126, 185, 290; Elector of, 24, 26n.; and Poland, 30, 35; population, 110; Austrian succession war, 174, 175, 178, 180; Seven Years War, 189–93; Napoleonic Wars, 330; and Vienna Settlement, 345
Scharnhorst, Gerhard Johann David von (1755–1813), 338
Scheldt estuary, 299
Schiller, Johann Christoph Friedrich von (1759–1805): *Sturm und Drang* period, 92; aesthetic theories, 93; principal writings, 94; nationalism, 95–96; attitude to French Revolution, 289
Schlözer, August Ludwig von (1735–1809), German historian, 289
Schwarzenberg, Karl Philip, Prince zu (1771–1820), Austrian field-marshal, 342; family, 102
Schweidniz (Silesia), 193

Science: revolution of the 17th century, 53–64; Newtonianism in the 18th century, 111–12; at the universities, 82, 157, 165; developments in biology and chemistry, 64, 112–13; and in electricity, 114

Scotland, 82

Scott, Sir George Gilbert (1811–78), architect, 232

Scott, Sir Walter (1771–1832), 232

Sebastopol, 137, 207

Sedan, 73, 297

Segovia, 21, 163

Ségur, Louis Philippe, Comte de (d. 1830), French ambassador at St Petersburg, 259

Self-denying Ordinance (May 1791), 293, 302, 314

Senegal, 197, 252

September Massacres (1792), 298

Serfdom: Russia, 43, 101–3, 134–5, 366–7; Poland, 102; Prussia, 102, 121, 338; Austria and Hungary, 145–6, 148, 290; Denmark, 170; relics of in France, 272–3, 281–2, 323

Seven Years War (1756–63), 122, 123, 124, 140, 159, 165, 200, 234, 235, 242, 243, 246, 252; Diplomatic Revolution and, 185–9; Frederick II's invasion of Saxony, 189–90; continental phase, 190–3; colonial phase, 193–7

Seville, 162, 163

Shaftesbury, Anthony Ashley Cooper, 1st Earl of (1621–83), 67n.

Shelburne, William Petty, Earl of (1737–1805), 222

Shuvalov, Peter, Russian finance minister, 136

Siberia, 40, 134, 139

Sicily, 16, 17, 18, 19, 23, 46, 47, 110–11, 331; under Charles III, 153–8

Sieyès, Emmanuel-Joseph (1748–1836), on the Third Estate, 283; constitution-making, 284, 300, 321; and the Directory, 317; coup de état of Brumaire, 319, 322

Silesia, 46, 118, 141, 142, 147, 184, 185; linen industry, 26; mines, 109, 123; Frederick II's invasion of, 173–9; Seven Years War, 188, 189, 190–3, 197

Sivaji (1627–80), Maratha chief, 49

Slavery, 306

Slave trade, 107, 182, 195

Smith, Adam (1723–1790), 77–78, 103, 105, 160; Sir William Sidney (1764–1840), British admiral, 319

Smolensk, 206

Smolny Institute, 138

Sobieski, John, King of Poland (1674–96), 29, 32

Social contract: Locke, 66–67, 86; Hume, 83–84; Rousseau, 86–87; in the American Revolution, 253–4; and the French Revolution, 282–3; in the Hungarian revolt of 1789, 289

Society of Jesus: see Jesuits

Soissons, 297

Solms, Count, Prussian ambassador in St Petersburg, 210

Soor, battle of (1745), 179

Sophia Alekseyeena (1657–1704), half-sister of Peter the Great, Regent of Russia, 1682–9, 38, 39, 40

Soufflot, Jacques Germain (1713–80), 231

South Sea Company, 16n., 49, 236

Spain, 47, 337; asiento, 14, 16, 17, 19, 49, 182, 184; Spanish succession war, 11–17, 20, 22; war v. France (1718), 17, 18; loss of Portugal and United Provinces, 20; under Philip V and Elizabeth Farnese, 20–24; Oropesa's reforms, 21–22; Orry's reforms, 22; Alberoni's reforms, 22–23; colonies, 23–24; Pragmatic Sanction, 47; under Charles III (1759–88), 158–64; population, 21, 161; the Church, 159–61, 266, 336; aristocracy, 161–2; economic development, 162–3; the arts, 163–4; Austrian succession war, 175, 180, 181; War of Jenkins' Ear, 49, 182–3; Seven Years War, 196–7; Family Compact with France (1761), 196; War of American Independence, 252–3; Nootka Sound dispute (1790), 291; war with Revolutionary France, 300, 313; and with England, 329; Trafalgar campaign, 329–30; and Continental System, 332; Peninsular War, 334–6; Constitution of 1812, 336; restoration of Bourbons, 348

Spanish Succession, War of (1702–13), 48; effect on France, 10, 233; course of, 11–17

Sparre, Karl, Swedish minister, 167

Spinoza, Benedictus de (1632–77), 92

Squillace, Marchese di, Neapolitan minister, 159

Staël, Madame de (1766–1817), 483

Stanhope, James, 1st Earl (1673–1721), 18

Stanislas Augustus: see Stanislas Poniatowski

Stanislas Poniatowski (Stanislas Augustus), King of Poland (1764–95; d. 1798), 30, 131, 200, 208–13

Starhemberg, Georg Adam, Count von, Austrian ambassador in Paris, 188, 189

Staszic, Stanislas, author of Warnings to Poland (1790), 212

Steam power, 109

Stein, Charlotte von (1742–1827), 92; Heinrich Friedrich Karl, Baron vom (1757–1831), 338
Stettin, 45, 128
Stockholm, 34, 166, 167, 169; treaty of (1720), 45
Strasbourg (Strassburg), 16
Strawberry Hill, 232
Streltsi, 38, 39, 40
Struensee, Johan Frederick (1731–72), 170
Stuart, James (1713–88), architect, 231
Sturm und Drang movement, 91–92, 93
Styria, 46
Suarez, German jurist, 120–1
Suez, 319
Svenskund, battle of (1790), 169
Sweden, 175, 199; alliance of Hanover (1725), 19; under Charles X (1654–60), 33; under Charles XI (1660–97), 33–34; population, 34, 100; military organization, 34; Charles XII's campaigns, 34–36; death of Charles XII, 36; disputed succession and Constitution of 1720, 37, 99–100, 165; Treaty of Nystadt, 37; aristocracy, 99–100; iron industry, 103; 'Age of liberty', 165; Seven Years War, 189, 191, 193; under Gustavus III (1771–92), 165–70; war with Russia, 168, 169, 290–1; Austrian succession war, 180–1; League of Armed neutrality (1780–83), 252; (1801), 333; and French Revolution, 290–1; and Napoleon, 332, 334; and Vienna Settlement, 345
Swedenborg, Emanuel (1688–1772), 166
Swinburne, Henry (1743–1803), author of Travels in the Two Sicilies (1783), 156
Switzerland, 258, 290, 319, 322, 328, 342
Szatmar, treaty of (1712), 46
Szlachta, 28, 29, 100, 102

Talleyrand-Périgord, Charles Maurice de (1754–1838), 264, 283, 331, 334, 336, 343, 345
Tallien, Jean Lambert (1767–1820), 310; and his wife, 311
Tanucci, Bernardo, Marchese (1698–1785), 154–5
Targowica Confederation, 213
Tarento, 329
Temple, William Johnson, 246
Terray, Joseph-Marie (1715–78), 244, 262
Terror, the: machinery set up, 300; expounded by Robespierre, 303, 364–5; psychology of, 304–5; victims, 305; Law of Prairial, 307–8; end of, 311; the 'White' Terror, 313

Teschen, treaty of (1779), 206
Tessin, Comte de, 229
Theodore III, Tsar of Russia (1676–82), 38
Theresianum, 151
Thermidorian reaction, 310–15
Thiers, Louis Adolphe (1797–1877), 269
Third Estate in France: attitude of the King to, 261; bourgeoisie, 265, 268–9; urban working classes, 270–1; peasants, 271–3; in the Estates-General, 277–9; Tennis Court Oath, 278; the Great Fear, 279–80; fall of the Bastille, 280–1; Sieyès's What is the Third Estate?, 283. See also French Revolution.
Thomson, James (1700–48), British poet, author of 'The Seasons', 91
Thorn, fortress of, 35, 210, 212, 213
Thornhill, Sir James (1676–1734), 226n.
Thugut, Johann Amadeus Francis de Paula, Baron (1736–1818), 205
Ticonderoga, battle of (1758), 194
Tiepolo, Giovanni Battista (1696–1770), 164, 229
Tilsit, treaty of (1807), 331, 336
Tobago, 197, 252
Tocqueville, Alexis Henri Charles Maurice Clerel, Comte de (1805–59), 233, 237, 257, 268, 269
Toledo, silk industry of, 21, 162
Toleration: demanded by philosophes, 72–74, 258; in Prussia, 124–5; in Russia, 138; in Habsburg Empire, 148–50; slow acceptance in France, 258; during the French Revolution, 283, 306, 311; under Napoleon I, 323, 325
Torgau, battle of (1760), 192
Toulon, 15, 315, 329
Toulouse, 336
Tournai, 15, 295
Townsend, Joseph (1739–1816), 163
Townshend, Charles, 2nd Viscount (1674–1738), 18, 224
Trafalgar, battle of (1805), 330
Transylvania, 31, 47, 144, 146
Treitschke, Heinrich von (1834–96), 95
Trèves (Trier), Elector of, 26n., 291
Trieste, 147
Triple Alliance: 1717 (England, France, Holland), 18; 1788 (England, Prussia, Holland), 207
Triumvirate (Barnave, Duport, Alexandre de Lambeth), 283, 293
Tudela, 163
Tuileries, 284, 288; storming of, 296–7; iron chest, 299; expulsion of Girondin deputies from, 301; decoration of, 327

King
DEAD OF JERICHO

Chief Inspector Morse is a very clever man. He likes using his brain; that's why he is a detective. But he has three weaknesses: beer, women, and Mozart. He can't say 'no' to any of them. As a result he doesn't always do the things policemen ought to do – and he does many things that policemen ought not to do. In fact, he behaves very much like an ordinary person, like you or me.

This is what makes Morse so special. A detective needs to understand people, and Morse does understand people because he enjoys the same pleasures and he suffers the same pains. He is clever, but he is human. He is strong, but he is weak – and his weaknesses are the same as ours. He represents a very human kind of justice. He does not take revenge; he listens, and understands, and does what must be done.